# Readings in Managerial Economics Accounting & Financial Analysis

# READINGS IN MANAGERIAL ECONOMICS ACCOUNTING & FINANCIAL ANALYSIS

2nd Edition


***Dr. R. K. Mishra***

Dean,
Institute of Public Enterprise,
Osmania University Campus,
Hyderabad - 500 001.

***Dr. B. Naveen***

Knowledge Manager,
Centre for Good Governance,
Dr. MCR HRD IAP Campus,
Jubilee Hills, Hyderabad - 500 033.



BSP **BS Publications**

A unit of **BSP Books Pvt., Ltd.**

4-4-309/316, Giriraj Lane, Sultan Bazar,
Hyderabad - 500 095.
Phone : 040 - 23445605, 23445688

***Published by :***

**BS Publications**
A unit of **BSP Books Pvt., Ltd.**

4-4-309/316, Giriraj Lane, Sultan Bazar,
Hyderabad - 500 095
Phone : 040 - 23445605, 23445688
**e-mail : info@bspbooks.net**

**ISBN : 978-93-52300-30-3 (HB)**

*Dedicated to*

***Prof. T. Navaneeth Rao***

President, Institute of Public Enterprise,
Chairman, Swamy Ramanada Theertha Institute for Rural Development,
Former Vice-Chancellor of Osmania University
Chairman, Education Reforms Committee, European Commission

*Who is a Constant Source of Inspiration to Management Teachers and Researchers in Social Sciences*

# Preface

## *Second Edition*

The first edition of this book namely "Readings in Accounting, Finance and Costing" was written to facilitate the understanding of finance and accounting function among the non-finance executives of public enterprises in India. The Country is engaged in the task of rapid development and the management educational institutions, technical educational institutions offering engineering courses and corporate sector have to make tremendous contribution in this pursuit. More than 2,000 management educational institutions and 3,000 engineering educational institutions are involved in offering management courses. The basic understanding of the economics, accounting, costing and finance is a prerequisite to complete any such course. In line with this development, the authors felt it necessary to revise the previous edition of the book by incorporating, among other things, an exclusive chapter on Managerial Economics.

Both the technical and non-technical personnel have to have an understanding of the dynamics of a healthy bottom line. The second edition of this book has been prepared by giving due regard to this fact. A number of new additions have been made to enable the reader to cultivate the requisite understanding of the economics, accounting, costing and finance inputs that are necessary to take myriad decisions regarding the tactical and strategic functioning of an enterprise.

We are sure the book would be of immense benefit to the students of engineering, management and finance courses. The non-finance executives in the public and private sectors, Central and State governments, non-profit organisations and NGOs, and municipal organisations would also find the book of great use in adding to their understanding of economics and finance related issues.

We dedicate this book to Prof.T.Navaneeth Rao, President, Institute of Public Enterprise. His encouragement and support has been our great asset. We also thank Prof.K.Harigopal, Director, IPE in motivating us to work on issues related to economics, accounting and finance. We thank Ms.S.Lalitha, A.O (Research), Ms.Ch.Lakshmi Kumari, Research Associate and Ms.J.Kiranmai, Research Assistant to provide the research backup.

The authors have taken much care in bringing the book error free, however some typographical mistakes may have crept in. If any, the same will be rectified in the next reprint.

Finally, we thank Mr. Nikhil Shah, Mr. K. S. Raju and Mr. Naresh of B.S Publications for bringing out this book in time and also benefitting us with their advice, related to the various aspects of publishing this book.

Authors
July 6th, 2004

## *First Edition*

This volume contains some essential readings in Accounting, Costing and Finance. These have been prepared to enable non-finance executives in public enterprises to understand the implications of their decision making in financial terms and improve their interface with finance executives. The bottom line figure in the profit and loss account of a public enterprise is the product of decisions taken by numerous executives in public enterprises. Most of such executives belong to areas other than finance.

We are sure this volume would go a long way in facilitating the understanding of finance function among non-finance executives. We express our thanks to Mr.A.V.Nageshwara Rao and Mr.K.S.Narayana for their assistance in the preparation of this volume.

*Authors*
August 2nd, 1989

# Contents

# 1

# Managerial Economics : Concepts, Issues and Tools

A not unreasonable question you might ask is, 'what is use the knowledge of economics to a businessman or businesswomen?' The answer is in two parts: the first is a 'consumption' benefit, the second an 'investment' benefit.

To start with, it is important to understand how the market economy functions: what its strengths and weakness are; how all the different parts of the economy relate to each other through the market mechanism; and what we as a society can do to modify this market mechanism to serve us better. This is the consumption benefit.

What are the 'investment' benefits? The major benefit that a comprehension of economics can bestow on the manager is an understanding of how economists tackle problems and an adoption of the economist's approach. The world in which the economist operates is a very complex world because it is the real world. To understand this world, the economists build models that attempt to capture the core of the problem being investigated; without this capability, rigorous analysis of the problem is impossible.

Major managerial decisions for a successful company must be treated in a similar fashion. If your company is contemplating setting up a plant abroad and you have to decide on warehouse, establishment of a research and development center, a legal department, and international exchange department-to name but a few; you will not find the answers to these problems in an economics text book. What you will find, however, is a methodology for setting out the major issues to be resolved, and a method and tools for analyzing such a complicated problem.

The pattern of the section on economics is to introduce economic concepts and theories, apply these to real-world problems, and finally to evaluate economics polices based on the theories. Multiple choice questions at the end of each chapter allow self-testing of how well fundamental concepts and principles have been mastered. Accompanying cases or real problems permit testing of analytical ability in economics and help to develop the higher-order skills of synthesis and evaluation.

In all aspects of life, scarcity exists both for individuals and societies. Since all living creatures have wants, that they attempt to satisfy but limited means of satisfying these wants, choices have to be made. Economics is the subject that studies how individuals and society tackle such a problem. For many individuals and societies, the making of choices is not an unpleasant experience. Where to go on holiday, which restaurant to try, which gifts to choose, how to design the new university library, where to locate new roads and shopping centers, are the activities that, although normally facing budgetary restrictions, are not matters of life and death. For a large portion of the world's population, however, many choices are matters of life and death. Even in more developed countries, scarcity imposes some cruel dilemmas.

In many underdeveloped countries in the world, the problem of scarcity is stark and striking. Insufficient income is generated to keep people alive for very long: children starve and die; medical services are non-existent; housing and sanitation consist of broken huts, slums, open sewers. Attempts to make life better for future generations by building towns and factories can mean fewer resources allocated to the wants of the current generation. How many people would approve, or be willing to take the decision of sacrificing the lives, say, of fifty per cent of the children in the village so that those who remain and their children-could have more of their wants satisfied in the future?

All of these problems, which necessitate choices, arise from scarcity. The fact that scarcity is relative, that the bulk of the people living in the developed world are incomparably better off than millions of people existing in abject poverty in the poorer countries, does not diminish the need of choice, though the implications of certain choices have more serious consequences.

Different societies in the world handle the scarcity-choice problem in different ways. Some countries have relied on a small group of individuals making the major economic decisions: those are the centrally planned economies. Others have utilized the market system in which the forces of demand and supply impersonally resolve the scarcity-choice issue: those are the capitalist, or free enterprise, economies. Others, primarily societies in the less developed world, have relied on traditional methods of economic organization in which the positions of individuals in a society determine primarily their jobs and rewards. No country in the world today provides a pure example of one of the above types of economic systems. In planned economies such as China, a significant amount of economic activity, especially in agriculture, takes place in a traditional framework. In capitalist countries such as Japan, Germany, the United Kingdom and the USA, governments are responsible for planning and carrying out many economic tasks, however market is the major player. Countries such as Norway and Sweden lie somewhere in between the above two groups, with a larger share of economic activity being undertaken by government.

The primary focus here is on the functioning of the free-enterprises type of economies. The principal reason for this is that over 80 per cent of the world's output is produced by nations that are primarily free-enterprise economies. A second reason is that many of the Eastern bloc countries, which previously adhered to a planning type of economy, are now embracing the market system.

The approach is to develop answers to questions such as: how would a completely free-enterprise system work? Would the outcomes for such an economy be desirable for any activity where a free-enterprise system will not provide the goods and services people want most ? Can government interference in the economy make it function more effectively? Who gains and who loses when the government more than is desirable? Who gains and who loses when the government interferes?

## Scarcity and Choice

All living creatures have wants, which they attempt to satisfy. Wants are not limited to basic subsistence items. Similarly, people's wants for housing, clothing, food, transportation, recreation and art exceed what is needed just to sustain human life. Not many decades ago, the families which are now high income group, lived in small houses consisting of a room and kitchen with outside toilet facilities. For most families today in developed countries, houses are spacious and convenient and meet much more than basic shelter requirements. Over a time the wants of a society changed; fortunately, so does the ability to satisfy them.

Whether human wants are determined by the need to survive (bread and water), the desire for pleasure (good food and wine), or gluttony (Roman style eating orgies) is not a primary concern of an economist. Economist takes human wants as given and does not pass value judgments about whether people should want the things they do want. The main focus of economist is on how societies providing the items that satisfy such want. So, the economist is concerned primarily with how society can best use its available means to achieve its given wants.

It is possible to conceptualize a world in which all of society's wants are fully satisfied, but such a paradise has never been observed. Consider only the materialistic side of such a world. Not only would there have to be a sufficient (infinite?) supply of all the goods and services that each and every person wanted but also sufficient time to consume and enjoy them. The richest person in today's world faces scarcity: for example, the form of a limited number of years in lifetime and the unwillingness of owners of unique assets to part with them. From a practical view point, it does not matter whether we envisage a world in which human wants are infinite or one in which human wants are finite but greater than resources can satisfy; in both case we finish up with a world of scarcity. It is only in such a world that economics has any meaning.

Items that satisfy some wants are provided by nature without human effort. Air, rain, beautiful scenery and sunset can increase human well being without human effort. They are known as 'free goods'. Other items that increase well being however, require considerable co-ordination of effort on the part of many thousands of individuals. Producing a car or sending a satellite around mars is not a gift of nature. Thus, with the exception of the free goods provided by nature, the ability of individuals or nations to provide the goods and services that help satisfy wants is limited by the resources under their command. Not all students can earn above 90% marks in every subject because of resource constraints – time and ability. Similarly, life expectancy is low in many parts of the world because of inadequate supplies of food, shelter and medicines.

A 'resource' is defined as, any thing that helps produce the goods and services people want. The wheat farmer's fields are resources, as are his tractors, fertilizer and seed. All of which are required to produce the wheat that people want.

It is the dual existence of insatiable wants and limited resources that produces what economists call the fundamental fact of scarcity. Because of scarcity, all individuals and nations face the same problem, namely the allocation of limited resources among the goods and services that are desired. Students have to decide how to allocate their time among study, sports, and sleeping activities. Households have to decide how to allocate their income among food, clothing, health services, and education, transportation, and leisure activities. A nation has to decide how to allocate its labour force, lands, factories and other resources to produce national defense (jets, nuclear submarines, army, navy and air force personnel), health services (medical schools, hospitals, clinics), educational services (pre- school playgroups, university campuses, audio-visual equipment, computers, teachers), transportation services (motorways, aircraft, private cars, railways), food and drink.

Economics is the study of how individuals and nations use resources under their command to satisfy their wants as fully as possible or to maximize their welfare (or utility) given to their resource constraints. Economics, therefore, is concerned with scarcity and choice. Scarcity exists because there are insufficient resources to satisfy all wants fully. The need for choice arises because resources allocated to the satisfaction of one want cannot, by definition, be available to satisfy other wants simultaneously. A child with only Rs.10.00 to spend in a sweet shop has a resource constraint, i.e. Rs.10.00 Given that the child wants many different types of sweets, that child has a choice problem. A Rupee spent on ice cream means no chocolate bar.

Some wants can be satisfied without the need for choice. This is possible only when the resources required for producing continuously those goods that satisfy such wants are not scarce. Water and fresh air are regarded as free goods. This is no longer true in many parts of the world. These bounties of nature are required at different times, in different locations and in differing amounts. For example, in many part of the world the rainfall is sufficient to provide for agricultural water, which is then often stored, piped and sprinkled in field. In other words, water in such locations is not a free good: the use of the resources required to transport that must be paid for irrigation.

## Preferences, Resources and Economic Efficiency

To satisfy wants as fully as possible, given limited resources, nations must make choices. No matter how a nation is organized, no matter which political philosophy is followed, the choices all nations face are common. The economic decisions to be made involving choices are:

(a) What goods and services to produce?

(b) How to produce the selected goods and services; and

(c) What share of these goods and services are to be given to each individual or household.

These are the 'what',' how', and 'for whom' problems. Although common to all nations, they are tackled in a wide variety of ways.

Education provides a striking example involving the above three problems. How much education should be provided in a nation and of what should it consist? How should educational services be produced? Should there be more teachers and smaller classes, a greater use of video tapes and computer assisted learning, or should students study distance-learning courses at home?

Who should receive higher education-any one who wishes, only the most intelligent members of society, or only those who are prepared to pay? In some countries, over fifty percent of the college age population participate in the higher education process. In other nations the proportion of the college age population going to universities is less than one per cent. Some countries do not have universities, and in some areas of the less developed countries no elementary schools exist.

To use a nation's resource as effectively as possible implies producing the goods and services that will satisfy the people's wants as fully as possible, which in turn implies taking account of the people's preferences. Thus to achieve the highest possible level of utility in a society from given resources means assigning priorities to the potential set of goods and services that could be made available. In deciding how to spend the weekly budget, a household will try to choose that set of goods and services (from the many possible sets that could be purchased with that budget) that will provide the highest possible level of utility: the set it hopes to choose is the affordable combination of food, drink, clothing, recreation, etc., compared with all of the sets rejected, that is best suited to the preferences of the household.

If a given amount of goods were allocated randomly among a group of individuals, it might be possible to increase utility levels without increasing the amount of goods, through voluntary exchange. For example, during World War II prisoners in camps sometimes received Red Cross parcels containing tinned milk, jam, butter, tinned meat, chocolate and cigarettes. Each prisoner received an identical package but had his own individual preferences. Prisoner who did not smoke but liked chocolate could raise their utility levels by exchanging cigarettes for chocolate with prisoners who smoked but did not like chocolate. Both groups could become better of through exchange without any increase in the total amount of chocolate and cigarettes. We can see from this example that by exchanging a good with a low level of utility for a good with a high level of utility, an individual can increase his total utility level. The voluntary exchange is possible only if such a condition holds for al least two individual, so both will benefit. A point will reach ultimately where all possible exchanges that can increase utility will have been made. Then utility can be increased only if additional goods or resources become available.

This system of exchange is vital to the welfare of most countries in the world today. In the field of international trade, Scotland exports whisky to France, which in turn exports wine to Scotland. The bulk of the world is dependent on the oil exporting nations to provide fuel for transport, heating and industrial need. Russia, one of the world's major caviar produces and exports, buys food from the USA, Canada and Europe. Such exchanges among nations increase people's utilities by accommodating differences in preferences.

It is in the interest of a nation to use as few resources as possible as in the production of any one good. The fewer the resources employed in producing a good and consequently, the more fully nations wants can be satisfied. The term 'engineering efficiency' (or 'technical efficiency') describes a situation in which a good of stated quality is produced using the fewest possible resources. For building a bridge over a river, there is a minimum amount of steel necessary to ensure that the bridge will not collapse when fully utilized. However, it would be complete waste of steel to keep adding support structures to a bridge in order for it to bear, say, several 100-tonne trucks if no such vehicles will ever use the bridge. It would be a waste-technical inefficiency-since steel has many alternative uses.

The concept of economic efficiency is more complex then the concept of engineering efficiency. For economic efficiency to prevail in the allocation of nation's resources, not only must the least amount of resources be used in production of each good and service but that set of goods and services that is produced must be the set that satisfies wants as fully as possible. Country could build 100 bridges in a manner that was efficient from an engineering viewpoint but could be using resources poorly from the viewpoint of economic efficiency. This would be the case if the bridges, despite being engineering-efficient, yielded less satisfaction to the society that the other goods that could have been produced with the resources used to produce some or all of the bridges. If building 100 bridges, however, did constitute an economically efficient allocation of resources, it would mean that not only was each bridge constructed in an engineering – efficient fashion but the alternative goods foregone would have yielded less satisfaction than 100 bridges.

### Marginal Analysis and Opportunity Cost

One possible way to solve problems in which economic efficiency is the goal to consider the potential welfare from every possible resources allocation and choose that allocation that yields the highest welfare. Consider Table 1.1, which shows the scores a student will achieve in a two-hour economics final examination for different allocations of time between objective questions (maximum score 33 points) and essay questions (maximum score 60 points). The limited resource is two hours of examination time, the goal is score maximization, and the choices are different allocations of time to objective and essay questions.

Total score is at a maximum when 40 minutes are allocated to objective questions and the remaining 80 minutes allocated to essays. Since no other allocation yields a higher total, this is the most efficient use of the two hours of examination time.

**Table 1.1** Examination scores

| Objective Questions | | Essay Questions | | Total Score |
|---|---|---|---|---|
| Time Spent (minutes) | Score | Time Spent (minutes) | Score | |
| 120 | 33 | 0 | 0 | 33 |
| 100 | 32 | 20 | 23 | 55 |
| 80 | 29 | 40 | 38 | 67 |
| 60 | 25 | 60 | 48 | 73 |
| 40 | 20 | 80 | 55 | 75 |
| 20 | 11 | 100 | 58 | 69 |
| 0 | 0 | 120 | 60 | 60 |

The disadvantages of such an approach are that, first, it may not be feasible always to consider every possible allocation of resources and, second, the calculations could be very time consuming. As the number of options considered increases, the number of possible permutations approaches infinity. An alternative way to find the optimal allocation of limited resources is to start with a particular allocation and to determine how total utility or welfare changes as the allocation of resources changes. If total utility increases because of the reallocation, then the change should be made; if there is no change in the allocation of resources that will result in an increase of utility, then the optima allocation already exists.

In Table 1.1 consider the allocation of time of 80 minutes on objective questions, yielding 29 marks, and the remaining 40 minutes on essay questions, yielding 38 marks, a decrease in time of 20 minutes on objective questions costs the student 4 marks on these questions, but 20 minutes more allocated to essays gains the student 10 marks. The net gain in marks (utility) of 6 (10 - 4) is positive, indicating that the change is worthwhile, i.e., the new allocation of 60 minutes to objective question and 60 minutes to essay questions is superior to the former 80-40 allocation. But is it optimal? Consider a further reallocation of 20 minutes, i.e. 40 minutes on objective and 80 minutes on essay questions. The net gain is 2 marks (7-5). A further change of 20 minutes results in a decrease of 6 marks (-9+3). Thus 40 minutes to objective questions and 80 minutes to essays is the optimal time allocation. Making an incremental or small change in that allocation causes benefits and costs (gains and losses) to occur. The gain from the incremental change is called the *marginal benefit*. The loss from the change is called the *marginal cost*. Any action or activity in which the marginal benefits exceed the marginal costs will, if undertaken, result in an increase in total utility or well being.

The technique of considering incremental change in resource allocation and weighing the marginal benefits and marginal costs is known as marginal analysis. Marginal analysis, therefore, is a useful technique for solving problems involving optimization. Because optimization problems in economics contain constraints, e.g., income, time, labour or materials, they are called constrained maximization problems. In the analysis of such problems, economists, business people and other decision makers, use marginal analysis widely and it can be important in avoiding costly and common mistakes.

Table 1.2 contains hypothetical data on the benefits and costs of different length of a motorway extension.

**Table 1.2** Extension of motorway

| | 1 kms | 2 kms | 3 kms | 4 kms | 5 kms |
|---|---|---|---|---|---|
| **Total benefit (Rs. Lakhs)** | 2 | 5 | 9 | 12 | 13 |
| **Total cost (Rs. Lakhs)** | 1 | 2.5 | 4 | 6 | 8 |

One might conclude that the five km extension should be built because total benefits (Rs.13 Lakhs) exceed total costs (Rs. 8 Lakhs) and this, therefore, must be an efficient way to allocate resources. The marginal analysis approach shows the error in the logic: for the first km, total and marginal benefits are equal (Rs. 2 Lakhs) as are total and marginal costs (Rs. 1 Lakhs) and so, since marginal benefit exceeds marginal costs, the first mile should be built. In adding a second km, corresponding marginal costs are Rs. 1.5 Lakhs (Rs. 2.5 Lakhs – Rs. 1.0 Lakhs), whereas marginal benefits amount to Rs.3.0 Lakhs (Rs. 5.0 Lakhs – Rs. 2.0 Lakhs). Thus, the km is worth adding as are, by similar reasoning, the third and fourth km. However, for the fifth km the marginal benefit is Rs.1 Lakh (Rs. 13 Lakh – Rs.12 Lakh) and the marginal cost is Rs. 2 Lakh (Rs. 8 Lakhs – Rs. 6 Lakhs). Since the marginal cost exceeds the marginal benefit, the activity of building the fifth km-should not take place despite the fact that the total benefit of five additional kms of motorway exceeds the total cost. Only four km of additional motorway should be built.

When considering the best use of resources the alternative goods or outputs that could have been produced must be considered, since in allocating a resource to any one activity, all alternative uses of that specific resource are sacrificed. Two hours spent in playing tennis are no longer available for watching television, eating or studying. The real cost to society of any activity undertaken is the best alternative foregone. Economists call the best alternative foregone the opportunity cost of the activity undertaken. Imagine an economy with adequate natural water supplies that has resources to build an additional school or an additional hospital but not both. It decides to build the school since it concludes that the marginal benefit from a school exceeds the marginal benefits from a hospital. The opportunity cost of the school is not the money required to finance the building for the school or the resources themselves; the opportunity cost of the school is the hospital – the best alternative foregone. Assume that the same resources could be used to build a reservoir. The reservoir is a distinctly inferior alternative to the hospital since the country has an ample water supply. Thus the opportunity cost of the school is not the reservoir because the reservoir would provide too low an assessment of the opportunity cost of building the school. Similarly, in the previous example of the allocation of time between objective and essay questions (see Table 1.1), the opportunity cost of time allocated to objective questions was time allocated to essay questions, not day-dreaming during the examination, which would have had low marginal benefits in terms of final score.

### Different Economics Systems

There are three methods of solving the scarcity-choice problem: by tradition, by command, and by markets. All societies today utilize each of the methods; what distinguishes different nations is the relative weights or reliance placed on each of the methods.

In traditional economies, the set of goods and services to be produced and the methods of production typically are determined by social custom and habits established over time. The traditional method of resource allocation, common in feudal times, is the principal solution to the economic problem in many undeveloped societies; it is also prevalent in certain rural and agricultural communities in developing nations. Under this system, most economic activity is concerned with eating, clothing and housing wants. Many of the societies are largely self sufficient at a relatively low standard of living, with some trade taking place with the 'outside' world. Since there is a heavy reliance on nature for much of the output produced, changes in output are caused chiefly by the vagaries of weather. Too little or too much rain can significantly affect crops and, consequently, the standards of living. Methods of production in agriculture and fishing, for example, are often primitive, with specific tasks being assigned to different members of the community.

How the output is distributed within such societies is often determined by birthrights and other social factors, and changes in the social order occur infrequently and slowly.

While not often recognized as a significant factor in developed nations, the traditional method does still exits, especially in economic organization within the home. In the last four decades, economic organization within the home has undergone significant change. The tradition of men being the primary wage earner and wives doing the cooking, housekeeping and dressmaking, has altered as participation of women in the labour force has approached that of men. Despite dramatic changes, however, the responsibility of weekly shopping and cooking in many homes still lies in the female domain. Many children are assigned certain tasks such as room tidying and setting and clearing the table. The willingness of children to 'volunteer for extra duties' has been noted to increase markedly, albeit briefly, when they pass their driving tests. The male in the home typically takes care of minor repairs and has the responsibility of making sure cars are functioning. In some households the female is in charge of the accounts, in other the male. The pattern varies significantly over households, but whatever the pattern much of the household economy functions along traditional organizational lines.

In the command solution to the scarcity problem, the set of goods and services to be produced is determined by a central ruling body or bodies. Once the set has been determined, it is treated as a target. A plan, often of five years in duration, is drawn up to implement the choice decision. Drawing up such a plan for an economy is an extremely complex problem. Suppose 5000 tractors are assigned a high priority in the plan, the resources requirements for them of machine tools, steel, rubber, paint and labour have to be specified as they do for all other goods and services in the plan and matched against available resources. If resources appear insufficient, choice as to what should be omitted or reduced have to be made; if surplus resources exist, the plan has to be revised in the opposite direction. Errors in planning can be extremely costly: if sufficient spare parts for machine tools, for example, are not fully planned for tractor output could be reduced, food output in turn could be less than planned, which in turn could have repercussions throughout the whole economy. Because of unforeseen elements, a degree of slack, or flexibility, must be built into every plan. Some allowance is made normally for individuals and managers to adjust the deployment of resources; incentives are often provided to utilities resources more effectively and increase output above the level stipulated in the plan.

Stipulating wage and salary levels for different types of workers and income allowances for people not in the labour forces, and solve the problem of the distribution of goods and services basically also by fixing the prices of goods and services. When the plans 'go wrong', two things happen. First, since there is no compulsion for people to spend all of their incomes, some goods produced and available in the stores may not find buyers, i.e. such goods are not in accordance with consumers' wishes. The prices may be reduces; the goods may be withdrawn. Conversely, consumers may not be able to buy the goods they want because they may not be available in sufficient quantities at the fixed price to satisfy all the consumers' demands. Thus queues are not uncommon in planned economies want,' first come, first served' becomes the distribution method superimposed upon the price mechanism. Black markets, many of which are prohibited in planned economies, form. Penalties can be levied on people dealing in such markets. In a similar vein, foreign travelers to certain planned economies are warned in advance of their trip that foreign-currency dealing with residents are prohibited and subject to fines, confiscation of property, and imprisonment.

In most planned economies significant economic activities, especially in agriculture, are conducted through free markets, farmers are permitted to sell part of their output in local towns and villages, and are allowed to keep the income earned.

In the market (capitalist/free-enterprise) solution to the scarcity-choice problem, which sets of goods and services are produced is determined by the interaction of consumers who are willing to pay for them and producers who are willing to supply them in response to market price. Consumers wishing to maximize their welfare bid for the goods that most satisfy their wants. Producers wishing to maximize their welfare (profits) produce the goods and services that they believe consumers most want.

Markets are the places where consumers and producer 'meet' and where prices are determined and exchange of goods and services takes place. Some markets are highly localized while some are international-oil, wheat, and gold, for instance.

Competition for resources to produce goods and services determines the prices of these resources and consequently, the distribution of income among resource owners in capitalist societies. Those people with resources in greatest demand will receive the largest incomes and consequently will be able to buy more goods and services that individuals with fewer resources or those who earn a lower return in resource markets. People with higher incomes will have more 'money votes' and consequently a greater say in the set of goods and services produced. Thus, the capitalist system is one in which every money vote, into every person, is equal. It is one that permits concentration of income and wealth. It is one that rewards individuals not according to their needs but according to the values of the contribution of their resources to production. It is one in which individuals have freedom to own resources, to offer them or withhold them from the market, and to choose where such resources will be employed. Those individuals who have no resources that can command a return, or meager resources that earn for a low income, have to rely on the charity of upper income groups or through government action, a transfer of income to purchase the goods and services they want.

The capitalist system also has to rely on government or some other form of collective action to produce certain goods (such as national defense) that are unlikely to be forthcoming in the correct quantities through individual's action. Similarly collective action is necessary to deal with national or international problems such as pollution. Thus all economies today that fall in the capitalist camp still have significant sectors of government control or planning.

Although there are few, in any, examples of purely traditional, planned or market economies in the world today, societies or nations are so classified according to the type of solution predominantly used to allocate resources, a concomitant of how resources are allocated in resource ownership. In market economies, individuals own resources or private groups of individuals, in command economies buy the state, and in traditional economies by both the dividing lines are blurred. In all capitalist countries, the national government and state or local governments own resources; in planned economies some private property and resources are owned by individuals.

Furthermore, as time passes, the classification of a society does not necessarily remain fixed. It changes as the solutions to the problem of what to produce, how to produce it, and how to distribute production alter in response to developments in the overall economic, political and historical context within which the nation exists. For example, in the thirteenth century Britain had a feudal type of economic system operating largely in the traditional mode. The industrial revolution of the eighteenth century enabled Britain to become the 'workshop of the worked' and to emerge as the first and most advanced of the market economies.

From the end of World War II up to 1978, a larger proportion of allocative decisions were made through the command mode as a result of the Labour Party policies. This trend was reversed, however, as a result of the 1979 and subsequent Conservative Party election victories, many state owned resources were privatized and market forces played an ever-increasing role in resource allocation. There was no reversal of this role when the 1997 UK general election witnessed the return of the Labour Party.

The last three decades also have witnessed a greater market element operating in the command economies of Russia, Romania, other Eastern bloc countries, and many of the emerging nations of the world, this trend culminating in the break up of the Commenter trading bloc and commitment of the old command economies to the market system.

### Summary

We have attempted in this chapter to impress upon the reader that it is the dual existence of insatiable wants and limited resources that produce for all societies, the fundamental fact of scarcity and consequently the need for choice. Resources used to satisfy one want are no longer available to satisfy other. The decisions to be faced by all societies are the 'what', 'how' and 'for who' decisions.

A useful tool for analyzing problems involving maximization is marginal analysis-a technique that pervades all aspects of economics so that it is important that you master the concept at this stage.

You are now aware that not all societies solve the 'what', 'how', and 'for whom' problems in the same way and you know the differences among them.

One useful tool for analyzing output decisions facing an economy at a point in time and also over time is the production possibilities curve.

## Review Questions

**1.1 Which of the following is correct ?**

*The concept of scarcity means that resources :*

(a) are not available in sufficient quantities to satisfy any individual's wants.
(b) are not available in sufficient quantities to satisfy all wants for them.
(c) cannot be increased in quantity to any significant extent.
(d) are of primary importance in satisfying the wants of society.

**1.2 It has been said that the fundamental fact of scarcity is no longer applicable to the US economy. Which of the following is correct ?**

*This statement is :*

(a) true, because the US is one of the richest countries in the world.
(b) true, because the resources that are scarce in the US can be imported from abroad.
(c) false, because not all the wants of all US citizens are fully satisfied.
(d) false, because a significant number of families in the US have incomes below what is known as the poverty level.

**1.3 Examples of free goods are :**

(i) A free type with every four purchased.
(ii) A crystal drinking glass with every 20 liters of petrol.
(iii) Fresh air in an air conditioned building in Oxford Street.

**Which of the following is correct ?**

(a) II only.
(b) II and III only.
(c) I,II and III
(d) Not I, not II and not III.

**1.4 Which of the following is correct ?**

*The fact that individuals tastes and preferences differ implies that :*

(a) No two individuals ever buy the same quantities of any given good in a given time period.
(b) Free exchange of goods and services can increase society's welfare without an increase in the quantities of goods and services available.
(c) Any individuals wants can never be fully satisfied until all of a nations resources are efficiently utilized.
(d) A nation's wants can never be fully satisfied.

**1.5 A given quantity of goods can be produced in a variety of ways using different amounts of two resources, A and B.**

Method 1 uses 5 units of A and 10 Units of B.

Method 2 uses 10 units of A and 4 units of B.

Method 3 uses 6 units of A and 4 units of B.

**Which of the following statements is correct regarding engineering efficiency ?**

(a) Method 2 is more efficient than method 1.
(b) Method 3 is more efficient than method 2.
(c) Method 3 is more efficient than method 2 and method 1.
(d) Insufficient information exists to determine whether one method is more efficient than any other.

**1.6 An economically efficient society that is capable of producing more goods and services in year 2 thadn in year 1 must :**

(i) have access to superior productive techniques in year 2.
(ii) have more resources available in year 2.

**Which of the following is correct ?**

(a) (i) only.
(b) (ii) only.
(c) (i) or (ii) both (i) and (ii).
(d) Neither (i) nor (ii).

**1.7 A government has completed a cost benefit study showing that the annual value of the services from an additional 100 kms of motorway would be 400 Crores and the annual value of the services from an additional airport would be Rs. 300 Crores. To achieve the most efficient use of resources, what should the government do ?**

(a) Construct only 75 km of motorway (that is three quarters of 100).
(b) Construct only the 100 kms of motorway.
(c) Construct both the 100 kms of motorway and the airport.
(d) Not necessarily construct either any additional motorway or the airport.

**1.8 'The problem facing the Government is whether to build a new motorway system or to improve public transport throughout the country during the next three years. Resources for both projects are not available. It must be one of the other'.**

**Which of the following is correct ?**

The opportunity cost of the new motorway system mentioned in the preceding paragraph is:

(a) greater than the economy can afford.

(b) and improved public transport system.

(c) the money required to pay for it.

(d) the resources required to build it.

**1.9 The following table shows the extra daily benefit and costs that would be derived from adding successive terminals at an airport in order to increase passenger handling capacity.**

| | Additional capacity | Additional benefits (Rs. Lakhs) | Additional costs (Rs. Lakhs) |
|---|---|---|---|
| First terminal | 1000 | 45000 | 40000 |
| Second terminal | 1000 | 35000 | 25000 |
| Third terminal | 1000 | 25000 | 20000 |
| Fourth terminal | 1000 | 15000 | 18000 |

How large an expansion program should the airport undertake to maximize net benefit (total benefit minus total cost) and why ?

(a) Build one terminal that provide the greatest marginal benefit.

(b) Build two terminals since that is the level of expansion where the difference between marginal benefit and marginal cost is greatest.

(c) Build three terminals since that is the largest number of new terminals for which marginal benefit exceeds marginal cost.

(d) Build four terminals since the program would involve the largest total benefit and the lowest marginal cost.

**1.10 Consider the following statements :**

(i) For centrally planned economies, since all members of the labour force are allocated jobs, scarcity is not a problem.

(ii) For capitalist economies, since workers occasionally become unemployed, scarcity is not always a problem.

(iii) For both centrally planned and market economies, since resources are insufficient to satisfy all wants, scarcity is a problem.

**Which of the following is correct ?**

(a) I only.

(b) II and III

(c) III only.

(d) Not I, not II and not III.

**1.11 In the present program of a National Health Service (medical services provided by the government at zero cost to patients), the total benefits exceed total cost. The government's goal is efficient allocation of resources. Which of the following is correct ?**

It should be undertaken and increase in expenditure on medical services only if:

(a) The total benefit derived form all medical services would still exceed the total cost.

(b) The total benefit derived form all medical services would exceed that of any other good.

(c) The benefit from the extra medical services would outweigh the cost of doing with less of other goods.

(d) Such expenditures improve people's health independently of the costs.

**1.12 Consider the following statement :**

(i) The opportunity cost of a unit of land is the value it would create when put to its best alternative use.

(ii) The opportunity cost of a good is the value of all other goods that must be foregone in order to produce it.

**Which of the following is correct ?**

(a) I only.

(b) II only.

(c) Both I and II.

(d) Neither I nor II.

**1.13 Which of the following is correct ? To satisfy wants as fully as possible, a society must :**

(a) Choose the best set of goods and services from all feasible sets.

(b) Produce various sets of goods and services then choose one set.

(c) Ensure that free goods are available to all members of society.

(d) Ensure that luxury goods are produced only when necessities are freely available to all.

**1.14 Two individuals who both had baskets containing oranges and applets were observed exchanging voluntarily three apples for two oranges. Which of the following are correct ?**

(a) There were more apples than oranges before the exchange in one individual's basket.

(b) Both individuals benefited from the exchange.

(c) One individual benefited more than the other from the exchange.

(d) One individual prefers oranges to apples and the other prefers apples to orange.

**1.15 An economy is operating in an economically efficient manner when:**

(i) goods and services are being produced using the least amount of resources.

(ii) No individual's utility could be increased.

(iii) Society's wants are being satisfied as fully as possible.

**Which of the following is correct?**

(a) I and II only.

(b) I and III only.

(c) II and III only.

(d) I, II, and III.

**1.16 The following are three statements pertaining to the nature of the kinds of economies: traditional, command and market :**

(i) What, how and for whom goods and services are produced are problems common to traditional, command and market economies.

(ii) In traditional, command and market economies all land is owned privately but other resources may be privately and/or collectively owned.

(iii) In traditional and command economies each individual receives the same amount of goods and services, whereas in market economies individuals receive and amount of goods and services equivalent to the resources each owns.

**Which of the following statements is correct ?**

(a) I only

(b) I and II only.

(c) I and III only.

(d) I, II and III.

## Case Study

### Marginal Analysis and Noise Pollution.

This case is an application of the concept of marginal analysis. Before you tackle it, you should understand:

(a) Total benefit;

(b) Total cost;

(c) Marginal benefit;

(d) Marginal cost; and

(e) The rule for efficient resources allocation.

The case shows that the application of the basic economic concept of marginal analysis can demonstrate the error in an apparently common sense conclusion.

### *How to Deal with Noise Pollution*

There are certain sounds or noises that give some people pleasure-the disco in full swing, or the grand opera chorus. There are other noises, equally loud, that cause displeasure-motorcycles without silencer, and jet aircraft. The traffic on many motorways passing through built up areas causes noise levels that result in resident's complaint. Often action is taken to reduce such noise to tolerable levels.

How can marginal analysis help a society make sensible decisions in reducing noise pollution? Noise can be measure on a decibel (dB(A)) scale. For noise levels below 68 on the scale, people seldom complain, whereas permanent ear damage can result at levels above 90 decibels if an individual is exposed to such levels over a period of time.(you might think about this if you are a rock music fan, and you might also note the earmuffs worn by ground personnel at airports).

Suppose that the residents of housing estate decide to investigate reducing the noise level from the motorway passing near their housing estate. The average noise level is 85 on the dB(A) scale. The options shown in the table below are available to the residents to reduce motorway noise. They may choose one or more.

| Options | Marginal change in noise level(db(A)) | Cost (Rs.)* |
|---|---|---|
| 1. (a) Build concrete wall 2 meters high | –10 | 160000 |
| (b) Build concrete wall 3 meters high | –12 | 190000 |
| (c) Build concrete wall 4 meters high | –13 | 230000 |
| 2. Reduce speed limit by 10mph and enforce new limit through police control | –3 | 90000 |
| 3. Resurface road | –2 | 70000 |
| 4. Rebuild the road 4 meters below its Existing level | –10 | 2500000 |

*Total cost divided by estimated number of years of useful life.

The residents decide that they are prepared to pay, collectively, Rs. 31,000 annually for each dB(A) that noise is reduced until a level of 68 is reached, and nothing thereafter for further noise reduction.

The local council, conducting its own investigation, proposes that a 4 meter wall be built (option 1 (c)) but that no other option be considered. Its reasoning is that the annual total cost of the 4 meter wall would be Rs. 2,30,000 and the annual total benefit Rs. 4,03,000, and it points out that no there option yields such a large total benefit.

***In light of all this information, assess the following question.***

1. What is the difference in monetary terms between the total benefit and the total cost of each option ?
2. Which options should be excluded on the basic that total cost is higher than total benefits ?
3. For which options does marginal benefit exceed marginal cost ?
4. Which option should be chosen to reduce noise pollution in an economically efficient manner ?
5. What is the mistake the Council made in arriving at its decision ?
6. Does the economic solution to the problem mean that the residents will suffer no noise pollution ?

# 2

# Economic Systems and Basic Tenets

Economics can be subdivided into two main branches of study: microeconomics and macroeconomics. Because it is a complete and difficult subject, we shall begin by making simplifying assumptions about the world in which we live and gradually relax those assumptions as our knowledge of fundamental concepts and ideas grows. The purpose of this module is to provide an overview of economics.

Micro is derived from the Greek word micros, meaning small, and 'macro' from macros, meaning large. Microeconomics is concerned with the behaviour of particular items: e.g., the price of personal computers relative to the price of horror comics, the salaries of lawyers relative to the wages of farm labourers, the employment of resources in the car industry compared with the shipping industry, the behaviour of household in spending their incomes, the behaviour of business firms in hiring resources to produce different goods and services. Macroeconomics is concerned with the big picture, with aggregates in the economy: e.g., the level of a nation's output, the national unemployment rate, the inflation rate. In addition, macroeconomics is concerned with government policy making, the use of taxes and transfer, the level of government expenditure, and control of the money supply.

International economics also has micro and macro components. The micro portion is concerned with exports and imports of goods and services, tariffs, quotas, and exchange rates. The macro portion is concerned with the balance of trade (i.e. all exports and imports summed), the balance of payments (i.e. the balance of trade plus capital flows), and policy making to affect exchange rates.

The basic theory of microeconomics is the theory of demand and supply. The interaction of demand and supply determines the price of a commodity and the quantity bought and sold. Resource allocation occurs in response to price signals. The basic theory of macroeconomics is the theory of the circular flow of national income. How well off a nation can be depends upon the nation's potential to produce goods and services, which in turn depends upon the quality and quantity of its stock of natural and man made resources and the quality and quantity of its labour force. How well off a nation is depends upon how fully it utilizes its potential.

International trade allows a nation to exchange the goods and services it produces for goods and services produced by other nations. International flows of goods, services, and resources allow world output to be large than it otherwise would be.

## Strengths and Weaknesses of the Capitalist System

Every nation faces the same problem: using its resources to produce those goods and services that will maximize its well-being or utility. Every nation has a capital stock. It consists of nature's endowment (a rare land, forests, rivers, mineral deposits) and man made resources, our inheritance from past generations (road, building, factories, machine tools). Every nation also has a labour force-that proportion of the population that is able and willing to work at going wage rates and working conditions.

Part of that labour force consists of entrepreneurs and managers whose job is to combine capital and labour to produce the goods and services the people want most. How large that flow of goods and services will depend upon the quality and quantity of the capital stock and the labour force and how well these are deployed. In market economies it is the price mechanism that provides the signals that indicate how these resources should be deployed to produce the goods and services that will maximize society's utility given the resource constraint. How does the system operate ?

To understand the underlying principles, let us assume we have something that does not exist anywhere in the world, namely a pure market economy in which all resources are owned by households (consumers) and all production is carried out by firms-also, of course, owned by households. There is no government sector, no taxes and transfers, and no international trade.

Let's imagine that you decide to start a firm from the savings you have accumulated by hard work. You might also borrow money from neighbours with a promise to pay interest to start your firm, or you may make your neighbours part-owners of the firm with a promise to pay dividends from future profits. You decide to manufacture wheelbarrows with square wheels. You build a factory and buy machine tools and raw materials with your savings, hire labour and start producing wheelbarrows. After a week or so you start to worry; you are producing wheelbarrows, they are piling up in inventory but no one wants to buy them-why ? Because they are useless: they cannot be pushed, and when full cannot be pulled. Your chief engineer at the first managers meeting suggests that the product could be significantly improved if round wheels were substituted for square wheels. You concur. Now will you sell your wheelbarrows? That will depend upon the quality of your wheelbarrows and the price of your wheelbarrows compared with the quality and price of wheelbarrows produced by other firms, and also on the demand for wheelbarrows in the driven home: if you produce goods and services that no one wants, you will go out of business because there is demand for the product you are producing, your product had to be better or atlest as good as the same product produced by your competitors and priced no higher than theirs.

Let us change the scenario. Let us imagine that you invent the first wheelbarrow and your prototype has a round wheel. Orders come flooding in faster than you can cope with, and consumers anxious to obtain this marvelous machine keep offering higher prices that you initially advertised. Each week you sell to the highest bidders and your profit per wheelbarrow – the difference between cost of production and selling price – keeps increasing. What will happen is not very surprising. Other resources owner, observing your success, move into the wheelbarrow business. They too build factories, hire resources and start producing wheelbarrows, hoping to share in the large profits in this industry. As more and more wheelbarrows are produced, consumers discover that they do not have to bid as high as previously to obtain a wheelbarrow. Thus the price of wheelbarrows starts to fall. When will it stop falling? It will stop falling when resources stop moving into the industry. When will they do that? They will do that when the returns that could be earned in other industries are higher. These returns include payments to the entrepreneurs who are attempting to ensure the resources are deployed optimally. Then the wheelbarrow industry will settle down with the 'correct' number of firms satisfying the demand for wheelbarrows. There will be a 'going price' for a standard wheelbarrow, and each producing company will have to be as efficient as its competitors just to ensure it stays in business.

What is happening in the wheelbarrow industry in our example is happening in all other industries simultaneously. Resources are constantly moving from industry to industry as consumer tastes and preferences change, as technology change, and as new industries emerge and old industries die out. Resource owners are motivated to seek the highest returns from their resources since this strategy, if successful, will yield the highest income. Likewise entrepreneurs of businesses are motivated to hire resource at the lowest prices, combine them as efficiently as possible to produce the goods and services people want, and sell them at the highest prices possible since this will yield the maximum return on their efforts. Consumer with the incomes earned from hiring out their resources (for many, their labour services only) will seek out the lowest prices for the goods means the more they have to spend on all there goods and services and consequently the higher the real standard of living they will enjoy.

Prices tell consumers how far their budgets can stretch and consequently how well off they are. Process tell business firms how resources are also business firms costs and consequently, for a given level of production, inform business what their total costs will be. Putting expected revenues and excepted costs together determines expected profits and indicates whether such a business venture is potentially worthwhile.

All of these prices mentioned, whether they be of goods and services or resources, are determined in a market economy by the forces of competition-consumers competing amongst themselves to buy and businesses competing are allocated in the market economy to produce the goods and services consumer want most. In a perfect world the basket of goods and services reflect the value to society of the scarce resource used in their production. Unfortunately, the world is not perfect and, even if it were, the price mechanism would still not produce the ideal basket of goods and services. The first question is why ? The second question is can we 'interfere' with the price mechanism in a market economy and come closer to producing this optimal basket of goods and services?

Before we tackle those questions, it is worthwhile observing some facts about the world in which we live. Approximately 83 per cent of the world's output is produced and consumed by economies. However, about 19 percent of the world's population enjoys the 83 percent of the world's output, i.e., those capitalist nations comprise 19 per cent of the world's population. Reliance on market forces in the world today is growing as many socialist government economies are attempting to switch from a group of planners deciding what goods and services to produce to the market mechanism making such decisions. Today Russia, Poland, and Hungary, to name but a few, are moving towards the capitalist camp elements of capitalism, are being promoted in China, the current flagship of planned economies. Even with in market economies, socialist parties are rapidly embracing the merit results of the market system. The reason is simple: the market economy may not be perfect but, given the apparent basic nature of mankind, namely a 'selfish' motivation to improve his lot in life, the market economy currently appears to offer the best chance of converting such a desire into reality.

In the immediate post World War II period, however, the market economy appeared to have more opponents than supporters. Socialist parties were voted into power so as to correct the evils and inequities caused by the free-market 'jungle', and many resource allocation decisions formerly undertaken by the market became the province of governments of central planners. What were, and still are, the criticisms of the market economy ?

## Criticisms of the Market Economy

Criticisms of the market economy can be summarized under five headings, as follows.

**(a)** ***Wrong goods and services :*** You don't have to be an economist to realize that the capitalist system *produces* the wrong bundle of goods and services. There are plenty of flick knives, horror comic and pornographic magazines available in the economy. There is a shortage of hospitals, schools and clean streets.

**(b)** ***The fallacy of consumer sovereignty*** **:** Economists of a free market economy, may tell you that consumers voting with their dollar bill ultimately determine how resources are allocated in order to produce the most desired goods and services, but this is a myth. It is the power of advertising agencies hired by companies that persuades, consumers to buy goods and services they do not really want.

**(c)** ***The pollution problem*** **:** If the capitalist system is so great, how come the free-market economies are the world's biggest polluters-noise, air and water! The world's major capitalist economy is the USA, within which California-a state with an output valued at more than the output of most economies in the world-house Los Angeles, a city in which air can be hazardous to your health.

**(d)** ***Poverty amongst plenty*** **:** Still within the USA, if the market economy is one of the mankind's greatest inventions, how is it possible for such an economy to laud the merits of the price system when 35 million people in its population live in dire poverty?

(e) ***Inflation and unemployment*** : Economist used to tell us that we had a choice: the economy could run at full employment but we would suffer from inflation, or we could have a zero inflation rate but that would necessitate some unemployment. What we have witnessed in the recent past is the worst of both worlds-inflation plus unemployment, i.e. stagflation. Will stagflation re-emerge ?'

***These are the major attacks. Are they supported empirically ?***

(a) Flick knives, horror comic and pornographic literature are not difficult to find. They are available in most cities of the capitalist world. Is there a shortage of hospitals, good schools and clean streets? The answer is 'yes'. In many countries there are queues for medical operations, university and college places are limited, and many streets are dirty and ill-paved

(b) Is low per cent of total national output spent on advertising excessive ? That is the level of advertising for several capitalist economies, the bulk of which is spent on newspapers, magazines, direct mail and at the point of sale, rather that on TV and radio. Some advertising is obviously useful: it provides information about the characteristics of goods, including price, and also informs us about new product – for example, buying 'worthless' breakfast cereal to keep the children happy because each package contains a plastic green turtle, or being aware of the insignificant differences between pure (generic) aspirin and the many branded aspirins compare with the price differences. In contrast to these instances, companies have gone bankrupt despite massive advertising campaigns to persuade consumers to buy products.

(c) Pollution is undoubtedly a current major concern in the world's capitalist economies. It is not, however, pressing concern to the Brazilian farmer engaged in cutting down a couple of acres of rain forest so that he can grow sufficient crop to keep his family alive. The world's major polluters are the developed economies. Los Angeles, in the USA, has a population of 12 million people and an accompanying population of eight million cars and trucks – the major cause of pollution. Visibility in the Los Angeles basin is normally restricted to three miles, and children often have to stay indoors on summer days. Approximately 70 per cent of the Los Angeles city area its concrete jungle-is devoted to the automobile.

Furthermore, many beaches throughout the world are health hazards, fish cannot breed in many of our rivers, and acid rain is blamed for the destruction of forests. We also have noise pollution in factories, at airports, and in towns and cities. 'Green parties' and scientists of the greenhouse effect warn us continually. Pollution exists.

(d) While the poverty levels in capitalist countries are 'insignificant' compared with poverty levels in countries such as Bangladesh and the Sudan, where mass starvation is the normal state, there is no doubt that many people in capitalist economies live below normally accepted definitions of the poverty line. Many of these people are homeless, ill – clad, ill – fed, and in poor health, unable to find jobs and dependent upon the state or charities for a meager income.

(e) In the mid 60s, governments and economists congratulated themselves on the success of their policies because many economies achieved full employment accompanied by very little inflation. However, in the 70s and 80s we observed and experienced in many capitalist countries stagflation, that is high unemployment and simultaneously high inflation, for USA and the UK. In the early 2000, these two countries had low inflation and low unemployment rates and were the envy of the other major capitalist nations-where the inflation but not the unemployment, problem appeared to have solved.

Thus there is little doubt that empirical evidence supports these criticisms of the market economy. What can be done about those weaknesses? People on the political 'left' maintain the answer is relatively simple: have the government solve the problems where the price mechanism fails by:

(a) Banning 'bad' goods and services and providing 'good' goods and services, which the market mechanism does not;
(b) Established advertising standards to prove useful information to house holds and to prohibit misleading and persuasive advertisements;
(c) Setting and enforcing pollution standards;
(d) Establishing poverty levels and providing goods and services to the poor so that every household enjoys a reasonable living standard; and
(e) Controlling wages and prices in times of inflation, and becoming an employer of the last resort, i.e. creating jobs through government expenditure when unemployment threatens.

People on the political 'right' also maintain that the solution is simple: problems exist in the world's market economies because there is too much government in these economies. If greater reliance were placed on market forces, the bulk of the problems or apparent weaknesses would disappear.

Who is correct? The answer is that there are some areas of economic activity where reliance on the market mechanism will not provide an efficient allocation of resources and consequently will prevent a nation enjoying the optimal basket of goods and services. On the other hand, significant inefficiency and inactive problems arise when government controls areas of economic activity. Before you decide where you lie on the political spectrum of the 'correct amount of government interference' in the market economy, let us consider the areas of market failure or partial failure.

## Public Goods

Before we discuss public goods, let us consider private goods. A private good is one that you buy and consume and for which the act of consumption affects no one else. For example, consider a good bottle of maltova retailing for Rs. 150. In making the decision to buy and consume maltova, you will apply marginal analysis, i.e., the extra utility you receive from allocating that Rs. 150 to other goods and services ? If the answer is 'yes', you have to do is find some one who has a bottle of good malt whisky but who would prefer to exchange it for Rs. 150. Such people are not hard to find-you find them in liquor stores. Both you and liquor store owner benefit from the exchange of one bottle for Rs. 150; if this was not the case, no exchange would take place.

A public good is different. If you buy a public good, other people can consume and enjoy it without paying for it. If someone else buys it, you can consume it without paying for it. This causes a problem as far as the efficient allocation of economic resources is concerned.

Consider a housing estate A, B, C and D live in an exclusive housing community. Independently, each hears that a series of robberies has occurred in neighboring estates. Again, independently, each considers whether or not it is worthwhile to hire a security firm to patrol the area. Each uses marginal analysis in weighing up the extra cost of such protection, Rs.120 per day, against the benefits of not being robbed. Each concludes that protection is a good buy and suddenly there are four protection vehicles patrolling the street. The robber also uses marginal analysis to decide that the ABCD community is not a fruitful area of robbing activity, given the amount of protection.

A suggests that B,C and D get rid of their protection, since one patrolling vehicle is adequate, and that each share the Rs.200 cost, i.e. Rs. 50 each. All agree. The patrol vehicle continues to circle the street, thus protecting A, the non-contributor, as well as B,C and D, who are paying for the services. We have a public good in the community. A few weeks later, B drops out and C and D now bear the cost. Each paying Rs. 100. The following week C drops out and poor old D, who wishes to remain protected, carries the whole Rs. 200 cost. A, B and C are 'free riders'. If they had been ignorant of each others actions, there would have been too many resources in the protection business in this community – three unnecessary security vehicles - and an inefficient use of resources.

Thus when public goods are involved, two issues have to be faced: how much of a given public good should be bought and who should pay for it? The price mechanism will not solve this problem. Is it possible to have too many resources committed, e.g., four security vehicles, but also possible to have too few as each person waits for his neighbor to buy the good ? Do we consume many public goods? The answer is 'yes'. National defense, police and fire services, the judicial system and lighthouse are all examples of public goods. To solve the scarcity-choice problem in this context requires some type of collective action, and government, be it local, state or national, is often the collective agent that makes the decision.

Different political parties offer different bundles of public goods in their election manifestos and different tax structures to pay for them. For example a political party might stress the need for a large national defense commitment, including the most sophisticated weapons system, and private health services and a tax structure in which the highest marginal tax is for private health services, and a tax structure in which the highest marginal tax rate (i.e. the amount of income taxes payable on the last rupee earned) is 30 per cent. An opposition party might argue for minimal national defense, a national health service and a very progressive tax structure with high marginal tax rates, e.g., 60 per cent for individuals earning more that Rs. 10,00,000 per annum. Hopefully, we are showing in this simple but realistic example how societies and their political systems can modify the market mechanism to affect both the allocation of resources and the distribution of disposable (after tax/transfer) income.

## Externalities

Externalities occur when the actions of an individual or firm confer benefits/losses to individuals of firms not directly involved in that action.

After having just finished a meal in a restaurant and decided to have a cigarette with coffee, you find all the neighboring tables are filled with non-smokers. Should you smoke? Should you be allowed to smoke? Allowed by whom ? The restaurant owner or the law? Suppose on the market there exists a Rs.50 widget that, if placed on the end of a cigarette, prohibits the emission of noxious fumes. Who should buy the widget in the restaurant, the smoker or the non-smokers? The smoker, the non-smokers will argue. But why should the smoker buy clean air for the non-smoker? If the non-smoker wants clean air in the restaurant, shouldn't they be prepared to pay for it?

### Economies of Scale

A third cause of market failure involves economics of scale. Economics of scale arise when, as a firm's level of output expands, the unit cost of producing output falls.

It is important to realize that economies of scale are a form of market failure requiring a 'collective' solution. The problem that immediately presents itself is that, with a guaranteed return, there is no incentive to minimize costs.

### Income Distribution

The fourth weakness of the price mechanism is a different animal altogether, involving the distribution of income. As seen earlier in this module income in the form of wages, salaries, rent, interest and dividends flow from firms to resource owners. Thus, how large and individual's or household's income can be will be determined by the value of resources owned. Households whose resources are in short supply and that are eagerly sought after by firms will have 'large' incomes. At the other end of the spectrum, households with no marketable resources will have zero income. The demand for services produced form these resources. For most households in capitalist or market economies, their principal resource is their labour. A proportion of the population, however, owns stock and share, or equity, in companies, firms or financial institutions, i.e., they are part owners of the capital stock of these companies and earn interest and dividends on such resources. Others own land and property, which in turn earn rent.

In market economies, returns to resource owners are determined by the forces of demand and supply, just as the prices of goods and services are determined by demand and supply forces.

Income distribution is depicted by a curve known as the Lorenz curve, named after its inventor Konrad Lorenz who devised the graphical presentation at the turn of the twentieth century. The Lorenz curve shows the cumulative percentage of incomes of any given cumulative percentage of households. Households are numbered on the horizontal axis from the lowest to the highest incomes. Thus the lowest 20 percent receive 35 per cent of national income. If every household receive an identical income, the resulting Lorenz curve would be represented by the solid 45° line.

How should income be distributed? Or, to put the question another way, what proportion of the good and services produced should flow to what proportion of the population? Is this equitable ? Questions of justice or equity are value judgements. Your opinion is a valid as a professional economist's opinion, or as a clergyman's, or as a film star's. There is no 'right' of 'wrong' income distribution in economics. How income should be distributed is not an unimportant question but it is a question not subjectable to economic analysis. Economists can evaluate the marginal benefits and marginal costs of adopting various strategies or polices to change the income distribution, but they have no expertise, only personal opinions, in stating what the 'ideal' income distribution is.

### Macroeconomics - an overview

How large the flow of national output can be/will be derived by, the quality and quantity of the capital stock and the quantity and quality of the labour force. It is obvious that if part of the capital stock is lying idle and part of the labour force is unemployed, national output will be less than its potential. As a result, households will enjoy fewer goods and services than the economy could produce.

To understand basic macroeconomics, we shall ignore, temporarily, the international sector. The reason for the large consumption sector is obvious. Consumption is the basic rationale for economic activity, i.e., using scarce resources to produce the goods and services that we enjoy. Why produce government goods? They are part of the goods and services we also enjoy – national defence, fire and police protection, are public goods. Thus they can be considered consumption goods also. But why produce investment goods? The reason is that we wish to enjoy a higher standard of living in the future. If we did not produce any investment goods, our capital stock would decline, building and factories would disintegrate, and machine tools would wear out. National output, remember, is a function of the quality and quantity of the capital stock and the labour force. Thus if we wish to enjoy increased living standards in the future, we must sacrifice some consumption today and allocate a proportion of our resources to increase the quality and quantity of the capital stock and/or the labour forces.

In addition, as technological change takes place, it does not occur in a vacuum but is embodied in new capital equipment. For example, we live currently in the computer age, a quite remarkable technological innovation, consider work processing. We cannot take an old Olivetti typewriter and 'add on' a word processing package. The marvelous economies and increases in output realizable from developments in word processing, are achievable only by building computers that can exploit the technological breakthrough. Similarly you cannot attach a jet engine to the Wright brothers aeroplane or attach a petrol engine to horse's rear end to revive the horse and carriage trade. Technological change has contributed more to improve living standards in the past two centuries than has the increase in the size of the labour force or the size of the capital stock. The realization of the benefits of new inventions requires incorporation of technological change into new capital goods. How much current consumption should be sacrificed for future consumption, therefore, is a decision every society must face. For less developed economies with low living standards, this can be a very painful choice.

Let us return to our economy with unemployment resources, ignoring the desirability of economic growth temporarily, how can we, or governments representing us, get the economy to full employment and avoid wasting resources. The tools available come under two classifications: fiscal policy and monetary policy. Fiscal policy consists of changing government expenditure and/or tax rates. Monetary policy consists of changing the money supply or interest rates. Let us consider each in turn via some examples.

To cure the unemployment problem (people plus part of the capital stock), the government announces a large road building program and invites tender for 1000 km of motorway. A contract is awarded. Construction companies hire unemployed labour and order new road-building equipment, and the road is built. With the incomes earned, the people involved in building the road spend part of the income earned on large variety of goods and services. This in turn stimulates further economic activity. Firms have to produce more goods and services to meet the increased demand, which involves hiring more people and perhaps buying more capital goods. Thus a multiplier process produces many more goods and services and creates many more jobs that are created by the initial expenditure on the road system. Alternatively, the government considers to cut income tax rates. Households now have a higher disposable income. They spend more, i.e. buy more goods and services, which in turn creates more revenue for the firms supplying these goods and services and therefore more income for the labour forces and owners of these firms, who also will spend more of their enhanced incomes. In other words, the multiplier process is in operation again.

Suppose the decision is made to ignore fiscal policy and concentrate on monetary policy. The money supply is increased, the price of money (the interest rate) falls, and this in turn can affect both firms and households. Take firms first. The cost of borrowing money falls. Investment projects that were not profitable when the expected rate of return was 15 per cent per annum and the cost of borrowing money falls. Investment expenditure increases. The firms that produce these capital goods experienced more orders, hire more people, and again the multiplier process goes into operation. Now let's consider households. Lower interest rates means increased demand for houses, washing machines, cars anything affected by the cost of borrowing. Increased demand leads to more goods and services being produced and ultimately more jobs, and consequently a reduced rate of unemployment of both the labour force and the capital stock.

This all sounds quite simple. All we have to do is to measure the unemployment rate of the labour force and the capital and estimate by how much we have to stimulate the economy through fiscal or monetary policy and bang right there. Then we achieve full employment, making the best use of our resources. You will not be surprised to learn that the real world is not quite so simple. What are the problems? There are many and they are complex.

First, we are not shooting at a fixed target. The potential of the economy changes over time; it is not static but very dynamic. Technology changes occur continuously; new industries expand; old industries decline. People emigrate and immigrate. People join the labour forces; people retire from the labour force. Firms decide to expand their capacity and build new factories and new office blocks; others contract. Foreign nations decide to invest in certain countries; some countries impose barriers to keep out foreign investment.

Second, it is difficult to predict households, and firms' behaviours. Tastes and preferences change; what was in fashion last year is not in fashion this year. Firms make investment decisions based on what they expect households to buy in the future. Some get it right; some get it wrong. Predicting the level and direction of investment expenditure is fraught with hazards; investment expenditure is the most volatile component of national income.

Third, we have no control over the outside world on which we are dependent for the supply of goods and services. Suppose we are an oil importing economy in which oil and its derivatives are essential to many of our industries. The price of oil doubles; in the immediate future we have no alternative fuels. The concomitant effects can be severe. Households buy the same amount of oil and related products despite the twofold price increase. Given their budget constraints; the demands for other goods and services plummet, workers are laid off and the economy is in a recession.

Fourth, discovering exactly - or even approximately - how close the economy is to producing at its potential involves time lags; taking 'corrective' action involves time lags; benefitting from the implementation of the 'correct' fiscal and monetary policies also involves time lags before full utilization of resources is achieved. And remember the making of fiscal and monetary policy is done in economies in which potential national output is increasing.

Fifth, no modern capitalist system lives in isolation; what is happening in other economies can have a significant affect. A recession in the rest of the world, for instance in a market for our exports, affects domestic employment of both labour and capital goods. Uncertainty about the state of our economy can cause capital flights affecting the balance of payments, the exchange rate, the demands for our exports with a 12 to 18 month lag, employment opportunities and the utilization of our capital stock.

These are the concepts and issues that we shall analyse and discuss in the macroeconomic section of the course. Lest you believe such problems are not too complex, imagine how you deal with such complexities if the starting position of your economy is one of high ware and force inflation, a large government budget deficit, high unemployment, a large balance of trade deficit and the stated objectives are a full employment economy, zero inflation, a balanced budget, exports equal to imports and a stable exchange rate. And that is economics!

# 3

# Demand

In this module, we shall start by studying how a household allocates its income to make itself as well off as possible. For most households, income is a scarce resource. This can be supplemented by using saving and/or by borrowing against future income, but, temporarily ignoring such supplements, we shall assume a household has a limited amount of income at some given time period. Thus a household has budget constraint. What the household attempts to do is to allocate this limited income on goods and services that create the greatest household satisfaction, or, using economic jargon, to maximize utility subject to a budget constraint.

There are many ways to allocate the limited income. The household has many wants that it wishes to satisfy. Companies or firms have produced, or can produce, many goods and services that they would like the household to buy. But the household cannot buy them all because it has a budget constraint. An allocation of Rs.1000 to the purchase of food in a week is no longer available for car repairs or clothes.

Subject to legal considerations, most people in market economies are free to allocate their income as they wish. It is this consumer freedom that is the cornerstone of a market economy. As we shall seem, it is consumer spending patterns that indicate to companies while goods and services households consider most desirable, i.e., it is the 'voting' with rupee notes on the part of households that encourages companies to produce the goods and services people want. Most companies respond to consumers preferences as expressed through their spending patterns by hiring the necessary resources to produce the desired goods and services. But they do not do so because of love for their fellow men; they do so because they can make a profit on such transactions. These are the driving forces of a capitalist or market of free-enterprise economy: consumers trying to maximize utility from hiring resources to produce the goods and services consumer want most.

Is our assumption of consumer rationality - that households know their own best interests - valid ? So people argue 'no' and further argue that there should be limits on the goods and services for which consumers can freely bid through a market mechanism. What do you think? Should consumer be allowed to buy alcohol and tobacco? What about soft drugs, hard drugs, sporting rifles and sub-machine-guns ?

In a similar vein, should consumer be forced to buy certain goods and services? What about seat belts and crash helmets if they drive cars or motor cycle ? What about paying taxes for national defence and police services, and what about paying taxes to build schools and have teacher if those paying have no children ? What about personal insurance contributions ? What about car insurance, medical insurance, property insurance ?

The answer to some of these questions are value judgments; but for there, as we shall see, a market economy - with each household pursuing its own self interest - will not produce the optimal basket of goods and services through the market mechanism. No matter what your personal opinion about the desirability of alcohol part of their income to these goods and, in response to consumer spending, manufacturers do produce such goods.

We shall start by assuming that consumers know their own best interests and study how consumers signal with rupee notes to indicate their preferences to manufacturers. Manufacturers are concerned with people's preferences only to the extent that these preferences are backed by rupee notes.

In the ensuing discussion we shall make no distinction between the household and the individual, even though many households consist of more than one individual, each with differing tastes and preferences. In other words, we shall assume the household consists of more than one individual, each with differing tastes and preferences. In other words, we shall assume the household as an individual consumer and in know of its tastes and preferences. Many teenagers might well dispute this point and argue that insufficient weight is given to their wants in allocating the household budget – for example, too many carrots and not enough Coca-Cola, and undoubtedly insufficient resources allocate to the family car (or cars) when the driving test is passed, despite an increased willingness on their part to put out the rubbish and perform a multitude of household tasks.

### *The Theory of Consumer Choice*

The rational consumer attempts to maximize utility or satisfaction subject to a budget constraint. Thus the household will change its expenditure pattern, i.e., buy a different combination of goods and services in some given time period, only if the change can yield a higher level of satisfaction. Only then will the household be in equilibrium. Of course, the tastes and preferences change over them, albeit slowly, and new goods and services are constantly appearing on the market, but the principle of attempting to maximize utility remains. When will the consumer be in equilibrium? This state will be reached when the utility received for the last rupee spent on any good or services just equals the utility received form the last rupee spent on any other good or service. Then, and only then, will there be no gain in total utility from a reallocation of expenditure.

As an individual consumes more of a good in given time period, total utility increase, but at a decreasing rate. The extra utility derived from consuming an additional unit of good is known as marginal utility. Marginal utility decreases as the consumption of good increase. This is known as the Law of Diminishing Marginal Utility. A tennis player at the end of a five- set match will obtain more utility from the first mouthful of waste than from the second, more from the second that from the third and so on. At some stage, say by the sixth mouthful, his thirst will have gone and he will obtain no more utility from additional water – and at the point he stops drinking.

The existence of diminishing marginal utility means that an individual can increase total utility by purchasing a combination of goods and services rather than by allocating the budget of one good only. Total utility can be increased by reallocation expenditure from goods with lower marginal utility to goods with higher marginal utility. Suppose you were dining out in a Rs.20 per helping, marginal utility is at work. You are much more likely to select a variety of items from the menu in order to maximize total utility given your tastes and preferences and your Rs.40 budget constraint. It is the desire to maximize satisfaction that stops you telling the waiter to bring you Rs.40 worth of food in any order.

The rule for efficient consumer behavior, i.e., for choosing the combination of goods that would yield the highest level of utility from a given budget is that the budget is allocated so that the last rupee spent on each good yields the same, utility. What if one good (good A) is twice as expensive as another good (good B)? in that case the lot unit of good A consumed will have to yield twice the level of utility of the last unit of good B consumed. Thus to be in equilibrium, i.e. maximizing total utility, the following condition must hold :

$$\frac{\text{Marginal Utility of Good A}}{\text{Price of Good A}} = \frac{\text{Marginal Utility of Good B}}{\text{Price of Good B}}$$

$$= \ldots\ldots = \frac{\text{Marginal Utility of Good Z}}{\text{Price of Good Z}}$$

That is :

$$\frac{MU_A}{P_A} = \frac{MU_R}{P_B} = \ldots = \frac{MU_Z}{P_Z}$$

Suppose an individual allocated his income on two goods only, goods A and B, such that :

$$\frac{MU_A}{P_A} > \frac{MU_B}{P_B}$$

How could he/she increase total utility be buying more of A and less of B. Given the law of Diminishing Marginal Utility, as more of A is bought, the marginal utility of A decreases. Simultaneously, as less of B is bought, its marginal utility increases. Thus by a reallocation of the budget from A to B, $MU_A$ declines and $MU_B$ increases. There will be one combination of A and B purchases at which :

$$\frac{MU_A}{P_A} = \frac{MU_B}{P_B}$$

With this combination, the last dollar spent on A and the last dollar spent on B provide the same utility, and so total utility is maximized. And other combination yields a lower level of total utility.

Suppose in America if a person decides to visit the latest wine bar in town with a budget of $500. This wine bar serves only local wine at $20 per glass and cheese sandwiches at $10 each. He like both wine and cheese. How should he allocate his $500 on wine and sandwiches? To maximize utility he should consume wine and sandwiches in such amounts that the last dollar spent on each yields the same utility, i.e.,

$$\frac{MUwine}{\$20} = \frac{MUsandwiches}{\$10}$$

The utility of the last glass of wine must therefore be twice the utility of the last cheese sandwich.

Further, suppose that the owner of the wine bar, attempting to attract the customers in future, gives $50 voucher that he must spend that night on wine and sandwiches. With this additional budget he can now purchase more of each, both wine and sandwiches. However, the marginal utility of both wine and sandwiches will decline as you consume more – remember the Law of Diminishing Marginal Utility – although total utility will rise. In his new equilibrium position, it must still be true that.

$$\frac{MUwine}{\$20} = \frac{MUsandwiches}{\$10}$$

Although this of course assumes he can still make rational choices despite the amount of wine consumed!

Assume now that he is in equilibrium in his wine and cheese world on his $10 per night budget, and thus :

$$\frac{MU_W}{P_W} = \frac{MU_S}{P_S}$$

To attract more customers, the owner of the wine bar reduces the price of a glass of wine, i.e. $P_w$ goes down. As far as you are concerned this will cause disequilibrium, with

$$\frac{MU_W}{P_W} = \frac{MU_S}{P_S}$$

To restore equilibrium, i.e., to make

$$\frac{MU_W}{P_W} = \frac{MU_S}{P_S}$$

Again, he must reallocate his budget between wine and sandwiches – buying more wine and fewer sandwiches than previously. As he will consume more wine, the marginal utility of wine will decrease and as he consumes fewer sandwiches the marginal utility of sandwiches will increase, and when equality is restored he will be back in equilibrium but better off than before because the reduction in the price of one of his staple foods is similar, but not identical, to the owner giving his the $50 voucher. He will have experienced an increase in real income and his total utility will have increased in both ways, so that even though his income has not increased, he can buy more with it.

What these examples show is that both income (budget) and prices affect the quantities of goods he buy. These are not the only factors, however, that affect his purchases or demands for different goods and services.

### *Individual (household) Demand*

The quantity of a particular good that an individual buys in any given time period depends on a large number of factors. For example, the amount of vacation or holidays purchased by a upper middle class household in a year may depend upon:

(a) The price of a week in Ooty versus two weeks in Manali;
(b) The prices of other goods that could be bought instead of a vacation, for example a second hand car;
(c) Household income;
(d) Size and age distribution of the family;
(e) State of health;
(f) Expected weather conditions; and
(g) Price of tickets.

Similarly, the amount of milk a household buys in a day will depend upon a large number of factors. The price of milk will be important, but so also will be the price of alternatives, e.g., butter. Household income, in low, may dedicate, no milk at all is purchased.

To isolate and measure the influence of any one factor on potential purchases of a particular good, it is necessary to hold constant all other factors affecting in tuition fees and wanted to investigate the impact this would have on student applications. Further, suppose that, simultaneously, educational grants and family income were increasing. This would make accurate calculation of the impact of increased fees difficult. Similarly if an electronic company's sales of personal computers are lagging and it is considering an increase in its advertising budget, measuring the effectiveness of such expenditure will have to be disentangled from all factors affecting PCs, e.g., economic recession, competing products, after sales service levels, expectations of more advanced machines, foreign exchange rates, interest rates and the investment plans of customers.

In studying demand, we shall select one variable initially and assume all other factors affecting demand for the good in question are held constant. We shall then investigate how changes in the selected variable affect demand for this good. Economists use the Latin expression *ceter paribus* (with other things remaining equal or unchanged, sometimes abbreviated *cet. Par.*). When investigating such a relationship, we shall encounter this expression throughout the study of economics.

Because of the importance of prices in providing information to consumers and producers of goods and services, and because it has an effect on their behaviour, we shall concentrate initially on the relationship between the price and the quantity of a good that an individual would be willing to buy in a given time period. This relationship is known as individual demand for a good.

Thus, the demand curve does not describe an event, i.e., it does not tell us how much biryani an individual actually bought; it is a hypothetical relationship concerning what our individual would be prepared to buy at each price, in a given time period, *cet. Par.*

Our individual is now in a sweet shop, mindful of the household budget constraint, looking at potential purchases. The sweet looks fresh and is priced at Rs.60 per kilo. Just as he is about to buy 2 kilos, the hotelier replaces the Rs.60 per kilo sign with a Rs. 40 per kilo sign, explaining that it is Saturday and he does not want to be left with unsold sweet over the weekend. Our purchaser is delighted and selects to buy 3 kilos now instead of 2. Has the individuals his demand curve changed? No. All he has done is move to a new position on his demand curve. In everything determining the position of the demand curve remains unaltered, i.e. if all the *ceters* remain pares, then neither the position nor shape of the demand curve changes.

The typical demand curve is negatively in-line to price axis: at higher prices lower quantities would be purchased; at lower prices higher quantities would be purchased. There are two reasons for this negative slop. First, at higher price the individual is unable to purchase as many units of goods as one normally purchases because of the budget or income constraint. Second, at higher prices the individual substitutes relatively cheaper goods for the good in question. The decrease in quantity of a food (good X) that would be purchased at a higher price, is therefore, a combination of two effects: an income / budget effect and a substitution effect.

The income and substitution effects can be isolated. A higher price of good X will, *cet. Par.* Lower and individuals total utility because it decreases the quantities of goods he (or she) is able to purchase, i.e., he suffers a loss in real income. An equivalent loss in total utility could be caused by money income (budget) being reduced by a certain amount and prices of all goods, including X, remaining unchanged. Such a reduction in money income would lower the purchase of good X i.e., the income effect leads to a reduction in the quantity of X purchased.

The difference between the lower quantity of X purchased because of a price increase in X and the decrease in quantity due to the income effect is the substitution effect. Alternatively, the substitution effect is the decrease in the quantity of good X purchased that results from the change in the price of X relative to other goods, if one were to compensate the individual for the resulting change in his real income.

Consider an individual who chooses to work 5 days a week at Rs. 100 per day. He does not work additional days per week because he considers that each day of leisure is worth at least Rs. 100 i.e. Rs. 100 (the daily wage rate) is what he gives up for every day of leisure he enjoys. If the wage rate was to increase to Rs. 150 per day, would he work more or less than 5 days per week? The answer depends on the relative strengths of the income and substitution effect.

If he were to continue working 5 days per week, his weekly income would increase from Rs. 500 to Rs. 600. At the higher income he would buy more of all goods, including leisure. If he 'buys' more leisure, it means that he will reduce the number of days worked per week; therefore, the income effect could lead to reduction in days worked. However, the price of leisure does not remain constant. The cost of a day of leisure now rise to Rs. 100 per day because that is what it costs the individual to 'buy' and a day of leisure. At a higher price for leisure, the individual will substitute relatively cheaper goods. But buying less leisure is equivalent to working more days. Therefore, the substitution effect would lead to and increase in days worked. Thus in this example the income effect (buy more leisure) and the substitution effect (buy less leisure) work in opposite direction. It is not possible to know a *priori* for a given individuals preferences for leisure versus income. However, the effect on the average worker over time is clear: days worked by the average individual have decreased over the past 10 years from over 60 days to under 5 days a week, and from this it appears that the income effect has outweighed the substitution effect.

The substitution effect is always negative, in other words the increase in the price of a good will always lead to the substitution of relatively cheaper goods for that good. The income effect may be positive or negative. For 'normal' goods the decrease in real income caused by an increase in the price of a good will lead to a smaller quantity being purchased and the increase in real income caused by a decrease in price will lead to a larger quantity being purchased, so that the income effect is positive since changes in real income and quantity purchased are of the same sign. Thus for normal good the positive income effect reinforces the negative substitution effect and the demand curves of such goods always slope downwards from left to right. Thus, for instance, where part of a household weekly budget is allocated to chicken, meat and fish and the price of chicken falls, not only will more chicken be purchased because real income will have risen but more chicken will also be purchased as it is substituted for relatively more expensive meat and fish, i.e., the income and substitution effects reinforce each other leading to more chicken being purchased at lower prices and exhibiting the normally sloped demand curve of chicken.

An increase in real income may be caused by an increase in money income (budget) while the prices of goods remain constant, or by a decrease in the prices of goods, while income remains constant. And so far as 'inferior good', the quantity purchased falls when real income rises. As a family's money income rises and the prices of all goods remain the same, the family's real income will also rise. When this occurs, the purchases of cheap cuts of meat, for example usually decline. Another example of an inferior good is low cost housing, since, with higher incomes, families switch to superior housing.

For inferior goods, the negative substitution effect of price change counteracts and generally exceeds the income effect, i.e., the change in the relative price of good X leads to a change in the quantity of good X purchased, and this is greater than the change in the quantity of good X purchased, because of the change in real income caused by the price of X changing. The demand curve is therefore still normally sloped. For example, assume margarine is an inferior good. While a decrease in the price of margarine may lead to a family substituting margarine for milk, the resulting increase in real income may cause more milk and less margarine to be purchased. The substitution effect, i.e., margarine for milk, as a rule outweighs the income effects, which for this good is negative and which causes less margarines to be purchased because of rising real income. Thus the demand curve for margarine will be normally sloped even though it is an inferior good, such that a lower price of margarine will be accompanied by a larger quantity purchased, *cet. par.*

There is one famous example where the income effect exceeds the substitution effect and where, over a range of prices and real income, a non-normal demand curve can be produced. This type of good is known as a Giffen good: at higher prices a larger quantity is purchased, though the range of prices for which this condition holds is limited.

In nineteenth century Ireland, it is alleged that the bulk of family income was spent on potatoes because all the people could afford for this only. However, when the potato crop was exceptionally large and the price of potatoes fell considerably, Irish peasants experienced a significant rise in real income. The same number of potatoes could be bought for much less and with the money left over Irish families could buy vegetables and meat. However, the purchase of other foodstuffs meant that fewer potatoes were required and thus their purchases could be reduced. Thus at lower process fewer potatoes were purchased, and this was caused by the very large income effect.

There is no empirical evidence that such a good ever existed but students being students, like exceptions, and if Victorian economist Sir Robert Geffen's hypothesis about the 1845 Irish potato famine helps clarify income and substitution effects. I am all for Sir Robert. With the exception of people who spend a large proportion of their incomes only on food, it is very difficult to imagine a family in advanced economies today for whom changes in the price of any one good could have such a dramatic effect on their real income.

Movements along a typical demand curve indicate that higher quantities are purchased as price falls, i.e., the quantity purchased varies as price varies. Prices and quantities are, not surprisingly; know in this context as variables. All factors other than price that affect purchases and that we assume to be unchanged in constructing a demand curve are know as parameters. Given that the parameter are fixed, the quantity of a good purchased will therefore depend on the price of that good; quantity becomes the dependent variable. Because it is highly unlikely in most markets that any single individual's purchase of a good will affect the price of that good, price is know as the independent variable.

Thus the position and shape of a demand curve will depend upon the parameters; and if any change occurs in any one of the parameters, the position and shape of the demand curve will change. We stated earlier that household tastes and preferences ultimately determine how resources are allocated in capitalist economies. In constructing an individual curve, tastes and preferences are considered to be parameters, in the other they are assumed to be unchanged in a given time period. Over time, however, tastes and preference do change, consequently the position and shape of demand curves shift. This can lead to price changes, of at least signals to producers, forcing them to redeploy resources if they wish to stay in business.

To simplify our analysis above, we have concentrated on a relatively brief time period, i.e., one week. For many households, one week or one-month is a convenient planning period, because they are paid weekly or monthly, have a weekly or monthly budget constraint, and plan expenditures accordingly. Many household decisions, however, require to be analysed over a longer period – for example, the decision to borrow money over a period of 25 years so as to purchase a house. Similarly the ability of students to borrow money, and maintain a level of consumption above current income – and the willingness of lenders to lend money to such students – is based on expectations of both students and lenders that a student's future income will be sufficient to pay back the sum borrowed plus interest. However, the principals of utility maximization given budget or income constraints remain in force.

Earlier we argued that utility maximization dictated that

$$= \frac{MU_a}{P_a} = \frac{MU_b}{P_b} = \ldots = \frac{MU_z}{P_z}$$

And that as an individual consumes more of a good in any given time period, total utility increase but marginal utility decreases. What then is the connection between utility theory and our downward-sloping demand curve? The law of Diminishing Marginal Utility implicitly argues that an individual will only be willing to buy more of a good if the price falls.

Suppose you are in equilibrium and consequently maximizing your utility in a two-good world in which you allocate your budget on biryani (b) and Tea (t), with biryani costing Rs.20 per plate and tea costing Rs.5. Then

$$\frac{MU_b}{P_b} = \frac{MU_t}{P_t}$$

Further, suppose that at those prices

$$\frac{MU_b}{P_b} = \frac{MU_t}{P_t} = \frac{4}{1}$$

If the price of biryani is reduced to Rs. 10 per plate, then

$$\frac{MU_b}{P_b} \text{ would become } \frac{8}{1}$$

So that the last Rs. 5 spent on biryani will now yield approximately twice as much satisfaction since you can now buy two plates instead of one. However,

$$\frac{MU_t}{P_t} \text{ would become } \frac{4}{1}$$

And spending less on tea reduces utility by 4 while spending on biryani increases utility by almost 8, giving a net gain of 4 (+8-4). Nevertheless, as you consume more biryani and less tea, the marginal utility of biryani will decline and the marginal utility of tea will increase. You will continue to reallocate expenditure until you are back in equilibrium, i.e., until

$$\frac{MU_b}{P_b} = \text{again equals } \frac{MU_t}{P_t}$$

Thus your demand curve for biryani will be negatively inclined to the price axis. The same reasoning applies to the tea, or any other good or service.

So far we have concentrated on individual demand. In markets where there are large number of firms (suppliers), the individual demand for any product can be assumed to have a negligible influence on both the price and quantity bought and sold of that good. Whether or not you buy a tea packet one day in your local supermarket does not significantly affect the sales or profits of the supermarket selling approximately 500 tea packets per day.

However, when we consider total demand in any given market, we are adding together all of the individual demands. Total market demand is something about which companies are very concerned.

### Summary

The keystone of the market mechanism is the determination of prices. To understand this mechanism requires you to appreciate the interaction between demand and supply. This module has introduced you to the first of these and you have learned to distinguish between movements along a demand curve and shifts in a demand curve, and the relevant factors involved in both.

The importance of the concept of elasticity is reflected in its relationship to total expenditure, a concept vital to both firms and governments in setting prices and taxes. You now understand the meaning of equilibrium conditions for maximizing consumers utility and how expenditure on good and service changes as prices, incomes and other related factors change. Such an understanding is a necessary condition for grasping the meaning of 'economy efficiency' in a market economy.

## Review Questions

**3.1 The concept of demand is described by**

(i) How fully a good satisfies and individual's wants.

(ii) How much of a good and individual would be prepared to buy

**Which of the following is correct?**

(a) (i) only

(b) (ii) only

(c) Both (i) and (ii)

(d) Neither (i) nor (ii)

**3.2 In a household with given food budget, factors that will affect how fully the family's wants for food are satisfied, are:**

(i) The prices of foodstuffs.
(ii) The prices of non-foodstuffs.
(iii) Total household income.

**Which of the following is correct?**

(a) (i) only.
(b) (i) and (ii) only.
(c) (i), (ii) and (iii).
(d) not (i), not (ii), not (iii).

**3.3 A traveller arrives at an airport and discovers that the taxi fare to the city center is Rs.50.00. The additional economic variables that will influence the average individuals decision whether or not to hire a taxi are :**

(i) the price of the airport bus to the city.
(ii) the individuals income.
(iii) the price of a new taxi.

**Which of the following is correct ?**

(a) (i) only.
(b) (i) and (ii) only.
(c) (i) and (iii) only.
(d) (i), (ii) and (iii).

**3.4 In some countries, such as Saudi Arabia, the sale of alcohol is prohibited. Which of the following is correct? It can be concluded that :**

(a) In those countries no individuals has any demand for alcohol.
(b) Law makers in those countries believe that the consumption of alcohol is harmful to society.
(c) There are no benefits from drinking alcohol.
(d) Individuals collectively in those countries have no demand for alcohol.

**3.5 On a desert island, only two foods are available, fish and coconuts. On some days a castaway eats well; on other days he goes hungry. On any given day :**

(i) The higher the marginal utilities of fish and coconuts the hungrier he is.
(ii) The lower the marginal utilities of fish and coconuts the hungrier he is.
(iii) When the marginal utilities are zero, his total utility is zero.

**Which of the following is correct?**

(a) (i) only.
(b) (ii) only.
(c) (i) and (iii) only.
(d) (ii) and (iii) only.

**3.6 In a village in Ireland in the nineteenth century, all income was earned by producing linen and all family income was spent on food. When the price of meat fell, family F bought fewer potatoes and said it was better off. Family G said it was neither better nor worse off in the same circumstances. Assuming the 'law of diminishing marginal utility' to hold, it follows that :**

(i) Family F's marginal utility of meat must have fallen.
(ii) Family G must not have consumed any meat either before or after the price change.

**Which of the following is correct ?**

(a) (i) only.
(b) (ii) only.
(c) Both (i) and (ii).
(d) Neither (i) nor (ii).

**3.7 A consumer's typical demand curve is downward sloping to the quantity axis because:**

(i) At lower prices the consumer buys more of the good in question in place of other goods that are now relatively more expensive.
(ii) At lower price the consumer can buy all she bought of the good at the higher price, and with the money left over she can still buy more.

**Which of the following is correct?**

(a) (i) only
(b) (ii) only
(c) Both (i) and (ii)
(d) Neither (i) nor (ii)

**3.8 An individual's demand curve for beer could shift because of :**

(i) A change in the price of the beer.
(ii) A change in the price of wine.
(iii) A change in the individual's income.

**Which of the following is correct ?**

(a) (i) only
(b) (i) and (iii) only
(c) (i) and (iii) only
(d) (i), (ii) and (iii)

**3.9 If chicken is a substitute for mutton and egg is a complementary good to mutton.**

**Which of the following is correct?**

An increase in the price of mutton, *cet. par.*, will lead to:

(a) A decrease in the quantity of chicken demanded.

(b) An increase in the quantity of chicken demanded and an increase in the quantity of egg demanded.

(c) A decrease in the quantity of egg demanded.

(d) An increase in the quantity of egg demanded and a decrease in the quantity of chicken demanded.

**3.10 Travelling in Kolkata, most people use either the Metro train system or the bus. Suppose all Metro train fares are doubled but bus fares remained unchanged. How would the Metro train fare affect the total fare revenue?**

(a) It would increase for buses but might increase or decrease for the Metro.

(b) It would increase for the Metro but might increase or decrease for buses.

(c) It would increase for both Metro and bus travel.

(d) It would increase for the Metro and remain unchanged for buses.

# 4

# The Market

A market exists when individuals, households and firms who want to buy a good or service are in contact with firms or institutions willing to supply that good or service. Some markets are highly localized; others are international. For example, the village mandi is small (few transactions because there are only a few households in the village) and highly localize (all vendors are from the village selling their local produce). In contrast, coffee, coca, sugar, shipping, cars, copper and steel are bought and sold at the wholesale level in the international markets by dealers from many countries throughout the world.

Markets exist for resources as well as for goods and services. Most major cities have newspapers containing a property section and the stock market. The property section contains information not only on houses, flats, and commercial property for sale, but also on properties for rent. Sometimes a 'fixed' price for a piece of property is advertised, i.e., the first person to offer that price secures the property; sometimes an offer over price is stipulated with a closing date for offers. Sometimes offers are invited, counter offers are made, and then yet more counter offers until a price is agreed between buyer and seller. Furthermore, the property section can contain accommodation/property wanted advertisements accompanied by price ranges. The stock market is concerned with the buying and selling of pieces of companies, denoted by shares. The major companies in the world are quoted on the international stock markets and the number of shares traded in these companies each day are recorded and published as are the prices at which the exchanges took place. 'Bid' and 'offer' prices (as the buying and selling prices are known) are also published. With the advent of sophisticated computers, data on world transactions are recorded and available as they are made.

In markets in which exchange takes place, the competition, (either implicit (e.g. a supermarket) of explicit (the stock market) among buyers to buy and among sellers to sell, determines the price or prices and the quantities that are bought and sold. Market prices provide information to buyers attempting to maximize profit from the production and sale of goods, services and resources.

While the decisions of supplier determine which resources are employed and consequently which goods and service are produced and how much of each good and service is produced, economic efficiency requires that resources are allocated to the production of those goods and services that satisfy society's wants as fully as possible. Prices indicate to suppliers society's preference for different goods and services; and to survive in a competitive world, it is to these prices that suppliers must respond in their decision-making process. Thus, ultimately, prices of air travel in the past three decades has been a major contributing factor to the number of people seeking vacations abroad, especially in countries offering sun and surf. This in turn has spawned construction of massive hotel and apartment complexes near previously deserted beaches and has attracted resources to vacation related activities eating, drinking, and dancing.

In a market economy, system of interrelated markets for goods and services determines how resources are allocated, and it operates without and centralized planning mechanism or central decision-making body. In such economies, millions of households daily buy various quantities of food materials, including rice, wheat, cereals, meat, milk, coffee, tea, fresh fruits, frozen vegetables, fresh vegetables etc. Retail outlets of every size, from small corner grocery stores to giant supermarket chains, regularly estimate how much of each kind of food materials they will sell, and place orders with wholesalers, who in turn place orders that filter down to the primary suppliers. These suppliers base production plans for food materials on estimated consumer demand and allocate resources to the supply of various kinds of food materials.

The relative quantity of food materials bought by households are not decided by some central plane, nor are the resources allocated to the production of food material decided by a planning mechanism instead the pattern of resource allocation is the outcome of lakhs of households expressing their preference for various kinds of food materials in markets and the decisions of independent suppliers to hire resources to produce the food materials to satisfy these households.

The magic of the price mechanism makes such a meal possible at almost any time. Take an example ! If you are having a fish curry in an economy restaurant in Mumbai. Spare a thought for the number of interrelated markets involved in delivering your meal. It was caught by a fisherman moving in deep sea in his old boat taking a lot of risk; then selling the fish to a middle merchant at the shore at a low price, who in turn makes a booty with the fish he purchased at the shore from fishermen by selling to a wholesaler. All the fish the wholesaler purchased from various merchants was transported by road to a packing house. Where it was packed. Refrigerated and trucked to the restaurant in Mumbai. It was then eventually served to you in the restaurant at a price of Rs. 15.00. All these markets just to satisfy your demand for a piece of fish curry and costing you only Rs. 15.00! That is the magic of the price mechanism.

### Market Supply and Demand

Let us now see how the price of a good and the quantity exchanged are determined in a market. A market demand curve relates the quantities of a good that individuals would be prepared to buy at different prices; a market supply curve relates the quantities of a good suppliers would be prepared to sell at different prices. A necessary condition for exchange to take place in a market is that there must be at least one common price at which suppliers would be prepared to sell a quantity of good and at which individuals would be prepared to buy a quantity of the good.

Table 4.1 contains data relating to hypothetical demand and supply schedules for sandwiches in Delhi.

**Table 4.1** Market demand and supply schedules for sandwiches in Delhi

| Price (Rs.) | Quantity demanded ('000 per week) | Quantity supplied ('000 per week) |
|---|---|---|
| 5.00 | 180 | 0 |
| 5.50 | 150 | 30 |
| 6.00 | 120 | 60 |
| 6.50 | 90 | 90 |
| 7.00 | 60 | 120 |
| 7.50 | 30 | 150 |
| 8.00 | 0 | 180 |

Exchange could take place in this market at price above Rs.5.00 pound and below Rs.8.00. This is because at least one consumer would be prepared to buy a sandwich and at least one supplier would be prepared to sell a sandwich at all prices within this range. Exchange will be possible at a price of Rs.7.50 pound, for example, since consumers would be prepared to buy 30,000 sandwiches per week and firms would be willing to supply 1,50,000 sandwiches per week at the price. At a price of Rs.5.50, exchange would also be possible since consumers would be willing to pay 1,50,000 sandwiches per week and supplier would be willing to sell 30,000 sandwiches per week at that price. It would not be possible, however, for exchange to take place at Rs.5.00, because although individuals would be willing to buy 1,80,000 sandwiches per week at that price, no firms would be willing to sell sandwiches at that price.

The reason that exchange takes place in a market is that both buyers and sellers benefit. Assuming rational behaviour, and consumer who is prepared to buy a unit of food at certain price must prefer that food to cash; otherwise there would be no incentive for him to sacrifice cash in order to acquire the good. Similarly, any producer who is prepared to supply a unit of good has no incentive to participate in exchange. In the market for sandwiches illustrated in Table 4.1. Consumers would be prepared to buy 1,20,000 sandwiches at a price of Rs.6.00, and at that price producers would be willing to supply 60,000 sandwiches. Both consumers and producers would gain through exchange. Consumers who wish to buy at Rs.6.00 would gain more satisfaction from a sandwich than from Rs.6.00. Producers who would be prepared to sell at Rs.6.00 would prefer Rs.6.00 received from the sale of each sandwich to the sandwiches themselves.

Even where a market demand schedule form and a market supply schedule of a good exists, exchange would be impossible if there were no common price at which at least one consumer was prepared to buy a unit of the good and atleast one producer was willing to supply a unit of that good. Suppose the electronics industry developed a new micro television set with a one inch square screen to be worn on the wrist, and suppose that the market demand and supply schedules are as shown in Table 4.2.

**Table 4.2** Market demand and supply schedules for micro TV sets.

| Price(Rs.) | Quantity demanded (per week) | Quantity supplied (per week) |
|---|---|---|
| 5000 | 200 | 0 |
| 10000 | 100 | 0 |
| 15000 | 0 | 0 |
| 20000 | 0 | 0 |
| 25000 | 0 | 100 |
| 30000 | 0 | 200 |
| 35000 | 0 | 300 |

Exchange would not be possible in this market because there is no common price at which both consumers and producers would be prepared to buy and sell the micro-TV sets. Consumers would be willing to buy certain quantities of these sets at prices of Rs. 10000 and below; producers would only be prepared to supply the TV sets at prices of Rs. 25000 and above.

## The Operation of Markets

If a price causes excess demand or excess supply to exist in a market, forces in the market will change the price of the good and the quantity bought and sold. These forces will eventually eliminate any excess demand or excess supply. If, at a given price, excess supply were to exist in a market, competition among suppliers would force down the price of the good. Simultaneously, at lower prices a larger quantity of the good will be demanded. Thus at lower price the excess supply will be reduced. Eventually, a price would be reached at which excess supply will be zero.

It is possible for at least one sandwich to be offered for sale and to be demanded at any price above Rs.5.00 and below Rs.8.00. This is because at least one supplier is prepared to sell a sandwich for at least Rs.5.00. While at least one buyer is prepared to pay up to Rs.8.00 for a sandwich. If one buyer and one seller agreed to terms of exchange within this price range, and if the terms of exchange were known to all other potential buyers and sellers in the market, they would act on the information provided.

If one sandwich were sold to a consumer for Rs.7.00 and as a result all suppliers attempted to sell sandwiches for Rs.7.00 each, some suppliers would discover that they could not find customers at that price. This is because excess supply would exist at Rs.7.00 since 60,000 more sandwiches would be offered for sale than consumers would wish to buy. Some suppliers who could not find individuals wishing to buy sandwiches at Rs.7.00 would be willing to lower their asking price prepared to sell sandwiches at prices less than Rs.7.00. But this act of lowering the price would provide information to all other buyers and sellers in the market. Buyers who are prepared to pay Rs.7.00 or more for sandwiches will seek those suppliers offering sandwich for sale at less than Rs.7.00. Additionally, at lower prices some consumers will buy more sandwiches. Others who would not buy at the higher prices will now be prepared to purchase sandwiches.

At Rs.6.50 each, the quantity consumers would be prepared to buy is 90,000 per week, and this exactly equals the quantity that firms would be prepared to supply. The excess supply that originally existed at Rs.7.00 would therefore be eliminated.

If, at a given price, excess demand were to exist in a market, competition between consumers would force up the price of a good. Simultaneously, at higher prices, suppliers would be willing to sell a greater quantity of the good. Thus at higher prices excess demand would be reduced. Eventually, a price would be reached at which excess demand will be eliminated. In our example, if the original exchange between one buyer and seller in the market for sandwiches were agreed at Rs.6.00, and as a result all sellers decided to ask for a price of Rs.6.00 for sandwiches, some potential buyers would find it impossible to obtain them. This is because consumers would desire excess demand of Rs.6.00, since 60,000 more sandwiches, would be desired by the consumers than firms would be prepared to supply. Those individuals who could not obtain sandwiches would be willing to bid up the price of sandwiches because, as indicated by the demand curve, some consumers would be prepared to pay prices above Rs.6.00 to obtain sandwiches. But those individuals who pay more that Rs.6.00 each for sandwiches would provide information to all other buyers and sellers in the market. Suppliers who are prepared to sell sandwiches for Rs.7.00 or less will seek those consumers who are prepared to pay more than Rs.7.00 to obtain sandwiches. Additionally, at higher prices some suppliers will supply more sandwiches. Other suppliers who would not supply sandwiches at lower prices will now be prepared to supply sandwiches.

At Rs.6.50 each, the quantity consumers in total would be prepared to buy would exactly equal the quantity firms would be willing to supply, i.e. 90,000 per week. The excess demand which originally existed at Rs.6.00 would therefore be eliminated.

When the forces that act to eliminate excess demand or excess supply exactly offset each other, a market is defined as being in equilibrium. The price at which equilibrium occurs in a market is the price that allows all individuals who wish to buy a good to obtain as much as they wish at that price, and enables all producers who wish to sell the good as much as they wish at that price. The price at which the intentions of all potential buyers and sellers are exactly matched is called the equilibrium price, and the potential quantity of the good which the two sides wish to buy and sell at that price is called the equilibrium quantity.

The equilibrium price of sandwiches in this market is Rs.6.50, since all buyers who wish to purchase sandwiches at Rs.6.50 each are able to do so and all firms who wish to sell at Rs.6.50 each are able to find buyers. The quantity bought and sold at Rs.6.50 in 90,000 per week and there are no unsatisfied buyers or sellers. In this market, 90,000 sandwiches per week is the equilibrium quantity.

When exchange takes place in a market, gain accrue to both consumers and producers. If such gains did not exist, there would be no incentive for exchange to take place. A demand curve relates the quantities of a good individuals would buy a different prices, and it also related the maximum prices that individuals would be willing to pay for different quantities of a good at a price that is less than they would be prepared to pay, they would derive and additional gain from exchange. This additional gain is called '*consumer surplus*' and can be measured by the difference between the price individuals actually pay for units of good and the higher prices they would be prepared to pay.

The equilibrium price of sandwiches is Rs.6.50 and the equilibrium quantity is 90,000 per week. This means that price of Rs.7.00 is paid by every individual for every sandwich bought. But according to the downward sloping demand curve, some consumers would have been prepared to pay more for sandwiches.

For example, one individual would be prepared to pay up to Rs.8.00 for the first sandwich, but he has to pay only Rs.6.50. He has a consumer surplus of Rs.1.50. Similarly, for successive quantities up to 90,000 per week there is a difference between the price of Rs.6.50 that consumers pay for sandwiches and the price they would be willing to pay. This difference, as described above, is called consumer surplus.

A supply curve relates to the various quantities of a good that suppliers would be prepared to sell at different prices, and it also relates to the minimum prices at which suppliers would be prepared to sell different quantities of a good. If suppliers can sell units of a good at a price that is higher than they would be prepared to accept, they derive an additional gain from exchange. This additional gain is called 'producer surplus' and can be measured by the difference between the price suppliers actually receive for selling units of a good and the lower prices they would be prepared to accept.

For example, one supplier would be prepared to sell a sandwich for just over Rs.5.00, but in fact receives Rs.6.50. He has a producer surplus of Rs.1.50. Similarly, for successive quantities of sandwiches up to 90,000 there is a difference between the price suppliers actually received and the prices they would be prepared to accept. This difference is called producer surplus.

An example of how both consumer and producer surpluses provide the motivating forces in a market to achieve equilibrium is provided by Myron Joseph's role-playing wheat game. This educational experiment is based on a hypothetical wheat market in which a class of economics students adopts the role of dealers, half of whom buy and half of whom sell wheat. In the experiment, a card is given by the teacher to each student, requiring him or her to buy or sell 1000 units of wheat for not more or less than a certain price, as shown in Table 4.3.

Students are told that when the fictional market opens, they should adopt the role of dealer for clients and attempt to do the best they can in a transaction.

**Table 4.3** Distribution of instruction cards

| Price (Rs.) | Number of buyers (Not less then the price) | Number of seller (Not less then the price) |
|---|---|---|
| 12.80 | 4 | 2 |
| 12.60 | 4 | 2 |
| 12.40 | 4 | 2 |
| 12.20 | 4 | 2 |
| 12.00 | 4 | 2 |
| 11.80 | 4 | 2 |
| 11.60 | 2 | 4 |
| 11.40 | 2 | 4 |
| 11.20 | 2 | 4 |
| 11.00 | 2 | 4 |

Once the game commences, students are free to contact each other to discuss terms of exchange. Each time an exchange is agreed, the teacher makes the price known to all students, and those students who have completed a deal may then pick up fresh cards and then start again. After a certain time, the market is closed and the whole class can then see the range of prices at which exchange actually took place and the number of transactions that were recorded at each price. Table 4.4 shows the results from one experiment conducted by Ramesh.

**Table 4.4** Distribution of Transactions

| Prices (Rs.) | Number of Transactions |
|---|---|
| 12.60 | 1 |
| 12.50 | 0 |
| 12.40 | 1 |
| 12.30 | 0 |
| 12.20 | 6 |
| 12.10 | 1 |
| 12.00 | 15 |
| 11.90 | 25 |
| 11.80 | 27 |

*Contd. Table 4.1*

| Prices (Rs.) | Number of Transactions |
|---|---|
| 11.70 | 20 |
| 11.60 | 16 |
| 11.50 | 13 |
| 11.40 | 5 |
| 11.30 | 1 |
| 11.20 | 3 |
| 11.10 | 0 |
| 11.00 | 1 |

According to Ramesh, the initial exchanges were agreed at a wide range of prices. But then there was a tendency for prices to move towards a theoretical equilibrium level of Rs. 11.80. By the end of the game virtually every exchange was agreed at or close to Rs. 11.80.

This game illustrates the role of information in markets, since the disparity in prices soon disappeared once the terms of each exchange became known to all buyers and sellers. Any exchange at prices well above Rs. 11.80 (which would have enlarged the area of producer surplus if all deals were made at that price) resulted in fervent competition among sellers, which in turn drove prices down. Conversely exchanges arranged at prices well below Rs. 11.80 (which would have extended the area of consumer surplus if all exchanges had taken place at that price) resulted in keen competition among buyers, which in turn drove prices up. Eventually, equilibrium would be reached.

## Changes in Market Equilibrium

If a market were in equilibrium and if any of the condition determining demand or supply were to change, forces would establish a different equilibrium price and/or a different equilibrium quantity. Assuming that the supply conditions of a good remain unchanged, an increase in demand would lead to an increase in equilibrium price and an increase in equilibrium quantity, while a decrease in demand would lead to decrease in equilibrium quantity.

The new equilibrium price and equilibrium quantity would be determined as a result of shift in the demand curve and a movement along an unchanged supply curve. In similar fashion, with the demand conditions for a good remaining unchanged, an increase in supply would lead to a fall in equilibrium price and an increase in equilibrium quantity, while a decrease in supply would lead Tories in equilibrium price and a fall in equilibrium quantity.

Also, the new equilibrium price and equilibrium quantity would be determined as a result of a shift in the supply curve and a movement along an unchanged demand curve. If there were an increase in demand for a good and simultaneously an increase in supply of the good, however, could rise, fall or remain the same, depending on the extent to which demand increased relative to supply.

If the demand for a good were to increase and the supply of the good were to decrease simultaneously, the equilibrium price of the good would rise. The equilibrium quantity of the good would rise. The equilibrium quantity of the good might increase, decrease or remain the same, depending on the extent of the relative changes in demand and supply.

If the supply of a good were to increase and the demand for the good were to decrease simultaneously, the equilibrium price of the good would fall but the equilibrium quantity might increase, decrease or remain at the same level.

If the demand for a good and the supply of a good were both to decrease, the equilibrium quantity of the good would fall, but equilibrium price might increase, decrease or remain at its original level.

## Intervention in the Market

Market intervention or market regulation occurs when a non-market force causes the price and quantity of a good bought and sold in a competitive market to be different from the price/quantity combination that would occur if the market were allowed to operate freely.

Tickets, for major sporting events such as cricket or football matches at Hyderabad, are priced below the level that would occur if the forces of supply and demand were allowed to operate freely. The result is that more people wish to buy tickets at the prevailing price than there are tickets available. Conversely, minimum wage laws in some countries, which stipulate that employees must be paid at least a stipulated minimum per day, provide an example of the price in a resource market that is set above the equilibrium level, where more people are willing to work at the stipulated minimum than there are jobs available.

## Price Ceilings

When the price of a good is fixed below the equilibrium level, a price ceiling is said to exit in the market for the good. Price alone will be an inadequate mechanism for allocating the available supply of the good among potential buyers, and other allocative mechanism (such as first come-first served, reliance of suppliers preferences, or rationing) may be employed.

When world famous pop groups stage a concert, the price of the tickets is often below the equilibrium price that would be established if tickets were sold without restriction in a competitive market.

Some way would have to be found for allocating the available 2000 tickets among potential buyers who appeared; this is why large queues are often seen when tickets for major events go on sale. Alternatively, the concert organizers might allocate some of the 2000 tickets according to their own preferences, e.g. to personal friends, and other show business personalities. As a third option, a system of rationing might be used whereby each individual would be allowed to purchase only a limited number of tickets.

When price ceilings are in operation and excess demand exists, a black market, in which units of a good are exchanged for prices higher than the fixed level, tends to develop. Black markets, despite being illegal in many countries, sever the function of establishing equilibrium prices and quantities in a market. If the black market is 'perfect', the higher price will be the equilibrium price, where all buyers who want a ticket at that price can do so. The motivation for exchange at black market prices exists because, as shown by the downward sloping demand curve, some individuals are prepared to pay much higher prices than others to obtain units of a good, and there is no guarantee that those individuals who are willing to pay higher prices actually receive any units of the good by the initial allocation.

## Review Questions

**4.1 Which of the following is correct?**

**A market for a good, service or resources exists when:**

(a) There is a specific location where trade can take place.
(b) Individuals have something that they can sell.
(c) Individuals wish to buy something.
(d) Potential buyers are in communication with potential sellers.

**4.2 Suppose the market for a newly developed gold plated pens were represented by the demand and supply schedules below:**

| Price (Rs.) | Quantity (Demanded per day) | Quantity (Supplied per day) |
|---|---|---|
| 600 | 0 | 1000 |
| 500 | 0 | 700 |
| 400 | 0 | 350 |
| 300 | 0 | 0 |
| 250 | 0 | 0 |
| 200 | 50 | 0 |
| 150 | 100 | 0 |
| 100 | 150 | 0 |
| 50 | 250 | 0 |

**Which of the following is correct?**

(a) Equilibrium quantity would lie between 50 and 350 pens per day.

(b) No exchange would occur.

(c) Suppliers would have to lower their prices to Rs. 200 since that is the maximum price consumer are willing to pay.

(d) Consumers would have to pay Rs. 400 to obtain pens since that is the minimum price at which suppliers are prepared to sell.

**4.3 The price system reacts to excess demand for a good in the short run by**

(a) Lowering the price and profits of firms producing the good.

(b) Raising the price and producer profits

(c) Lowering the price but increasing producer profits.

(d) Raising the price but lowering producer profits.

**4.4 When influenza tablet first became available in India, the government set the price equal to the cost of production. At that price, output was insufficient to fulfil orders and the government regulated the distribution of the tablet. Which of the following correct if the tablet had been sold privately without government intervention?**

(a) The price would have been higher.

(b) The price would have lower.

(c) The price would have been the same.

(d) Whether the price would have been higher of lower cannot be determine from the information.

**4.5 If the equilibrium price prevails in the market for a good**

(i) No consumers would buy units of the good if the price were higher

(ii) Excess demand and excess supply are both zero.

(iii) No producers would sell units of the good if the price were lower.

**Which of the following is correct ?**

(a) (i) only.

(b) (ii) only.

(c) (i) and (iii) only.

(d) (i), (ii) and (iii).

**4.6 A city has decided to build 5000 dwelling units and to lease them to low income residents at a rental below cost and the going rate in the private market. Other things (such as population) being the same, which of the following effects would you expect this to have on the market for private housing?**

(a) A decrease in rent, followed later by a decrease in the quantity supplied.

(b) A decrease in tenants, followed by an increase in rents.

(c) An increase in rents, followed later by an increase in the quantity supplied.

(d) No effect, because the low income persons who will be eligible for the 5000 city build dwelling units cannot afford private housing.

**4.7 Assume the market for golf clubs to be initially in equilibrium. If there were a considerable increase in the number of people wishing to take up golf and simultaneously, a decrease in every golf club manufacturers production costs due to the use of a new metal compound, which of the following would be correct?**

(a) The equilibrium price of golf clubs might rise, fall or remain at the same level, but the equilibrium quantity would increase.

(b) The equilibrium price of golf clubs would rise, but the equilibrium quantity might increase, decrease or remain at the same level.

(c) The equilibrium price of golf club would fall, and the equilibrium quantity would increase.

(d) The equilibrium price of golf clubs would fall, but the equilibrium quantity might increase, decrease or remain at the same level.

**4.8 Suppose a government wants to raise money by means of a tax levied on each unit of a good bought and sold. The government wants the incidence of the tax to fall mainly on buyers, not producers. It also wants to disturb the quantity bought and sold as little as possible. Which of the following demand or supply curves meets these requirements?**

(a) Highly inelastic supply.

(b) Highly elastic demand.

(c) Highly elastic supply.

(d) Highly inelastic demand.

**4.9 If a government were to increase the sales tax on new cars, what would be the effect on the equilibrium price and equilibrium quantity of second hand cars?**

(a) Both increased equilibrium price and equilibrium quantity.

(b) Equilibrium price would decrease but equilibrium quantity would increase.

(c) Equilibrium price would increase but equilibrium quantity might increase, remain the same, or decrease.

(d) There would be no affect, since the second hand market is independent of the new car market and the sales tax applies only to new cars.

**4.10 Assume the market for motor bikes to be in equilibrium. If the demand for new motor bikes were suddenly to increase, which of the following would happen in the market (immediate) time period?**

| | Equilibrium price | Equilibrium quantity |
|---|---|---|
| (a) | No change | No change |
| (b) | Increase | Increase |
| (c) | Increase | No change |
| (d) | No change | Decrease |

**4.11 Suppose that the market for tomatoes were initially in equilibrium, but that costs of production for every supplier were to rise as a result of a significant increase in wages paid to all workers in the farms. Which of the following would occur?**

| | | |
|---|---|---|
| (a) | Increase | Increase |
| (b) | Increase | Decrease |
| (c) | Decrease | Increase |
| (d) | Decrease | Decrease |

# 5

# Forms, Structures and Sources of Finance for Business Organisations

## Forms of Business (Enterprise) Organization

In India there are both, private and public enterprises. The forms of private business in our country are :

1. Sole Proprietorship
2. Joint Hindu Family Firm
3. Partnership Firm
4. Joint Stock Company, and
5. Co-operative Organization

From the above mentioned forms of business 1 and 2 do not fall into the category of either medium or large scale enterprises, except in the rarest of cases.

## Partnership Firm

In India as in most other parts of the world, it is seen that as a business grows beyond the capacity of sole proprietorship and joint Hindu family firm, it becomes necessary to form a partnership. The Indian Partnership Act, 1932 provides for the registration of firms with the Registrar of Firms appointed by the government. The registration of a partnership firm is not compulsory. But an unregistered firm suffers from certain disabilities. Therefore registration of a partnership firm is considered desirable, and at times a requirement of the lenders.

### Joint Stock Company

The definition of a joint stock company, in India, is similar to that followed in other countries. It is an incorporated and voluntary association with a distinctive name, perpetual succession, limited liability and common seal, and usually having a joint capital divided into transferable shares of a fixed value. The companies can further be classified into the following kinds of companies on the basis of their mode of incorporation :

1. Chartered Company
2. Statutory Company
3. Registered or Incorporated Company

In India the companies are also classified from the light of public interest or membership :

1. Private Company
2. Public Company
3. Government Company

On the basis of inter-company relationships, companies are of two types :

1. Holding Company
2. Subsidiary Company

From the point of view of nationality, companies may be divided into two categories :

1. National or Domestic Company
2. Multinational or Transnational Company

In India, companies are governed by the Companies Act, 1956. This Act provides for the standard procedures relating to the affairs of a company such as modes of winding up, liquidation of a company etc.

### Co-operative Enterprise

In India co-operative organization grew as a means of protecting the interests of the relatively weaker sections of society against exploitation by big businesses operating for the maximization of profits.

According to the Co-operative societies Act, 1912, co-operative organization is "a society which has its objectives, the promotion of the interests of its members in accordance with the principles of co-operation." In addition to the above mentioned Act, such societies are also governed by the various state Co-operative Societies Acts. Co-operative organizations are suitable generally for medium and small-sized business operations. They do not generally graduate to being a large scale industrial operation.

The requirements of registration for the above mentioned forms of business organizations are as follows:

1. ***Sole Proprietorship*** : Sole proprietorship is easiest to organize as no legal formalities are required for starting it. No agreement is to be made for constituting such a business entity and registration of the firm is not essential, except for claiming benefits available to small sector units. However, a formal license may be required from the municipal corporation or Health Department in some cases, e.g., liquor, drugs, etc.

   Although no registration is mandatory under the central acts, yet these corporate bodies may be registered under the local shop and establishment acts, and other laws for licensing requirements.

2. ***Joint Hindu Family Firm*** : This is a peculiar form of business found in India. In this form of business ownership, all members of a Hindu undivided family do business jointly under the control of the head of the family who is known as the 'Karta'. No registration is necessary for this form of business. Some kind of statutory control on the working of the Hindu Undivided Family can be maintained by following the specific conditions, as laid down in the Income Tax Act. This is a peculiar business entity having its origin in personal law of the Hindus, and is peculiar to the Hindu Trading Community and their families.

3. ***Partnership Firm*** : In the case of partnership firm, although statutorily registration is not compulsory, however, an unregistered firm suffers from certain limitations. A partnership firm can be registered at any time by filing a statement in the prescribed form. The form should be duly signed by all the partners. It should be sent to the Registrar of Firms along with the prescribed fee. On receipt of the statement and the fees, the Registrar makes an entry in the Register of Firms. The firm is considered to be registered when the entry is made.

4. ***Joint Stock Company*** : A company is an incorporated or registered association of persons. One person cannot constitute a company under the law. In a public company, at least seven persons and in a private company at least two persons are required. A company can be formed only after fulfilling legal formalities and its incorporation under the Act is essential, before it can commence its business. A company registered under the companies Act is called Registered or Incorporated company. Such companies are most common in practice.

5. *Co-operative Enterprise* : No association of persons use the word cooperative in its name without being registered under the Co-operative Societies Act, 1912 or under the Co-operative Societies Act of a state government. In order to get a co-operative registered, an application in the prescribed form must be submitted to the Registrar of Co-operative societies of the state in which the society's registered office is to be situated. Any ten persons above the age of 18 years and having common interest may submit a joint application for being formed into a co-operative society.

**Minimal Capitalization Requirements for these Enterprises**

There are no prescribed or statutory capitalization requirements for the small forms of business such as sole proprietorships and the Joint Hindu Family firms. None of the regulating Acts such as the Companies Act or the Partnership Act list any such requirements. Capital adequacy or stipulations are industry specific, and not industry or size specific. The classification of Small Scale Sector unit is now dependant on the total owned capital of the undertaking. A medium scale enterprise will be an undertaking, which has more capital than that of a small scale unit viz. capital in excess of its size.

**Main features of the Business Organizations**

1. *Sole Proprietorship* : This is a form of business ownership under which a single person supplies the capital, uses his own skill, receives all the profits and bears all risks of business. He may borrow money and may employ workers but he alone owns and controls the business.

   The basic feature is that it is owned and controlled by a single individual. He receives all the profits and risks all of his property in the success or failure of the enterprise. The sole proprietor is not only the exclusive owner of the business, but also its founder and controller. In India as in most other countries Sole proprietorship is the simplest and the oldest form of business enterprise. This form of business is free from legal formalities and regulations, relating to incorporation and establishment. Those enterprises which are aided units and which require support from government, and other sponsored institutions have to comply with conditions specified by such government bodies granting support to the small scale sector. Such support may be in the form of concessional capital or procurement of controlled commodities or marketing support. Under the Income Tax Act, a sole proprietor must get his/her accounts duly audited, in case, annual sales turnover or gross receipts exceed Rs. 40 lakhs in case of business and Rs. 10 lakhs in case of profession.

2. *Joint Hindu Family* : The business of a Hindu Undivided Family is managed by the senior most male member or father. He is known as the Karta, or Manager. As the head of the joint family, the Karta has full control over the affairs of the family business and serves as the custodian of the firm's assets.

Other members of the Hindu Undivided Family cannot question his judgment, if the Karta has acted in the name of the family and for its benefit. The only remedy available to them then is to demand partition of the ancestral property. Family business is considered a part and parcel of the ancestral property and, therefore the family business is the subject matter of co-parcenary interest. The rights and liabilities of co-partners are determined by the general rules and traditional conventions of the Hindu Law.

3. ***Partnership*** : The basic features, and how the partnership is formed has been explained above. As far as the management is concerned, there can be different kinds of partnerships such as a partnership at will, particular partnership and joint ventures. The law does not permit the formation of a limited partnership or limited liability partnership in India. It is common to appoint a managing partner and empower such a person with its powers of day to day management and give such authority to act on behalf of the firm in terms of the specific authorities and powers conferred upon the managing partner. Such a person then binds the firm and other partners on the basic legal principle of mutual agency. The Institute of Chartered Accountants lays down the Standards for accounting and auditing in India. These standards are to be applied, irrespective of the size or type of industry in India.

4. ***Settlement of Accounts on Dissolution*** : When a partnership firm is dissolved, its assets are disposed off, and a partner has unlimited liability as in the case for a sole proprietorship and HUF. The proceeds therefrom are utilized in paying the creditors. If the amount realized by sale of assets is not sufficient to discharge the claims of the creditors in full, the deficiency can be recovered proportionately from the personal properties of the partners. If any partner becomes insolvent, the remaining solvent partners will bear the loss in their capital ratio. In case the assets of the firm are more than sufficient to meet the liabilities in full, then the surplus may be utilized to pay off the loans and capitals contributed by the partners. Section 48 of the Partnership Act, 1932 lays down the following procedure for the settlement of accounts between partners after the dissolution of the firm:

   (i) Losses including deficiencies of capital should be made good out of profits, then out of capital, and if need be, out of personal contributions of partners in their profit sharing ratios in that order.

   (ii) The assets of the firm including any sum contributed by partners to make up deficiencies will be applied for settling the debts of the firm, in the following order, subject to any agreement to the contrary;

      (a) First, in paying of the debts of the firm due to third parties;

      (b) Then in paying to each partner rateably any advances or loans given by him in addition to or apart from his capital contribution;

(c) If any surplus is available after discharging the above liabilities, the capital contributed by the partners may be returned, if possible, in full or otherwise ratebly;

(d) The surplus, if any, shall be divided among the partners in their profit-sharing ratios.

3. ***Joint Stock Companies*** : In a private company, the minimum number of members is 2 and the maximum is 50. In a public company minimum number of members is 7 and there is no maximum limit prescribed by law. A company has to comply with several legal requirements and it must submit reports to the Government. Also every member does not participate actively in the day to day management.

The company is managed by a Board of Directors consisting of elected representatives/nominees of the members. There is a divorce between ownership and management of a company. A company must maintain its accounts in the prescribed form and must get them audited by a qualified auditor. The form of accounts of a company are specified under the companies Act. The responsibilities of an internal auditor and external auditor are prescribed by law. Manufacturing companies and other specified notified companies have compulsory audits and cost audit obligations by law. Tax audits are required to be conducted for companies having an income over specific limits. The lenders more than the Registrar of companies or the Department of Company Affairs, stipulate commercial conditions for debt equity ratios and debt service reserve obligations. There are ceilings prescribed for intercorporate investments and loans and strict rules for receiving public deposits and monies. The companies Act lays down stringent provisions for the regulation of the process of running a company. One of the most important developments in this direction was the Constitution of Board of Company Law Administration, by virtue of section 10E which was inserted by section 4 of the companies (Amendment) Act (LIII of 1963)(w.e.f.1-1-1964). This is also referred to as company Law Board (CLB). The CLB exercises its powers and functions as under:

(a) The Companies Act, 1956

(b) Securities Contracts (regulation) Act, 1956

In addition to this the CLB also exercises powers under Code of Civil Procedure, 1908. The following sections of the Companies Act, 1956 are important for the statutory regulation of a Company in India:

Section 17-Special resolution and confirmation by CLB required for alteration of memorandum. Section 150 to section 158- These sections provide for the maintenance of registers of members and debenture-holders. Section 159 to section 164- annual returns to be made by companies having share capitals. Section 209 to section 223- accounts, companies are required to keep at their registered offices books of accounts. These books of accounts can be inspected by the Registrar of Companies (ROC) as well as authorities such as the Reserve Bank of India. Section 224 to section 233-Audits, these sections provide for the appointment and remuneration of auditors, their qualifications, their mode of appointment and other procedural requirements. Section 234-According to this section where, on perusing any document which a company is required to submit to him under this Act, the Registrar is of the opinion that any information or explanation is necessary with respect to any matter to which such document purports to relate, he may, by a written order, call on the company submitting the document to furnish in writing, such information or explanation, within such time as he may specify in the order. This section along with Section 235 is of critical importance in statutory regulation of the running of a company. Section 235-Investigation of the company, by virtue of this section the Government can on the report of the ROC under Section 234 appoint one or more competent persons as inspectors to investigate the affairs of a company and to report in such a manner as the Central Government may direct. Section 388B to Section 388E-These sections describe the powers of Central Government to remove managerial personnel from office on the recommendation of the Company Law Board. Lenders required more controlled forms of organization to lend larger amounts, and often stipulate conversion from partnership or limited companies for securing the fund raising and capital market tapping capacity of corporate borrowers.

### A-2 Controls and Influences

The most important influence on the types of business organization in India is the organization of banking institutions in India. The banking institutions have been strongly influenced by social, political and cultural influences, the political influence culminating in the nationalization of all the major banks in 1969. Historically, however, the banker has been an indispensable pillar of Indian society. He may have been miring in the good old days, when self-sufficiency was the law of the land. Money lending has been a traditional activity for several centuries in India, and recovery procedures have been strict, and at times harsh in the agricultural and rural sector in India. However, in the present scenario banks and money lenders have to be licensed to carry on the business in India and they are regulated by the usury laws also. In India, traditionally most modern business organizations, right from a simple company to an imposing conglomerate, have at times had their genesis in the Hindu undivided business. Such businesses being closely held, and fiercely proud, have hesitated to approach the formal institutions for credit. It is this factor that encouraged and sustained in India, an informal system of disbursing credit, in the form of the unregulated money lender, a practice which is still prevalent in the country. This has also encouraged, in recent times, the growth of co-operative banking institutions in India. The traditional antipathy amongst Indian business to approach the banks may be attributed to the concept of usury or high rate of interest, which was widely prevalent in India. Most experts attribute usury to the state of insecurity in India, and the risk involved on account of the low financial status of the borrowers. It was this factor which prevented the Indian business from approaching the financial institutions for reconstruction and left him to totter on the brink of insolvency and financial ruin.

Although the practice of the indigenous banker is fact dwindling each year as he is unable to adjust to the requirements of modern banking conditions, it must be presumed that the private banker is not yet extinct. His activities have been generally in agriculture, retail trade sectors and is spread amongst the various classes of small borrowers. The co-operative banking institutions are also playing an important role in reducing the role of the indigenous money lender.

With the growth of these co-operative banks and other institutions such as the IFCI, SFC's ICICI, IDBI etc., there are several banking opportunities available to enterprise in India. The above named institutions are operating various schemes of assistance to industrial units such as Direct Assistance, Indirect Assistance. Another feature, influencing, the way in which business enterprises operate has been the entry of the private banks. This entry has been led by the entry of the foreign banks such as the Bank of America, Hong Kong & Shanghai Bank, Deutsche Bank, Standard Chartered Bank, Citibank etc. These banks have employed specialized techniques of risk evaluation and the monitoring of the financial health of their clients. They have been maintaining entire departments for these feasibility studies and for monitoring domestic enterprises. This inturn has led many business enterprises to improve their credit-worthiness or to atleast work in that direction. Political influences have affected the corporate environment, and businessmen are requiring government to be more business sensitive. The large business houses were identified with India's freedom movement and this did influence the business licenses issued to them. However, their influence has waned and technology and the introduction of outside competition from foreign sources has diminished their dominance. The nexus or the relationships between the businessmen and the politicians has usually transcended the business of ideology and party affiliations. Political influence is more evident, when large scale unemployment is feared and the government is known to have inducted labour protection laws to prevent unemployment and closures; both with a view to alleviate poverty and unemployment and with an eye on the "vote banks" of labour. Banks in India can at best invest up to 30% of the capital and free reserves in any company. For prudential norms and capital adequacy purposes, they usually invest less than this amount (usually in the range of 15% to 25%) in any single enterprise or group. Cultural influences were of great importance in the pre-independence days.

When business and trade was restricted to certain communities, however with every passing decade since 1947, even this cultural hesitation of the foreign influence is waning.

# 6

# Finance Function

## The Finance Function

The finance function in any enterprise carries the primary responsibility for advising the management on policies concerning the acquisition and use of funds. It is also responsible for maintaining a financial information system, which is so essential for planning and controlling the enterprise operations and also for measuring its performance in financial terms. The circular issued by the Bureau of Public Enterprises (see : Appendix A) broadly covers the functions and responsibilities of the Financial Adviser & Chief Accounts Officer (FA & CAO) in a public enterprise. The position of private sector enterprises, in this regard, is not any different. He not only renders financial but also exercises financial controls. He is recognized as the principal staff officer to the Chief Executive on all financial matters. This paper attempts an overview of financial management, in terms of its main components, namely, acquisition of funds, use of funds, planning systems and control systems.

## Acquisition of Funds

### (a) *Long-term sources*

The financial executive has a dual responsibility with regard to the acquisition of funds. He advises on the choice of appropriate sources of funds and then take steps to procure the funds from the chosen sources. The funds employed in the enterprise may be classified into two groups, as long-term funds and short-term funds. The long-term sources are further classified as debt and equity. Successful enterprises seek debt in preference to equity for reasons of cost, convenience and control. Debt is a less expensive source, since tax savings are possible on interest paid. Servicing equity, on the other hand, entails payment of tax. The overall cost of capital, therefore, varies in inverse proportion to the debt component in the capital structure of the structure of the enterprise. Secondly, debt is relatively more convenient to obtain when needed and to redeem when not required. Debt does not also result in any dilution of control over the affairs of the enterprises, since lenders do not acquire any voting rights. Lastly, the low-cost debt provides a leverage, which helps achieving a higher rate of return on Equity.

There are, however, definite limits to debt financing. debt involves financial risks. They need to be commensurate with the business risks arise from likely changes in demand for the product, emergence of competition or imposition of controls over prices imports, exports etc. The financial risk grows in proportion to the debt component in the capital structure. Excessive borrowings will render the corporate equity riskier and potential investors become more and more reluctant to go in for that equity. It is, therefore, essential to match the two risks and set definite limits to debt financing.

Limits to debt are fixed keeping in mind three interrelated standards, namely, industrial norms, debt servicing capacity and the cash adequacy during recession.

Each industry adheres to certain norms of capitalization on the basis of its asset structure and magnitudes as well as volatility of its earnings in the long run. It is for this reason that utilities like power industry can afford to employ higher doses of debt. Industries which are earning are subject to high risk of obsolescence prefer self-financing and go in for a large equity base which can withstand the shocks. The second factor, namely, the debt servicing capacity is taken as a fraction of the annual cash accruals. Conservative bankers insist on debt service coverage ranging from 200 to 300 per cent. The cash adequacy standard is a variant if debt service capacity standard and is based in cash flows expected during the recession period. The objective is to ensure the required capacity to service the debt even under the worst circumstances. The three norms together guide the management in deciding on the limits up to which it can seek funds in the form of debt.

It may be relevant to have a closer look at the equity-debt proportion in the capital structure of Central Government undertakings in India. The statement placed in Appendix B summarizes the position as on March 31, of a fiscal year. There are very few instances where the debt is more than the equity and even in these cases, the excess is due to the erosion of Not Worth because of accumulated deficits. The aggregate position conforms more or less to the age-old policy of the government to maintain a 1:1 ratio for debt and equity.

## Recent Changes in Government Policy

Until the year 1968, the Government of India followed the policy of insisting on the debt-equity ratio of 1:1, unless there were exceptional reasons to deviate from that form. The Committee on Public Undertaking (67-68) (Lok Sabha) fifteen report recommended in that year that such a rigidity should be avoided and that if the undertaking made out a strong case for relaxation, it should be concerned. The BPE issued a circular later suggesting an interrelated approach to the fixation of debt-equity norms. The suggestion was that the norm should follow logically from the funds flow projections made in the feasibility reports and the detailed project reports and that the debt level should be related to the service capacity of the project.

The term-lending institution in India follow a somewhat more liberal policy. They stretch up to a debt-equity ratio of 2:1. Capital-intensive projects for manufacture of items like paper, cement, chemicals, etc. Press for a 3:1 ratio on the ground that the capital requirement are high and the level of profitability can service a higher level of debt and also help achieving a more satisfactory return on the equity component of the capital.

### (b) *Short-term Sources*

The current assets held by on enterprise are financed mainly from short-term sources. However, the long-term sources are supposed to provide the margin money and also take care of investments in the core current assets. Bank borrowings in the form of overdrafts for cash credit, suppliers, credit and other current liabilities constitute the major sources of shortterm finance available to an enterprise. Bank borrowings have become so expensive now-a-days that they are exerting a restraining influence on the enterprises. They are trying to manage their current assets more efficiently and are at the same time, looking for alternative and less expensive sources of short-term finance.

The Government follows the policy of asking the PEs to obtain their credit requirements from the Nationalised Banks. In those cases where the enterprise is short of margin money the Government extends a guarantee to cover the deficit. When they find it impossible to obtain their total requirements of working capital from the banks, the Government will provide short-term loans for a specified period.

## Use of Funds

### (a) *Investments in long-term assets*

The enterprise employ their capital partly in fixed and partly in current assets. The financial executive has to ensure that the funds at the disposal of the enterprise are judiciously employed and that the proposals for further investments are economically feasible and justifiable. The investments in fixed assets involve substantial long-term commitments in terms if finance as well as technology. The proposal for each investment is to be, therefore, subjected to a Cost Benefit Analysis.

PEs have to convince the Administrative Ministry, Finance Ministry and the Parliament that the proposed investments are worthwhile and that they conform to the pubic policies and priorities.

A professional analyst has a number of techniques at his disposal for carrying out the Cost Benefit Analysis. The following four techniques have found practical applications :

(a) Average Rate of Return (b) Pay back period

(c) Internal Rate of Return (IRR) (d) Net Present Value (NPV)

While analytical techniques are necessary what is more important is the need for estimating the future cash flows are realistically as possible. The final decision can be as estimated for several years ahead, there are bound to be distortions and biases creeping into these estimates. The agencies at the higher levels are supposed to possess the expertise should ensure the competence required for developing realistic project estimates. The sophisticated techniques of analysis should not act as a cover for unrealistic estimates.

The finance theory attempts to tackle the problems of risk and uncertainty in the estimates by applying various correctives. One is to vary the discounting rate in keeping with the degree of risk. The riskier investments may be subjected to a higher rate of discount. The second method suggests modifying the expected cash flows by using a factor known as "Certainty Equivalent-Co-effecient" which reflects the management perception of the risk in the project. The third approach is to use probability distributions and ranges of estimates for investments, cost and cash flows. If the investment decisions are sequential, business schools recommend the use of "Decision Tree" which enables staking optimal decisions at various points and then aggregating them into a main decision by the process of "Backward Induction". In essence, all the statistical techniques try to shed light on the dispersion of possible outcomes of an investment project. While the conventional techniques use single estimates of outcome.

There is a mistaken notion among the finance professionals in the country that all these techniques cannot be applied in the developing countries because the risk and uncertainties are extremely high. But experience indicates that most of the public sector projects in India enjoy protected market and abundant funds. This may not reflect the general situation. The techniques can at least do positive good when used imaginatively. They compel the management to take into account all factors relevant to the decision-making and to indicate the sensitivity of the project viability to the several errors, which may creep into the estimates. The on set of an economic liberalisation and the initiation of the second generation economic reforms at the state level are bridging the gap between the free-market economics and India

the Indian corporates in the public sector have to use the sophisticated techniques in their decisions making on the capital expenditure proposals.

### Short-Term Investments

Major investment decisions may be subject to external pressure on the enterprise. But the decisions on current asset holding fall well within the scope of internal management. Investments in inventory can be regulated to ensure that excess stocks and stock-outs are avoided. Similarly efficient management of trade credit will enable keeping the investments in sundry debtors to the absolute minimum. Better management of cash officers scope for reducing the interest burden on the enterprise.

The technique of ABC analysis, Economic Order Quantity, Re-ordering Level, Standardization, Value analysis, etc. help managing the current assets more efficiently. The financial executives coordinates the use of the techniques since they eventually help him manage the fund completed to current assets.

### Planning Systems

The planning process in the enterprise includes planning, long range corporate planning performance budgeting. It also covers economic and financial analysis needed for short-term decisions.

*Strategic Planing* refers to planning major strategies concerning expansion, diversification, taking up manufacture of new products, entering new markets, etc. The financial executive plays a crucial role in marshalling the relevant costs and benefits and in advising the management on the long-term financial implications in terms of outlays and resultant cash flows expected. He works closely with the team engaged in the strategic planning process. In fact use of the investments decisions discussed earlier are integral part of strategic planning.

Long Range Corporate Planning is the process of developing a time bound plan for achieving the objectives of an enterprise over a period of five or more years. It takes into account all the on-going activities as well as the new projects being taken up and prepares an integrated total plan for the enterprise as a whole. Here again the financial executive plays a major role in assimilating the data, appraising the alternative and developing master budgets and financial forecasts for covering the plan period.

The performance budget is a corporate plan. It is prepared in greater detail and sets physical and financial targets for each responsibility center and builds efficiency norms into them. The budget thus serves as in instrument of planning as control. The profitability need not necessarily be the guiding index of performance. What is needed is a system for review and target setting for each segment of the enterprise.

The Management by objectives may be adopted for formulating and implementing the performance budget. These budgets enable decentralization of authority and centralization of control. Budget also helps management by exception.

### Operating Decisions

There are very few decisions at the enterprise level, which do not affect its funds. It is therefore, logical for the financial executive to have a say in those decisions. Leaving aside the investment decision mentioned earlier the operating decisions cover a wide range of problems such as:-

(a) Capacity Utilization
(b) Pricing
(c) Product-mix
(d) Credit policy
(e) Overtime working
(f) Shift-working
(g) Incentives, etc.

Most of these decisions entail cost-volume profit analysis and also the use of incremental costs and opportunity costs in the analysis. Decisions even on these issues are sometimes governed by considerations of Public policy.

### Government Policy

BPE perceives budgeting as essentially a managerial process of setting physical and financial targets, appraising and reporting performance. It has prescribed proforma statements for Revenue Budget, Capital Expenditure budget and cash Budget. It recommends quarterly review of profit and loss account and balance sheet by the Board and expenditure review once in six months. It also recommends review of the achievements of physical targets every month and investments of variations.

### Control Systems

Budgetary control and Standard Costing systems provide the basis for monitoring enterprise performance at all levels. They introduce a participative element in the target-setting exercise.

The financial executive is expected to develop an integrated system, which incorporate statuary accounting as well as management accounting systems. The system has to be so designed as to generate data for compelling periodical reports to be sent to the Administrative Ministry, Finance Ministry, and Planning Commission etc. It should also provide information to enterprise managers at all levels about their achievements vis-à-vis plans and targets. These managers need assistance in identifying and analyzing cost variances as well as profit variances.

Internal Audit is considered to be an integral part of finance function in most of the public enterprises. It is an internal appraisal and is mainly concerned with the evaluation of the effectiveness of other managerial controls including systems and procedures. The external auditors rely very much on the internal audit for ensuring the credibility of basis transactions and records.

The financial executive coordinates with statutory auditors in carrying out the external audit once a year. Public Enterprises are audited directly by the Controller and Auditor General of India (CAG) or by Chartered Accountants appointed by him as Auditors. In the latter case he has power to carry out a supplementary test audit. There is an audit board, which coordinates the external audit work in respect of Central Sector undertakings in India.

### Reporting

The routine periodical reports generated by the Finance include both internal reports and external reports. Internal reports are meant for the information of managers at all levels and contain budget and actual comparisons for the period, along with cummulative data. The objective is to help the managers initiating corrective action where necessary. BPE introduced in 1975 the "Integrated Reporting Systems". It includes 22 reports to be sent to Administrative Ministry, BPE and Planning Commission with the following periodicity:

| | |
|---|---|
| Monthly | 5 |
| Quarterly | 10 |
| Half-Yearly | 4 |
| Yearly | 3 |
| **Total** | **22** |

## Appendix A

### Main Functions/Responsibilities of Financial Adviser

1. The Term '*Financial Adviser*' used in this note would refer to the Finance Director or the Financial Adviser and Chief Accounts Officer, were there is no full time Finance Director i.e., the top post in the Finance side.

   The Financial Adviser has both 'staff and line' functions. Expect for exerting line authority over his own department, Financial Adviser fills a staff role, which is his major role.

2. The accounting function is usually 'staff' with responsibilities for providing line managers and also other staff managers with specialized services. This includes advice in areas of budgeting, controlling, pricing and special decisions. The line functions would include the organization of his own office to enable him to render the staff functions and also to maintain cost and financial accounts.

3. The Financial Adviser should be responsible as the Principal Staff Officer to the Chief Executive on all financial matters. The Financial Adviser, where there is no full time Financial Director, should invariably be invited to be present at the meeting of the Board of Directors. In many cases there has been delegation of financial powers. For exercising these powers, the Board of Directors may determine matters which will be reserved (i) for concurrence of the financial adviser such as (a) proposals requiring the sanction of Government (b) departures from approved plan; (ii) reserved for consultation with the Financial Advisers and (iii) those on which the Financial Adviser need not be consulted.

4. ***The responsibilities of the Financial Adviser, interalia include the following:***

   (i) Determines the financial resources required to meet the company's operating programme.

   (ii) Forecasts how much of the requirements would be met by internal generation of funds by the company and how much will have to be obtained outside the firm.

   (iii) Develops the best plans to obtain the external funds needed.

   (iv) Establishes and maintain a system of financial control governing the allocation and use of funds.

   (v) Formulates programmes to provide most effective profit-volume cost.

   (vi) Analyses the financial results of all operations, report the facts to top management and make recommendations concerning future operations.

   (vii) Carry-outs special studies with a view to reduce costs, improve efficiency and profitability.

5. ***The above are dealt with in detail hereunder :***

**(a)** ***Feasibility studies and project reports.***

In regard to capital expenditure relating to new projects or expansions feasibility studies and detailed project report are to be prepared by the Management and these should be examined by the Financial Adviser interalia to ensure.

(i) That the capital expenditure proposed would be in furtherance of the objectives for which the enterprises have been established;

(ii) That the expenditure proposed to be incurred is reasonable;

(iii) That the expenditure would result in ensuring reasonable profits;

(iv) The overall economic viability of the proposal;

(v) That the financial resources for meeting the expenditure would be available

**(b)** ***Budgeting***

***The Financial Adviser will be the principal coordinating officer for :***

(i) Long term operating budget covering a period of 10 years indicating the likely profit/loss year during the period;

(ii) Preparation of longterm capital expenditure budget covering a period of about 10 years and advises the management in regard to the timing to the incurrence of capital expenditure

(iii) Capital cxpenditure budget in regard to the capital expenditure that is expected to be incurred during the year;

(iv) The preparation of the annual operating budget;

(v) The budget returns that flow out of the comprehensive budgetary system in operation

For the benefit of various levels of management, he would analyse variations between budget figures and the expenditure incurred and comment on the causes that led to such variations to facilitate the management to control expenditure by the application of the principle of exception.

**(c)** ***Cash flow statement***

Based on the longterm budget the Financial Adviser would prepare a cash flow statement indicating the inflow of cash during the period. Similarly, he will also prepare a detailed monthly cash flow statement for the year based on the annual budgets.

**(d)** ***Working capital***

He will also make an assessment of the total working capital requirements for the fiscal year and advise the management regarding the source of financing and the working capital requirements.

**(e)** ***Purchases***

He will be associated on all the matters relating to purchase of equipments, raw materials, etc. He would also lay down suitable procedure for purchases to ensure that adequate control is exercised over such purchases and that there are no uneconomic purchases.

**(f)** ***Pricing Policies***

He will also advise the Chief Executive on the pricing policies to be followed in the organization - in regard to the selling prices of products, inter-departmental issues, changing of material to jobs, etc.

(g) *Service conditions*

He will advise the management on all service matters having financial implications, such as scale of pay, dearness allowance, bonus, gratuity etc.

He will organize an effective internal audit department and will process the reports submitted by the internal auditor and place the same before the Board through the Chief Executive. He will ensure that the annual accounts are prepared in time according to provisions of law. He will attempt to all matters relating to the statutory audit and the audit by the comptroller and Audit General. He will be custodian of the each of the company. He will be the principal disbursing officer and in discharging this duty he will ensure that adequate financial control is exercised over allocation and use of funds in accordance with the approved programme and budgets and with due regard to policies and regulations laid down by the Board. He will be responsible for attending to all matters relating to the company. He may make up from time to time social studies particularly with reference to cost reduction, economic in administration and other overhead expenditure and such other areas, which have bearing on the profitability of the company. He would also furnish to the management, prospective costs of the products to enable the management to determine the optimum product mix.

## Reporting

The preparation of the following quarterly reports included in the reporting system would be the responsibility of Financial Adviser:

- (i) Resources employed
- (ii) Summary of cash flow for the quarter
- (iii) Forecast of cash for the next quarter
- (iv) Capital expenditure incurred during the quarter compared with sanctioned amount, budget estimates, etc.
- (v) Profit and loss account for the quarter
- (vi) Ratios of (a) overheads to sales; (b) stocks to sales; (c) debtors to sales; (d) capital employed to sales.
- (vii) Expenditure on the specific items of overheads items included therein.
- (viii) Cost of production of item completed during the period together with variations, if any with standards established.
- (ix) Any other report prescribed by the undertaking relating to financial cost matters.

The above management reporting should, however, be within the organization and rendered to the Board of Directors through the Managing Director and the Financial Adviser should rely on the tools and services available within the organization and parallel system should not be developed for this purpose.

The Financial Adviser on the other hand, should also bear in mind the fact that he is a part of the management team and that he has much responsibility in ensuring best approach of the enterprise as any other principal staff officer of the enterprise. His entire approach to problems of the enterprise should be an integrated one and his efforts should be such as to bringing optimum results.

## Appendix B

Groupwise Analysis of Investment in Central Government Undertakings (Rs/Crores)

| Sl. No. | Name | Paidup capital | Loan | Total | Debt in % to Total |
|---|---|---|---|---|---|
| 1. | Enterprise under Construction | 13184 | 42864 | 174718 | 24.53 |
| 2. | Steel | 350382 | 221342 | 571724 | 38.71 |
| 3. | Minerals & Metals | 172529 | 121150 | 293679 | 41.25 |
| 4. | Coal | 212987 | 193895 | 403882 | 47.65 |
| 5. | Power | 182131 | 68940 | 81071 | 85.04 |
| 6. | Petroleum | 67697 | 309727 | 377424 | 82.06 |
| 7. | Chemical & Pharmaceuticals | 243877 | 155397 | 399274 | 38.92 |
| 8. | Heavy Engineering | 53707 | 111466 | 165169 | 67.49 |
| 9. | Medium & Light Engineering | 25722 | 33025 | 58747 | 56.22 |
| 10. | Transportation & Equipment | 37312 | 80572 | 117664 | 68.35 |
| 11. | Consumer Goods | 42894 | 37242 | 80136 | 46.97 |
| 12. | Agro-based Industries | 2741 | 879 | 3620 | 24.28 |
| 13. | Textiles | 25921 | 60086 | 86007 | 69.86 |
| 14. | Trading & Marketing Services | 41562 | 40755 | 82317 | 49.51 |
| 15. | Transportation Services | 29096 | 190405 | 219481 | 86.75 |
| 16. | Contract & Construction Services | 8444 | 18140 | 26584 | 86.24 |
| 17. | Industrial Development & Technical Consultancy Services | 1858 | 7561 | 9419 | 80.27 |
| 18. | Development of Small Industry | 1350 | 3436 | 4786 | 71.79 |
| 19. | Tourist Services | 4263 | 3925 | 8185 | 47.95 |
| 20. | Financial Services | 19856 | 163719 | 183578 | 89.18 |
| 21. | Section 25 Companies | 292 | 8014 | 8306 | 96.48 |
| 22. | Insurance Companies | 12100 | ----- | 12100 | ------ |
| | **Total** | **1668546** | **1872540** | **541088** | **53.00** |

**(Source : Bureau of Public Enterprises, Govt. of India, New Delhi)**

# 7

# Conceptual Framework of Accounting; Concepts & Conventions; and a Glimpse of Contents of Financial Statements

## Introduction

The book-keeping is an art of recording methodically and systematically transactions involving or relating to money or money's worth. Book-keeping and accountancy practically mean the same thing although the term 'Accountancy' is usually used for accounting work of a higher order.

Accounting has been defined as a part of recording, classifying and summarizing in a significant manner and in terms of money, transactions and events which are, in part, at least, of financial character and interpreting the results thereof. The rules of financial accounting are generally applicable to all commercial enterprise and for the sake of uniformity, the financial accounting is subjected to certain principles, concepts, conventions, developed by accountants over a period of time, to serve as 'grammar rules' to the languages of 'accounting'. The financial statements are the final product of the financial accounting process. For better understanding and interpretation of the financial statements it is essential to bear in mind the concepts and conventions of accounting, the details of which are discussed as under:

The accountants in order to make their language namely,' accounting convey the same meaning to all people, as far as practicable, and to make it meaningful business language on a number of concepts which they attempt to follow. These are :

**(i)** ***Business Entity Concept*** **:** The accountant treats the business as distinct from the persons who owns it; it then becomes possible to record transactions of the business with the proprietor also. It is the business, which owns the property (assets). It is the business, which owes money to outsiders.

This concept has now been extended to accounting separately for various divisions of a firm in order to ascertain the results for each division separately. It has been of immense value in determining responsibility center-responsibility accounting.

**(ii)** ***Money-Measurement Concept*** **:** In the accounting process only those transactions are recorded which can be expressed in momentary terms (though quantitative records are also kept). An event, even though important like a quarrel between two functionaries like finance manager and production manager will not be recorded unless its monetary effect can be measured with a fair degree of accuracy.

**(iii)** ***Cost Concepts*** **:** Transactions are recorded in the books of account at the amounts actually involved. Suppose a firm purchases an asset for Rs.1,00,000 only. This cost will be the basis for all subsequent accounting of the assets. The market value of this asset may be more than the cost price or less then the cost price. The accounting is on the basis of historical costs only.

**(iv)** ***Going Concern Concepts*** **:** It is assumed that the business will exist for a long time and transactions are recorded from this point of view. It is this that necessitates distinction between expenditure that will render benefit over a long period and what whose benefit will be exhausted quickly, say, within the year. Of course, if it is certain that the business will exist only for a limited time, the accounting record will keep the expected life in view.

**(v)** ***Dual-Aspect Concept*** **:** Each transaction has two aspects: If a business has acquires an asset, it must have resulted in one of the following:

(a) Some other assets have been given up;

(b) The obligation to pay for it has arisen;

(c) There has been a profit, leading to an increasing the amount that the business owes to the proprietor, or

(d) The proprietor has contributed money for the acquisition of the asset.

The reverse is absolute. If for instance there is an increase in the money owed to others there must have been an increase in assets or a loss. At any time:

Assets = Liabilities + Capital; or Capital = Assets – Liabilities.

In other words, capital, i.e. the owner's share of the assets of the firm, is always what is left out of assets after paying off outsiders. A transaction must affect one of the three things mentioned above.

(vi) ***Realisation Concept*** : The accounting is a historical record of transactions. It records what has happened. It does not anticipate adverse effects of events that have already occurred are usually recorded. Unless money has been realized either cash has been received or a legal obligation to pay has been assumed by the customer, no sale can be said to have taken place and no profit or income can be said to have arisen.

(vii) ***Accrual Concept*** : All transactions recorded in the accounting records do not necessarily mean cash flow. All transactions, eventhough not yet settled in cash, must be taken into account. When once the workers have worked for a month, wages are accounted for, whether the wages were received by the workers or not. The accountant only endeavors to relate expenditure to the accounting only periods by assessing the extent to which the goods or services acquired were actually usual in the period.

## Matching Income and Expenditure Concept

In determining the income of any business, expired costs should be matched with references in the accounting periods to which both are applicable.

## Conventions

In order to make the message contained in the financial statements the income statement (profit and loss account) and the statement showing the financial position (balance sheet) – dealt and meaningful, these are drawn up according to the below mentioned conventions:

(i) ***Consistency*** : The accounting practices should remain the same from one year to another. For instance, it would be proper to value stock in trade according to one method one year and according to another method next year. If a change becomes necessary, the change and its effect should be slated clearly.

(ii) ***Disclosure*** : Apart from the legal requirements, good accounting practice also demands that all significant information should be disclosed. Not only various assets, for example, have to be stated but also the mode of valuation should be disclosed. Various types of revenues and expenses must also be stated separately. Whether something should be disclosed or not will depend on whether it is a material or not.

**(iii)** ***Conservatism*** **:** The financial statements are usually drawn upon rather a conservative basis. But at the same time window dressing i.e. showing a position better than what it is, is not permitted. It is also not proper to show position substantially worse than what it is.

**(iv)** ***Periodicity*** **:** Even though it is assumed that business will continue for a long time it is necessary to keep accounts in such a manner as to permit results being ascertained and presented periodically, usually, yearly.

As is already mentioned the above are only concepts and conventions developed by the accountants over a period of time. In order to arrive at a global consensus Standards Committee (IASC) of which the Institute of Chartered Accountants of India and the Institute of Cost & Works Accountants of India are associate members of the above. International body of Accountants is formed to arrive at the global consensus with the member countries in the matter of influencing accounting policies. The IASC has so far recognized the cost concept, accrual concept and the consistency convention as fundamental assumptions.

Besides the above, broadly the entire accounting system is categorized into two parts viz. Single entry book keeping system (ii) and double entry book keeping system.

### Single Entry System

According to this system all the transaction are recorded only on a single entry basis. For example, the government transact the payments into the government's treasury are mainly dealt on single entry book.

### Double Entry System

This system advocates that every transaction has two fold effects, in other aspect, in other words, it indicates that for every debit, there is corresponding credit. For example if cash purchases are made for Rs. 5,000 cash might have gone out from the enterprise and more or less equivalent amount of goods might have been received, the debit credit mechanism centers round these transactions. However, debit and credit take different transformations under various types of accounts viz., personal accounts, real accounts and nominal accounts. Further the accounts are broadly categorized in two ways i.e., personal accounts and impersonal accounts. Impersonal accounts are further divided into two categories viz. Real accounts and nominal accounts as under:

**ACCOUNTS**

- Personal Accounts
- Impersonal Accounts
  - Real Accounts
  - Nominal Accounts

### Personal Accounts

These record the transactions with persons, companies, banks and institutional accounts only. In these transactions one happens to be giver and another to be a receiver in all such cases. To record these transactions the following rule is to be adopted:

### Debit the Receiver and Credit the Giver

*Real Accounts*

These are concerned about assets, liabilities, cash etc. The assets are of two types, fixed assets and current assets. Fixed assets are those which are essential for running day-to-day operations. Thus all these assets come under this category. Under these transactions as assets are brought into the business, it is debited and if it is debited and if it is taken away from the business, it is credited. In all as such cases, the debit and credit take the transformation under this rule.

Debit what comes in (assets, liabilities, cash)

Credit what goes out (assets, liabilities, cash)

### Nominal Accounts

These accounts record the transactions relating to revenue, income and loss. The debit-credit rule in this category is:

***Rule :*** Debit all expenses and losses, credit all gains and profits.

In order to record all the above business transactions any enterprise has to maintain a set of books of account, which are discussed in detail as under.

The books of account are further categorized into two parts:

(i) Books of primary entry; and (ii) Books of Secondary entry. Certain books like cash book, bank book, journal are know as books of primary entry. Petty cash book is know as book of secondary entry.

### Cash Book

Cash book is one of the most important books of primary entry. It records all sorts of cash transactions involving sales, purchases, payments etc. The cash book normally has two sides – the left hand side is known as receipts and the right hand side of is known as payments. Every day the net cash balance as at the close of the day is to be worked out by deducing the payments from that of the receipts.

### Journal

Normally all the credit transactions are to be incorporated in this book depending upon size and nature of all the transactions. Journal could be further categorized as purchases journal and sales journal in which the credit purchases and credit sales could be recorded respectively. Some of the outstanding expenses at the close of the accounting year could also be incorporated in the final accounts with the help of passing a journal entry and suitably incorporating the same in the journal.

## General Ledger

This book contains a consulate account of balances in respect of each account in the primary ledgers viz., Debtors Ledger, Creditors Ledger etc. This is the genesis for the preparation of trial balance, an essential document responsible for the compilation of profit and loss and balance sheet.

**(i)** ***Debtors Ledger*** **:** This ledger incorporates all the credit transactions pertaining to sales. In this book each customer's account is chronologically maintained with running balances of payments and receipts. At the end of the financial year, a single and consolidated amount is posted into the general ledger taking care of the credit sales transactions.

**(ii)** ***Creditors Ledger*** **:** In this book all the credit transactions like purchases are posted party wise. This has also a running account of credit received for the suppliers as well as the payments made to them from time to time. At the close of the financial year a single amount incorporating all the balance shall be posted into the general ledger.

**(iii)** ***Sales Day Book*** **:** In this book all the transactions of credit sales are recorded from this book, the entries could be made into the ledger.

**(iv)** ***Purchase Day Book*** **:** In this book the credit purchases are recorded. From this book, the postings are made into the ledger.

In this way transactions could be posted in suitable subsidiary ledgers with respective control accounts incorporated in the general ledger.

## Trial Balance

When the transactions are properly posted into the cash book and general ledger, an attempt is made for the preparation of the most important document called trial balance. The trial balance is the itemised list of all ledger balances, cash balances at the close of the accounting year. Since the accounting system is to be followed on the double entry basis, it is imperative that all debits must tally with all the credits. Therefore, in the trial balance where there are two sides like debit and credit, both the debits and credits must tally to ensure arithmetical accuracy of the transactions. Sometimes though the trial balance tallies with regards to debits are credits, it is not a conclusive proof that all entries are properly recorded in the books of accounts. Sometimes there may be mistakes like compensating errors, errors of omission which may result in the agreement of trial balance nevertheless vitiate true and fair view of the accounts. This is a most important document since it is the genesis for preparation of final accounts, i.e., profit and loss accounts which tells the profit or loss for a particular period as a whole, the balance sheet that indicates a true and fair view of the state of affairs of the enterprise. Therefore, every care must be exercised in order to ensure that the balance is correct and fair in all respects.

Before compiling the final accounts it is essential to demarcate different types of expenditure which are briefly discussed as under:

*The expenditure is mainly categorized into three parts:*

1. Capital expenditure
2. Revenue expenditure.
3. Deferred revenue expenditure.

1. ***Capital Expenditure*** **:** In order to establish that a particular expenditure belongs to capital expenditure, the transaction must satisfy the following tests :
   (i) The expenditure should result in the form of acquisition of asset.
   (ii) The benefit of which should extend over a number of years-say beyond 8 to 10 years. Some of the examples of capital expenditures are the purchase of machinery, land and buildings and vehicles etc.
2. ***Revenue Expenditure*** **:** This is that of the expenditure which is incurred for running the day-to-day business operations of the enterprises. Some of the examples of revenue expenditure are – salaries and wages, power, fuel, depreciation, repairs and maintenance etc.
3. ***Deferred Revenue Expenditure*** **:** This is that part of expenditure which lies between capital expenditure and revenue expenditure. Sometimes a substantial amount in the form of revenue expenditure may have to be incurred, nevertheless extending the benefits over a period of 4 to 5 years and that kind of expenditure may have to incur about Rs.5 lakhs in a particular year towards sales advertisement charges. Nevertheless, the benefit may extend for a period of 5 years and in such cases it is desirable to charge a deferred amount of Rs.1 lakh per year over a period of 5 years.

But it is practically very difficult in some cases to establish a particular expenditure, as what sort of expenditure is that? Be it revenue or capital or differed revenue, the type of expenditure varies from industry to industry. For example, in a motor car manufacturing company, the motor cars are shown as their current assets and the charges incurred for manufacturing them are treated as revenue charges while the enterprises purchasing the same vehicles treat them as fixed assets classifying that expenditure as capital expenditure.

### Financial Statements

The objects of book keeping accountancy is to present a clear financial picture of the state of affairs of a firm. This picture consists of two statements mainly. One statement summaries that income and expenses showing how much profit the firm has earned in a particular period or how much has been the loss during the period. The other statement sets out what the firm possess (assets), how much the firm owes to other (liabilities) and how much belongs to the proprietors (capital). The first statement is known as 'profit and loss account' and the second one is called 'balance sheet'.

### The Balance Sheet

The first of the two major or financial statements, the balance sheet, is a statement of the sources and the ways in which these resources are invested at a specified date. Thus, it is an elaboration of the static form of the accounting equation.

Assets = Liabilities + Capital. Every balance sheet is composed of those three main elements. A very simple form of the balance sheet is given in Chapter 10 on page 159.

### Assets

Assets are the resources of the business enterprise. They include both monetary assets (cash and claim to cash) and rights to future services. Assets are conventionally classified on the balance sheet in three major categories, fixed assets and other assets.

### Fixed Assets

The fixed assets classification is reserved for long term tangible assets used in the operation of the business, such as land and furniture. These assets are retained by a business enterprise for fairly longer periods with a view to carrying on the business.

### Investments

Investments are classified as current or fixed assets according to their nature and object in view. Investments in the form of government securities and marketable securities are treated as current assets. If the investments are not readily marketable or permanent controlling substantial interest in other companies, they are not convertible into cash and as such are not included in current assets.

### Current Assets

Current assets are defined as cash and assets which can be converted into cash or used up within the next operating cycle of the enterprise. Since the operating cycle is usually taken to be one year in order to correspond with the convention of annual reporting, the usual time limit on current assets is one year. Typically included in current assets are inventories, sundry debtors (accounts receivable) cash, advances and prepaid expenses. These represent, for the most part, the liquid assets of the enterprise.

Inventories are of four basic types. The merchandise enterprise, one that buys and sells goods, deals which are referred to merchandise inventory or simply merchandise. The amount of merchandise inventory on hand at the balance date appears on the balance sheet as a current asset. The manufacturing enterprise, on the other hand, usually has three types of inventories on hand. Finished goods inventory is the amount of completed product on hand awaiting sale to customers. Work in process, as the name implies represents goods, which are partially completed and require further processing before becoming finished goods inventory. Raw materials used in the manufacturing process.

All the four types of inventory, when they are present, are usually included in current assets on the balance sheet.

### Sundry Debtors

Sundry Debtors represent amount due against sales in the normal course of day to day operations. The amount due from sundry debtors varies with industry and trade practices.

Sundry debtors are normally shown on the balance sheet with an amount deducted called allowance for doubtful debts. This is an estimate of the portion of the total amounts receivable which is not expected to be collected.

Cash includes coin and currency on hand as well as cash on deposit in banks which can be readily withdrawn. Cash in banks which is set aside for special purposes and thus is not readily available for normal business should not be included in current assets.

### Other Assets

The 'other assets' include all assets which do not fall into any category of assets mentioned above. These include intangible assets like goodwill and fictitious assets like preliminary expenses, deferred revenue expenditure etc.

### Liabilities

Liabilities have been defined as sources of enterprise resources obtained front non-owners. They are also defined as the debts of the business enterprise.

### Capital

Capital measures the amount of enterprise resources contributed by owners and accumulated through successful operations. Hence the classification of capital varies with the legal structure of the enterprise. The capital sections of balance sheets for three basic business structures viz, the sole proprietorship, the partnership, and the corporation are discussed as under:

### Capital in a Proprietary Concern

A sole proprietorship is a business owned entirely by one person. Legally, there is no essential distinction between a sole proprietorship and its owner, but economically, the owner himself has made a distinction between his personal and business of the sole proprietor and treats his business activities as an accounting entity. The equity of the proprietor in this accounting entity constitutes his capital.

Conventionally, a sole proprietor's capital account reflects investments made by the owner, plus amounts of net income minus withdrawn by the owner during the accounting periods are reflected in the withdrawals account.

A typical balance sheet presentation would appear as shown below :

Capital (beginning of the period)...

Add (investment during the period)...

Net income for the period...

Less withdrawals during the period

Capital (end of the period)

### Capital in a Partnership Concern

A partnership is an association of two or more persons in a business enterprise. Legally the partnership is not recognized as a separate entity although the laws does recognize that partners may act on behalf of each other. Economically, however, the partnership does exist as an entity separate from time, its owners. This same entity is used for accounting purposes.

Obviously, it is necessary to keep the ownership interest of various partnerships separated. This causes the capital section of a partnership balance sheet to resemble a sole proprietor's capital section multiplied by the number of partners in the enterprise.

### Capital in a Limited Company

A company registered under the Companies Act is recognized at law as an entity separated from its owners. Legally, it is an artificial person, able through its officers to enter into contracts due and be used, etc., just as a natural person can do. This legal status of the company brings about certain restrictions on the reporting of corporate to report separately its share capital, which cannot legally be distributed to its owners in the form of dividends, and the amount, which can legally be so distributed.

A corporation may issue two different types of shares, Equity shares and preferences shares.

A typical capital section of a limited company appears in Chapter 10 on page 159.

### Reserves and Surpluses

Reserves are with special reference to limited companies divided into two main classes.

(a) Capital reserves and

(b) Revenue reserves.

A capital reserve arises out of profits not directly related to the business, For example, premium on issue of shares, profits on forfeiture of share etc., are credited to capital reserve.

Revenue reserves are again divided into classes general reserves and specific reserves.

General reserves are created by setting aside profits in order to strengthen the general financial position of the company. Such profits are available for distribution as divided. For this reasons, reserve is often described as a 'Free Reserve'.

Specific reserves are also created by setting aside profits, are available for specific purposes or because of specific obligations. Therefore even though a specific reserve is a revenue reserve, is not immediately available for divided.

If reserves are invested outside the business in securities and such securities are earmarked for particular purpose denoted by the reserve, the reserve will be called "*reserve fund*".

### Secured Loans

Since the cost of debt funds is cheaper in order to finance the operations of a business enterprise, moneys are borrowed against the security of the properties of the company. These loans may be raised from the public or banks or financial institutions.

### Unsecured Loans

Unsecured loans are those loans which are not backed by any security. There are certain restrictions on acceptance on unsecured loans by limited companies.

### Current Liabilities and Provisions

Current liabilities consist of obligations incurred in the normal course, if business is payable within a period of one year. For example, payments due to supplies for the materials supplied by them are short-term obligations.

During the course of business, an enterprise might have incurred an obligation to pay for some services etc., which were not discharged before the end of accounting period. A part of the profits are set apart to meet such expense. Thus a provision is the amount set aside out of profits to meet any liability of which the amount cannot be determined, either substantial accuracy. Provision for taxation, provision for expenses etc, are a few examples.

### Profit and Loss Account

One of the aims of accountancy is to ascertain periodically, say yearly, how much profit a business enterprise has earned. This is done by preparing a financial statement called profit and loss account. Into this account all revenue items, both income and expenses are transferred. The net result would be profit if the income exceeds expenses. It will be a loss if the expenses exceed the income.

The following principles are followed while preparing a profit and loss account.

(a) Only revenue receipts and revenue expenditure are taken into account.

(b) Expenses and income relating only to the period for which the accounts are being prepared should be considered.

(c) All expenses and income relating to the period concerned should be considered even if the expense has not been paid in cash or the income has not yet been received.

The following is a simple proforma of the profit and loss account of a manufacturing company.

**Profit & Loss Account for the period ended**

| | Rs. | | Rs. |
|---|---|---|---|
| To Opening Stock : | | By sales less returns | 1,85,000 |
| Raw Materials | 10,000 | By closing stocks: | |
| Work-in-Process | 5,000 | Raw materials | 15,000 |
| Finished Goods | 30,080 | work-in-process | 5,000 |
| | | Finished goods | 36,000 |
| | 45,000 | | 56,000 |
| To Raw Material Purchased | 85,000 | | |
| To Manufacturing Overheads | 33,000 | | |
| Gross Profit | 78,000 | | |
| | 2,41,000 | | 2,41,000 |
| | | By gross profit b/d 78,000 | |
| To Admistrative Overheads | 12,000 | | |
| To Selling Overheads | 14,000 | | |
| To Operation Profit | 52,000 | | |
| | 78,000 | | |
| To Interest | 16,000 | By Operating Profit | 52,000 |
| To Net Profit | 76,000 | By Non-operating Income | 40,000 |
| | 92,000 | | 92,000 |

## Relationship of the Income Statement and Balance Sheet

The income statement and balance sheet must be considered as related statements. The obvious mechanical relationship between the two statements lies in the addition of net income for the period to retained earning, but the relationship has sleeper implications.

The balance sheet is a static statement, reporting assets, liabilities, and capital of a specified time. The income statement is a dynamic statement, reporting the results of operations over a specified period of time. Two different views on the relationship between the two statements correspond to the relative importance attached to them.

For many years, the balance sheet was thought of as primary financial statement. Users of the statements, particularly bankers and others creditors, relied heavily on the amounts and composition of assets, liabilities and capital reported on the balance sheet. The income statement was considered merely a link between successive balance sheet.

Later, the income statements came to be considered as the primary financial statement, and the balance sheet as a sort of stopping point between successive income statements. This view is enhanced in part by the reorganization that the balance sheet consists largely of unexercised costs rather than realizable market values. In addition, creditors and investors alike have come to recognize the going concern aspects of the enterprise, which leads to increasing reliance on the income statement.

More recently, users of financial statements seem to be exhibiting renewed interest in the balance sheet. The income statement, however, has not lost any of its prestige. Apparently, the two statements are beginning to be considered as related statements, which in fact they are. Joint consideration of the two statements yields much more meaningful information than reliance on either to the exclusion of the other.

## Conclusion

An attempt has been made in this paper to discuss in general the contents of a balance sheet and a profit and loss account. While there is no law prescribing the format and content of those financial statements by a sole proprietary concern and/or a partnership concern, the Companies Act, 1956 stipulates the manner in which these statements have to be prepared. Similarly, in respect of statutory bodies like Electricity Board, Road Transport Corporation etc, directives are given in the respective statutes under which they came into being, as to the manner in which these statements have to be prepared. However, the contents of the information given in the financial statements, both by the statutory bodies and the limited companies is basically the same.

## Exercises

**1. Enter the following information in the proper books of Ratnam Enterprises for the month of January, 2004.**

| Date | Particulars |
|---|---|
| 01-01-04 | Balances as at January-1-2004: |
| | **Assets** |
| | Buildings, Rs. 1,38,000; |
| | Accumulated Depreciation (24,000); |
| | Inventory, Rs. 51,900; |
| | Cash at Bank, Rs. 7,620; |
| | Cash in hand Rs. 860; |
| | Accounts Receivable: Shyam & Company Rs. 1,460,<br>Maruti & Co. Rs. 1,260; |
| | Furniture Rs. 1,500. |
| | **Liabilities** |
| | Loan (Interest of 6% per annum) Rs.20,000; |
| | Accounts payable; Laxmi and Co., Rs. 6,000,<br>JK Keyboards, Rs. 32,000. |
| | Owner's Equity : Share Capital, Rs. 1,00,000;<br>General Reserve, Rs. 15,000; |
| | Profit and Loss Account, Rs. 5,600. |
| 03-01-04 | Withdrew from bank Rs. 1,500. |
| 04-01-04 | Salaries and Wages paid, Rs. 1,435. |
| 07-01-04 | Bought 20 manual typewriters from Laxmi and Co., Rs. 4,400. |
| 08-01-04 | Paid freight on typewriters purchase, Rs. 300. |
| 09-01-04 | Returned 5 typewriters to Laxmi and Co. as defective. |
| 17-01-04 | Paid Laxmi and Co. by cheque in full settlement of amount due on January-1-2004, Rs. 5,850. |

18-01-04 Received from Maruti & Co. by cheque in full settlement, Rs. 1,235 and deposited in Bank.

19-01-04 Bought of Tumbi office needs, office supplies, Rs. 1,000.

24-01-04 Sales to Krishna and Bros. Rs. 14,000

24-01-04 Paid cash to Raju Repair Works for repairs to building, Rs. 250.

25-01-04 Purchases, from AST Computers Rs. 3,500.

26-01-04 Received from Shyam and company on account, cheque for Rs. 2,000 and deposited in Bank.

27-01-04 Cash Sales at an auction, Rs. 47,500

27-01-04 Paid to JK Keyboards in full settlement, Rs. 31,400

28-01-04 Serviced office machines of City Bank, and billed them Rs. 1,200.

31-01-04 Paid warehouse rent, Rs. 1,500.

31-01-04 Bank charges for the month, Rs. 35.

31-01-04 Received Rs. 1,600 in cash for repairs to office machines of Desu Co.

**Additional Information for Adjustments**

(a) Value of inventory at the end of January, Rs. 38,700

(b) Salaries and Wages for the month of January unpaid, Rs. 2,000.

(c) Rent paid on January 31, covered three months, January-March.

(d) No interest was paid on the loan during the month.

(e) Buildings have a useful life of 20 years, and a salvage value of Rs. 18,000. Depreciation is charged in equal amounts each month.

(f) Office supplies used during the month, Rs. 600.

(g) Monthly maintenance services were rendered to State Insurance Agency. This is under an annual contract, and the customer would pay at the rate of Rs. 1,000 per month for the whole year's services.

(h) Repair work for Desu Co. could not be started in January, but is expected to be completed during February.

**Solution :**

## CASH BOOK

| Date | Particulars | Discount Rs. | Bank Rs. | Cash Rs. | Date | Particulars | Discount Rs. | Bank Rs. | Cash Rs. |
|---|---|---|---|---|---|---|---|---|---|
| 1-Jan 2004 | To Balance | | 7,650 | 860 | 3-Jan 2004 | By Cash | | 1,500 | |
| 3 | To Bank | | | 1,500 | 4 | By Salaries and Wages | | | 1,435 |
| 18 | To A/R: Maruti & Co. | 25 | 1,235 | | 8 | By Freight | 150 | 5,850 | 300 |
| 26 | To A/R Shyam, & Co. | | 2,000 | | 18 | By A/P Raju Repair Works | | | 250 |
| 27 | To Sales Revenue | | 47,500 | | 24 | By Repair Expenses | | | 31,400 |
| 31 | To Service Revenue | | 1,600 | | 27 | By A/P JK Keyboards | | | 230 |
| | | | | | 29 | By Advertising Expense | | | 1,500 |
| | | | | | 31 | By Rent Expense | | 35 | |
| | | | | | | By Bank charges | | 3,470 | 16,345 |
| | | 25 | 10,855 | 51,460 | | By Balance c/d | 750 | 10,855 | 51,460 |
| Feb .1 | To Balance b/d | | 3,470 | 16,345 | | | | | |

## Sales Book

| Date | Customer | Total Rs. | Sales revenue Rs. | Service revenue Rs. |
|---|---|---|---|---|
| 17-Jan-2004 | Shyam &Co. | 6,000 | 6,000 | |
| 24-Jan-2004 | Maxwell Co. | 14,000 | 14,000 | |
| 28-Jan-2004 | City Bank | 1,200 | | 1,200 |
| 31-Jan-2004 | Libra&Co. | 18,000 | 18,000 | |
| | | **39,200** | **38,000** | **1,200** |

## Purchases Book

| Date | Supplier | Details | Total | Purchases Rs. | Supplies Rs. |
|---|---|---|---|---|---|
| 17-Jan-2004 | Laxmi and Co. | 20 Typewriters | 4,400 | 4,400 | |
| 19-Jan-2004 | Tumbi Office | Office Supplies | 1,000 | | 1,000 |
| 25-Jan-2004 | AST Computers | | 3,500 | 3,500 | |
| | | | **8,900** | **7,900** | **1,000** |

## Purchases returns Book

| Date | Supplier | Details | Purchase Returns Rs. |
|---|---|---|---|
| 9-Jan-2004 | Laxmi and Co. | 5 Typewriters | 1,100 |
| | | | 1,100 |

## General Ledger

### Sales Revenue

| Date | Particulars | Dr.<br>Rs. | Date | Particulars | Cr.<br>Rs. |
|---|---|---|---|---|---|
| 31-Jan-2004 | To Balance | 85,500 | 27-Jan-2004 | By Cash | 47,500 |
| | | | 31-Jan-2004 | By Credit | 38,000 |
| | | **85,500** | | | **85,500** |
| | | | | By Balance | 85,500 |

### Service Revenue

| Date | Particulars | Dr.<br>Rs. | Date | Particulars | Cr.<br>Rs. |
|---|---|---|---|---|---|
| 31-Jan-2004 | To Balance | 2,800 | 31-Jan-2004 | By Cash | 1,600 |
| | To Unearned Rev | 1,600 | | By A/R | 1,200 |
| | To Balance | 2,200 | | By A/R | 1,000 |
| | | **3,800** | | **3,800** | |
| | | | 1-Feb-2004 | By Balance | 2,200 |

### Purchases

| Date | Particulars | Dr.<br>Rs. | Date | Particulars | Cr.<br>Rs. |
|---|---|---|---|---|---|
| 31-Jan-2004 | To A/P | 7,900 | 31-Jan-2004 | By Balance | 7,900 |
| | | 7,900 | | | |
| 1-Feb-2004 | To Balance | | | | 7,900 |

### Supplies

| Date | Particulars | Dr.<br>Rs. | Date | Particulars | Cr.<br>Rs. |
|---|---|---|---|---|---|
| 31-Jan-2004 | To A/P | 1,000 | 31-Jan-2004 | By Supplies exp | 600 |
| | | | | By Balance | 400 |
| | | 1,000 | | | 100 |
| 1-Feb-2004 | To Balance | 400 | | | |

**General Ledger** ***Contd.....***

### Purchase Returns

| Date | Particulars | Dr. Rs. | Date | Particulars | Cr. Rs. |
|---|---|---|---|---|---|
| 31-Jan-2004 | To Balance | 1,100 | 31-Jan-2004 | By A/P | 1,100 |
| | | 1,100 | | | 1,100 |
| | | | 1-Feb-2004 | | 1,100 |

### Salaries and Wages Expense

| Date | Particulars | Dr. Rs. | Date | Particulars | Cr. Rs. |
|---|---|---|---|---|---|
| 4-Jan-2004 | To Cash | 1,435 | 31-Jan-2004 | By Balance | 3,435 |
| 31-Jan-2004 | To Wages Payable | 2,000 | | | |
| | | **3,435** | | | **3,435** |
| 1-Feb-2004 | To Balance | 3,435 | | | |

### Freight

| Date | Particulars | Dr. Rs. | Date | Particulars | Cr. Rs. |
|---|---|---|---|---|---|
| 8-Jan-2004 | To Cash | 300 | 31-Jan-2004 | By Balance | 300 |
| | | **300** | | | |
| 1-Feb-2004 | To Balance | 300 | | | |

### Discount

| Date | Particulars | Dr. Rs. | Date | Particulars | Cr. Rs. |
|---|---|---|---|---|---|
| 31-Jan-2004 | To Cash | 25 | 31-Jan-2004 | By Cash | 750 |
| 31-Jan-2004 | To Balance | 725 | | | |
| | | **750** | | | **750** |
| | | | 1-Feb-2004 | By Balance | 725 |

**General Ledger** ***Contd.....***

## Repairs Expense

| Date | Particulars | Dr. Rs. | Date | Particulars | Cr. Rs. |
|---|---|---|---|---|---|
| 24-Jan-2004 | To Cash | 250 | 31-Jan-2004 | By Balance | 250 |
| | | **250** | | | **250** |
| 1-Feb-2004 | To Balance | 250 | | | |

## Advertisement Expense

| Date | Particulars | Dr. Rs. | Date | Particulars | Cr. Rs. |
|---|---|---|---|---|---|
| 24-Jan-2004 | To Cash | 250 | 31-Jan-2004 | By Balance | 250 |
| | | **230** | | | **230** |
| 1-Feb-2004 | | 230 | | | |

## Rent Expenses

| Date | Particulars | Dr. Rs. | Date | Particulars | Cr. Rs. |
|---|---|---|---|---|---|
| 31-Jan-2004 | To Cash | 1,500 | 31-Jan-2004 | By Prepad rent | 1,000 |
| | | | | By Balance | 500 |
| | | **1,500** | | | **1,500** |
| 1-Feb-2004 | To Balance | 500 | | | |

## Bank Charges

| Date | Particulars | Dr. Rs. | Date | Particulars | Cr. Rs. |
|---|---|---|---|---|---|
| 31-Jan-2004 | To Cash | 35 | 31-Jan-2004 | By Balance | 35 |
| | | 35 | | | 35 |
| 1-Feb-2004 | To Balance | 35 | | | |

**General Ledger** ***Contd.....***

### Buildings

| Date | Particulars | Dr. Rs. | Date | Particulars | Cr. Rs. |
|---|---|---|---|---|---|
| 1-Jan-2004 | To Balance | 1,38,000 | 31-Jan-2004 | By Balance | 1,38,000 |
| | | 1,38,000 | | | 1,38,000 |
| 1-Feb-2004 | To Balance | 1,38,000 | | | |

### Inventory

| Date | Particulars | Dr. Rs. | Date | Particulars | Cr. Rs. |
|---|---|---|---|---|---|
| 1-Jan-2004 | To Balance | 51,900 | 31-Jan-2004 | By Balance | 51,900 |
| | | 51,900 | | | 51,900 |
| 1-Feb-2004 | To Balance | 51,900 | | | |

### Furniture

| Date | Particulars | Dr. Rs. | Date | Particulars | Cr. Rs. |
|---|---|---|---|---|---|
| 1-Jan-2004 | To Balance | 1,500 | 31-Jan-2004 | By Balance | 1,500 |
| | | **1,500** | | | **1,500** |
| 1-Feb-2004 | To Balance | 1,500 | | | |

### Accounts Receivable Control

| Date | Particulars | Dr. Rs. | Date | Particulars | Cr. Rs. |
|---|---|---|---|---|---|
| 1-Jan-2004 | To Balance | 2,720 | 31-Jan-2004 | By Bank | 1,235 |
| 31-Jan-2004 | To Sales | 39,200 | | By Discount | 25 |
| | To Service Rev. | 1,000 | 26-Jan-2004 | By Bank | 2,000 |
| | | | 31-Jan-2004 | By Balance | 39,600 |
| | **42,920** | | | | **42,920** |
| 1-Feb-2004 | To Balance | 39,660 | | | |

**General Ledger** ***Contd.....***

### Accounts Payable Control

| Date | Particulars | Dr. Rs. | Date | Particulars | Cr. Rs. |
|---|---|---|---|---|---|
| 18-Jan-2004 | By Bank | 5,850 | 1-Jan-2004 | By Balance | 38,000 |
| | By Discount | 150 | 31-Jan-2004 | By Purchase | 7,900 |
| 27-Jan-2004 | By Bank | 31,400 | | By Supplies | 1,000 |
| | By Discount | 600 | | | |
| 31-Jan-2004 | To Purchase Returns | 1,100 | | | |
| | To Balance | 7,800 | | | |
| | | 46,900 | | | 46,900 |
| | | | 1-Feb-2004 | By Balance | 7,800 |

### Loan

| Date | Particulars | Dr. Rs. | Date | Particulars | Cr. Rs. |
|---|---|---|---|---|---|
| 1-Jan, 2004 | To Balance | 20,000 | 31-Jan, 2004 | By Balance | 20,000 |
| | | 20,000 | | | 20,000 |
| | | | 1-Feb-2004 | By Balance | 20,000 |

### Accumulated Depreciation

| Date | Particulars | Dr. Rs. | Date | Particulars | Cr. Rs. |
|---|---|---|---|---|---|
| | | | 1-Jan-2004 | By Balance | 24,000 |
| 31-Jan, 2004 | To Balance | 24,500 | 31-Jan-2004 | ByDepexp | 500 |
| | | 24,500 | | | 24,500 |
| | | | 1-Feb-2004 | By Balance | 24,500 |

**General Ledger** ***Contd.....***

### Share Capital

| Date | Particulars | Dr. Rs. | Date | Particulars | Cr. Rs. |
|---|---|---|---|---|---|
| 31-Jan-2004 | To Balance | 1,00,000 | 1-Jan-2004 | By Balance | 1,00,000 |
| | | 1,00,000 | | | 1,00,000 |
| | | | 1-Feb-2004 | To Balance | 1,00,000 |

### General Reserve

| Date | Particulars | Dr. Rs. | Date | Particulars | Cr. Rs. |
|---|---|---|---|---|---|
| 31-Jan-2004 | To Balance | 15,000 | 1-Jan-2004 | By Balance | 15,000 |
| | | 15,000 | | | 15,000 |
| | | | 1-Feb-2004 | To Balance | 15,000 |

### Profit and loss account

| Date | Particulars | Dr. Rs. | Date | Particulars | Cr. Rs. |
|---|---|---|---|---|---|
| 31-Jan-2004 | To Balance | 5,000 | 1-Jan-2004 | By Balance | 5,000 |
| | | 5,000 | | | 5,000 |
| | | | 1-Feb-2004 | To Balance | 5,000 |

### Salaries and wages

| Date | Particulars | Dr. Rs. | Date | Particulars | Cr. Rs. |
|---|---|---|---|---|---|
| 31-Jan-2004 | To Balance | 2,000 | 1-Jan-2004 | By Balance | 2,000 |
| | | 2,000 | | | 2,000 |
| | | | 1-Feb-2004 | To Balance | 2,000 |

### Prepaid rent

| Date | Particulars | Dr. Rs. | Date | Particulars | Cr. Rs. |
|---|---|---|---|---|---|
| 1-Jan-2004 | To Balance | 1,000 | 31-Jan-2004 | By Balance | 1,000 |
| | | 1,000 | | | 1,000 |
| 1-Feb-2004 | To Balance | 1,000 | | | |

**General Ledger** *Contd.....*

## Interest Expense

| Date | Particulars | Dr. Rs. | Date | Particulars | Cr. Rs. |
|---|---|---|---|---|---|
| 1-Jan-2004 | To Balance | 100 | 31-Jan-2004 | By Balance | 100 |
| | | 100 | | | 100 |
| 1-Feb-2004 | To Balance | 100 | | | |

## Interest Payable

| Date | Particulars | Dr. Rs. | Date | Particulars | Cr. Rs. |
|---|---|---|---|---|---|
| 31-Jan-2004 | To Balance | 100 | 31-Jan-2004 | By Interest Exp | 100 |
| | | 100 | | | 100 |
| | | | 1-Feb-2004 | By Balance | 100 |

## Depreciation Expense

| Date | Particulars | Dr. Rs. | Date | Particulars | Cr. Rs. |
|---|---|---|---|---|---|
| 31-Jan-2004 | To Account Dep | 500 | 31-Jan-2004 | By Balance | 500 |
| | | 500 | | | 500 |
| 1-Feb-2004 | To Balance | 500 | | | |

## Supplies Expense

| Date | Particulars | Dr. Rs. | Date | Particulars | Cr. Rs. |
|---|---|---|---|---|---|
| 31-Jan, 2004 | To Supplies | 600 | 31-Jan-2004 | BY Balance | 600 |
| | | 600 | | | 600 |
| 1-Feb-2004 | | 600 | | | |

## Unearned Revenue

| Date | Particulars | Dr. Rs. | Date | Particulars | Cr. Rs. |
|---|---|---|---|---|---|
| 31-Jan-2004 | To Balance | 1,600 | 31-Jan-2004 | By Service Rev | 1,600 |
| | | 1,600 | | | 1,600 |
| | | | 1-Feb-2004 | | 1,600 |

## Subsidary Ledger

### Accounts Receivable

| Date | Particulars | Dr. Rs. | Cr. Rs. | Balance Dr. Or Cr. |
|---|---|---|---|---|
| 1-Jan-2004 | To Balance | 1,460 | | 1,460 |
| 17-Jan-2004 | To Sales | 6,000 | | 7,460 |
| 26-Jan-2004 | By Cash | | 2,000 | 5,460 |

### Maruti and company

| Date | Particulars | Dr. Rs. | Cr. Rs. | Balance Dr. Or Cr. |
|---|---|---|---|---|
| 1-Jan-2004 | To Balance | 1,260 | | 1,260 |
| 18-Jan-2004 | By Cash | | 1,200 | 0 |
| 24-Jan-2004 | To Sales | 14,000 | | 14,000 |

### City bank

| Date | Particulars | Dr. Rs. | Cr. Rs. | Balance Dr. Or Cr. |
|---|---|---|---|---|
| 24-Jan-2004 | To Service | 1,200 | | 1,200 |

### Linga and Co.

| Date | Particulars | Dr. Rs. | Cr. Rs. | Balance Dr. Or Cr. |
|---|---|---|---|---|
| 31-Jan-2004 | To Sales | 18,000 | | 18,000 |

### Accounts Payable Subsidiary Ledger

| Date | Particulars | Dr. Rs. | Cr. Rs. | Balance Dr. Or Cr. |
|---|---|---|---|---|
| 1-Jan-2004 | By Balance | | 6,000 | 6,000 |
| 3-Jan-2004 | By Purchase | | 4,000 | 10,400 |
| 5-Jan-2004 | To Returns | 1,100 | | 9,300 |
| 18-Jan-2004 | To Cash | 6,000 | | 3,300 |

### JK Keyboards

| Date | Particulars | Dr. Rs. | Cr. Rs. | Balance Dr. Or Cr. |
|---|---|---|---|---|
| 1-Jan-2004 | By Balance | | 32,000 | 32,000 |
| 27-Jan-2004 | To Cash | 32,000 | | - |

**Subsidary Ledger** ***Contd.....***

**Sharp Brothers and company**

| Date | Particulars | Dr. Rs. | Cr. Rs. | Balance Dr. Or Cr. |
|---|---|---|---|---|
| 19-Jan-2004 | By Purchases | | 1,000 | 1,000 |

**AST Computers**

| Date | Particulars | Dr. Rs. | Cr. Rs. | Balance Dr. Or Cr. |
|---|---|---|---|---|
| 25-Jan-2004 | By Purchases | 3,500 | 3,500 | |

**Trail Balance: Accounts Receivable Subsidiary Ledger**

**January 31, 1990**

| Particular | Dr. |
|---|---|
| Shyam and Company | 5,460 |
| Maxwell and Company | 14,000 |
| City Bank | 1,200 |
| Libra and Company | 18,000 |
| | **38,660** |

**Trail Balance: Accounts Payable Subsidiary Ledger**

**January 31, 2004**

| Particular | Cr : |
|---|---|
| Laxmi and Co. | 3,300 |
| Sharp Bros and Company | 1,000 |
| Thomas Barnes and Company | 3,500 |
| | **7,800** |

## Journal Entries

| | Particulars | Dr. Rs. | Cr. Rs. |
|---|---|---|---|
| (a) | Ending Inventory | 38,700 | |
| | To Trading A/c | | 38,700 |
| (b) | Salaries and Wages Expense | 2,000 | |
| | To Salaries and Wages payable | | 2,000 |
| (c ) | Prepaid Rent | 1,000 | |
| | To Rent Expenses | | 1,000 |
| (d) | Interest Expense | 100 | |
| | To Interest Payable | | 100 |
| (e) | Depreciation Expense | 600 | |
| | To Accumulated Depreciation | | 600 |
| (f) | Suppliers expense | 1,000 | |
| | To Suppliers | | 1,000 |
| (g) | Accounts Receivable Control | 1,000 | |
| | To Service Revenue | | 1,000 |
| (h) | Service Revenue | 1,600 | |
| | To Unearned Revenue | | 1,600 |

## Smart office Machines Ltd. Trading Account for the Month January, 2004

| Particulars | | Dr. Rs. | Particulars | Cr. Rs. |
|---|---|---|---|---|
| To Beginning Inventory | | 51,900 | By Sales | 85,500 |
| | | | By Service Revenue | 2,200 |
| | | | By Ending Inventory | 38,700 |
| To Purchase | 7,900 | | | |
| Less: Returns | 1,100 | 6,800 | | |
| To Freight | | 300 | | |
| To Gross Profit | | 67,400 | | |
| | | **1,26,000** | | **1,26,000** |

### Profit and Loss Account for the Month of January, 2004

| Particulars | Dr. Rs. | Particulars | Cr. Rs. |
|---|---|---|---|
| To Salaries and wages | 3,435 | By Gross Profit | 67,400 |
| To Repairs | 250 | By Discount | 725 |
| To Advertisement | | | |
| To Rent Expense | 500 | | |
| To Bank Charges | 35 | | |
| To Interest | 100 | | |
| To Depreciation | 500 | | |
| To Supplies used | 600 | | |
| To Net profit transferred to p&l appropriation account | 62,475 | | |
| | **68,125** | | **68,125** |

### Profit and Loss appropriation Account for the month of January 2004

| Particulars | Dr. Rs. | Particulars | Cr. Rs. |
|---|---|---|---|
| To Balance transferred to Balance sheet | 68,075 | By Balance | 5,600 |
| | | By Net profit Transferred from Profit and Loss Account | 62,475 |
| | **68,075** | | **68,075** |

### BALANCE SHEET as at January, 2004

| Liabilities | Rs. | Assets | | Rs. |
|---|---|---|---|---|
| Share Capital | 10,0000 | Cash in hand and Bank | | 19,815 |
| General Reserve | 15,000 | Accounts Receivable | | 39,660 |
| Profit and Loss Account | 68,075 | Supplies | | 400 |
| **Out Standing :** | | Inventory | | 38,700 |
| Loan | 20,000 | Prepaid Rent | | 1,000 |
| Accounts Payable | 7,800 | Furniture | | 1,500 |
| Salaries & Wages | 2,000 | Building | 1,38,000 | |
| Interest | 100 | Less Depreciation | 24,500 | 1,13,500 |
| Unearned revenue | 1,600 | | | |
| | **2,14,575** | | | **2,14,575** |

**2. From the following Trial Balance of XYZ Ltd. as on December 31, 2003 prepare a Trading, Profit and Loss Account and a Balance Sheet as on that date.**

**Trading Balance of 'XYZ Ltd'**
**for the year ending December 31, 2003**

| Debit Balances | Rs. | Credit Balances | Rs. |
|---|---|---|---|
| Purchases | 75,000 | Sales | 1,00,000 |
| Stationary | 400 | Capital | 45,000 |
| Drawings | 800 | Bills payable | 15,700 |
| Bills receivable | 4,600 | Creditors | 27,400 |
| Delivery van | 11,000 | Commission | 600 |
| Income Tax | 1,200 | Discount | 800 |
| Salary | 2,800 | Purchases Return | 1,200 |
| Bad Debt | 300 | | |
| Cash in hand | 700 | | |
| Opening Stock | 30,000 | | |
| Commission | 900 | | |
| Office Expenses | 600 | | |
| Building | 25,000 | | |
| Patent | 6,000 | | |
| Trade Expenses | 200 | | |
| Fuel and Power | 1,000 | | |
| Insurance and Taxes | 1,300 | | |
| Carriage Inwards | 400 | | |
| Carriage Outwards | 500 | | |
| Plant and Machinery | 12,000 | | |
| Advertisement | 1,400 | | |
| Bank Balances | 4,600 | | |
| Sundry Debtors | 10,000 | | |
| | **1,90,700** | | **1,90,700** |

**Adjustments:**

1. Closing Stock Rs. 20,000
2. Outstanding salary Rs. 200 and Stationary Rs. 100
3. Insurance and Advertisement prepaid to the tune of Rs. 300 and Rs. 400 Respectively.
4. Depreciation plant and Machinery by 5%, Building by 2% and patent by 10%.
5. Provide Reserve for Bad and Doubtful Debts on Sundry Debtors at 5%.

**Solution :**

**Trading Account of XYZ Ltd**
**for the year ending December 31, 2003**

| Particulars | | Rs. | Particulars | Rs. |
|---|---|---|---|---|
| To Purchases | 75,000 | | By Sales | 1,00,000 |
| Less: Purchase Returns | 1,200 | 73,800 | By Closing Stock | 20,000 |
| To Opening Stock | | 30,000 | | |
| To Trade Expenses | | 200 | | |
| To Fuel and Power | | 1,000 | | |
| To Carriage Inwards | | 400 | | |
| To Gross Profit | | **14,600** | | |
| | | **1,20,000** | | **1,20,000** |

**Profit and Loss Account of XYZ Ltd**
**for the Year Ending December 31, 2003**

| Particulars | | Rs. | Particulars | Rs. |
|---|---|---|---|---|
| To Stationary | 400 | | By Gross Profit | 14,600 |
| | 100 | | By Commission | 600 |
| | | 500 | By Discount | 800 |
| To Salary | 2,800 | | | |
| Add: Outstanding | 200 | | | |
| | | 3,000 | | |
| To Reserve on Bad and doubtful debt | | 500 | | |
| To Bad Debt | | 300 | | |
| To Commission | | 900 | | |
| To Office Expenses | | 600 | | |
| To Depreciation :- | | | | |
| (a) Building @ 2% | 500 | | | |
| (b) Patent @ 10% | 600 | | | |
| (c) Plant and Machinery@ 5% | 600 | | | |
| | | 1,700 | | |
| To Insurance and Taxes | 1,300 | | | |
| Less Prepaid taxes | 300 | | | |
| | | 1,000 | | |
| To Carriage Outwards | | 500 | | |
| To Advertisement | 1,400 | | | |
| Less: Prepaid | 400 | | | |
| | | 1,000 | | |
| To Net Profit | | 6,000 | | |
| | | **16,000** | | **16,000** |

**Balance Sheet of XYZ Ltd.**
**for the year ending December 31, 2003**

| Liabilities | | Rs. | Assets | | Rs. |
|---|---|---|---|---|---|
| Bills Payable | | 15,700 | Cash in hand | | 700 |
| Sundry Creditors | | 27,400 | Cash at bank | | 4,000 |
| Salary Outstanding | | 200 | Bills Receivables | | 4,600 |
| Stationary Outstanding | | 100 | Closing Stock | | |
| | | | Sundry Debtors | 10,000 | |
| | | | Less RBDD | 500 | |
| Capital | 45,000 | | | | |
| Less : Drawings | 800 | | | | 9,500 |
| Less: Incometax | 200 | | Insurance Prepaid | | 300 |
| | | | Advertisement Prepaid | | 400 |
| | 43,000 | | Delivery Van | | 11,000 |
| Add : Net Profit | 6,000 | | Plant and Machinery | 12,000 | |
| | | 49,000 | Less : Depreciation | 600 | |
| | | | | | 11,400 |
| | | | Patent | 6,000 | |
| | | | Less : Depreciation | 600 | |
| | | | | | 5,400 |
| | | | Building | 25,000 | |
| | | | Less : Depreciation | 500 | |
| | | | | | 24,000 |
| | | **92,400** | | | **92,400** |

**3. From the following Trial Balance of Manohar and Co. prepare Trading and Profit and Loss Account and Balance sheet for the year ending December 31, 2003.**

**Trail balance of Manohar and Co. for the ending December 31, 2003**

| Debit Balances | Rs. | Credit Balances | Rs. |
|---|---|---|---|
| Stock | 12,000 | Capital | 75,000 |
| Fuel | 2,800 | Sales | 1,20,000 |
| Salaries | 5,600 | Depreciation Reserve | |
| Carriage | 2,500 | 1. Plant and Machinery | 4,000 |
| Furniture | 4,900 | 2. Furniture | 700 |
| Traveling Expenses | 1,500 | Outstanding Salaries | 300 |
| Purchases | 72,000 | Outstanding Rent and Taxes | 100 |
| Plant and Machinery | 40,000 | | |
| Sundry Debtors | 45,500 | Commission | 200 |
| Wages | 12,700 | Sundry Creditors | 36,000 |
| Drawings | 1,000 | Bills Payable | 15,200 |
| Cash in Hand | 3,800 | | |
| Cash at Bank | 38,000 | | |
| Rent and Taxes | 2,300 | | |
| Office Expenses | 3,500 | | |
| Trade Expenses | 1,400 | | |
| Insurance | 900 | | |
| Stationary | 2,000 | | |
| | **2,52,400** | | **2,52,400** |

**Adjustments :**

1. Stock as on 31.12.03 was Rs.30,000.
2. Goods worth Rs. 5000 were stolen on 10.10.03, but the insurance cover expired on 30.11.03, and was not renewed.
3. A portion of the Plant and Machinery whose book value Rs. 15,000 was disposed off in exchange of a new one for the value of Rs. 35,000 and a cheque for Rs. 25,000 issued in this respect on 28.12.03, was not passed through any of the books.
4. Provide Depreciation Reserve at 10% on Furniture and 5% on Plant and Machinery as per the Balance on 31.12.03.
5. Opening stock and closing stock include stationery worth Rs. 200 and Rs. 500 respectively. Further the stationery purchased for Rs. 700 was wrongly included under office expenses.
6. The proprietor has taken goods worth Rs. 500 for his personal use.
7. Outstanding salaries Rs. 850.

**Solution :**

**Trading Account of Manohar and Co.**
**for the year ending December 31, 2003**

| Particulars | | Rs. | Particulars | | Rs. |
|---|---|---|---|---|---|
| To Opening Stock | 12,000 | | By Sales | 1,20,900 | |
| Less: Stationary | 200 | | Add : Stolen Goods | 5,000 | |
| | | 11,800 | | | 1,25,900 |
| To Purchases | 72,000 | | By Closing Stock | 30,000 | |
| Less : Drawings | 500 | | Less: Stationary | 500 | |
| (Goods taken Proprietor) | | | | | |
| | | 71,500 | | | |
| To Fuel | | 2,800 | | | |
| To Carriage | | 2,500 | | | |
| To Wages | | 12,700 | | | |
| To Trade Expenses | | 1,400 | | | |
| To Gross Profit. | | 52,700 | | | |
| | | **1,55,400** | | | **1,55,400** |

**Profit and loss Account of Manohar and Co.**
**for the year ending December 31, 2003.**

| Particulars | | Rs. | Particulars | Rs. |
|---|---|---|---|---|
| To Loss of Stolen Goods | | 5,000 | By Gross Profit | 52,700 |
| To Loss in sale of Plant and Machinery | | 5,000 | By Commission | 200 |
| To Stationery | 2,000 | | | |
| Add: Included in Opening stock | 200 | | | |
| Add: Included in Office expenses | 700 | | | |
| | 2,900 | | | |
| Les: Included in Closing Stock | 500 | | | |
| | | 2,400 | | |
| To Salaries | 5,600 | | | |
| Less: Last Year Outstanding | 300 | | | |
| | 5,300 | | | |
| Add: This Year Outstanding | 850 | | | |
| | | 6,150 | | |
| To Rent and Taxes | 2,300 | | | |
| Less: Last year outstanding | 100 | | | |
| | | 2,200 | | |
| | | 1,500 | | |

*Contd.....*

| Particulars | | Rs. | Particulars | Rs. |
|---|---|---|---|---|
| To Travel Expen. | | | | |
| To Office Expenses | 3,500 | | | |
| Less: Stationery | 700 | | | |
| | | 2,800 | | |
| To Insurance | | 900 | | |
| To Depreciation Reserve | | | | |
| 1. Plant & Machinery | 3,000 | | | |
| 2. Furniture | 490 | | | |
| | | 3,490 | | |
| To Net Profit | | 23,460 | | |
| | | **52,900** | | **52,900** |

**Balance sheet of Manohar & Co.**
**for the year ending December 31, 2003.**

| Liabilities | | Rs. | Assets | | Rs. |
|---|---|---|---|---|---|
| Bills payable | | 15,200 | Cash in hand | | 3,800 |
| Sundry Creditors | | 36,000 | | | |
| Outstanding Salaries | | 850 | Cash at bank | 38,000 | |
| Depreciation Reserves | | | Less : Cheques | | |
| 1. Plant and Machinery | 4,000 | | issued but not | 25,000 | |
| Add : Further Reserves | 3,000 | | accounted | | |
| | | 7,000 | | | 13,000 |
| 2. Furniture | 700 | | Sundry Debtors | | 45,000 |
| Add : Further Reserves | 490 | | Closing stock | | 29,500 |
| | | 1,190 | Stock of stationery | | 500 |
| Capital | 75,000 | | Furniture | | 4,900 |
| Less Drawings | 1,000 | | Plant & Machinery | 40,000 | |
| Less: Goods taken by | | | Less : Sale of old | | |
| Proprietor | 500 | | Machinery | 15,000 | |
| | | | | 25,000 | |
| | 73,500 | | Add : New | | |
| Add Net Profit | 23,460 | | Machinery | 35,000 | |
| | | 96,960 | | | 60,000 |
| | | **1,57,200** | | | **1,57,200** |

# 8

# Computer Based Financial Accounting

## Introduction

The main function of accounting is to accumulate data in a manner that the amount of profit made or loss suffered during a period can be determined. The profitability and the financial position of the company is disclosed in the statement of account known as the profit and loss account and the balance sheet prepared at the end of the financial year. The various items of income or expenditure which arose during the period are detailed under different heads. One should properly differentiate the capital and revenues expenditure while preparing these statements.

## Ledgers

It is necessary to maintain separate ledgers for sundry debtors, sundry creditors, cash and bank, bills payable, bills receivable etc. The items, which are not pertaining to the above mentioned heads would be entered in a ledger called general ledger. All nominal and real accounts and the remaining personal accounts are opened in the general ledger. These ledgers should be balanced every month and a trial balance is prepared by taking the debit or credit balance.

### Profit & Loss Account

The first statement to be preferred from the trial balance is the trading account. The items which belongs to it like purchases, sales, opening stock, wages, returns, closing stock etc., are taken into this account. This account shows profit earns or gross loss suffered at the end of the year. In case of profit, the amount should be transferred to the credit side of profit and loss account and vice versa. In case of loss, it is further credited with items of income or gain, which have been earned during the period. While the account is debited with expenses relating to sales or administration, the balance of the account represents the net profit, our net loss of the account period should be transferred to the appropriation account.

### Appropriation Account

In this account, in addition to the balance brought forward from the previous period, the balance of profit or loss is also bought in whether it is debit or credit. Appropriation of profits which may take the form of transfer of reserves, interest on capital, payment of dividends in case of company is shown herein. The balance of this account will be transferred to the balance sheet.

### Balance Sheet

The balance sheet shows the financial position of the business at a given date by disclosing the amount of capital contributed and how the same has been invested and the values of assets and liabilities and their nature. Section 211 of the companies act 1956 makes it compulsory to prepare this statement set out in part I of schedule VI or as near thereof as circumstances admit or in such other form as may be approved by the Central Government generally or in any particular case.

### Computerized Preparation of Financial Statements

Any company accumulates huge amounts of data during the period of its financial year. The accounting function analyzes this data and prepares the necessary statements required under the Companies Act. This process takes anything between 3 to 6 months depending on the type and size of the company and volume of data. Till this job is completed one never knows clearly as to whether the company made any profit at all. So it will be used to computerize this process so as to reduce the amount of time taken in preparing the financial statements. For this purpose, many tailor made financial accounting software packages are available.

Here an earnest attempt has been made to develop a simplified financial accounting program to demonstrate the usefulness of such packages for preparation of financial statements.

This program is applicable to any limited company. The trial balance of any company is to input the program. Other data, which the user has to input are closing stock, purchases and or/sales returns, bad debts written off and depreciation percentage. Taking these as inputs the program generates the financial statements such as profit & loss account and balance sheet.

**Working Data**

**Table 8.1** Trial Balance

| | Debit<br>Rs. | Credit<br>Rs. |
|---|---|---|
| Profit & Loss A/c | | 2,00,000 |
| Plant & Machinery | 5,00,000 | |
| Furniture | 20,000 | |
| Sales | | 20,00,000 |
| Opening Stock | 30,00,000 | |
| Bank Overdraft | | 1,00,000 |
| Share Premium | | 3,60,000 |
| Share Capital | | 6,00,000 |
| Debtors | 10,00,000 | |
| Salaries & Wages | 2,00,000 | |
| Selling & Distribution expenses | 1,50,000 | |
| Creditors | | 4,15,000 |
| Income Tax | 3,00,000 | |
| Interim Dividend | 60,000 | |
| Purchases | 9,00,000 | |
| Buildings | 1,20,000 | |
| Investments | 1,00,000 | |
| Cash at Bank | 20,000 | |
| Cash in Hand | 3,000 | |
| Audit Fees | 2,000 | |
| | 36,75,000 | 36,75,000 |
| Closing Stock | Rs. 2,60,000 | |
| Bad Debts written off | Rs. 45,00 | |
| Depreciation Percentages : | | |
| Plant & Machinery | 10% | |
| Building | 12% | |
| Premises | 0% | |
| Furniture | 4% | |

**Table 8.2** Trial Balance

| | Debit Rs. | Credit Rs. |
|---|---|---|
| Share Capital | | 5,00,000 |
| General Reserve | | 1,50,000 |
| Debtors | 3,50,000 | |
| Salaries | 50,000 | |
| Interest | 10,000 | |
| Sales | | 35,00,000 |
| Opening Stock | 1,50,000 | |
| Purchases | 30,39,000 | |
| Cash in Hand | 3.000 | |
| Cash at Bank | 1,20,000 | |
| Audit & Legal Charges | 6,000 | |
| Profit & Loss A/c | | 1,25,000 |
| Creditors | | 2,25,000 |
| Premises | 80,000 | |
| Plant & Machinery | 70,000 | |
| Goodwill | 23,000 | |
| Advertisement | 30,000 | |
| Travelling expenses | 25,000 | |
| Trade Expenses | 1,500 | |
| Interim Dividend | 42,5000 | |
| | 45,00,000 | 45,00,000 |
| Closing Stock | Rs. 4,50,000 | |
| Bad Debts written off | Rs. 35,000 | |
| Depreciation Percentages for | | |
| Plant & Machinery | 6% | |
| Building | 0% | |
| Premises | 10% | |
| Furniture | 0% | |

**Table 8.3** Trial Balance

| | Debit Rs. | Credit Rs. |
|---|---|---|
| Share Capital | | 15,00,000 |
| Share premium | | 5,00,000 |
| General Reserve | | 7,00,000 |
| Bank Overdraft | | 1,82,000 |
| Creditors | | 2,61,000 |
| Interim Dividend | 70,000 | |
| Goodwill, Patents | 50,000 | |
| Buildings | 12,00,000 | |
| Plant & Machinery | 7,24,000 | |
| Investments | 2,00,000 | |
| Opening Stock | 6,74,000 | |
| Cast at Bank | 1,45,000 | |
| Cash in Hand | 41,000 | |
| Debtors | 10,66,000 | |
| Repairs & Renewals | 5,000 | |
| Sales | | 31,70,000 |
| Profit & Loss A/c | | 13,500 |
| Rent & Taxes | 10,000 | |
| Purchases | 18,95,000 | |
| Sales Returns | 10,000 | |
| Advertisements | 64,000 | |
| Travelling Expenses | 30,000 | |
| Interest | 14,000 | |
| Trade Expenses | 4,000 | |
| Audit Fee | 5,000 | |
| Income-tax paid | 75,000 | |
| Purhcases Return | | 4,000 |
| Premises | 50,000 | |
| Furniture | 40,000 | |
| Unexpired payments | 20,000 | |
| Salaries & Wages | 60,000 | |
| | 64,52,000 | 64,52,000 |
| Closing Stock | Rs. 3,50,000 | |
| Bad Debts written off | Rs. 45,000 | |
| Depreciation % for | | |
| Plant & Machinery | 16% | |
| Building | 18% | |
| Premises | 0% | |
| Furniture | 5% | |

# 9

# Finance and Accounting in Action

## How to use this Programme

| Question | Your Answer | Correct Answer |
|---|---|---|
| 1. Welcome to our programmed text on Finance and Accounting in Action. We hope that you will find our approach to learning instructive and enjoyable. | | |
| 2. Our objective is really quite simple. We want to keep you thinking as you respond to each new subject. We want your mind to be ____ (active/passive) as you fill in the missing words which make the questions and sentences complete. When you have written your answer in the white space provided in the middle of the page, look at the right-hand column for the correct answer. | | (We provide our answer here on the right, but look below one frame). |

| Question | Your Answer | Correct Answer |
|---|---|---|
| 3. You will note that we have put our answers on the right. However, we have moved them down one space alongside the next question so you won't be tempted to look ahead until you have written your________. | | Active (This is the answer to question for frame 2. Verify your answer. Then go ahead with frame 3). |
| 4. Cover the correct answer until you have read the question and answered it. Then verify the right-hand column to see if you had the same answer as we did. Then proceed to the next ________. | | Answer |
| 5. You will find as you go through the book, the questions get more and more difficult. Little by little we try to build on what you have _______. | | Question |
| 6. Since we do not want you to forget what you have read, you may find the same information repeated in several different ways. We have found that such repetition helps you to ______ what you have learned. | | Learned |
| 7. From time to time you will have to make a choice between the answers given. The choices are shown in the parentheses following the blank. Be sure and pick the best _____ (answer/question) and write it in the answer space in the centre of the page. | | Remember |
| 8. To review, our programmed text divides the material to be learned into a series of questions or frames. Each step requires you to make an active ______. | | Answer |

| Question | Your Answer | Correct Answer |
|---|---|---|
| 9. After answering each frame, compare your answer with ours to see if we agree. The important thing is to learn the underlying principles. Therefore, if your answer was different from ours but nevertheless a good synonym, you may consider your answer as ______ (right:wrong). | | Reply (or response) |
| 10. If you did not get the correct answer or a reasonable approximation be sure to reread the question so that you can understand the ________ (correct/incorrect) answer. | | Right |
| 11. Our text is divided into sections. Each begins with a summary which introduces the key points to be covered. These points are explained in detail by the frames which follow. If you cannot complete the assigned sections in the time allowed, be sure to read the ________. In this way you will cover the most important ideas. | | Correct |
| 12. By now you should have a good understanding of our method. You may now begin programmed text. Good Luck. | | Summaries |

# PART - I

## The Balance Sheet

### Summary

In evaluating the financial position of a business or an individual, we begin by examining the valuable things he owns. In accounting terms, valuable things owned by a business which have a measurable worth are called Assets. The assets of a business are financed by owners and by outsiders. As a result, each has a claim or equity against the assets of the business.

The claims of creditors or outsiders are called Liabilities. These often appear as debts or obligations to be paid to outsiders.

The owner's share or claim against assets of the business is called Owners Equity. This corresponds to the portion of the assets remaining after deducting liabilities due to be paid to outsiders.

The Assets of a business are equal to the claims against them. These claims are Liabilities and Owners Equity. ASSETS = LIABILITES + OWNERS EQUITY. The Accounting Report which shows the Assets of a business and the corresponding claims of Liabilities and Owners Equity at a given point in time is called as a Balance Sheet.

In order to avoid unpleasant surprises, accountants generally follow a conservative approach in valuing assets at cost or lower. Assets are valued under the assumption that the business is a 'Going Concern'. Accounting Reports show only those aspects of a business entitiy which can be expressed in monetary terms.

| Question | Your Answer | Correct Answer |
|---|---|---|
| 1. If you wish to evaluate the _____ position of an individual or a business, you might begin by examining the valuable things he owns. | | |
| 2. In accounting terms, _____ are valuable things owned by a business which have a measurable worth. | | Financial |
| 3. Health, happiness and reputation are valuable things indeed but the accountants would not class them as assets since their worth is difficult to ______. | | Assets |
| 4. Assets include cash or money and other valuable things. If you puchased, could you include it on your list of assets ? _____ (yes/no) | | Measure |
| 5. If you were using an automobile belonging to a friend, you could not include it in your list of assets because you do not _____ it. | | Yes |
| 6. If we purchase an automobile we could put it on our list of assets at its original cost or its resale value. Which if these possibilities is easiest to verify ? ______ (original cost/resale value) | | Own |
| 7. Costs are usually easier to document and less controversial than market valuse. For this reason, accounting reports are generally based on ______ (cost/market value). | | Original cost |

| Question | Your Answer | Correct Answer |
|---|---|---|
| 8. Accountants, like the rest of us, hate unpleasant surprises. Given the choice of valuing an asset at an optimistic (high) or a conservative (low) value, they would tend to pick the _____ (high/low) value. This approach avoids unpleasant discoveries later on. | | Cost |
| 9. When he enters the value of the automobile in his books, the accountant is usually most concerned with ____ (replacement value/original cost). | | Low (conservative) |
| 10. Unless the company is going out of business, assets are valued on the assumption that the company will remain in business indefinitely. This 'Going Concern' concept means that the accountant is concerned with the _____ (short/long) term worth of the assets. | | Original cost |
| 11. Examples of _____ include the following : cash, bank balance, debtors (amounts) owed to the business by its customers), stock (merchandise), land, buildings, machinery, patents, etc. | | Long |
| 12. Let's review : Assets are valuable things owned by a business which have a ______ worth. In accordance with the "______ concern" concept and the principle of conservatism, assets are generally valued at cost. | | Assets |

| Question | Your Answer | Correct Answer |
|---|---|---|
| 13. To determine the net worth of an individual you must know what he _____ to others as well as what he has. Amounts owed or due to be paid to others are called liabilities. | | Measurable Going |
| 14. Bank loans which have to be paid back at the end of month are ____ (assets, liabilities) | | Owes |
| 15. A creditor who extends you credit or loans you money has a claim against your _____ equal to the amount of the liability. | | Liabilities |
| 16. The obligation to pay others at some point in time is a _______. Examples include bank loans, creditors or accounts payale to suppliers, salaries payable, taxes payable, etc. | | Assets |
| 17. Assets less liabilities equals owners equity or net worth. The net worth. The net worth of an individual with 100 in assets and 50 in liabilities is ________. | | Liability |
| 18. Assets – Liabilities = Owners Equity. A company which has assets of 300 and owners equity of 75 has liabilities amounting to ______. | | 50 |
| 19. Owners Equity is the amount remaining after deducting liabilities from assets. When a company goes out of business and is liquidated, which claim is paid off first ? _____ (owners equity/ liabilities). | | 225 |
| 20. Assets–Liabilities = Owners Equity. Therefore, _____ = Liabilities + Owners Equity. | | Liabilities |

| Question | Your Answer | Correct Answer |
|---|---|---|
| 21. Assets equal the claims against them by outsiders and owners. This means a company with liabilities of 100 and owners equity of 200 has assets equal to ______. | | Assets |
| 22. Assets = _____ + Owners Equity. This basic equation serves as the basis for the accounting report called the Balance Sheet. Because, assets always equal claims, the balance sheet is always in 'balance'. | | 300 |
| 23. The statement which shows the assets of a business and the corresponding claims of liabilities and owners equity at a given point in time, is called a ________. Since components may change from time to time, a new balance sheet should be prepared periodically to show the new values on a specific date. | | Liabilities |
| 24. Refer to the simplified balance sheet shown below. Total assets amount to ______. Total claims of liabilities and owners equity amount to ______. Therefore the balance sheet ______ (does/does not) balance.<br>**Assets**<br>Cash 100<br>Land 900<br>1,000<br>**Claims**<br>Liabilities 600<br>Owners Equity 400<br>1,000 | | Balance sheet |

| Question | Your Answer | Correct Answer |
|---|---|---|
| 25. The Balance Sheet shows the Assets of a business at a particular point in time and the way they are financed through _____ and ____ _______. | | 1,000<br>1,000<br>does |
| 26. The Owners Equity of a business normally includes the original investment of the owners (share capital) plus profits or earnings accumulated in the business. In the example shown below. Owners Equity is equal to_____. Is owners Equity the same as cash ? ______ (yes/no).<br>**Assets**<br>Cash 50<br>Machinery 950<br>Total 1,000<br>**Claims**<br>Bank Loans 100<br>Note Payable 300<br>Share Capital 200<br>Accumulated Profit 400<br>Total 1,000 | | liabilities owners equity |
| 27. Prepare a simplified Balance Sheet using the following information: Bank Loan 50, Cash 50, Accum-lated Profit 150, Land 400, Mortgage Payable 200, Share Capital 50. Does the Balance Sheet balance ? ______ (yes/no). | | 600<br>no |

| Question | Your Answer | Correct Answer |
|---|---|---|
| 28. This completes this section. Please review the Summary before proceeding. | | **Assets**<br>Cash 50<br>Land 400<br>Total 450<br>**Claims**<br>Bank Loan 50<br>Mortage Payable 200<br>Share Capital 50<br>Accumulated Profit 150<br>Total 450<br>Yes |

## PART - II

### The Profit & Loss Account

#### Summary

The Profit & Loss Account shows the profit or loss made during the accounting period. The P & L account is often called an operating statement, earnings statement or income statement. In accordance with the matching principle, the P & L account matches revenues with corresponding costs and expenses to determine the profit or loss made during the accounting period. Where activities may extend over more than one period, the accountant's judgment may be required to determine the portions of revenues and expenses to be attributed or allocated to each period.

Accounting statements include both cash and credit transactions and payment may not take place during the accounting period. Cash and profit may not be the same.

The P & L account shows sales, costs, expenses and profits during the accounting period. Sales less costs equals gross profit. Gross profit less expenses and taxes equals net profit (or less) for the period.

| Question | Your Answer | Correct Answer |
|---|---|---|
| 1. The accounting report which shows the profit or loss made during the accounting period is called a _______ _______. | | |
| 2. ______ less costs and expenses equals profit or loss during the period. | | Profit & Loss account |
| 3. The P & L account is often called an earnings statement, operating statement or income statement. The P & L account matches revenues with corresponding costs and expenses to determine profit or losses made during the accounting _____. | | sales |
| 4. Assume we acquire goods at a cost of 100 and resell them at 300. If we record no other sales, costs or expenses during the period, we have made a profit of _____. (How much ?) | | period |
| 5. The cost of the merchandise sold to customers during a given accounting period is often called 'Cost of Goods Sold' in a production company or 'Cost of Sales' in a trading company which buys and sells goods. If we acquired goods for 100 and sold them for 300, sales amounted to _____ and Cost of Sales amounted to _______. | | 200 |

| Question | Your Answer | Correct Answer |
|---|---|---|
| 6. Sales less Cost of Sales equals Gross Profit. Assume we have Sales of 300 and Cost of Sales is 100. Complete the statement shown below :<br>Sales<br>Cost of Sales _______<br>Gross Profit | | 300<br>100 |
| 7. Sales less Cost of Sales equals ______ Profit. Gross Profit less Expenses equals Profit Before Taxes. Profit before taxes less taxes equals net profit. | | Sales 300<br>Cost of Sales 100<br>Gross Profit 200 |
| 8. Assume sales for the period are 300, Cost of Sales is 100, and we pay rent expenses for the month amounting to 50. Taxes for the period are 75. Using this information, complete the following P & L account :<br>Sales<br>Cost of Sales _______<br>Gross Profit<br>Expenses _______<br>Profit before Taxes<br>Taxes _______<br>Net Profit | | Gross |
| 9. Sales less Cost of Sales equals Gross Profit. Gross Profit less _______ equals Profit before Taxes. Profit before Taxes less equals _______ _______. | | Sales 300<br>Cost of Sales 100<br>Gross Profit 200<br>Expenses 50<br>Profit before<br>Taxes 150<br>Taxes 75<br>Net Profit 75 |

| Question | Your Answer | Correct Answer |
|---|---|---|
| 10. In the P & L account we have just seen, the costs of the merchandise sold appeared under the heading '__________'. Selling, General and Administrative items are often listed under the heading of 'Expenses'. | | Expenses Net Profit |
| 11. The presentation of the P & L account may vary from one company to the next. For example, Gross Profit is not always shown. Sales, costs or expenses may be shown by product or region. In a service company, costs may consist largely of salaries and personnel. The judgement of the _____ is an important factor in finding a presentation which will be of maximum use to users and decision-makers. | | Cost of Sales |
| 12. Financial Statements include both cash and credit transactions. In the case of a cash transaction, we may buy or sell now and payment is made immediately. In a credit transaction, we buy or sell now and payment is made ______ (now/later). | | Accountant |

| Question | Your Answer | Correct Answer |
|---|---|---|
| 13. Credit transactions imply a payment at a later date. If we acquire goods on credit for 100 and sell them for 200 during the accounting period on credit, we have made a gross profit of ______. If no payments are made or received during the period, our cash position is _____ (increased/decreased/unchanged). Cash and profit _____ (are/are not) the same. | | later |
| 14. On the P & L account we normally recognise revenues, costs and expenses when the goods have been sold, shipped and invoiced. If we buy goods for cash in Period I and sell them in Period III, the Sales and Costs will be shown on the P & L account for Period ________. | | 100 unchanted are not |
| 15. We have made an expenditure when we acquired an asset (goods) in Period I. In accordance with the recognition concept, we do not ______ revenues, costs and expenses until Period III when the goods have been sold, shipped and invoiced. | | III |
| 16. In a credit transaction we buy now and pay ______. In credit transactions, the date of payment is usually on the same as the date when revenues, costs and expenses are recognised. | | recognise |

| Question | Your Answer | Correct Answer |
|---|---|---|
| 17. If activities continue over more than one period, good judgement on the part of the _______ may be required to allocate revenues and corresponding costs and expenses to the proper accounting periods. | | later |
| 18. An expenditure in one period may not appear on the _____ _________ as a cost or an expense until a later period when it is matched against corresponding sales or revenues. | | accountant |
| 19. Sales less _____________ equals Gross Profit. Gross Profit less _____ equals Profit before Taxes. Profit before Taxes less _______ equals Net Profit. | | Profit & Loss account |
| 20. This completes this section. Please review the Summary before proceeding. | | Cost of Sales |

## PART - III

## Balance Sheet Transactions

### Summary

The balance sheet shows the assets of a business and the way they are financed through liabilities and owners equity. When a business event is recorded in monetary terms on the financial statements, it is called a transaction. On the balance sheet, each transaction has a dual effect. A change in any element on the balance sheet is always accompanied by at least one other offsetting change in another element. Dual entries mean that the balance sheet is always in balance because every change is always offset by another. Assets are always equal to liabilities and owners equity.

| Question | Your Answer | Correct Answer |
|---|---|---|
| 1. The accounting report which shows the assets of business and the way they are financed through liabilities and owners equity is called a ____________. | | |
| 2. The Balance Sheet is based on the following basic accounting equations : ______ = claims. Assets = Liabilities + Owners Equity. | | Balance Sheet |
| 3. 'Claims' are often called 'equities' because they could presumably be defended in a court of Law as 'Equity'. Owners claims against the business are called owners _______. | | Assets |
| 4. The dual aspect of accounting means that each event of transaction changes at least ______ accoutns on the balance sheet. | | Equity |
| 5. A few sample trnsactions will show you how the dual aspect works in practice. Assume a new company is formed by selling shares for 1000 in cash. Read the balance sheets shown below, study the changes. Does the correct balance sheet balance ? _______ (yes/no) | | Two |

| | Initial BS | Changes | Corrected BS |
|---|---|---|---|
| **Assets** | | | |
| Cash | 0 | + 1,000 | 1,000 |
| Total | 0 | + 1,000 | 1,000 |
| **Liabilities and owners Equity** | | | |
| Owners Equity | 0 | + 1,000 | 1,000 |
| Total | 0 | + 1,000 | 1,000 |

| Question | Your Answer | Correct Answer |
|---|---|---|
| 6. The same company purchases stock for 500 in cash. Correct the company's balance sheet to increase stock by 500 and decrease cash by 500. Make sure the new balance sheet is in balance by calculating the totals. | | Yes |

| | Opening BS | Changes | Corrected BS |
|---|---|---|---|
| Cash | 1,000 | – 500 | |
| Stock | 0 | + 500 | ____ |
| Total | 1,000 | 0 | |
| **Liabilities and owners Equity** | | | |
| Owners Equity | 1,000 | 0 | ____ |
| Total | 1,000 | 0 | |

| Question | Your Answer | Correct Answer | |
|---|---|---|---|
| 7. Transctions may be made for cash or credit. The same company buys additional stock for 400 on credit (Here stock and creditors go ____). Complete the corrected balance sheet shown below. | | Assets | |
| | | Cash | 500 |
| | | Stock | 500 |
| | | Total | 1,000 |

| | Opening BS | Changes | Corrected BS |
|---|---|---|---|
| **Assets** | | | |
| Cash | 500 | 0 | |
| Stock | 500 | + 400 | ____ |
| Total | 1,000 | + 400 | |
| **Liabilities and owners Equity** | | | |
| Creditors | 0 | + 400 | ____ |
| Owners Equity | 1,000 | 0 | |
| Total | 1,000 | + 400 | |

| **Liabilities & Owners Equity** | |
|---|---|
| Owners Equity | 1,000 |
| Total | 1,000 |

| Question | Your Answer | Correct Answer |
|---|---|---|
| 8. In the example just shown, the value of total assets onthe balance sheet has increased from 1,000 to ______. Total assets are now financed by _______ of liabilities and _____ of owners equity. The assets are financed in part by the owners and in part by the creditors. The balance sheet continues to _____. | | up<br>**Assets**<br>Cash 500<br>Stock 900<br>Total 1,400<br>**Liabilities & Owners Equity**<br>Creditors 400<br>Owners Equity 1,000<br>Total 1,400 |
| 9. Every credit transaction implies a later ________ transaction. | | 1,400<br>400<br>1,000<br>Balance |
| 10. When we buy goods on credit, the amount we owe the supplier appears on the balance sheet as a (n) _______ (asset/liability) called creditors. This is a debt to be repaid later. | | Cash |
| 11. When we reapy the creditors. cash goes _____ (up/down) and creditors go _____ (up/down). | | Liability |
| 12. Let us complete a credit transaction on the balance sheet and repay our supplier the 400 due in accounts payable. Correct the balance sheet below : | | down<br>down |

| | Opening BS | Changes | Corrected BS |
|---|---|---|---|
| **Assets** | | | |
| Cash | 500 | – 400 | |
| Stock | 900 | 0 | _____ |
| Total | 1,400 | – 400 | |
| **Liabilities and owners Equity** | | | |
| Creditors | 400 | – 400 | |
| Owners Equity | 1,000 | 0 | |
| Total | 1,400 | – 400 | |

| Question | Your Answer | Correct Answer |
|---|---|---|
| 13. Some transactions change only one side of the balance sheet. When we acquire goods for cash, we are merely exchanging one ___ (asset/liability) for another. Total assets remain equal to liabilities plus owners equity. | | **Assets**<br>Cash 100<br>Stock 900<br>Total 1,000<br>**Liabilities & Owners Equity**<br>Creditors 0<br>Owners Equity 1,000<br>Total 1,000 |
| 14. If we acquire goods on _______ (cash/credit), both sides of the balance sheet are influenced. Assets go up when we increase our stock and ______ go up when we make the corresponding increase in accounts payable to our creditors. The balance sheet continues to balance. | | Asset |
| 15. In accordance with the dual aspect of accounting, every transaction on the balance sheet influence at least _____ elements or accoutns. ____ are always equal to ______ plus owners equity. | | credit liabilities |
| 16. This completes this section. Please review the summary before proceeding. | | two assets liabilities |

# PART - IV

## Profits and Accumulated Profit

### Summary

The Profit & Loss account shows sales, costs and expenses incurred during the accounting period. Sales and revenues increase profits or earnings on the P & L account and cause a corresponding increase in accumulated profit on the Balance Sheet. Costs and expenses reduce profits on the P & L account and cause a corresponding decrease in accumulated profit on the Balance Sheet.

Profit and accumulated profit provide the links between the Balance Sheet and the P & L account. Profits increase accumulated profit on the Balance Sheet. Losses and dividends reduce accumulated profit on the Balance Sheet. The details of profits and losses during the period are shown on the P & L account. The details of dividends paid during the period appear on a separate accounting statement called the Statement of accumulated profit. This statement will be explained in detail in a later section.

| Question | Your Answer | Correct Answer |
|---|---|---|
| 1. The ____________ shows sales, costs, expenses and profits for the accounting period. | | |
| 2. Sales and revenues increase profits shown during the period on the P & L account. At the same time they cause a corresponding increase in accumulated profit on the __________. | | Profit & Loss account |
| 3. Costs and expenses _______ (increase/reduce) profits shown for the period on the Profit & Loss account and cause a corresponding decrease in ____ _______ shown in the Balance Sheet. | | Balance Sheet |
| 4. Some transactions appear only on the Balance Sheet and do not influence profits or losses shown on the P & L account. When a company buy goods from a supplier, profits are not changed and the purchase transaction _______ (does/does not) influence the P & L account. | | reduce accumulated profit |
| 5. At a later date, the goods just acquired will be sold, shipped and invoiced. At this time, revenues, costs and expenses are normally 'recognised' and the resulting profit (or loss) will be shown on the _________ _______ for the period. | | does not |
| 6. Transactions which relate to Sales, Costs and Expenses for the period influence both the _______ shown on the P & L account and the accumulated profit shown on the ________. | | Profit & Loss account |

| Question | Your Answer | Correct Answer |
|---|---|---|
| 7. The accumulated profit shown on Balance Sheet is profit which has been made by the company and retained for use in the business. Together with the original investment of the owners, it forms a part of _______ (liabilities/owners equity). | | Profits Balance Sheet |
| 8. The accumulated profit shown on the Balance Sheet represents the profits made since the founding of the company less any losses, adjustments or amounts which have been paid out in the form of dividends. The Profit & Loss account shows only the portion of these profits (or losses) which has been made during the accounting ______. | | Owners Equity |
| 9. We will now look at a few sample period transactions to show you how transactions covering sales, ________, and expenses influence accumulated profit on the Balance Sheet and Profits or Losses on the P & L account. | | |
| 10. In the Balance Sheet shown below, Assets equal _____. Liabilities equal ______. Owners equity equals _______.<br>**Assets**<br>Cash 500<br>Stock 500<br>Total 1,000<br>Liabilities and Owners Equity<br>Share Capital 1,000<br>Accumulated Profit 0<br>Total 1,000 | | Costs |

| Question | Your Answer | Correct Answer |
|---|---|---|
| 11. Assume a company sells goods (Stock) for 1.000 in cash. *To simplify the posting, we will divide this transaction into two parts* and record the revenue and cost production separately. First we will correct the Balance Sheet and Profit & Loss account below to record the revenue from the sale. (cash goes up, accumulated profits go up, sales and profits go up, each is changed by 1,000) | | 1,000<br>Zero<br>1,000 (Owners Equity equals share capital plus accumulated pro |

| | Opening | Changes | Closing |
|---|---|---|---|
| **Assets** | | | |
| Cash | 500 | + 1.000 | |
| Stock | 500 | 0 | ______ |
| Total | 1,000 | + 1,000 | |
| **Liabilities and owners Equity** | | | |
| Share Capital | 1,000 | 0 | |
| Accumulated Profit | 0 | + 1,000 | ______ |
| Total | 1,000 | + 1,000 | |
| **P & L account** | | | |
| Sales | 0 | + 1,000 | |
| Cost & Expenses | 0 | 0 | ______ |
| Profit | 0 | + 1,000 | |

| Question | Your Answer | Correct Answer |
|---|---|---|
| 12. Now we 'post' or enter the cost (500) of the stock sold on the Balance Sheet and the P & L account. (Costs go ______. Profits accumulated profit and stock go ______. Change these items by 500). | | **Assets**<br>Cash 1,500<br>Stock 500<br>Total 2,000 |

| | Opening | Changes | Corrected |
|---|---|---|---|
| **Assets** | | | |
| Cash | 1,500 | 0 | |
| Stock | 500 | – 500 | ______ |
| Total | 2,000 | – 500 | |
| Total | | | |
| **Liabilities and owners Equity** | | | |
| Share Capital | 1,000 | 0 | |
| Accumulated Profit | 1,000 | – 500 | ______ |
| Total | 2,000 | – 500 | |
| **P & L Account** | | | |
| Sales | 1,000 | 0 | |
| Cost & Expenses | 0 | + 500 | |
| Profits | 1,000 | – 500 | |

**Liabilities & Owners Equity**

| | |
|---|---|
| Shaer Capital | 1,000 |
| Accumulated Profit | 1,000 |
| | 2,000 |

**P & L account**

| | |
|---|---|
| Sales | 1,000 |
| Costs & Expenses | 0 |
| Profits | 1,000 |

| Question | Your Answer | Correct Answer |
|---|---|---|
| 13. You will note that changes in profits on the P & L account are matched by changes in accumulated profit on the Balance Sheet. This is true whenever we complete revenue, ______ or expense transactions on the Balance sheet and P & L account. | | Up. down<br><br>**Assets**<br>Cash 1,500<br>Stock 0<br>Total 1,500<br>**Liabilities & Owners Equity**<br>Share capital 1,000<br>Accumulated Profit 500<br>Total 1,500<br>**P & L account**<br>Sales 1,000<br>Costs & Expenses 500<br>Profits 1,500 |

| Question | Your Answer | Correct Answer |
|---|---|---|
| 14. Expense transactions are similar to cost transactions. Both costs and expenses _______ (increase/ decrease) profits on the P & L account and accumulated profit on the Balance Sheet. | | Cost |
| 15. Revenues increase _____ on the P & L account and ________ on the Balance Sheet. | | decrease |
| 16. The Balance Sheet shows the financial resources of a business at a given date in terms of assets, _______ and ____________. | | Profits<br>Accumulated profit |
| 17. The P & L account shows how a firm uses the resources at its disposal during the accounting period. The key elements which appear on the P & L accoutn are _____. costs, expenses and profits. | | Liabilities Owners Equity |
| 18. You will appreciate the fact that in any large business many thousands of transactions may occur during the accounting period. These may change hundreds of accounts. Extreme care and judgement on the part of the accountant is required to be sure that each transaction is posted to the correct ______. | | Sales |

| Question | Your Answer | Correct Answer |
|---|---|---|
| 19. In order to simplify the accounting process. Balance sheets and P & L accounts are normally prepared at the end of each reporting period. At this point, the balance of each account is calculated, adjustments made as required, and 'closing' entries made to prepare the required financial statements. | | account |
| 20. This ends this section. Please review the Summary now. | | |

**EXHIBIT II**

**Worksheets**

| Transactions | BALANCE SHEET (B.S) — ASSETS | | | | |
|---|---|---|---|---|---|
| | Fixed Assets | Stock | Debtors | Cash | Total Assets |
| 1. Sold shares for 20,000 in cash | | | | | |
| 2. Purchase Fixed Assets for 5,000 on credit | | | | | |
| 3. Purchase Stock for 15,000 on credit | | | | | |
| 4. Make cash down payment on stock of 5,000 | | | | | |
| 5. Obtain cash loan of 5,000 | | | | | |
| 6. Pay 5,000 cash to supplier of Fixed Assets | | | | | |
| 7. Wages and salaries of 10,000 paid in cash and charged to stock | | | | | |
| SUBTOTALS | | | | | |

**EXHIBIT II**

**Worksheets**

| Transactions | BALANCE SHEET (B.S) — OWNERS EQUITY + LIABILITIES | | | | PROFIT & LOSS ACCOUNT (P & L) | |
|---|---|---|---|---|---|---|
| | Share Capital | Accumulated Profit | Liabilities | Total (OE + L) | Title | Amount |
| 1. | | | | | | |
| 2. | | | | | | |
| 3. | | | | | | |
| 4. | | | | | | |
| 5. | | | | | | |
| 6. | | | | | | |
| 7. | | | | | | |
| SUB TOTALS | | | | | | |

**EXHIBIT II**

**Worksheets**

| Transactions | BALANCE SHEET (B.S) — ASSETS: Fixed Assets | Stock | Debtors | Cash | Total Assets |
|---|---|---|---|---|---|
| Balance Forward | | | | | |
| 8. Sale on credit of 10,000 posted to balance sheet and profit & loss account | | | | | |
| 9. Cost of sales 5,000 charged from stock to accumulated proft and profit & loss account | | | | | |
| 10. Calculate gross profit on profit & loss account | | | | | |
| 11. Pay rent expenses of 2,000 cash | | | | | |
| 12. Advertising expense of 1,000 on credit | | | | | |
| 13. Receive partial payment from customer of 1,000 cash | | | | | |
| 14. Calculate pretax profit as gross profit less expenses | | | | | |
| 15. Calculate tax liability as 50% of pretax profit | | | | | |
| 16. Calculate net profit (after taxes) | | | | | |
| 17. Calculate balance sheet totals | | | | | |

**EXHIBIT II**

**Worksheets**

| Transactions | BALANCE SHEET (B.S) — ASSETS: Share Capital | Accumulated Profit | Liabilities | Total | PROFIT & LOSS ACCOUNT (P & L): Title | Amount |
|---|---|---|---|---|---|---|
| Balance Forward | | | | | | |
| 8. | | | | | Sales = | |
| 9. | | | | | Cost of Sales = | |
| 10. | | | | | Gross Profit = | |
| 11. | | | | | Rent Expense = | |
| 12. | | | | | Advertising Expenses = | |
| 13. | | | | | | |
| 14. | | | | | Pretax profit = | |
| 15. | | | | | Taxes = | |
| 16. | | | | | Net profit = | |
| 17. | | | | | | |

# 10

# Financial Ratio Analysis : A Control Technique

RATIO is the relationship between two variables; it can be expressed in terms of ratio as 1:3 or as percentage as 33 1/3%, or as some number of times (two times).

The purpose of preparation and interpretation ratios is to epitomize and facilitate comparison with reference to periods, another organization or an industry average.

The ratios can be classified into five groups. They are:

1. Activity Ratios
2. Liquidity Ratios
3. Leverage Ratios
4. Profitability Ratios
5. Management Control/Guidance Ratios.

An attempt has been made in this writeup to explain these ratios with an illustration of the financial statements of ABC Manufacturing Co., which appears to be rather healthy in the absence of footnotes to the annual accounts.

But a glance at the footnotes of annual accounts of companies tell many fascinating sidelights on the financial story.

*Some examples of typical footnotes relate to:*

1. Changes in the company's method of depreciation.
2. Changes in the method of stock valuation.
3. Employment contracts, profit sharing, pension, retirement plans.
4. Contingent liabilities representing claims or law suits pending.
5. Converting loans into subsidiary/equity.

The financial statements are only valuable in vacuum. To be truly useful basis, they must be compared to competitors on year-to-year.

## Activity Ratios

(a) *Inventory Turnover Ratio*

$$\frac{\text{Cost of goods sold}}{\text{Average inventory}} \text{ (or) } \frac{\text{Cost of goods sold}}{1/2(\text{Opening Inventory} + \text{Closing Inventory})}$$

The inventory turnover ratio indicates how quickly the goods are sold by a business unit. It measures the number of times inventories are held and replaced during the period by comparing the cost of goods sold with the stock carried.

The higher ratio indicates that manufacturing activity is maintained with the help of a smaller stock and that there are lesser chances of the turning obsolete, unsaleable over-valued items. However, it may involve a disproportionate increase in selling and administrative expenses and may therefore be relatively less profitable unless the total gross profit is larger.

The low rate turnover is an unfavorable sign and indicates dull business or bad buying or over investment in relation to sales or over-stocking in expectation of higher prices or greater sales or unbalanced goods, overstated inventory valuation.

The inventory turnover also indicates the measure for the size or adequacies of optimum inventory holding of an enterprise.

The inventory ratio of ABC Manufacturing Co. Ltd., for the year 2003 is as follows:

(27) Cost of goods sold Rs. 82,00,000 (All the cost incurred to convert raw materials into finished goods such as raw materials, labour, factor overheads, supervision, rent, electricity, maintenance and repairs.)

(5) Average Inventories : $\frac{3,00,000 + 27,00,000}{2}$ = 28,50,000

2.88 times

(b) Sundry Debtors to Average Daily Sales = $\frac{\text{Sundry Debtors}}{\text{Sales}/365}$

The ratio shows the average time lag in days between sales and the collection of bills. It measures the period of credit and indicates the efficiency of the credit and collection policy. The ratio is also a test of solvency of collectibility and currency of trade debts. It provides a check on adequacy of the currency.

The debt collection period in respect of ABC Manufacturing Co., is as follows:

(26) Net Sales $\frac{11,000}{365}$ = Ave. daily sales = 30,137

(4) Sundry Debtors = $\frac{20,00,000}{30,137}$ = 66.36 days.

(c) Accounts Payable Turnover Ratio = $\frac{\text{Sundry Creditors} + \text{Bills Payable}}{\text{Purchases}} \div 365$

This ratio indicates at what interval the company pays to its suppliers. If the ratio shows on increasing trend, it indicates that the company is taking longer time to pay than previously. If it shows a declining trend it means that the company is now prompt in paying its creditors.

This ratio in respect of ABC Manufacturing Co. is as follows:

Code nos. $\frac{13+14}{21,644} = \frac{18,50,000}{21,644}$ = 85.48 days

* (Derived)

(*Closing stock 27,00,000 + Cost of sales : 82,00,000 – Op. Stock 30,000 = 79,00,000 ÷ 365 = 21,644)

(b) *Net Sales to Net fixed Assets*

The ratio measures the relationships between the amount invested in assets and the results accruing in terms of sales. It indicates the efficiency in the utilization of the assets of the company.

The ratio may show whether there is a tendency towards over-investment in assets. If larger investments in assets is not matched by a larger volume of sales and greater managerial efficiency, it may weaken the financial position, especially if the expansion is financed through current liabilities or borrowing.

The ratio in respects of ABC Mfg. Co. is as follows:

$$\frac{\text{Code 26}}{\text{Code 9}} = \frac{1110,00,000}{35,00,000} = 3.142 \text{ times}$$

Liquidity Ratios

(a) *Current Ratio*

This ratio indicates the solvency of the company and determines the short-term financial strength. The ratio of 2 : 1 is usually considered safe which means that even if the value of current assets were to shrink to one half, the creditors would receive payment in full. It is an index of debt paying ability of the company.

This ratio in respect of ABC Mfg. Co., is worked out as follows:

$$\text{Code 6} + \text{Code 17} = \frac{60,00,000}{25,00,000} = \frac{2.4}{1} \text{ or } 2.4 : 1$$

(b) *Acid Test or Quick Ratio*

This ratio applies more as a stringent test of solvency. It takes cash and other assets, which can be turned into cash, and other assets, which can be turned into cash at a short notice and compares them with current liabilities.

Inventories are excluded from quick assets because of the time required to sell goods and convert raw to finished goods. Marketable securities are added to cash and trade debts for purposes of calculating this ratio.

A quick ratio of 1:1 indicates that the company has goods short-term financial strength and that it can pay off its current liabilities at short notice.

The quick ratio in respect of ABC Mfg. Co. is worked out as follows :

Code 6 – Code 5 ÷ Code 17

$$\text{i.e., } \frac{60,00,000-27,00,000}{25,00,000} = \frac{1.32}{1} \text{ or } 1.32 : 1$$

**Leverage Ratio**

(a) *Debt : Equity Ratio*

This ratio indicates whether a company is debt biased or equity biased. This ratio is of interest to share holders, creditors and financial intuitions.

Debt/Equity ratio is the relationship between shareholders funds plus reserves and the total liabilities of an enterprise.

This ratio is important as companies these days prefer to borrow finance than by issuing more shares. Borrowing loan capital is cheaper in case profit making and incometax paying companies.

Financial institutions insist on a reasonable ratio like 2:1 between total liabilities and shareholders funds because, under condition of liquidation the bigger protection is possible for payment at least out of shareholders funds are available.

The debt equity ratio in respect of ABC Mfg. company is worked out as follows:

$$\text{Code 18} \div 45{,}00{,}000 \quad \frac{27{,}00{,}000}{45{,}00{,}000} = \frac{.6}{1} \text{ or } 1 : .6$$

(b) *Net fixed assets to long term debt*

The net fixed assets represent long term investment. This ratio is used to determine the extent to which the long term liabilities are covered by the company's long term investments in assets.

When the ratio is less than 1, it means longterm debt exceeds the fixed assets implying that a part of the working capital is supplied by longterm creditors.

When the ratio is more than 1, it means long term asset exceeds long term debt and creditors obligations finance only a part of the fixed assets.

An unduly low ratio signifies greater dependence on outside finance for funds and successful working is contingent on profitable trading and quick collection of debts. It must be borne in mind that the value of net fixed assets as per books might be significantly different form the actual value of the assets.

This ratio in respect of ABC Mfg. Co., so worked out as follows :

$$\text{Code 9} \div \text{Code 18} \quad \frac{35{,}00{,}000}{27{,}00{,}000} = \frac{1.29}{1} \text{ or } 1 : 1.29$$

(c) *Debt Service Coverage Ratio*

DSCR represents profits after tax + Non-cash expenditure like depreciation + Interest on term loan installment + dividend by term loan rapid + interest on term loan.

If the coverage is more than 2 times, the financial institutions regard this as safe norm for extending term loans. The reason being that the interest as weak as term loans is well covered by internal generation itself (Profit after Tax + Depreciation).

## Profitability Ratios

The profitability ratios are of interest to shareholders, top management and financial institutions and prospective investors.

(a) *Profit Margin on Sales*

$$\frac{\text{Profit before interest and depreciation and tax}}{\text{Sales}}$$

The percentage of profit to sales over the years within the same company can give useful information about an organization. If the profit margin is going up every year it clearly indicates a good trend.

Conversely if it were going down the years this would indicate a need for investigation which may reveal whether the cost of raw material has gone up or there had been no increase in selling price or there is greater wastage of materials during manufacturer.

This ratio for ABC Mfg. Co., is worked out as follows:

$$\frac{\text{Code 26} - \text{Code 27}}{\text{Code 26}} \times 100 = \frac{28{,}00{,}000}{110{,}00{,}000} \times 100 = 25.45\%$$

(b) *Operating Profit to Sales*

This ratio indicates how each rupee of sale there remained fross from operations. This ratio is significant in two ways.

In the first place we can compare it with the margin of profit in the previous year. Changes in profit margin can reflect changes in efficiency as well as changes in products manufactured or in types of customs served.

Secondly, we can also compare our company with other companies doing similar type of business.

Analysis also frequently uses operating cost ratio as a complement to margin of profit ratio.

In the case of ABC Mfg., Co., these ratios may worked out as under:

$$\text{For 2003} \quad \frac{\text{Operating Pr ofit}}{\text{Sales}} \quad \frac{\text{Code 30}}{\text{Code 26}} \quad \frac{110{,}00{,}000}{110{,}00{,}000} \times 100 = 10\%$$

$$\text{For 2004} \quad \frac{\text{Code 30}}{\text{Code 26}} \quad \frac{9{,}16{,}000}{102{,}00{,}000} \times 100 = 9\%$$

*Operating cost ratio is summarized as under :*

| | | Amount | Ratio |
|---|---|---|---|
| Code 26 Net Sales | Rs. | 110,00,000 | 100% |
| Code 27 - 29 Operating Costs | Rs. | 99,00,000 | 90% |
| Operating Profit | Rs. | 11,00,000 | 10% |

(c) *Return on capital employed*

$$\frac{\text{PBIT}}{\text{Total capital employed}}$$

The ratio indicates how efficiently the total capital employed to earn profits. Capital employed is represented by Net fixed assets + working capital

This ratio in respect of ABC Mfg. Co., Ltd., is arrived at as follows:

$$\frac{\text{Code} \quad 34}{\text{Code} \quad 9+(\text{Code } 6-\text{Code } 17)} = \frac{10{,}15{,}000}{35{,}00{,}000+35{,}00{,}000} \times 100 = 14.5\%$$

(d) *Return on Net Worth*

The ratio indicates how much of the profit is availabel for share holders funds. A shareholder who is anxious to know what his investment is going to give when he invests his funds can measure the same through this ratio.

This ratio in respect of ABC Mfg. Co., is as follows :

$$\frac{\text{Net Profit}}{\text{Net Worth}} = \frac{\text{Code 36} \quad 5{,}35{,}000}{44{,}00{,}000} \times 100 = 12.15\%$$

(e) *Return on Investment*

This ratio gives measurement of profit for internal use by top management. Profit is measured in relation to total investment – i.e., resources committed to operation. The objective of any commercial enterprise is to maximize the profits. Such maximization is possible either by optimizing the margin or the turnover of the investment or both. The operating assets are represented by Net Fixed Assets + Current Assets. This ratio indicates the deficiency utilization of company's operating assets.

This ratio can increase if revenue is kept constant and cost is reduced or by keeping cost constant increasing revenue.

This ratio in respect of ABC Mfg. Co., can be derived as follows:

$$\frac{\text{Net Operating Profit (P B I T)}}{\text{Operating Assets}} = \frac{\text{Code 34}}{\text{Code 9} + \text{Code 6}} \times 100$$

$$= \frac{10{,}15{,}000}{35{,}00{,}000 + 60{,}00{,}000} \times 100 = 10.68\%$$

## Management Control Ratios

(a) *Interest coverage ratio*

This ratio signifies the capacity of the company to meet its fixed data payment via, interest.

The higher the ratio the better it is for the company. This ratio when looked at in conjunction with the debt equity ratio can give a clue as to the further capacity of the firm to go in for debt financing.

*The formula for this ratio is as under*

$$\frac{\text{P B I T (Profit before interest and tax)}}{\text{Interest}}$$

This ratio for ABC Mfg. Co., is as follows :

$$\frac{\text{Code 32}}{\text{Code 33}} = \frac{11{,}50{,}000}{1{,}35{,}000} = 8.51 \text{ times.}$$

(b) *Dividend Coverage*

This ratio indicates the capacity of firm to pay higher dividends. It is more an indicator of the potential of the firm to declare higher dividends in future. If for every subsequent year of operation a higher ratio is matched with a higher dividend payment, the trend is considered to be healthy both from the point of view of the shareholders and also the point of view of the company.

This ratio in respect of ABC Mfg. Co., is as follows:

$$\frac{\text{PAT}}{\text{Equity Divided}} = \frac{\text{Code 46}}{\text{Code 44}} = \frac{5{,}35{,}000}{1{,}20{,}000} = 4.45 \text{ times.}$$

(c) *Net Assets Value*

For debentures, shares either preference or equity shares, net asset value represents the amount of corporate assets backing or protecting these securities.

The net book value per share can be looked upon as measuring the amount of money each share would receive if the company were liquidated, based on balance sheet value.

In respect of ABC Mfg. Co., the net asset value for equity shares can be worked out as under :

| Code | | | | |
|---|---|---|---|---|
| 12 | Total Assets | | Rs. | 97,00,000 |
| 11 | Less Intangible | | Rs. | 1,00,000 |
| | | | | 96,00,000 |
| | *Total Tangible Assets* | | | |
| 17 | Less : Current Liabilities | Rs. 25,00,000 | | |
| 18 | Long term liabilities | Rs. 27,00,000 | | |
| 20 | Preferential Shares | Rs. 6,00,000 | | |
| | | | Rs. | 58,00,000 |
| | | | Rs. | 38,00,000 |

Net Assets available for Equity Shareholders

$$\frac{38,00,000}{1,50,000} = \text{Rs. } 25.33 \text{ per share}$$

(d) *Earnings per share*

The share holder is often more concerned with the earnings per share (or rather prospective earnings per share) influence stock market prices.

The earnings per share are worked out as follows in respect of ABC Mfg. Co.,

| Code | | |
|---|---|---|
| 36 | Net Profit for the year | Rs. 5,35,000 |
| Less | Dividend requirements on preference share | Rs. 30,000 |
| | | Rs. 5,05,000 |

Earnings available for Equity shares

$$\text{Earnings per share} = \frac{\text{Earnings available}}{\text{No. of Equity Shares}} = \frac{5,05,000}{1,50,000} = \text{Rs. } 3.36$$

(e) *Price Earning Ratio*

The price and return on equity vary with a multitude of faction. One such factor is the relationship that exists between the earnings per share and the Market Price. It is called the price earning ratio and this is how it is calculated. If a share is selling at Rs. 25 and earning Rs. 2 per share, its price earning ratio is 12 1/2 to 1, usually shortened to 12 1/2 and the share is said to be selling at 12 1/2 times the earning. If the share should raise to 40, the price earning ratio would be Rs. 20 or if the share drops to 12 the price earning ratio would be a ridiculous 6.

Presuming that the Market value of the share of ABC Mfg. Co., is ruling at Rs. 25/- the price earning ratio is as follows :

$$\frac{25 \text{ Market Price}}{3.36 \text{ Earning Per Share}} = 7.45 \text{ times.}$$

However, we have to remember that this historical P/E multiple is a guide, not a guarantee.

***Conclusion***

Ratio analysis is a rough and ready tool to evaluate the present financial position and the previous financial position of a company. A thorough analysis enables the financial analyst to anticipate reaction of investors and creditors who use these techniques in evaluating the company.

The ratio are used in 3 basic ways

1. Comparative analysis with industry averages
2. Trend analysis and
3. Common size analysis.

Ratio analysis is a guide rather than a solution of present problems and future plans. Ratios are only symptoms to indicate the financial health of any enterprise, basing on which corrective action could be initiated with the supplementary data. It is not possible to suggest absolute ratios for a firm. There are such factors like competition, financial resources of the firm, company objectives which should be taken into consideration. Rigid set of ratios can do more harm than good. The ratio analysis and interpretation of the Financial results of the enterprises should only be done by a qualified financial analyst unless misleading results may emerge resulting more harm.

**Consolidated Profit and Loss Account for the year ended 31 March, 2004**

| **Code No.** | | **2004 Rs.** | **2003 Rs.** |
|---|---|---|---|
| 26 | Net Sales | 1,10,00,000 | 1,02,00,000 |
| | *Less :* Cost of Sales & Operating expenses | | |
| 27 | Cost of Goods sold | 82,00,000 | 76,00,000 |
| 28 | Depreciation | 3,00,000 | 2,75,000 |
| 29 | Selling & Administrating expenses | 14,00,000 | 13,00,000 |
| 30 | Operating Profit | 11,00,000 | 9,16,000 |
| 31 | Other Income Dividends & Interest | 50,000 | 27,000 |
| 32 | Total Income | 11,50,000 | 9,43,000 |
| 33 | Less: Interest on Debentures | 1,35,000 | 1,35,000 |
| 34 | Income before provision for income-tax | 10,15,000 | 8,08,000 |
| 35 | Less: Provision for income tax | 4,80,000 | 3,65,000 |
| 36 | Net profit for the year | 5,35,000 | 4,43,000 |

### Statement of Accumulated Retained Earnings

| Code No. | | | 2004 Rs. | 2003 Rs. |
|---|---|---|---|---|
| 39 | Balance April 1st | | 13,15,000 | 10,22,000 |
| 40 | Net profit for the year | | 5,35,000 | 4,43,000 |
| 41 | | Total | 18,50,000 | 14,65,000 |
| 42 | Less: Dividends paid on | | | |
| | (i) Preference share capital | | 30,000 | 30,000 |
| 44 | (ii) Equity Shares | | 1,20,000 | 1,20,000 |
| 45 | Balance as on 31st March | | 17,00,000 | 13,15,000 |

### Statement of Source and Application of Funds – 2004

| | | | |
|---|---|---|---|
| 46 | Funds were provided by ' Net income (36) | | 5,35,000 |
| | Non-cash expenditure – Depreciation (28) | | 3,00,000 |
| 48 | Total | | 8,35,000 |
| 49 | Funds were used for : | 30,000 | |
| 42 | Dividends on preferential shares | 1,20,000 | |
| 44 | Dividends on equity shares | 3,05,000 | |
| 7 | Plant & Equipment | 3,05,000 | |
| 10 | Sundry Assets i.e., loan Advance | 10,000 | |
| | | | 4,65,000 |
| | Increase in working capital | | 3,70,000 |

### Analysis of changes in Working Capital during – 2003

Changes in Current Assets

| | | | | |
|---|---|---|---|---|
| 55 | Cash (1) | | 1,50,000 | |
| 56 | Marketable securities | (2) | 3,90,000 | |
| 57 | Sundry debtors | (4) | 1,10,000 | |
| 58 | Inventories | (5) | 3,00,000 | |
| | | | Total Inc. | 3,40,000 |

### Changes in Current Liabilities

| | | | | |
|---|---|---|---|---|
| 59 | Sundry Creditors | (13) | 60,000 | |
| 60 | Bills/Hundies payable | (14) | 1,50,000 | |
| 61 | Accrued Interest | (15) | 30,000 | |
| 62 | Provision | (16) | 30,000 | |
| | | | Total | 30,000 |

(Increase in Working Capital = Rs. 3,40,000 + Rs. 30,000)

## Connotation of Terms Used and Interpretation of Certain Ratios by Financial Institutions

### I. Important ratios to be incorporated in appraisal reports/memoranda

**A. Balance Sheet Ratios**

(i) Debt equity ratio
(ii) Current ratio
(iii) % of stock of finished goods to annual sales
(iv) % of stock receivable to annual sales
(v) % of stocks of raw materials to annual consumption
(vi) Ratio of net block to equity
(vii) Ratio of net block to debt
(viii) Ratio of net block to longterm resources.

**B. Profit and Loss account ratios**

(i) % of gross profit to sales
(ii) % of operating profit to sales
(iii) % of profit (before tax and total interest) to capital employed
(iv) % of profit after tax (net profit) to equity capital
(v) % of raw materials to cost of production
(vi) % of salaries and wages to cost of production
(vii) % of interest to value of output.

**C. Important performance indicators**

In addition to giving ratios as at 'B' above, the following ratios/indicators may be given in respect of projections for the project:

(i) Gross value added to capital employed
(ii) Gross value added per worker (productivity per worker)
(iii) Investment per worker.

**D. Other important indicators**

(i) Debt service coverage ratio
(ii) Unit cost of production
(iii) Break even point
(iv) Internal rate of return
(v) Economic rate of return
(vi) Domestic rate of return

## A B C Manfacturing Comapany Limited Balance Sheet as at 31-3-2004

| Code No. | Liabilites | | 31-3-2004 Rs. | 31-3-2004 Rs. |
|---|---|---|---|---|
| 21 | ***Share capital*** | | | |
| | Authorised, Issued, Subscribed and paid-up 1,050,000 equity shares of Rs, 10/- each | | 15,00,000 | 15,00,000 |
| 20 | 5% Cumulative Redeembale Preference Shares of Rs. 100/- each Authorised Issued and paid-up. | | 6,00,000 | 6,00,000 |
| | ***Reserve & Surplus*** | | | |
| 22 | Capital Reserve | | 7,00,000 | 7,00,000 |
| 23 | Profit * Accumulated Earnings | | 17,00,000 | 13,15,000 |
| | Total Shareholders Funds | (A) | 45,00,000 | 41,15,000 |
| | ***Secured Loans*** | | | |
| 18 | Non-Covertible Funds | (B) | 27,00,000 | 27,00,000 |
| | ***Current Liabilities Provisions*** | | | |
| 13 | Sundry Creditors | | 10,00,000 | 9,40,000 |
| 14 | Bills/Hundies payable | | 8,50,000 | 10,00,000 |
| 15 | Interest accurued but not due | | 3,30,000 | 3,00,000 |
| 16 | Provision for income tax | | 3,20,000 | 3,00,000 |
| 17 | Total Current Liabilities | (C) | 25,00,000 | 25,30,000 |
| 19 | Total Liabilities | (B + C) | 52,00,000 | 52,30,000 |
| | Total liabilities and Shareholders Fund | (A + B + C) | 97,00,000 | 93,45,000 |

| Code No. | Liabilites | | 31-3-2004 Rs. | 31-3-2004 Rs. |
|---|---|---|---|---|
| 7 | ***Fixed Assets*** | | | |
| | (Property, plant and Equipment) Land | | 4,50,000 | 4,50,000 |
| | Buildings | | 38,00,000 | 36,00,000 |
| | Machinery | | 9,50,000 | 8,50,000 |
| | Office Equipment | | 1,00,000 | 95,000 |
| | | | 53,00,000 | 49,95,000 |
| 8 | *Less :* Accumulated Depreciation | | 18,00,000 | 15,00,000 |
| 9 | Net Fixed Assets | (D) | 35,00,000 | 34,95,000 |
| | ***Current Assets*** | | | |
| 2 | Marketable Securities at Cost | | | |
| | Market Value : | | | |
| | 2004 – Rs. 8,90,000 | | 8,50,000 | 4,60,000 |
| | 2003 – Rs. 4,80,000 | | 27,00,000 | 30,00,000 |
| 5 | Inventories | | | |
| 4 | ***Sundry Debtors*** | | | |
| | Less : Provision for Bad debts | | | |
| | 2004 - Rs.1,00,000 2003 - Rs. 95,000 | | 20,00,000 | 19,00,000 |
| 1 | Cash and Bank Balances | | 4,50,000 | 3,00,000 |
| 6 | Total Current Assets | (E) | 60,00,00 | 56,60,000 |
| 10 | Loan and Advances | (F) | 1,00,000 | 90,000 |
| 11 | Intangibles (Goodwill, patent, trademarks) | (G) | 1,00,000 | 1,00,000 |
| 12 | Total Assets | (D+E+F+G) | 97,00,000 | 93,45,000 |

## II. Guidelines for calculation of ratios connotation of terms used

### 1. Debt (Term liabilities)

(i) Long term loans/deposits (repayable after 12 months) including interest bearing unsecured loans from government/government agencies, promoters etc.
(ii) Debentures (convertible debentures to be treated as debt expect part of debentures which are compulsorily converted, irrespective of the period of maturity)
(iii) Deferred payment
(iv) Preference shares due for redemption between 2 and 3 years.

### 2. Equity (Owned funds)

(i) Ordinary share capital
(ii) Preference share capital due for redemption after 3 years
(iii) Premium on issue of shares
(iv) Free reserves and surplus less accumulated losses, arrears of depreciation, goodwill and miscellaneous expenses (i.e. preliminary expenses etc.,) to the extent not written off. Development rebate/ investment allowance reserve, debenture redemption reserve divided equalization reserve etc., should also be treated as free reserves. Reserves created out of revaluation of assets should not be taken as free reserves.
(v) Amount of Central/State subsidy.
(vi) Long-term interest-free unsecured loans from state government or government agencies (such as sales tax loans etc.) and promoters, usually subordinated, such loans may be treated as debt.)
(vii) Non-refundable deposits in the case of co-operatives.

### 3. Current assets

(a) Stocks of raw materials
(b) Stores
(c) Work-in-process
(d) Finished goods
(e) Book debts including on account of bills discounted.
(f) Bills and other receivable
(g) Loans and advances.
(h) Pre-paid expenses (such as advance payment of tax)
(i) Cash and deposit with banks.

**Note :** Investment is not to be included in current assets.

4. **Current Liabilities:**
   (a) Sundry creditors
   (b) Unpaid dividends
   (c) Provision for taxation
   (d) Bank borrowing for working capital including bills discounted.
   (e) Unsecured loans/deposits to the extent not treated as debt or equity.
   (f) Preference shares redeemable within one year
   (g) Other current liabilities and provisions.
5. **Stocks of finished goods:** Closing stocks of finished goods.
6. **Annual sales (net sales):** Income from sale of finished goods, net of excise duty less discounts and returns. Non-operating income need not be included in net sales; however, such income should be shown separately to form part of the turnover.
7. **Receivables:** The amount of receivable and/or sundry debtors as given in the balance sheet, including bills discounted.
8. **Stocks of raw materials:** Closing stocks of raw materials, chemicals and bought out components.
9. **Consumption of raw materials:** opening stocks plus purchases made during the years minus closing stocks or raw materials, chemicals and boughtout components.
10. **Net block:** Net fixed assets (gross fixed assets minus depreciation) plus capital work-in progress. Arrears of depreciation, if any, to be accounted for in full while preparing the analysis of balance sheets and profit and loss accounts even if not provided for in the accounts and shown as arrears (if necessary, give a suitable footnote)
11. **Net worth:**
    (a) Equity share capital (paidup value)
    (b) Preference share capital (paidup value)
    (c) Free reserves (i.e. reserves created out of revenue profits and not set aside specifically to meet depreciation, taxation or any other known liability, contingency or commitment); development rebate/investment allowance reserve, debenture redemption reserve, dividend equalization reserve etc., and Central/State subsidy should be treated as free reserves. Reserves created by revaluation of assets should not be taken as free reserves.
    (d) Surplus (if any) in profit and loss account.
    (e) Deduct from sum total of (a to d) intangible assets, goodwill etc., and deficit (if any) in profit and loss account.

12. **Gross profit:** Profit before interest, depreciation and tax.

13. **Operating profit:** Profit after interest and depreciation but before tax.

14. **Net Profit:** Profit after interest, depreciation and tax but including other income

15. **Capital employed (to be computed as at the beginning of the year) :**

    (a) Net worth (as given at 11 above)
    (b) Debentures
    (c) Long-term loans including interest free unsecured loans from State Government, Government agencies etc.
    (d) Deferred credits
    (e) Short-term loans such as bank borrowings etc.
    (f) Unsecured loans and deposits.

16. **Cost of production:**

    (a) Cost of raw materials, chemicals components and stores.
    (b) Utilities
    (c) Labour and plant overheads
    (d) Other factory overheads
    (e) Administrative expenses
    (f) Sales expenses
    (g) Royalty and know-hows payable

17. **Value of output:**

    Net sales realisation (not of excise duty and returns) plus value of closing stocks of finished goods and work-in-process *minus* value of opening stock of finished goods and work-in-process.

    i.e. Cost of production + interest + Depreciation.

18. **Gross value added:**

    Value of output *minus* cost of raw materials, fuel, power, water and other direct material inputs like consumables. Stores and spares etc. (net value added equals gross value added *minus* depreciation)

19. **Variable cost (for calculating break-even point):**

    (a) Raw materials
    (b) Bought-out components, chemicals etc.
    (c) Stores and Spares
    (d) Utilities (Power, water, fuel etc.)
    (e) Packing materials

(f) Interest on working capital borrowings
(g) Direct selling expenses
(h) Royalty (variable)
(i) Other expenses varying proportionately with output
(j) Contingencies relating to the above items.

**20. Fixed and semi variable cost (for calculating break-even point):**

(a) Wages and salaries
(b) Factory and plant overheads
(c) Repairs and maintenance
(d) Administrative expenses
(e) Interest on term liabilities
(f) Selling expenses (other than variable items)
(g) Fixed know-how fees/royalty payments
(h) Depreciation
(i) Contingency relating to the above items.

## III. Interpretation of Ratios

***Balance sheet ratios***

(i) Debt equity ratio $= \dfrac{\text{Term liabilities}}{\text{owned funds}}$

This ratio denotes the relationship between longterm debt and owned funds of a company and helps in assessing the capital gearing.

The following points may be noted while working out debt-equity ratio :

(a) In the case of existing companies having investments in other companies the extent to which such investments are considered to be non-realisable, may be deducted from the amount of equity. Whether an investment is non-realisable or not should be decided taking into account various relevant factors.

(b) Free reserves would mean reserves created out of revenue profits and not these set aside specifically to meet depreciation, taxation or any known liability, contingency or commitment. Reserves created by revaluation of assets should not be treated as free reserves.

(c) Debt-equity ratio should not be expressed in terms of percentage but as a ratio showing equity as 1 and calculating debt up to one decimal point. Also, expression of the ratio in the reverse order may be avoided.

(d) Debt-equity ratio may be worked out as on the date of completion of the project both for new as well as expansion cases.

(ii) Current ratio $= \dfrac{\text{Current assets}}{\text{Current liabilities}}$

This ratio is an indicator of a company's liquidity position and ability to meet current obligations.

**Note :** Current ratio should not be expressed in terms of percentage but as a ratio showing current liabilities as 1 and calculating current assets up to one decimal point.

(iii) % of stocks of finished goods to annual sales

$$= \frac{\text{Closing stocks of finised goods}}{\text{Net sales}} \times 100$$

This ratio reflects the funds blocked in finished goods in relation to sales. Quick turnover of stocks (or a low ratio of finished goods to sales) is an indicator of good management of production, sales and stock of finished goods.

(iv) % of receivables to annual sales

$$= \frac{\text{Re ceivables and/or sundry debtors including bills rediscounting}}{\text{Net sales}} \times 100$$

The ratio points to the average period of conversion of sundry debtors to cash i.e. the number of days credit enjoyed by sundry debtors or the credit period allowed and thus the money blocked with sundry debtors.

**Note :** Since receivables would normally include excise duty element, the ratio may be calculated on the basis of turnover including excise duty and where the elements of excise duty is significant, a specific mention may be made.

(v) % of stocks of raw materials to annual consumption =

$$\frac{\text{Closing stock of raw materials chemicals and components}}{\text{Consumption of raw materials chemicals and components}} \times 100$$

The ratio, revealing the cost structure, is an indicator of stocks of raw material to annual consumption and indicates the efficiency in inventory management.

(vi) Ratio of net block of equity $= \dfrac{\text{Net fixed assets}}{\text{Net worth}}$

This ratio indicates the extent to which the cost of fixed assets is met out of owned funds.

***Note :*** As indicated earlier, full depreciation should be accounted for even if not provided for in the accounts and shown as arrears.

(vii) Ratio of net block to debt = $\frac{\text{Net fixed assets}}{\text{Term liabilities}}$

This ratio indicates the extent to which cost of fixed assets is met out borrowed long-term funds.

(viii) Ratio of net block to long term resources = Net fixed assets + long term investments in subsidiary companies are financed out of long term resources, indicating the margin available for working capital.

**B. Profit & Loss Account ratios**

(i) % of gross profit to sales = $\frac{\text{Gross profit}}{\text{Net sales}} \times 100$

(ii) % of operating profit sales = $\frac{\text{Operating profit}}{\text{Net sales}} \times 100$

This ratio denotes the margin of profit on sales revealing the operational efficiency of the unit.

(iii) % of profit (before tax and interest) = $\frac{\text{Gross profit}}{\text{Capital employed}} \times 100$

to capital employed

As an indicator of return on investment, this ratio helps in assessing the merit of the project.

(iv) % of profit after tax (net profit) =

Profit after tax minus preference to equity capital =

$$\frac{\text{Profit after tax minus preference dividend for the year}}{\text{Equity share capital (Paidup value)}} \times 100$$

As this ratio is intended to be a measure of return on equity share capital, dividend payable (for the year) on preference capital is deducted from profit after tax.

(v) % of raw materials to cost of production =

$$\frac{\text{Cost of raw materials components and consumable stores}}{\text{Cost of production}} \times 100$$

(vi) % of salaries and wages to cost of production = $\frac{\text{Salaries and wages}}{\text{Cost of production}}$

(vii) % of interest to value of output = $\frac{\text{Total interest}}{\text{Value of output}} \times 100$

Ratios at (v) and (vi) above indicate the cost components of raw materials and salaries and wages in the cost of production and ratio at (vii) above indicates the share of interest payment in the value of output.

**C. Important performance indicators**

(i) Gross value added to capital employed = $\dfrac{\text{Gross value added}}{\text{Capital employed}}$

(ii) Gross value added per worker (productivity per worker) =

$$\frac{\text{Gross value added}}{\text{Number of workers and salaried employees}}$$

(iii) Investment per worker = $\dfrac{\text{Capital employed}}{\text{Number of workers and salaried employees}}$

These ratios reflect the capital intensity and labour productivity of the project.

**D. Other important indicators**

(i) Debt service coverage ratio (DSCR) =

$$\frac{\text{Profit after tax + Depreciation + interest on term borrowings and deferred credits}}{\text{Repayment (instalment of term borrowing and deferred credits) + interest on term borrowings and deferred credits}}$$

This ratio indicates the ability of the unit to meet its liabilities by way of payment of installments of term loans and interest thereon from out of cash accruals and forms the basis for the fixation of the repayment schedule in respect of the term loans raised for the project. DSCR may be calculated as an average for the total loan amount covering the whole repayment period after commencement of production. Hence, the values in the denominator and the numerator of the ratio may be taken as the sum-total of the values for the entire period of the proposed term loans commencing from the year in which commercial production starts. (DSCR may also be worked out as an average of the annual ratios).

(ii) Break-even point (at installed capacity)

$$= \frac{\text{Fixed and semi-variable cost}}{\text{Contribution (i.e sales } \mathit{Minus} \text{ variable cost)}} \times \text{Capacity utilisation (\%)} \times 100$$

Breakeven point is the point at which cost of production equals sales realisation. Normally, in the breakeven analysis, costs are segregated into fixed, semi-variable and variable components. It is assumed that in the short run, the fixed and semi-variable costs would not materially vary with level of output and that the variable costs vary directly with the level of output. In the case of highly capital-intensive projects like fertilizers, automobile tyres, paper, cement, petrochemicals etc., breakeven point may also be calculated on a cash basis (i.e.) excluding depreciation as a cost factor.

## Highlights of a Balance Sheet - Interpretation and Implication

I. (a) Name of the Company : Reliance Textile Industries Limited.

(b) Balance Sheet period : For the year ended 31-12-1998

(c) (i) Clause (g) of Schedule 'B' – Fixed Assets of Balance Sheet

(g) Depreciation is provided in accordance with the provisions of Section 205 (2) of the Companies Act, 1956. The company has hitherto been providing depreciation for the full year on additions to fixed assets, even though assets were installed and commissioned for part of the year. However, in view of legal opinion depreciation has been provided on the fixed assets installed during the year on pro-rata basis with reference to the period of use.

II. Points 13 and 14 of Schedule 'N' - Forming of Notes and Contingent Liabilities of *Balance Sheet* :

13. There has been a change in the mode of computation of depreciation in the current year as referred to in Note (g) of Schedule "E". Had depreciation for the year been provided on the same basis as in the previous year, the depreciation charged in the Profit & Loss Account would have been higher by Rs. 1633.56 lacs."

14. The company until last year used to capitalise interest on long term loans/ debenture/deferred payment arrangements obtained for procuring fixed assets till the date of commissioning of the assets. In the current year, the Company has capitalised :

    (a) Interest for the entire contracted period of loans availed of for acquisition of fixed assets of polyester yarn Project at Patalaganga.

    (b) Interest for the entire contracted period of loans availed of during the current year for acquisition of fixed assets of the Naroda Unit at Ahmedabad, on the following assumptions.

        (i) Interest accrues at the time of availment of the loan till the date of repayment of the said loan.

        (ii) All loans shall be repaid on due dates, and

        (iii) For Euro-Currency Loans, procured on fluctuating rates of interest based on LIBOR, the rate of interest will be (a) the rate prevailing on 31st December, 1982 in respect of Naroda Unit at Ahmedabad and (b) the rate prevailing on 31st October, 1982 in respect of polyester yarn project at Patalaganga.

As a result of the above change in the method of accounting the charge to the Profit & Loss Account on Account of depreciation is by Rs 100.54 lacs and on account of interest is lower by 183.22 lacs".

***Observation***

By change in the method of accounting with regard to change of Depreciation and Capitalisation of interest the company has overstated the profit to the extent of Rs. 1715.94 lacs as under :

| | | Rs. in Lacs |
|---|---|---|
| | Profit for the year as per profit and loss A/c | 2916.45 |
| *Less :* | Depreciation undercharged on account of Pro-rate charge as per Clause (g) of Schedule "B" | 1633.56 |
| *Add :* | Depreciation excess charged as per note 14 of | 1282.89 |
| | Schedule 'N' | 100.84 |
| | | 1383.73 |
| *Less :* | Undercharging of interest due to change in Accounting as per Note 14 of Schedule 'N' | 183.22 |
| | Real profit | 1200.51 |
| | | 2916.45 |
| | (–) | 1200.51 |
| | Overstatement of Profit | 1715.94 |

In addition to the above two changes in principle and convention of accounting the Company has not followed the higher rates of depreciation for the year ended 31-12-1983 as per the following note :

Point (f) - Schedule 'E' - Fixed Assets of

***Balance Sheet***

(f) "The Company has charged depreciation for the year on the basis of revised rates as prescribed by the Finance Act, 1999 in respect of assets put to use during the year. As per the legal advice, the Company has continued to provide depreciation in the accounts in respect of assets put to use in previous years on the same rates as adopted in past. Had depreciation been provided at enhanced rates, the charge for depreciation would have been higher by Rs. 61.73 lacs."

Further, with the impact of point 11 of Schedule 'N' the real profit for the year end 31-12-1999 stands as under :

Point 11 - Schedule 'N' - Notes and Contingent

*Liabilities*

11. The Company has continued during the year to capitalise "interest on Long Term Loans/Deferred Payment Arrangements obtained for procuring Fixed Assets for the entire contracted period of such loans availed of during the year on the following assumption.

   (i) Interest accrues at the time of availment of the loan till the date of repayment of the said loan.

   (ii) All loans shall be repaid on due dates, and

   (iii) For Euro-Currency loans procured on fluctuating rates of interest based on LIBOR, the rate of interest will be the rate prevailing on the relevant dates of respective years.

   The total amount of future interest capitalised till date in Rs. 9368.08 lacs (previous year Rs. 9007.76 lacs). Consequently the charge to Profit and Loss account on account of

   (i) Depreciation is higher by Rs. 612.20 lacs (previous year Rs. 100.84 lacs).

   (ii) Interest is lower by Rs. 788.82 lacs (previous year Rs. 183.22 lacs)."

| | | **Rs. in Lacs** |
|---|---|---|
| | Profit for the year as per Profit and Loss A/c | 3852.39 |
| *Less :* | Undercharge of Depreciation as per Note (f) of Schedule 'E' | 61.73 |
| | | 3790.66 |
| *Add :* | Higher charging of Depreciation as per Note (f) Schedule 'N' | 612.20 |
| | | 4402.86 |
| *Less :* | Undercharge of interest as per Note 11 of Schedule 'N' | 788.82 |
| | Actual Profit | 3614.04 |

Overstatement of profit – 3852.39 – 3614.04 = Rs. 238.35 lacs

11. (a) Name of the Company : Modern Threads (India) Ltd.

   (b) Balance Sheet period : 31-12-1998

   (c) Point 9 of schedule 11 - Notes of Balance Sheet

9. Interest of Rs. 2,93,77,232 for the entire contracted period of term loans and debentures from financial institutions and bank relating to acquisitions of fixed assets has been charged on such enhanced value of fixed assets.

Interest to the extent of Rs. 2,36,26,247 not due has been included under unsecured loans.

As a result of this capitalisation, interest charge for the period is less by Rs. 57,50,986 and the provision for depreciation is more by Rs. 18,12,603 and the resultant profit for the period is more by Rs. 39,38,384.

**(d) *Observation***

By change in the accounting policy the loss of the company is suppressed by Rs. 39.24 lacs as under :

| | Rs. in Lacs |
|---|---|
| Profit for the year as per profit and loss A/c | 13,838 |
| *Add :* Excess charge of depreciation as per point 9 Schedule 11 | 18,12,603 |
| | 18,26,441 |
| *Less :* Undercharge of interest Actual working loss for the period | – 57,50,936 |
| | – 39,24,495 |

III (a) Name of the Company : The Bombay Dyeing and Manufacturing Company Ltd.,

(b) Balance Sheet period : 30-9-1998

(c) Profit and loss account for 18 months ended 30-9-1998.

**Profit and Loss Account by 18 months ended 30th September, 2004.**

| | | | 12 months to 3-3-2003 |
|---|---|---|---|
| | **Schedule No.** | **Rs. in lacs** | **Rs. in lacs** |
| Income | | | |
| Sale of products and other income | 14 | 14,420,44 | 12,377,15 |
| Expenditure | | | |
| Manufacturing and other Expenses | 15 | 14,038,46 | 11,488,92 |
| Depreciation | | 534,66 | 395,44 |
| | | 14,573,12 | 11,884,36 |
| | | (152.68) | (492.79) |

| | | | |
|---|---|---|---|
| Profit/Loss on Sale of Fixed Assets | | | |
| (i) Flats (Previous year-land) | 445.67 | | 8.85 |
| | 0.76 | 446.43 | (0.06) |
| (ii) Other | | 10.44 | – |
| Profit on sale of investment | | 456.87 | 8.79 |
| Profit before tax | | 304.10 | 501.58 |
| Less : Transferred to investment allowance reserve | | 19.00 | 75.25 |
| | | 285.19 | 426.33 |
| Balance brought forward | | 0.13 | 0.51 |
| | | 285.32 | 426.84 |
| Appropriations | | | |
| Interim Dividend (Subject to Tax) | | – | 27.05 |
| Proposed Fina Dividend (Subject to tax) | | 104.09 | 118.65 |
| Transferred to General Reserve | | 81.00 | 281.00 |
| | | 185.09 | 426.71 |
| Balance Carried to Balance Sheet | | 100.23 | 0.13 |

**(d)** ***Observation***

1. The company has adopted 18 months period in order to cover up its poor working performance during the first 12 months.
2. While the company sustained losses from its main manufacturing activity, it balanced the results by sale of Flats thereby realising an amount of Rs. 445.67 lacs. This profit/surplus is of an unusual nature.
3. The gross margins are under pressure on main activity.

## Conclusion

The above cases are brought out as a matter of illustration to drive at the nature of window dressing that is normally adopted. One can observe from the cases of (a) change in method of depreciation from W.D.V. Method to straight line method right from inception of the company; (b) Revaluation of Assets; (c) Omission of clear liabilities and disclosure as contigent liabilities in lieu thereof; (d) changes in method of stock valuation; (e) conversion of loans into equity thereby projecting a better networth projection etc.

## Company Annual Report Data

Name of the Company : ______________________

Year ended : ______________________

Book closure date : ______________ AGM Date ______________

**I. *Profit and Loss Account (Summary)*** **(Rs. in lakhs)**

| | 19 | 19 | Remarks |
|---|---|---|---|
| 1. Net sales | | | |
| 2. Gross Profit (% to 1) | | | |
| 3. Interest | | | |
| 4. Depreciation | | | |
| 5. Profit before tax (% to 1) | | | |
| 6. Investment Allowance | | | |
| 7. Taxation | | | |
| 8. Net Profit (% to 1) | | | |
| 9. Earned Profit (6 + 8) | | | |
| 10. Earned Div. (%) | | | |
| 11. Paid Div. (%) | | | |

**II. *Balance Sheet (Summary)***

**(Rs. in lakhs)**

| | 19 | 19 | Remarks |
|---|---|---|---|
| 1. Equity Capital | | | |
| 2. Pref. Capital | | | |
| 3. Reserves and surpluses | | | |
| 4. Loss carried forward, if any | | | |
| 5. Net worth | | | |
| 6. (a) Debts & Long term loans | | | |
| (b) Short term borrowings | | | |
| 7. Gross block | | | |
| 8. Net block | | | |
| 9. Capital work-in-progress | | | |
| 10. Cont. liabilities | | | |

**III. *Brief comments on operation/problems, if any***

**IV. *Brief comments on Expansion/Diversification plants***

**V. *Summary of Agenda of AGM***

**VI. *Observations/Recommendations.***

## Analysis of Profit and Loss Account for the Period Ending

Name ____________________________________

| | | (Rs. in lakhs) | | | | |
|---|---|---|---|---|---|---|
| | | 19 | 19 | 19 | 19 | 19 |
| 1. | Sales | | | | | |
| | Less : Excise Duty Net Sales | | | | | |
| 2. | Add : Closing stock (Fin. Gds & St. in pr.) | | | | | |
| 3. | Less : Opening stock (Fin. Gds & St. in pr.) | | | | | |
| 4. | Adjusted sales & | | | | | |
| 5. | Add : Other income-normal % | ( ) | ( ) | ( ) | ( ) | ( ) |
| 6. | Total adjustment sales & Income % | ( ) | ( ) | ( ) | ( ) | ( ) |
| 7. | Raw materials and stores consumed & other manufacturing expen. % | ( ) | ( ) | ( ) | ( ) | ( ) |
| 8. | Power & Fuel % | ( ) | ( ) | ( ) | ( ) | ( ) |
| 9. | Repairs & Maintenance % | ( ) | ( ) | ( ) | ( ) | ( ) |
| 10. | Salaries, wages, etc. % | ( ) | ( ) | ( ) | ( ) | ( ) |
| 11. | Other expenses | ( ) | ( ) | ( ) | ( ) | ( ) |
| 12. | Profit before Int. & Dep. % | ( ) | ( ) | ( ) | ( ) | ( ) |
| 13. | Interest % | ( ) | ( ) | ( ) | ( ) | ( ) |
| 14. | Depreciation % | ( ) | ( ) | ( ) | ( ) | ( ) |
| 15. | Operating profit % | ( ) | ( ) | ( ) | ( ) | ( ) |
| 16. | (a) Add : Non-recurring Income/Prov.% | ( ) | ( ) | ( ) | ( ) | ( ) |
| | (b) Less : Non-recurring Exp/Prov. % | ( ) | ( ) | ( ) | ( ) | ( ) |
| 17. | Profit before tax (PBT) | ( ) | ( ) | ( ) | ( ) | ( ) |
| 18. | Provision for taxation % to 17 | ( ) | ( ) | ( ) | ( ) | ( ) |
| 19. | Net Profit after tax (PAT) | ( ) | ( ) | ( ) | ( ) | ( ) |
| 20. | Reserves brought in | | | | | |
| 21. | P/L brought forward | | | | | |
| 22. | Amount available for approxn (19 + 20 + 21 = 23 + 24 + 25 + 26) | | | | | |
| 23. | Preference dividend | | | | | |
| 24. | Ordinary dividend | | | | | |
| 25. | Transfers to Reserves | | | | | |
| 26. | P/L carried forward | | | | | |
| 27. | Equity capital | | | | | |
| 28. | Earnings Ratio (19 – 16a + 16b – 23) (%) | | | | | |
| 29. | Pd. equity dividend % | | | | | |

% to adjusted sales given in brackets.

Name ______________________________

**Analysis of Balance Sheet** (Rs. in lakhs)

As on ______________________________

| | 19 | 19 | 19 | 19 | 19 |
|---|---|---|---|---|---|
| 1. Capital : (a) Equity | | | | | |
| (b) Pref. | | | | | |
| 2. Reserves : (a) Capital | | | | | |
| (b) General | | | | | |
| (c) Others | | | | | |
| 3. Surplus/Def. in P & L Net worth | | | | | |
| 4. Long Term Liabilities | | | | | |
| (a) Debentures | | | | | |
| (b) Term loans/Mortages | | | | | |
| (c) Others | | | | | |
| SUB-TOTAL | | | | | |
| 5. Current Liabilities | | | | | |
| (a) O/D & Cash credits | | | | | |
| (b) Sundry and trade creditors | | | | | |
| (c) Provision for taxation | | | | | |
| (d) Proposed dividends | | | | | |
| (e) Other current liabilities | | | | | |
| SUB-TOTAL | | | | | |
| **Grand Total (A)** | | | | | |
| Assets | | | | | |
| 1. Fixed Assets - Gross | | | | | |
| 2. Less : Depreciation | | | | | |
| 3. Capital work-in-progress | | | | | |
| 4. Current Assets | | | | | |
| (a) Raw material stores & spares | | | | | |
| (b) stocks in process | | | | | |
| (c) finished goods | | | | | |
| (d) sundry & trade debtors | | | | | |
| (e) loans & advances | | | | | |
| (f) marketable invts. | | | | | |
| (g) cash and bank balance | | | | | |
| (h) other current assets | | | | | |
| SUB-TOTAL | | | | | |

5. Miscellaneous Assets
   - (a) Investments in Associates/Subs.
   - (b) Other Misc. Inv./Adv. Tax. etc.
6. Intangible Assets
   - (a) Goodwill, Patents etc.
   - (b) Misc. expenses
   - (c) Preliminary & pre-op-expenses
   - (d) Carried forward loss

   SUB-TOTAL

   **Grand Total (B)**

1. Long term Debt/Equity
2. Current Ratio
3. Asset cover
4. NAV (face value Rs.)
5. Secured loans
6. Cont. Liabilities.

# 11

# Working Capital Management*

## Introduction

The term 'working capital' can be defined, broadly speaking, in two different ways. One way is to define working capital as 'gross working capital', and the other to define it as 'net working capital'. Gross working capital is equal to the total of stocks of raw materials, work-in-progress, finished goods, stores and spare parts, monetary assets, and other items in the nature of tender deposits, deposits with customs, excise, and port authorities . Funds provided by external agencies , namely, trade creditors, are not deductable from the total of these items. Net working capital is equal to current assets minus current liabilities. Current liabilities represent the amount of working capital provided mainly by trade creditors. Gross working capital and net working capital are together the generally accepted meaning of the term 'working capital'. In an organization these concepts of working capital may sometimes lead to an overstatement of funds employed as working capital. The reasons are not far to seek. Quite often, it happens that some of the closing stocks are slow-moving debts. Similarly, there are deposits, which are

* Reproduced form "Topics in Accounting and Finance" by S. K. Chakraborty, K. K. Bhattacharya, S. K. Ghagh, M. K. Rao, Oxford University Press, 1976.

sticky in nature, in the sense that these deposits which are permanently with the deposited organization. In the conventional manner of calculating working capital, all these items are included.

Instead, if working capital is viewed as a coffer wherefrom all the operating expenses are to be met, these items are merely dead wood in the coffer and must be excluded. This concept of working capital is known as 'current working capital' and is a more appropriate term for use by a finance manager. This concept of working capital is complementary to the flow concept, which is an economic phenomenon germane to the modern approach in working capital management.

In addition to the concept of current working capital, can also think in terms of negative working capital. Negative working capital emerges where current liabilities exceed current assets. Such a situation is not entirely theoretical. Depending on the nature of the product and the competitive position, an entity can carry on its operations with creditors funds. The most benefiting example in India in today's inflationary situation is presented by the industry producing diesel engines. Diesel-engine manufacturers demand advance payment of 100 percent of bill for an engine to be delivered after an agreed period of time. The ability to extract advance payment from the customers results in carrying on operational activities with a very low working capital or, in an extreme case with negative working capital.

The different concepts of working capital have been presented as a prelude because they are very pertinent to the management of working capital in an inflationary situation. Later, more will be said on the operational aspects of these concepts.

## Approaches to Manage Working Capital

Two approaches are available for the management of working capital : (i) the conventional approach; and (ii) the operating cycle approach.

***Conventional Approach :*** This approach suggests that if one can manage the individual components of working capital efficiently and economically, there will be no idle funds or paucity of funds. The components of current working capital are: (i) inventory, (ii) receivables, (iii) sundry deposits, and (iv) sundry creditors. Separate techniques have been evolved for the management of each of these components. The mechanics of such management is a subject by itself and it is not within the scope of this paper. It is beyond doubt that the adoption of management techniques for inventory management, credit management, and payable management will result in greater profitability on capital employed. In India, most organizations manage working capital by adopting the conventional approach, though, by and large, emphasis has been on the management of sundry debtors. Management techniques for inventory control have not yet been practiced on a wide scale in India, presumably because of scarcity conditions prevailing in the economy, and instability in the purchasing power of money.

***Operating Approach :*** This approach to the management of working capital is a recent development in the area. It differs from the conventional approach in viewing working capital as a function of the volume of operating expenses. Working capital is needed to cater to the needs of carrying on operational activities and is not considered merely as security for creditors. It logically follows that under this approach there is no particular sanity in maintaining a current ratio of 2:1. Adherence to a current ratio of 2:1 involves carrying idle funds which may not contribute to the profitability of an entity. There has already been a departure from the conventional 2:1 ratio, and this departure has taken place because of the gradual recognition that working capital is needed to meet operational expenses and not merely as a security for creditors.

Linked with this perception, the usual course of development has been greater appreciation of the operating cycle approach. The operating cycle concept suggests that the optimum level of working capital is to be determined by the duration of the operating cycle and the operating expenses needed for completing the cycle. The duration of the operating cycle is equal to the number of days involved in the various stages, commencing from acquisition of raw materials and ending with realization of process. Thus, if the span of the cycle spreads over 91 days after availing itself of the number of days' credit allowed by the suppliers itself of the number of days' credit allowed by the suppliers of raw materials, and the operating expenses involved in the process amount for the year to Rs. 200 lakhs because the number of cycles in a year is four. The maintenance of working capital at less than Rs. 50 lakhs will amount to overtrading and will entail the risk of being a defaulter in paying the suppliers of raw materials, and thereby bringing productive activities to a halt. An overtrading situation may emerge from a management policy with regard to acquisition of inventory, the credit period allowed to sundry creditors. Whatever may be the reason for overtrading, it can be very well explained by the corporate sector in India, management does indulge in overtrading by augmenting the level of activity or by resorting to expansion projects diverting working capital from the existing activities. This unscientific approach to the problem can be effectively tackled by the use of the prevail if the amount of working capital exceeds Rs. 50 lakhs. The essence of an understanding condition is that the entity will have unutilized fund at its disposal. If we consider working capital as part of the capital employed, the existence of unproductive capital will mean lowering the rate of profitability. The operating cycle approach will detect the existence of idle funds without difficulty.

In India, the operating cycle approach has not yet been used on a very wide scale. Recently the Reserve Bank of India appointed a committee to streamline the procedure if determining the limit of credit which a banker can extend to an entity. It is indeed a welcome feature to apply the operating cycle concept to a greater extent when granting credit facilities to its clientele. The corporate sector in its own interest will also be compelled to adopt this approach in the not too distant future.

## Sources of Working Capital for the Corporate Sector in India

The sources of working capital are (i) internal sources; and (ii) external sources. The internal sources of working capital are retained income and depreciation. The external sources are (i) bankers; (ii) trade creditors; and (iii) other channels, namely, deposits accepted from the public. Discussion will center round the source of working capital from external agencies. There would have been no problem if these external sources has been willing to supply finance to an unlimited extent at a reasonably stable cost. In reality the situation is completely different. The banking sector in India is guided by the monetary policy of the Reserve Bank of India. In framing its policy the Reserve Bank of India takes note of various purposes for which credit facilities are availed of by sectors of the economy. The credit policy recently announced by them has aimed at curbing the inflationary tendency, and with that end in view, fresh accommodation of credit facilities is extremely difficult to arrange, except for certain selected types of industries. The cost of credit has also moved upward appreciably. Because of the inflationary spell sweeping over the economy, the corporate sector finds itself in a difficult position in raising additional funds for working capital. Bank doors are closed, the possibility of maneuvering with creditors is being narrowed down day by day, and the ability of the public to save is declining. The corporate growth is being adversely affected, and this affects the growth of the economy as well. In such a situation corporate management's role has to be geared up, and all avenues must be explored as to how to operate with as low a working capital as possible.

The measures to be discussed here is suggesting ways out of the present difficult situation are: short-term and quasi-long-term in nature. The long-term solution of the problem is of a different character and can be achieved only with the concerted action of all partners in the economy, including the framers of monetary policy and fiscal policy. International developments also play a dominant role in the process.

## Cost Control Measures

From the short -term view, the following cost control measures may be experimented with an order to arrest the ever-increasing demand for working capital which is required even to continue at the existing level of activity.

***The production front :*** Greater discipline will have to be enforced in all segments of the production front and may be attempted in the following ways:

(a) The possibility of using substitute raw materials without affection quality, must be explored in all seriousness. In other words, greater use must be made of the techniques of industrial engineering. Research activities may be carried on at various national institutes with financial contributions from the government and the corporate sector. The incidence of cost to be borne by an individual unit will be much less than in a situation where it is required to implement the R and D programme out of its own resources co-operative action in the area of R and D can also be initiated industry-wise. An All India Institute of Packaging has already come into existence and an institution of this nature may go a long way towards reducing packaging costs to an appreciable extent. There is need for more institutes of this type. The corporate sector must come forward with the requisite initiative and financial participation.

(b) Then, greater productivity from the working force must be achieved. The Indian economy is at the moment plagued with a shortage of power. The total available time during which a factory can run its operations is regulated by, among other factors, the supplier of power, i.e., the respective state electricity boards. Within these constraints an attempt must be made, either by persuasion or by offering greater monetary benefit to workmen, to achieve greater productivity. An incentive scheme on the production front may be introduced after having considered the cost/benefit aspects of such a scheme. Many organizations have already in the meantime, introduced incentive schemes, and some of them have proved to be extremely effective in augmenting the firm's productivity. The wage bill represents the cost of labour. Wages, though considered a variable cost in all accounting literature, have tended to become semifixed in nature because of inroads of various legislative measures adopted by both the State and Central Governments in recent times. If productivity can increase, value added will be up with the incidence of the same amount of wage bill. The cost of labour per unit of production will decline. Before going in for any incentive scheme, the cost involved must be weighed against the benefit to be derived from increasing the productivity of the firm.

***Monitoring the Cost Element*** : Of late, in the cost structure of a corporate body the proportion of managed cost is on the increase. This trend is understandable considering the environment in which a business enterprise functions today. Managed costs are one form of fixed costs and in an age of technological advancement and sophistication, expenses such as office decoration, advertisement, and the salaries of management experts in different areas, become a necessary evil. These expenses are also in the nature of sunk cost and once committed to them, it is very difficult to retreat. The only way to minimize the cost impact of such items is to ensure the maximum possible use of facilities already created and available at the behest of a business entity.

A complete embargo on expenses of this may be enforced in times of inflation. The Board of Directors must play a very vigilant role in giving sanction to any expenditure belonging to the managed cost area. It is agreed that it may not be possible to do away with all types of managed costs. In some cases this may even assume the character of a behavioral problem, in the sense that a benefit may be denied to one executive while another executive of the same rank has been enjoying that benefit. The Board of Directors must move very cautiously and may achieve the desired result by having a free and frank discussion with the outer executives about the financial health of the organization and the difficult situation in which the company has been placed as a result of the inflationary spiral in the economy. In other words, what is required is not a patchy, ***ad hoc*** decision by the Board of Directors but the formulation of a clear-cut policy on prestigious expenditure. Such a policy will have general application, irrespective of class of employee or cadre. An attempt in this direction is now being made in government departments and the public sector undertakings. Exact quantification of the result achieved in such undertakings may not be possible at this stage because of the volume involved in collating the necessary information. The corporate sector may be in a position to quantify annual savings of cost as a result of a policy on the control of managed costs.

## Sales and Collection

In an inflationary situation, the increasing pressure to augment working capital will be some extent is neutralized if the span of the operation cycle can be reduced. Greater turnover at shorter duration and quicker realization of sundry debts will go a long way in easing the situation. All the monetary weapons available to a business unit must be used with greater vigour and purpose.

***Discount Policy*** : A discount policy must be evolved realistically, and services to customers must be improved to the maximum possible extent. Also, the credit policy will have to be formulated in close liaison with the discount policy. Higher discount rates may be offered in order to ensure quicker realization of sundry debts. The discount will then become the cost of quicker realization of debts. Against this cost benefit must be weighted so that the offer of a higher rate of discount does not affect and become a losing proposition.

The quality of credit management must be upgraded. In times of prosperity it matters little whether or not a customer pays at the end of the agreed period. Quite often the fact of default by a customer goes unnoticed. Such a luxury can hardly be afforded, however, in the present inflationary situation. Credit management must be established on sound footing covering all its aspects, namely, organizational, operational, and review. A separate credit department may be created with proper staff at its disposal. Credit-rating procedure must be introduced and utmost care should be exercised when granting credit especially to those parties who are slow paymasters or new customers. It is understandable that the establishment of a separate department may analise costs, which in the short-term view may appear to be out of proportion to the benefit to be derived. Taking a long-term view, however, it is beyond doubt that benefit will outweigh the cost in the not too distant future.

***Recovery from Sundry Debtors*** : The debtor's ledger will have to be scanned meticulously, and the payment patterns of big customers must be analyzed. The capacity to pay in time and the ability to sustain a payment habit are important factors to be considered. Slow-moving accounts must be spotted and steps taken to get back the amount blocked in those accounts. If necessary, a very high rate of discount may be offered as an inducement to the slow-moving parties. Here again, a behavioral problem may crop up in those organizations, which have introduced a performance appraisal system and inventive schemes on the sales front. Sales personnel will be generally unwilling to devote their time and effort to the collection of slow-moving disputed accounts. One of the reasons is that the amount of discount offered will be treated as cost of collection and as attributable to the concerned sales personnel. This, in turn, will have an adverse effect on their performance appraisal. In order to circumvent this motivational bottle-neck, a policy will have to be evolved which should categorically spell out that bad debts arising out of collection of slow-moving accounts will not figure in the performance appraisal process of any sales personnel. On the other hand, special incentives may be arranged for those sales personnel but for whose efforts even a part of debts which were considered wholly irrecoverable would not have been realized. It has been empirically observed that such an attitude on the part of the management will achieve another invaluable purpose. The sales personnel may thus be motivated to spend a part of their time and effort for the realization of slow-moving and disputed accounts. This will be a great feat for the management indeed.

### Slow - Moving Stocks and Stores

There is another important area, which receives inadequate attention in normal times. Only when there is a pressure on working capital does the management becomes conscious of the existence of slow-moving and obsolete stocks. It then tends to adopt ***ad hoc*** measures, which are grossly inadequate. What is desirable in the formulation of a clear-cut policy with regard to the disposal of slow-moving and obsolete stocks. Industries producing consumer goods are more agile in the matter, but the need is also pressing for industries producing durable and semi-durable products. To meet this need the following steps are suggested:

(a) Stock statements must be scanned by senior management officials at regular intervals. The officials should be those who are not concerned directly with management of sticks. A concise list of old and slow-moving stocks may also be placed before the monthly Board meeting, a management information format being devised for the purpose.

(b) The Board should take a constructive view of the situation and not merely play the role of critic or a fault-finding missing. It should expedite the framing of guidelines for dealing with the stocks. If occasion demands, the stock may be disposed of even at throw-away prices. As a result, there will be an inflow of cash, to some extent at least, which would not have been possible in the absence of a clear-cut policy decision. The concerned functional director must be on guard at all times against the possibility of further accumulation of slow-moving and obsolete stocks.

(c) Similarly, a policy should be evolved for slow-moving and obsolete stores, spare parts, and loose tools. There are organizations, which carry forward these items from one year to another, and funds are thus locked up unnecessarily. What is unfortunate is top management's failure to frame guidelines for dealing with slow-moving stress and spare parts. Cases can still be found where stores and spare parts are carried forward from one period to another, even though the product line for which these stores and spare parts were acquired may have already been discontinued. Part of the funds thus blocked in stores and spare parts, is not current working capital and represents non-current working capital. Non-current working capital of this type can be converted into current working capital by taking a policy decision for the disposal of these items at a discounted price; this will improve the fund position. Here also there is a pressing need for the installation of a management information system to reflect the position of slow-moving and obsolete stores and spares parts. A statement on a monthly basis can be presented before the Board meeting so that appropriate decisions can be taken in time.

### Scheduling of Payments to Creditors

The management of payables is as important as credit management. The management of payables implies:

(a) Ability to pay suppliers of material as and when payment becomes due;

(b) Selection of suppliers for identical raw materials;

(c) Choice between dependence on a mono-supplier or on multi-suppliers;

(d) Payment policy to large suppliers vis-à-vis small suppliers, since small supplier should not be exploited because of their weak bargaining power;

(e) Increase in bargaining power in relation to the suppliers by being able to pay in time and building up a reputation in the market. The organization backed by reputation acquired over a period of time will find more than one willing supplier at its disposal. Consequently, the organization may bargain for longer credit period from its suppliers.

Some of the components of payables management are quasi-long-term phenomena and may not be possible to achieve at short notice. Of all the components, the ability to pay creditors as and when payment falls due are of paramount important, as otherwise the very existence of the business entity may be at stake. Various techniques have been evolved for the purpose and are now made use of in India. Two such techniques are :

(a) Preparation of cash-flow statement; and

(b) Preparation of a fund flow statement. Both these statements summarize the total inflow of funds and the total outflow of funds projected during a future period.

If the two flows match, no problem arises. Problems creep in only when the projected cash outflow exceeds the cash inflow. In such a situation, steps must be taken to bridge the gap between the two flows, either by seeking additional accommodating from the bank for a very limited period, or by postponing payments to creditors to the maximum extent possible, or by deferring purchase of avoidable items including those of a capital nature. In time of inflation, cash forecasts should be prepared at short intervals, even twice a month, if necessary.

## Control over Branches

Strict control over branches in a molt-branch organization; Branches sometimes enjoy considerable autonomy is managing their own affairs. If must be ensured that this autonomy is not misused. Close coordination between the central office and the branches must be established so as to transmit to the branches policy decisions in sundry matters without leaving room for controversy and ambiguity. Scope for achieving economy in branch operations must be made use of to the maximum possible extent. One fruitful exercise may be a close scrutiny of power delegated to branches with regard to managed cost items. Other accepted modes of control, namely, timely receipts, may also yield desirable results in the form of reducing the branches constant demand for working capital. Other procedural matters like remittance of fund, or collection of disputed debts at a discount, must be streamlined so as to avoid the possibility of any delay in inflow of cash. To achieve this end, what is of importance is a clear-cut organization cost demarcation responsibility centers.

## Expansion and Diversification

Launching of expansion projects/diversification plans. Any expansion project of diversification plan will need some amount of permanent working capital at the initial stage. This additional working capital may be obtained from the banking sector or the term lending institutions, in which case the magnitude of the problem is reduced. The main factor to be taken care of is that in times of inflation there is every possibility that the original estimate for working capital may prove to be under-projected. This is now a common feature in all new companies in India. In the case of projects for which some funds have already been committed, the ways out of such an adverse situation, are:

(a) Persuade the banker to increase the amount of accommodation originally sanctioned.
(b) Approach the term lending institution for refixation of sanctioned loan amount.
(c) Rephasing of expansion project/diversification plans, which may mean delayed completion of the project.
(d) In extreme cases, shareholders may be approached for further investment in right shares.

The utmost care is also to be exercised at the very initial stage of the decision to undertake an expansion or diversification project. It must be ensured that the project outlay includes adequate provision for working capital. This, it is agreed, is an extremely difficult task, particularly in an economy torn by ergative inflationary tenancies. A rough measurement of the amount required is possible by keeping an eye on the trend of change in prices during the immediate past and projection this trend in the future. The probability analysis technique can also be applied in order to reduce the risk of being over-run in relation to the working capital requirements contemplated in the project. Such monitoring of any expansion project or diversification plan must of course, be discharged efficiently.

## Additional Steps

The following additional steps may be taken to complement the range of steps described which a company may take for the management of its working capital:

(a) Dislodgment of investment held outside the business except trade investments; trade investments have some intangible benefits in addition to a series of tangible benefits. It is felt that investments other than trade investments may be realized to supplement working capital in an inflationary situation.

(b) Sale and lease arrangements for immovable property: During the past few decades the prices of land and building have gone up considerably. Negotiations may be made with estate/investment companies for the sale of buildings and lease back to the company on a rental basis. This method has been practiced successfully in the United Kingdom. In India, it has not yet been practiced to a very large extent, but a few cases have been tried, and not without success. It is believed that with the growth of investment companies. This will prove to be a very useful source of finance for well-established companies in the not distant future.

(c) The use of bank guarantee instead of placing deposits with government departments and other bodies. Bank guarantees or deposits are acceptable securities for government contract work. Instead of parting with liquidity in the form of deposits, a bank guarantee should be used as far as possible. Arrangements may be made with the bankers for increase of guarantee limit under appropriate circumstances.

(d) Advance to customer should be kept at the lowest possible amount.

(e) Public deposits may be accepted within the guidelines framed by the Reserve Bank of India. It has been seen that a credit squeeze has, in the recent act, been one of the monetary measures adopted during inflation by the central bank of a country. In view of the existing credit squeeze in India, the corporate sector has to a large extent been making efforts to supplement resources with deposits from the public. In recent times, there has been a steep rise in the volume of such deposits accepted by the corporate sector.

There is no objection to resorting to this mode of financing because the cost of deposits in the form of interest after tax may still be knows than the return, which the company expects to earn by utilizing public deposits. Sound financial management is a sine qua non for being able to service debts in the form of public deposits. Otherwise, the very existence of the entity may be at stake.

(f) Uneconomic product lines may be discontinued depending on the amount of contribution generated by an individual product line.

## A Package Programme

The above observations constitute a package program for management of working capital when a tight money condition prevails in the country. Any program will prove futile unless it is duly backed by financial discipline throughout the organization. Austerity will have to be practiced not only at the lower and middle levels of management, but also at the highest level. In fact, the policy framers should produce a demonstration effect, which will tickle down the lines. Wastage will be avoided, and growth and profitability will be achieved.

## Operating Cycle Method of Computing Working Capital

The conventional definition of working capital adopts a balance sheet view of resources for sustaining the current operations of the firm. However, the balance Sheet is a static position statement of the firm on certain date, and it fails to indicate the dynamic flow of values occurring in the firm throughout a period. The real dynamics of the pressures on cash flows are contained in the firm's income or profit and loss statement which contains all the operations cycle concept of working capital discussed here. It is basically a profit and loss statement which contains all the operational inflows and outflows discussed here. Also a profit and loss account - based tool.

The following methodology has been used in determining the length of the operating cycle period.

1. ***Materials in storage period :*** This measures the average time bought items remain in store prior to being released into the production stream. The following steps are involved in calculating it: (a) materials consumed during the year, say M; (b) average daily rate of materials consumption, M/365; (c) average materials inventory during the year, i.e., (opening inventory + closing inventory /2, say I; (d) M number of days materials remain in storage = I / (M/365).

   Materials consumed during the year could be readily found out with the help of opening and closing stock and raw materials purchase figures.

2. ***Conversion process period :*** This measures the time taken on average to carry to the basic manufacturing processes converting materials inputs into finished goods. The steps involved are: (a) cost of finished goods production during the year, say, C; (b) average daily cost of finished goods produced = C/365; (c) average work-in-process during the year, i.e., (opening WIP + closing WIP/2, say, W; (d) average conversion time = W/ (C/365).

Into cost of finished goods produced, will go opening WIP, material consumed, and all manufacturing expenses including wages, less closing WIP. The manufacturing expenses may have to be unearthed from scheduled to the profit and loss account. The pace of the conversion process is determined largely by the state of the technological efficiency and supervisory abilities in the firm.

The degree of completing of work-in-progress on the opening and closing dates will influence the number of days for this phase of the operating cycle. This illustrates below with simple figures where the same quantities of opening and closing WIPS are assumed 50 per cent and 25 per cent completed for the first period, and for the second period 25 per cent and 50 per cent completed respectively.

| | **Year 1** | **Year 2** |
|---|---|---|
| | **Rs.** | **Rs.** |
| Opening | 100 | 50 |
| Manufacturing expenses | 600 | 600 |
| | 700 | 650 |
| Closing WIP | 50 | 150 |
| Cost of finished goods produced | 650 | 550 |
| Average WIP | 75 | 75 |
| Therefore conversion period | $75 \div \frac{650}{365}$ | $75 \div \frac{550}{365}$ |
| | i.e., 42 days | i.e., 50 days |

The difference of eight days reflects the relative efficiencies of conversion in the two years.

3. ***Finished goods in storage period :*** Sometime usually elapses before finished goods move out of the manufactures warehouse to the customer. This is particularly so for firms which produce for stock and not against orders. How speedily these movements take place depends upon the nature of the product(s), market(s), the season of the year, the effective of sales and marketing tactics, and so on. Calculation of this period follows the following sequence:
   (a) Cost of finished good sold during the year, say F;
   (b) Average daily cost of finished goods sold = F/365;

(c) Average finished goods inventory during the year, i.e., (opening stock of finished goods + closing stock of finished goods) /2, say G;

(d) Therefore average period during which finished goods remain in warehouse = G/F/365).

The cost of finished goods sold during the year is obtained by adding to the cost of finished goods produced in the year (already calculated in 2(a) above), the opening stock of finished goods and all administrative and selling expenses and deduction the closing stock of finished good at the end of the year. The splitting of administrative expenses into manufacturing and selling expense categories has been regarded as not being practically very meaningful in the context. It is also assumed that finished goods inventory valuation is done on full cost or absorption cost basis.

4. ***Debtor's collection period :*** Depending on the commercial conventions of trade for an industry in varying economic environments, and also on the firm's own credit policies, the conversion of debtors into cash (stage 3 above being that of conversion of finished goods into debtors) will consume sometime. Since published accounts do not usually show the break-up of sales to be on credit. The calculation then is as follows;

(a) Average daily sales during the year, i.e., (total net sales during the year/ 365, say, S;

(b) Average debtor's balance during the year i.e., (opening balance + closing balance) /2; say D;

(c) Therefore average collection period of debtor's balance = D/S.

Since excise duty is payable by the firm on its sales, which is later on recovered from customers, two alternatives are possible. Either net sale of excise duty be considered in which case the amount of excise duty should be considered, and the amount of excise duty should be excluded in computing cost of goods sold. Or gross sales value including excise duty is taken, in which case the amount of duty should be added to the cost of goods sold. There will be some variation in both the finished goods in storage and the debtor's collection periods according to the particular alternative adopted.

5. ***Creditors liquidation period :*** The same mix of commercial and policy considerations as in stage 4 above also govern the period of credit obtained from the suppliers to the firm. The computation is as follows:

(a) Average daily purchase during the year, i.e., (total net purchases in the year)/365, say F;

(b) Average creditors balance during the year, i.e., (opening balance + closing balance)/2, say, C;

(c) Therefore average credit period obtained from supplies = C/P. This period goes to the advantage of the firm and to that ten is to be offset against the sub-total of the first our phases of the operation cycle period.

Thus, taking together the above five calculations, the operation cycle period is derived as follows:

I/M/365 + W/(C+365) + G/(F/365 + D/S –C/P = OC

**Operating Cycle Example**

| Sl.No. | Year / Particulars | 2004 |
|---|---|---|
| | | **Days** |
| 1 | Raw material in store | 134.4 |
| 2 | Conversion period | 18.5 |
| 3 | Finished goods in store | 31.5 |
| 4 | Debtors collection period | 24.4 |
| | less | 208.8 |
| 5 | Creditors payments period | 58.7 |
| 6 | Operating cycle period | 150.1 |
| 7 | Number of operation cycles per year (365/row 6) | 2.431 |
| | | **Rs. (millions)** |
| 8 | Cash working capital requirement | 65.00 |

## Tandon and Chore Committe Recommendations *

Financing of working capital had always been an exclusive domain of commercial banks. Too much emphasis on security by the banks directed the flow of credit to affluent sections of society with the result that economic resources of the country were concentrated in a few hands. Projects promoted by technically qualified entrepreneurs with no tangible security to offer to the bank found it difficult to raise finance for the working capital required by them. With the nationalisation of banks an entirely new breed of entrepreneurs made a demand on bank credit. Small sector and other segments of priority sector were to be the major beneficiary of nationalisation and were preferred claimants of credit. This resulted in an unexpected demand of lendable funds of banks and naturally called for a reform in the policies of banks to orient them to the new development role assigned to banking industry.

* Reproduced from the Reports of Tandon Committee (1975) and Chore Committee (1980)

Another important factor, which called for reforms, was the inbuilt weakness in the cash credit system linked with emphasis on security. The limits were directly fixed on the basis of security available in the account which in many cases resulted in double finance. Banks also had no control over the level of advances at any particular time. It was not related to how much a bank can lend at a particular time but was linked to the decision of the borrower to borrow at that time. A major part of credit limits sanctioned by the bank remained unutilised and there was a strong tendency within the banks to oversell the credit. It was noted as at the end of June 1974 that total limits sanctioned by the banking industry was far in excess of its total deposits. Bank could afford this over-selling as 43% of the limits sanctioned by them remained unutilised. Any unexpected demand within the sanctioned limits could prove disastrous and had the capacity to put the entire banking industry out of gear. This fear was proved true in late 1973 when a sudden demand on bank credit was made due to unprecedented rate of inflation and the banks had to arbitrarily freeze the credit limits of their borrowers.

In view of such situations obtaining at that time Reserve Bank of India constituted a 'Study Group' with Prakash Tandon as chairman in July, 1974 to frame necessary guidelines on bank credit with the following terms of reference:

- To suggest guidelines for commercial banks to follow up and supervise credit from the point of view of ensuring proper end-use of funds and keeping a watch on the safety of the advances and to suggest the type of operational data and other information that may be obtained by banks periodically from such borrowers and by the Reserve Bank of India from the lending banks,
- To make recommendations for obtaining periodically forecasts from borrowers of (a) business/production plans, (b) credit needs,
- To make suggestions for prescribing inventory norms for different industries both in the private and public sectors and indicate the broad criteria for deviating from these norms,
- To suggest criteria regarding satisfactory capital structure and sound financial basis in relation to borrowings,
- To make recommendations regarding the sources for financing the minimum working capital requirements,
- To make recommendations as to whether the existing pattern of financing working capital requirements of cash credit/ overdraft system etc., requires to be modified, if so, to suggest suitable modifications, and
- To make recommendations on any other related matter as the Group may consider relevant to the subject to enquiry or any other allied matter which may be specifically referred to it by the Reserve Bank of India.

Based upon these terms of reference the group attempted to identify the various constituents of working capital that could be financed by the banks and suggested norms for build up of inventory. Far reaching recommendations on the style of lending and improvement in the present system of cash credit were also made. These recommendations were mostly accepted by Reserve Bank and were referred to banks for implementation in late 1975. Many modifications have since been suggested by 'Chore Committee' nevertheless the basis of the recommendations of Tandon Commit- tee, have been retained. The recommendations of the group are in the following paragraphs.

## Level of Current Assets

Working capital requirement of any unit is directly related to the level of current assets with the unit. As the main emphasis by the banks had been on security, the limits were sanctioned on the basis of the value of inventory held by the unit and no attempt whatsoever was made to assess its requirement. The Group analysed the inventory build up of various units and classified the inventory as under:

(i) Flabby inventory, comprising finished goods, raw materials and stores held because of poor working capital management and inefficient distribution.

(ii) Profit-making inventory, representing stocks of raw materials and finished goods held for realising stock profits.

(iii) Safety inventory providing for failures in supplies, unexpected spurt in demand etc., in effect an insurance cover.

(iv) Normal inventory, based on a production plan, lead-time of supplies and economic ordering levels. Normal inventories will fluctuate primarily with change in production plan. Normal inventory also includes reasonable factor of safety.

Some excessive inventory may also have to be built up sometimes due to factors beyond the control of management as in case of bunched imports etc. Flabby and profit-making inventory are both non-productive and should be discouraged. Normal inventory includes an element of safety and it should be the endeavour of any management not to hold any excess inventory over its normal requirements. To arrive at this normal level of inventory, 'Tandon Group' suggested norms for 15 different kind of industries covering a major part of all industries in the country and the norms related to

- raw materials
- goods in process
- finished goods
- receivables.

which together make for bulk of the current assets of any unit. These norms have since been changed for a few industries. The norms presently in force for all groups of industries as per the above recommendations are given in Chapter 13, 241-243 pp.

### Flexibility from Norms

The norms suggested by the 'Group' are not rigid or absolute. Norms were made to be applicable uniformly to private and public sector for all units having working capital limits of Rs. 10.00 lakhs and above. The normal deviations from the norms may be allowed in circumstances, which are beyond the control of the borrowers. The deviation in norms was envisaged in the following circumstances:

1. bunched receipt of raw materials including imports,
2. power cuts, strikes and other unavoidable interruptions in the process of production,
3. transport delays and bottle necks,
4. accumulation of finished goods due to non-availability of shipping space for exports or other disruptions in sales but not under circum- stances where a sales stimulation is needed through reduction in prices,
5. build up of stocks of finished goods such as machinery, due to failure on the part of purchasers for whom those were specifically manufactured to take delivery, and
6. need to cover full or substantial requirement of raw materials for specific export contract of short duration.

The above criteria for deviation of norms is not to be taken for granted. Specific and particular reasons have to he stated before any deviation is permitted. It has also been prescribed at the same time that these norms are the maximum permitted level of inventories which a unit can hold and this level should not, therefore, he taken as entitlement. If a unit is working will inventory level which is below these suggested norms there is no reason why the unit should not continue to do the same in future. The assessment of working capital in such cases would he computed on the basis of existing level.

The various components of working capital as suggested by the Group have already been assessed by us in the 'Assessment of Working Capital' However, while computing the requirement of current assets by the unit, we had permitted all inventories on lI1e basis of average holding by the until as derived from its past performance. The 'Group' suggested an improvement on that method and we shall now attempt to work out the requirement of that unit in view of the norms suggested by the Group. Let us take that until as an Engineering unit manufacturing consumer durables The norms prescribed for such units by the Group are as under:

| | |
|---|---|
| Raw materials | 2 months |
| Stock-in-process | ¾ months |
| Finished goods and receivables | 2 ½ months |

On this basis the permitted level of inventory will be calculated as under

2 months requirement of raw materials = 2 × 290.58 = Rs. 581.16 lakh.

3/4 months of stock-in-process = $3/4 \times \frac{4326.1}{12}$ = Rs. 270.4 lakhs

But the unit is working with average stock in process of 2.68 weeks and will be permitted to hold the inventory level upto that value only.

Thus stock in process = Rs. 222.96 lakhs.

2 ½ months finished goods and receivables = Rs. $\frac{5}{2} \times \frac{5315.82}{12}$ = Rs. 1107.46 lakhs.

We may also permit stores and spares up to Rs. 10.00 lakhs. The total working capital will now be worked out as under:

| | On average basis | after application of norms |
|---|---|---|
| Raw Materials | 611.22 | 581.16 |
| Stores | 10.00 | 10.00 |
| Stock-in-process | 222.96 | 222.96 |
| Finished goods | 478.05 | |
| Bills receivables/debtors | 735.35 | 1107.46 |
| Total | 2057.58 | 1921.58 |

The excess level of inventory with the unit is thus Rs. 2057.58 Rs. 1921.58 = Rs. 136.00 lakhs.

As per tile norms the unit should be allowed to hold inventory upto Rs. 1923.51 lakhs only and the unit must make efforts to reduce its holding.

## Approach to Lending

The second aspect of tile recommendations of the Group related to the style of credit. It was stipulated that the unit should finance a part of its current assets from owned funds and term liabilities. It prescribed a mini- mum margin of 250/" to be brought in by the unit from its owned funds and long-term liabilities and suggested 3 different methods of lending to arrive at the contribution of the borrower in tile above manner The three methods of lending as suggested by tile Group were as under:

Method I. The borrower should bring in 20% of the net working capital (current assets -current liabilities including bank borrowing) from its owned and long-term liabilities.

Method II. The borrower should finance 25% of all current assets from owned funds and long term liabilities and tile balance be financed by the bank.

Method III. The hard core current assets i.e. the current assets which are permanently required by tile unit for its functioning must be exclusively financed by tile borrower The borrower should also provide 25% for tile remaining current assets and only the balance will be financed by the bank.

Let us now consider the following example to illustrate the application of all the above three methods:

| Current liabilities | | Current assets | |
|---|---|---|---|
| Creditors for purchase | 200 | Raw materials | 300 |
| Other current liabilities | 80 | Stock in process | 100 |
| Bank borrowings | 400 | Finished goods | 150 |
| Receivable and book debts | 100 | Other current assets | 50 |
| | 680 | | 700 |

In this example

Total current assets TCA = Rs. 700 lakhs

Other current liabilities OCL = Rs. 280 lakhs

(OCL)

**Lending under Method I :**

| | |
|---|---|
| Total current assets | 700 |
| Less : Other current liabilities | 280 |
| Working capital gap | 420 |
| 25% of the above as margin from long term sources | 150 |
| Maximum permissible bank borrowings | 400 |
| Excess borrowings | 85 |

**Lending under Method II :**

| | |
|---|---|
| Total current assets | 700 |
| 25% above as margin from long-term sources | 175 |
| Less: Other current liabilities | 525 |
| | 280 |
| | 245 |
| Working capital gap | 420 |
| Excess borrowings | 175 |

**Lending under Method III :**

| | |
|---|---|
| Total current assets | 700 |
| Less: Core current assets (assumed figure) from long-term sources | 160 |
| Real current assets | 540 |
| 25% above from long-term sources | 135 |
| | 405 |
| Less : Other current liabilities | 208 |
| | 125 |
| Working capital gap | 420 |
| Excess borrowings | 295 |

It would be noticed from above that contribution from long-term sources is to be progressively increased as we move from first method of lending to the third method of lending and the ideal set up by the group was to bring all the borrowers to third method in a phased manner. All the existing and new borrowers were to conform to first method to start with. Due to various difficulties in assessing the core assets, the third method of lending has been discarded and as per recommendations of 'Chore Committee' all the borrowers have now to conform to second method of lending. It would also be noticed that first method corresponds to a minimum current ratio of 1:1 while the second method ensures a minimum current ratio of 1.33:1.

As a first step now the existing units have to adjust the excess borrowings by bringing in additional capital or arranging the funds from long-term sources. However, keeping in view the difficulties, which the existing borrowers would have faced due to this sudden change. it was proposed that a separate 'working capital loan' representing excess borrowing may he granted to such units.

The repayment of the loan may he fixed according lo cash generating capacity of the unit hut in any case tile repayment should not go beyond five years. By proposing this temporary adjustment the long-term sources of tile unit were strengthened and at the same time it was also ensured that contribution from borrower was brought lo desirable level in a phased manner.

On the basis of above-discussion we shall now attempt to work out the working capital limits of our exercise as given in the Assessment of Working Capital. We have by now calculated as under:

| | |
|---|---|
| The level of inventories as per the past records | 2057.58 |
| The maximum level of inventories as per the norms suggested by Group | 1923.58 |
| Expected level of creditors for purchase | 441.04 |
| Working capital limits already available | 1323.76 |
| Other current assets | 35.84 |
| Other current liabilities | 190.66 |

The current assets and liabilities may now be arranged as under:

| **Liabilities** | | **Assets** | |
|---|---|---|---|
| Creditors for purchase | 441.04 | Inventories | 1923.58 |
| Other current liabilities | 190.66 | Other current assets | 35.84 |
| OCL | 631.70 | | |
| Working capital limits from bank | 1323.76 | | |
| | 1955.46 | | 1959.42 |

| | | |
|---|---|---|
| Method I : | Total current assets | 1959.42 |
| | Less: Other current liabilities | 631.70 |
| | Working capital gap | 1327.72 |
| | Less 25% of working capital gas as margin from long-term sources | 331.95 |
| | Maximum permissible bank finance | 995.79 |
| | Excess borrowing | 327.97 |
| Method II : | Total current assets | 1959.42 |
| | Less: 25% of above as margin from long-term sources | 489.85 |
| | | 1469.57 |
| | Less: Other current liabilities | 631.70 |
| | | 837.87 |
| | Working capital gap | 1327.72 |
| | Maximum permissible bank finance | 489.85 |

### Style of Credit

The third important aspect of Group's recommendations related lo the style of credit. Recommendations in this regard had four basic ingredients as under:

(i) Financing inventories, which is already in excess of stipulated norms.

(ii) Treatment to be given lo borrowings which arc already in excess of maximum permissible bank finance.

(iii) New structure of cash credit facility.

(iv) Financing the sales receivables.

### Financing inventories in excess norms

The banks would not normally extend any credit facilities against inventories in excess of norms and the units might be granted a short time say 2 months to 6 months to liquidate those excess stocks. This will result in the unit holding inventories as per the norms.

### Treatment to be given to the excess borrowings

All units would first of all be brought to conform to first method of lending. However, no slip back would be permitted if any unit is already on the second method. The unit is progressively to be moved from first method to second method.

The borrowings, in excess of the permitted bank finance, should normally be adjusted by the unit by arranging funds from long-term sources by way of additional capital etc. In cases where it is not possible for the unit to arrange for funds for liquidating the excess borrowings, the bank may consider to amortise these dues by granting a short-term working capital loan. The repayment of working capital may be fixed according to the cash generating and capital raising capacity of the unit. To induce the units for early adjustment of working capital loan, it was suggested that a higher interest may be charged on the loan component as compared to the interest on normal working capital limits.

The units were required to bring in matching funds from their long- term sources at the time of enhancement in their working capital limits.

### New Structure of Cash Credit Facility

Cash credit limit is considered a short-term facility payable on demand. But in practice it is rarely so. A part of facility, being the minimum requirement at all times, is used almost permanently. It was, therefore, suggested that this part representing permanent requirement of the unit may be sanctioned as a loan and the balance amount of limit may be permitted as cash credit facility. The total cash credit facility is thus to be bifurcated in two parts -a loan component representing fixed requirement and running account facility representing the fluctuating requirement of the unit. It was further provided that the loan component may be charged at a rate of interest, which is lower by 1 % than that charged on the fluctuating components. This provision was considered necessary to induce the borrowers to have proper financial planning to envisage the level of borrowings for their fixed requirements.

### Financing the Sales Receivables

It was suggested 1liat the sales may he financed through the medium of hills instead of granting running limits against debtors. Monitoring of credit facilities granted as purchase/discount of hills is far easier and the seller is also aware of the due date for realisation of its dues, which is not possible in case of finance against hook debts.

The Group further suggested that banks should endeavour to grant credit facilities to the purchasers as far as possible and seller should be paid immediately after sale. This type of financing can also he arranged through the medium of bills and is popularly known as 'Drawee Bill Scheme'. The seller will be paid immediately on presentation of the bill and the liability against these bills will he on account of the buyer as part of his working capital limits. On due date the bills will be paid to the bank by the buyer. This mechanism was considered better as it not only ensures end use of funds but also imposes a discipline in respect of payments for purchases. The Group, however, did not give any specific recommendations in the matter and left it to concerned banks for implementation of the scheme.

### New Information System

Under the cash credit system the borrowers can draw upto the sanctioned limit at his own option subject to the availability of drawing power. The limit is generally fixed for a period of one year. The Group recommended fixation of quarterly operative limits on the basis of quarterly budget and performance data to be furnished by the borrower every quarter. These quarterly operative statements and funds flow statements were parts of the annual projected operating plan submitted at the time of sanction. Actual drawings within the sanctioned limit were to be determined on the basis of inflow and outflow of funds on the basis of quarterly operating statements. The Group prescribed standard pro forma for submission of the quarterly data and thus introduced a new information system and brought in a new concept of 'operating limits' within the overall sanctioned limit. The concept of 'operating limits' is now well established though the underlying pro forma have been suitably modified subsequently.

It is important to note that recommendations of the 'Group' formed the basis of first ever attempt to fix and operative credit limits on a scientific basis. Most of the recommendations of the 'Group' were accepted and implemented by Reserve Bank of India. Many modifications/changes have also since been accepted but the basic format of lending as suggested by the 'Group' has remained intact.

The quality of lending improved considerably but the cash credit system continued to pose few difficulties. Bifurcation of working capital limit in two parts as demand loan and a fluctuating cash credit component, as suggested by Tandon Group, was not effected by many banks It was therefore, considered necessary by Reserve Bank to review the system of cash credit in all its aspects and for this purpose a 'Working Group' headed by K.B. Chore was appointed in 1979. The terms of reference to the 'Group' were as follows.

To review the operation of cash credit system in recent years particularly with reference to the gap between sanctioned credit limits and the extent of their utilization.

In the light of the review, to suggest:

(a) modifications in the system with a view of making the system more amenable to rational management of funds by commercial banks, and/or

(b) alternative types of credit facilities which would ensure greater credit discipline and also enable banks to relate credit limits to increase in output or other productive activities, and

To make recommendations on any other related matter as tile 'Group' may consider germane to the subject.

The 'Group' gave its recommendations in 1979. Important recommendations, which were accepted by Reserve Bank and have a direct bearing on credit limits of the borrowers, are discussed below.

## No Structural Changes-Continuation of Cash Credit Loan and Bills Facilities

No structural changes in the lending system are considered necessary and working capital credit limits are to be sanctioned as a combination of cash credit, loans and bills facilities as hitherto. However, a directional change is necessary and the cash credit limit is to be supplemented by loan and bill facility wherever possible.

## Review of Borrowal Accounts

All borrowal accounts enjoying total working capital credit limits of Rs. 10 lakhs and above from the entire banking system must be reviewed at least once in a year. The review is necessary not only to ensure the continued viability of the borrower but also to assess the need-based requirement for credit limits.

## Bifurcation of Cash Credit Limit

The scheme of bifurcating the cash credit limit in two parts as demand loan and variable cash credit portion as recommended by 'Tandon Group' and accepted by Reserve Bank is scrapped as it did not find any acceptance either at borrower's level or at bank's level. The scheme was basically suggested to enable the banks to have proper credit planning. The objective is now desired to be achieved by streamlining and strengthening the information system.

## Application of Second Method of Lending

The permitted level of inventories with various groups of industries is to be determined as per the norms of 'Tandon Group'. However, the borrowers have to enhance their contributions in the working capital and for this purpose all the borrowal accounts with working capital limits of Rs. 50 lakhs and above from the entire banking system are to be placed under the second method of lending recommended by 'Tandon Committee.' Under the second method the borrowers have to contribute a mini- mum of 25% of total current assets from long-term sources ensuring a minimum current ratio of 1.33:1.

Exemption from second method of lending were permitted in case of new companies floated prior to 8th December, 1980 or companies showing signs of incipient sickness/companies having finalised modernisation/ expansion programmes etc., prior to implementation of Chore Committee recommendations. However all these units were eventually to be brought to second method within a maximum period of 3 years.

## Working Capital Term Loan

A few borrowers on being placed on second method of lending may not be able to bring in the additional contributions immediately. The banks may sanction 'Working Capital Term Loan' (WCTL) which may be placed on liquidation basis within a maximum time of 5 years. The method to be adopted for segregating excess borrowings on this account would be the same as already discussed under 'Tandon Group'. Higher interest at a rate which may be 1 % more than the normal rate charged on cash credit a/c subject to the ceiling rate may be charged 011 WCTL to induce the borrowers for its early adjustment at the discretion of the bank.

### 'Peak Level' and 'Normal Non-Peak Level' limits

Separate appraisal and fixation of credit limits for 'peak level' and normal 'non-peak level' must be necessary and the periods during which the separate limits will be in operation must also be specified. The past trend in utilisation of limits by the borrower must be taken into consideration at the time of fixing up these limits. 'Peak Level' requirements are relevant only not for seasonal agro based industries but assume importance even in industries producing consumer goods like fan, refrigerators, woollens etc. Demand of funds may also be created due to purchase of raw material in lot, payment of tax, bonus to staff, dividend etc. at a particular point of time. All these factors are required to be taken into cognisance while fixing 'peak level' and 'normal lion-peak lever credit limits.

### Adhoc or Temporary Limits

Any requests for ad hoc/temporary credit limits are to be discouraged positively by the banks. However, in exceptional circumstances the adhoc limits may be granted for a predetermined short duration and disbursed through a separate demand loan or 'non-operable cash credit account'. Such limits shall also attract a higher rate of interest, which may be fixed at a rate, which is 1 % more than the normal rate charged on the account except in exceptional circumstances such as natural calamities where additional interest may not be charged. Further, more interest rates on preshipment/postshipment credit are subject to directives issued by Reserve Bank of India and any adhoc/temporary limit sanctioned under these categories will conform to those directives. No additional charge of 1 % will thus be leviable on such adhoc/temporary limits sanctioned for export purposes.

The borrowers in such cases will also be required to bring in matching additional contribution. The banks may, however, allow these limits with- out insisting on corresponding additional contributions from those borrowers who are not in a position to do so.

### Sanctioning of Additional Limits

In a few borrowal accounts it may become necessary to sanction additional credit limits on account of increased production. WCTL component is not to be enhanced in such cases and the borrower should bring in additional matching contribution to conform to second method of lending.

A flexible approach in this regard may however, be taken by the banks if the additional limits are sanctioned to enable the borrower to meet obligation of experts under a specific export contract. Additional contribution from the exporter under the second method of lending may not be insisted upon in such cases.

### Fixation of Operative Limits

The operative limits will be fixed by the banks within the overall sanctioned limits on the basis of quarterly information submitted by the borrower in Form I was already discussed before the commencement of a quarter. This statement will form the basis of quarterly review of the account and the operative limit indicated by the borrower should virtually set the level of drawings in the account in that quarter subject to a tolerance of 10% either way.

Any excess/under utilisation of operative limit beyond tile tolerance level should be taken as irregularity revealing defective planning by the borrower and calling for some corrective measures to avoid recurrence of such irregularities in future.

The concept of 'operative limit' is desired to be set up on a more formal basis and it is compulsory for all borrowers enjoying working capital credit limits of Rs. 50 lakhs and above to submit tile quarterly operating statements before the commencement of the quarter. If a borrower does not submit the returns within the prescribed time limits, the banks may charge a penal interest of one percent per annum on the total outstanding for the period of default in submission of statements. The penalty is to be followed by a notice to the borrower to freeze the account if the default persists. Even in consortium accounts, the operations in cash credit accounts of the borrower may be frozen if the quarterly operative returns are not submitted. No additional limits shall be sanctioned for such defaulting borrowers. The borrowers are, therefore, required to make necessary arrangements for timely compilation and submission of quarterly statements to the bank.

### Cash Credit Limits Against Book Debts

Sales are financed either by allowing purchase/discount facilities of bills drawn by the seller or simply as cash credit facility against book debts. The facility of cash credit against book debts is to be discouraged and such limits are to be converted to bill purchase discount facilities wherever possible.

### Drawee Bill Scheme

It has been recommended by 'Tandon Committee' as well that a part of cash credit facility for purchase of raw material should be allowed by the banks under 'Drawee Bill Scheme'. This concept has been put on a formal basis and it is now recommended that 50% of the cash credit limit against raw materials to manufacturing unit must be allowed by Drawee bills only. It would be interesting to clearly understand the mechanism of 'drawee bills' and also the method suggested for fixation of limits and drawing power under this system.

The drawee bill scheme may operate under two different methods as under :

### Acceptance System

The seller may draw a bill on the bank of the buyer who shall accept it under an arrangement with the buyer. The seller can discount the bill with his banker. Seller's Hank would obtain payment of the hill from the buyer's bank on due date. The buyer's bank will maintain a separate liability account on behalf of the buyer to keep record of all bills accepted by the bank on its behalf. On due date the buyer's hank will debit the bill amount in the cash credit account of the buyer.

### Bill Discounting System

Under this system the buyer's bank will himself discount the bills drawn by the seller and will keep the liability in a separate account against the buyer. On due date the amount will be debited in the account of the buyer.

Under both the above systems the seller gets the payment immediately after supply of goods. The liability for acceptance discount of bills is held in a separate account by the bank (buyer's) on account of the buyer under the scheme and the bill amount is eventually debited to buyer's account on due date.

The stocks represented by accepted/discounted bills are to be shown separately and accounted for as such while determining the drawing power in an account. The possible method that can be adopted by the bank to determine the drawing power is illustrated below:

| | |
|---|---|
| Limit sanctioned against raw material | Rs. 400 lakhs |
| Amount earmarked for Drawee bills @ 50% | Rs. 200 lakhs |
| Amount available for drawings in cash credit amount | Rs. 200 lakhs |
| Margin on stocks | 25% |
| Stocks with the borrower are as follows: | |
| Total stocks | Rs. 350 lakhs |
| Out of which unpaid stocks represented by accepted/discounted bills | Rs. 150 lakhs |
| The drawing power can now be determined as under: | |
| Total stocks | Rs. 350 lakhs |
| Drawing power @ 75% | Rs. 262 lakhs |
| Amount earmarked for accepted/discounted bills | Rs. 150 lakhs |
| D.P. Available against stocks | Rs. 112 lakhs |

In the calculation of drawing power as above it must be noted that margin requirements for drawee bill facility has also been considered in advance which has considerably reduced the available drawing power against stocks.

The second method of calculating drawing power, which is more liberal, could be as under:

| | |
|---|---|
| Total stocks | Rs. 350 lakhs |
| Stocks earmarked for accepted discount bills | Rs. 150 lakhs |
| Stocks paid for | Rs. 200 lakhs |
| Drawing power @ 75% | Rs. 150 lakhs |

Under this method borrower is entitled for a higher D.P. hut will have to provide the margin of 25% on the due date of the bill when it is debited to the account otherwise the cash credit account will become irregular at the time of debit.

The most notable contributions from 'Chore Committee' can he summed up as under:

Application of second method of lending to all borrowal accounts enjoying working capital credit limits of Rs. 50 lakhs and above from the entire banking system.

Scrapping of the scheme of bifurcation of cash credit limit into two parts as demand loan and fluctuating cash credit account.

Formalisation to the system of operative limit and strengthening of submission of quarterly information by the borrowers.

A new direction of implementation of 'Drawee Bill Scheme' by making it compulsory to allocate 50% of the cash credit limit against raw materials to be utilized by way of Drawee bills.

These methods have not only brought in better financial planning by the banks but have also helped the borrowers to have a planned and budgeted approach to their production and operating schedules.

# 12

# Management of Working Capital in ECIL - A Case Study

The objective of this case study is to highlight the policies and practices of working capital management pursued by the Electronics Corporation of India Ltd. (ECIL) a large public sector undertaking in the medium and light engineering industry category. An attempt is made here to make a detailed analysis of the strategies adopted by the company for planning, monitoring, controlling and financing working capital and derive the critical areas where greater attention is needed for better management. The case study is divided into three parts: the general working environment is discussed in the Part I, a detailed analysis of working capital components is made in Part II and finally, the issues central to the case are summarized in Part III.

## An Introduction to ECIL

The Electronics Corporation of India Ltd., is a leading company in the medium and light engineering industry group in the public sector, manufacturing electronic items like computers, communication and control systems, consumer electronics, instruments, and so on. Registered as a public limited company on April 1967, it has come a long way in developing and strengthening the base of the electronics industry in India. Prior to this, the Indian electronics industry was confined to the activities of production of a few components for radio receiver sets based on foreign collaboration and assembly operations at that time.

The Bhaba Atomic Research Centre took a pioneering role of initiating research and development in massive way to design and develop electronics system, instruments and components with the broad objective of indigenously meeting the requirement of nuclear science and develop electronics capability for other industries.

The establishment of ECIL in the public sector was specifically intended to meet the above growing needs. With the well defined objectives of developing an indigenous base in the field of electronics, contributing substantially to the process of technological self-reliance, by producing quality electronics and placing above all the commercial goal of earning adequate return on capital employed, the company has been able to chart an independent course of action for itself. Opting for self-reliance at every level of its operation, which has helped it to get off the ground without any foreign collaboration, it has convincingly demonstrated the techno-economic viability of indigenous technology.

## Organisation Structure

ECIL is organized into seven semi-autonomous business groups. Each business group is a profit centre equipped with manufacturing, marketing and finance function and producing a specific product range and headed by a General Manager. The General Manager of each business group is responsible for the profit/loss, production, sales and management of the group as a profit centre. All business groups are supported by the Central functional and service department like personnel, administration, accounts and finance. It has developed a system by which enough autonomy is provided to each group in planning, monitoring and controlling their operations. This is a unique blend of decentralization of authority within a Central system. ECIL employed a work force of over 8,000 which includes about 2000 qualified and experienced engineers.

## Product Groups

The production of the company covers a wide range of sophisticated and precession electronics items, instruments and components. Its product range account for over 250 products in seven groups. The activities and product lines of each group are as follows:

### 1. Consumer Electronics Group (CEG)

ECIL manufacturers commercial TV receiver sets in the sphere of mass media. Popularly known as the EC TV, the product has come to be acknowledged as the leading brand in the country.

2. **Communication System Group (CMSG)**

   This group manufactures microwave communication antenna for providing network communication for the ministry of defence. ECIL has recently supplied troop-scatter antennas including associated feeds for the Indo-USSR troop scatter link which has a pathway of 692 Kms making it the longest in the world. It has also the distinction of successfully completing India's second satellite earth station for overseas communication. Besides, the company also makes a range of trans receivers, for use as vehicular stations by police, railways, fire brigade, airports, industries and other transport organizations. ECIL's facsimile trans receiver has found wide acceptance for rapid transmission of information.

3. **Computers Group (CMG)**

   This group is engaged in designing, development, manufacture, installation and commissioning of 16 bit and 32 bit third generation main frame computers and 8 bit and 16 bit micro computers for scientific and business applications. ECIL has a series of indigenous firsts to its credit such as first micro computer, first COBAI and FORTRAN compilor, first store and forward Telegraph Systems, etc.

4. **Instruments Group (IG)**

   ECIL's range of instruments encompasses nuclear instruments, industrial instruments, medical instruments, test and measuring instruments, and microwave instruments for use in industry, research, education and medicine.

5. **Components Groups(CG)**

   The Company offers a variety of professional grade components. These include carbon film, metal film, wire wound resistors, trimming and precision cells, silicon power transistors, small signal transistors, tantalum capacitors, etc.

6. **Control Systems Group (CSG)**

   This group undertakes on a turnkey basis design, manufacture, installation and commissioning of computer-based and non-computer based control system for thermal and nuclear power plants, chemical, fertilizers, steel and other process industries.

7. **Military System Group (MSG)**

   The group manufactured specific electronic items as required by the defence department. However, ECIL's involvement in production of defence electronics items is very small. Because another public sector electronics company, namely Bharat Electronics Ltd., is specifically engaged in producing these items.

### Importance of the Product Groups and their relative position

An analysis of the share of various groups in total value of production, total income and contribution to Central administrative expenses reveal that four groups, namely, CEG, CNSG, CMG and CSG, relatively occupy higher positions than others

(Table. 12.1). While these two groups account for about 77.48% of the total value of production, components, and military systems group together constitute only 10.2% with the former playing an insignificant role (1.79%). The percentage distribution of income for all these groups also closely follow, the same pattern as that of value of production.

**Table. 12.1** ECIL's product groups and their relative positions

| Product Groups | Percentage share in value of production | Percentage share in income | Percentage share in contribution to to administrative expenses | Manufacturing cycle in months |
|---|---|---|---|---|
| Consumer electronics | 27.72 | 28.23 | 24.36 | 1 |
| Communication systems | 15.05 | 13.17 | 11.79 | 9 (Major project 36 months) |
| Computer | 16.62 | 16.85 | 12.83 | 9 |
| Instruments | 12.21 | 12.54 | 19.37 | 7 |
| Components | 8.53 | 8.26 | 0.49 | 4 |
| Control Systems | 18.08 | 19.08 | 23.16 | 18 |
| Military systems | 1.79 | 1.87 | 8.00 | 2 |
| | **100.00** | **100.00** | **100.00** | |

Source : Revised Budget Estimates of ECI1L, 1986-87

It is common place that longer the manufacturing cycle, the higher is the investment in the working capital. It is significant to note that the consumer electronics group, which has highest share in income and value of production, has the shortest manufacturing cycle of one month.

On the other hand, the control and communication systems groups are mostly job-oriented and they have a very long manufacturing cycle. Considering the relative shares of product groups by way of contribution to general and administrative expenses, CEG stands first with 24.36% closely followed by the controls group (22.16%). On the whole the four groups, namely CEG, CSG computers and CNSG need to pay a greater attention to the management of working capital.

## Working Capital Policies and Practices

### Working Capital Trend

A declining trend is clearly visible in the percentage of current assets to net total assets during 1983-84to 1985-86 as per the published data and in 1987 and 1988.

as revealed by the figures (Table 12.2). In any case, an investment of over 80% in the current assets in all these years is certainly not an ideal situation. It seems that this fact has not been given due consideration in preparing the budget. This is because the ratio of current assets to net total assets for 1986-87 (80.35%) is slightly higher than that of 1985-86. Similarly, the current ratio has constantly been increasing and has reached 175.38% in 1985-86. The budget figures for 1987 and 1988 shows further increase in the ratio. Considering the recent trend of maintaining a current ratio of 1.5 or less in the private sector electronics industry, the trend is reportedly high and unfavourable. No reversal of the situation is noticed in the quick ratio which is fluctuating between 76 to 80%. The root cause behind this behaviour of quick ratio is changes in the level of debtors. A slow declining trend is visible in the level of working capital as related to turnover and value of production. It means that company forsees some improvement in this area during 1987-88. In the revised estimates of 1986-87 shows these variables at a higher figure than 1985-86.

**Table. 12.2** Working capital trend in ECIL during 1984-85 – 1987-88

**(Rs.in lakhs)**

| Particulars | 1983-84 | 1984-85 | 1985-86 | 1986-87* | 1987-88* |
|---|---|---|---|---|---|
| A. Current assets, loans and advances | 8896.01 | 9538.45 | 11537.80 | 11876.00 | 11921.40 |
| Less current liabilities and trade dues excluding bank borrowing | 5324.80 | 5526.99 | 6211.74 | 5656.00 | 5909.36 |
| Working capital | 3571.21 | 4011.46 | 5326.06 | 6220.00 | 6012.04 |
| B. (i) Percentage of current assets to | | | | | |
| (a) Net total assets | 88.28 | 87.94 | 80.18 | 80.35 | 79.39 |
| (b) Current liabilities | 167.07 | 171.89 | 175.38 | 209.97 | 201.37 |
| (ii) Percentage of quick assets to current liabilities | 77.33 | 72.90 | 77.22 | 86.74 | 78.89 |
| (iii) Working capital representing No. of months of value of production | 6.00 | 5.80 | 5.30 | 5.70 | 5.20 |
| (iv) Working capital as a percentage of turnover | 48.70 | 48.00 | 42.00 | 43.85 | 38.26 |

Source: Annual Reports of ECIL for 1983-84 through 1985-86 and budget Estimates for 1986-87 and 1987-88

* Budget estimates

### Inventory and its components

The broad picture of inventories is contained in Table 12.3 are the major findings emerging out of the trend of inventories can be outlined as follows :

**Table. 12.3** Inventories in ECIL

| A. Inventories | 1984 | 1985 | 1986 | 1987 | 1988 |
|---|---|---|---|---|---|
| 1. Raw materials, stores and spares and packing materials | 2345.95 (49.84) | 2508.08 (46.71) | 2973.06 (46.27) | 3808.53 (55.17) | 4033.23 (56.19) |
| 2. Loose tools (including tools in use) | 28.61 (0.61) | 25.15 (0.47) | 23.15 (0.36) | - | - |
| 3. Work-in-progress (including manufactured stock) | 439.15 (30.57) | 1683.10 (31.35) | 2045.45 (31.83) | 1685.21 (24.41) | 1736.91 (24.20) |
| 4. Finished stock | 399.77 (8.49) | 539.38 (10.93) | 702.62 (10.41) | 741.44 (10.74) | 739.44 (10.30) |
| 5. Material in transit | 476.81 (10.14) (0.35) | 598.78 (11.15) (0.27) | 668.47 (10.41) (10.41) | 668.47 (9.68) - | 668.47 (9.31) - |
| | 4707.17 | 5369.29 | 6425.74 | 6903.65 | 7176.05 |

| Inventory Ratios | 1984 | 1985 | 1986 | 1987 | 1988 |
|---|---|---|---|---|---|
| (a) Stock of raw materials stores and spares equivalent to months of consumption | 9.34 | 8.52 | 6.14 | 6.9 | 6.17 |
| (b) Work in process expressed in months of value of production | 2.35 | 2.36 | 1.99 | 1.85 | 1.65 |
| (c) Finished goods expressed as months of sale | 0.66 | 0.77 | 0.67 | 0.63 | 0.67 |

Source : Annual reports of ECIL from 1983-84 to 1985-86 and budget estimates for 1986-87 and 1987-88

(i) Raw materials including materials in transit, construction materials and loose tools constitute about 60 to 65% of the total inventory. The budget figures for 1987 and 1988 also reflect an increase in the component over previous years. Considering the results of consumption requirement the level of raw materials have substantially decrease.d from 9.34 months in 1984 to 6.14 in 1986.

(ii) The work in process constitutes on an average, 31% of the total inventory for the three years upto 1986 and budget reveals planned improvement in this area bringing it down to 24%. This is also reflected in the figure of WIP expressed in months of value of production.

(iii) The percentage of finished goods inventory is more or less stable for all the years. The same trend is also noticed in the figure of finished goods turnover.

The major component of inventory is the raw materials where a tight control is needed to reduce the overall investment. However, ECIL is pursuing a well defined inventory control proceed for the last three to four years. The salient features of the existing inventory control system are:

(i) Each group enjoys the autonomy of devising their own ways of controlling inventories under the overall supervision of the General Manager. The Manager, materials and stores; is entrusted with the task of verifying, ordering, maintaining and recording the movement of stores.

(ii) The stores accounting is mechanized using an EDP system. The store issues are charged to consumption on weighted average method.

(iii) ABC analysis is carried out for main inventories and VED analysis for stores and spares. The breakup of each category of inventory based on value and quantity is showed as under:

| | Based on value (%) | Based on quantity (%) |
|---|---|---|
| A | 65 | 2 |
| B | 28 | 77 |
| C | 7 | 21 |
| | 100 | 100 |

*VED refers to vital, essential and desirable

(iv) The minimum, maximum and reordering levels are fixed for all standardized and repetitively manufactured products and fed to the EDP system, brings out the slow moving items for review and subsequent action.

(v) The purchase function is completely decentralized and looked after by the integrated materials management department of each group. This has resulted in consideration, in reduction in the lead time for procuring of raw materials in the lat two years. The placement of purchase orders are also streamlined.

(vi) Recently the corporation has installed a Data Base Management System (DBMS) for online decisions and control operation. The materials management department furnishes the details regarding consumption, receipts, issues and transfers to system for assessing overall situation and taking quick decisions.

(vii) There is a great risk of certain inventories becoming slow moving or non-moving in an electronics company due to product obsolescence, design modifications, improvements and so on. According to 1986 data, the value of obsolete and stagnant raw materials constitute about 3% of total raw materials and that of non-moving finished goods forms about 5% of total finished goods in ECIL. For constant review of control of such items, the Corporation has devised a special policy where the indentor is required to take all possible care and precautions for raising purchase requisitions for barest minimum quantity of requirement, indicating the period over which it will be drawn on receipt. In case, the minimum quantity offered is more than the requirement, the indentor is required and the excess quantity so indented and the possible alternatives if any, it can be put to.

(viii) The major reasons cited by the authorities for excess time include bureaucratic delays and changes in customer's requirement. Similarly, the factors responsible for accumulation of inventories beyond reasonable levels were found out to be market fluctuations, abandoned and stalled projects, discontinued product lines, keeping stores and spares in respect of past sales to meet future demand, delays in custom and import licences etc.

### Debtors

As a multi-product organization, ECIL is catering to the needs of customers including Government departments, undertakings and private parties, the former category consisting of 95% of total sales. The terms and conditions of sales, credit policy and credit limit vary for both types of customers. But in the areas of sales realization, the dues from the Government departments outstanding for two years or more is one the rise (Table. 12.4). Its percentage in the total debtors aged for more than one year has increased form 25.2% in 1983-84 to 33.1% in 1984-85 and 48.06% in 1985-86.

**Table. 12.4** Debtors outstanding for one year an more from 1983-84 To 1985-86

| Particulars | 1984 | | 1985 | | 1986 | |
|---|---|---|---|---|---|---|
| | Govt.under-takings | Others | Govt.under-takings | Others | Govt.under-takings | Others |
| Outstanding for one year but less than two years | 365.37 | 55.58 | 375.89 | 54.96 | 281.16 | 35.64 |
| Outstanding for two years but less than three years | 85.24 | 24.71 | 155.41 | 27.79 | 223.44 | 16.76 |
| Outstanding for three years and more | 38.12 | 4.49 | 33.71 | 5.63 | 41.94 | 21.57 |
| Debtors expressed as months of sales | 4.76 | | 3.77 | | 2.78 | |

Source : Annual Reports of ECIL from 1983-84 to 1985-86

The credit terms for the Government department state that 95% payment is to be made against despatch of documents, inspection or proof of despatch and the balance of 5% being payable within a period of 30 days from the date of receipt of goods. For orders of significant value, an advance of 20% to 50% is generally quoted. In such orders inspection is made by customers at ECIL and 95% payment is requested before dispatching the system for installation and commissioning. The installation and commissioning charges are quoted separately and are payable in full along with 95% payment.

Considering these terms the increasing levels of debtors due for more than two years is highly unsatisfactory. Explaining the situation, the authorities points out that :

(a) the first instalment of 90 to 95% is realized well in time, but the balance amount linked to installation, is held up for a longer period due to non-availability of site with facilities required for commissioning.

(b) the customers sometimes enhance their orders and desire to make payment for the enhanced portion together with the remainder resulting in the hold up.

(c) When there is a serious deficit in the supplies like manuals, instructions, a small component, etc., the customers withhold the balance payment.

(d) The funds in the Government sector is more associated with the lapsing/ closing of the financial year. This results in non-availability of funds with the customers at the appropriate time leading to further waiting period.

(e) Procedural delays also result in over dues.

According to the Board's direction the debtors should stand at a maximum of two months sale. As against this, the debtors stood at 4.76 months, 3.77months and 2.78 months of sale for the three years from 1984 through 1986. Though a declining trend is clearly noticed certainly more effort is needed in this direction.

## Sources of Working Finance

Working capital is generally financed through long term external sources, short term external sources and internal sources. That is, the major sources are commercial banks, loans from Government and internally generated funds. Commercial banks extend financial assistance in the form of term loans or cash credit facilities. The common method of providing working capital term loan is against pledge of inventory and hypothecation of inventories and book debts.

The trend of financing working capital* in ECIL for the period of study reveals that the company has gradually reduced its dependence on borrowed funds for the purpose (Table. 12.5). The internal source is steadily emerging as the single most important source for working capital followed by cash credit. The share of internal funds in the working capital has gone up from 42.68% in 1984 to 70.9% in 1986 and budget figure of 1987 and 1988 reveal a relatively low proportion of about

**Table. 12.5 Financing of Working Capital in ECIL from 1984-1988**

**(Rs.in lakhs)**

| | 1984 | 1985 | 1986 | 1987** | 1988** |
|---|---|---|---|---|---|
| Working Capital | 3571.21 | 4011.46 | 5326.06 | 6023.88 | 6012.04 |
| Financed by : | | | | | |
| A. Borrowed Funds : | | | | | |
| (i) Cash credit | 1802.62 | 1601.60 | 1058.38 | 2805.01 | 2805.01 |
| (ii) Loans from Government | 190.58 | 60.00 | 192.00 | | |
| (iii) Loans from financial institutions | 54.00 | 18.00 | 300.00 | | |
| Total: (i + ii + iii) | | | | | |
| B. Internal Sources | 1524.11 | 2331.86 | 3775.68 | 3218.87 | 3207.03 |
| Total (A+B) | 3571.21 | 4011.46 | 5326.06 | 6023.88 | 6012.04 |

Source: Annual Reports of ECIL from 1983-84 through 1985-86 and Budget estimates for 1986-87 and 1987-88

** Budget Estimates

53%. Further, among the borrowed sources, the proportion of loans from financial institutions and Government has increased in 1986 over the previous two years. It is quite evident that the company is shifting to those two sources as against use of cash credit. The reason for this tilt could be related due to higher interest rate on cash credit (17.5%) and many legal stipulations**. At present the cash credit limit enjoyed by the company is of the order of 21.5 crores with a limit of 2.5 crores for cheques/bills discounting facilities. The cash credit utilization statement at the end of December 1986 show that roughly 46% of the limit remained to be utilized during the next three months i.e., upto March 1987 (Table. 12.6).

* The term working capital refers to net working capital, i.e. current assets and loans and advances less current liabilities excluding bank borrowings. Hence, the trade dues and creditors do not become a source.

** The interest rate for Government loan is about 12.5% and that for the loans from financial institutions is about 14.0%.

The revised estimate in the 1986-87 budget revealed the planned use of cash credit to the tune of 20.6 crores. This means that there is no need for ECIL to ask for a higher cash credit limit for 1987 or 1988.

**Table. 12.6 Bank-wise position of cash/credit utilisation at the end of December 1986**

**(Rs.in lakhs)**

| Name of the Bank | Limit | Utilisation | Percentage |
|---|---|---|---|
| S.B.I | 11.65.00 | 469.78 | |
| I.O.B | 450.00 | 346.42 | |
| P.N.B. | 200.00 | 103.25 | |
| Syndicate Bank | 200.00 | 136.32 | |
| Dena Bank | 135.00 | 111.72 | |
| **TOTAL** | **2150.00** | **1166.88** | |

Source: Status report of ECIL, December 1986

As per the first method of lending suggested by Tandon Committee, ECIL's actual borrowings is much less than the permissible level (Table. 11.7). Similarly, according to the second method of lending (Table. 11.8) the company's actual borrowing is less than the permissible level in 1986 and the same trend is planned for 1987 situation automatically brings in the concept of cost. Should the company make use of more internal funds than required and reduce the level of borrowings to less than the permissible limit ? In order to develop a proper proposition, the cost of both borrowed funds and owned funds was worked out. Based on the 1986 figure, the cost of borrowed funds was found to be 7.29% and internal fund as 16.47%. It was also seen that the ratio of net profit to net worth for the last three years i.e. 1984 and 1985 was 1.35% and 8.73% respectively. This implies that recently ECIL's profitability is steadily improving and making the cost of internal funds very high. Thus in the situation of a good profit trend, the actual and planned use of more internal funds for working capital does not seem to be cost effective particularly under the condition of a narrow fixed capital base* it should as well try for more borrowed funds and divert its internal funds for acquisition of mere fixed assets. This is also the time when ECIL should go in for other sources of funding such as public deposit which would be less costly in comparison to internal funds. Another advantage with the public deposit source is that it does not come under the category of bank borrowings for applying Tandon Committee Norms. Thus a replanning is required for balancing between different sources for meeting working capital needs.

* Fixed Assets Constitute about 20-22% of the total assets.

**Table. 11.7** Financing of working capital as per tandon committee norms first method

| | 1984 | 1985 | 1986 | 1987 | 1988 |
|---|---|---|---|---|---|
| Working Capital Gap | 3571.21 | 4011.46 | 5326.06 | 6023.88 | 6012.04 |
| Minimum internal (25%) finance | 892.80 | 1002.86 | 1331.52 | 1505.97 | 1503.01 |
| Actual internal finance | 1524.11 | 2331.86 | 3775.68 | 3218.87 | 3207.03 |
| Difference | +631.31 | +1329.09 | –2444.16 | +1712.90 | +1704.02 |
| Permissible borrowing (75% of working capital gap) | 2678.41 | 3008.60 | 3994.54 | 4517.91 | 4509.03 |
| Actual borrowing | 2047.2 | 1679.60 | 1550.38 | 2805.01 | 2805.01 |
| Difference | –631.21 | –139.00 | –2444.16 | –1712.90 | –1704.02 |

**Table. 11.8** Financing of working capital as per tandon committee norms - 1984 - 1986

**(Rs.in lakhs)**

| | 1984 | 1985 | 1986 | 1987* | 1988* |
|---|---|---|---|---|---|
| Current Assets (a) | 8896.01 | 9538.45 | 11537.80 | 11876.00 | 11921.00 |
| 75% of current assets (b) | 6672.00 | 7153.84 | 8653.35 | 8907.00 | 8941.05 |
| Non-bank current liabilities (c ) | 5324.80 | 5526.99 | 6211.74 | 5656.34 | 5909.36 |
| Permissible bank finance (b – c) | 1347.20 | 1626.85 | 2441.61 | 3250.66 | 3031.69 |
| Actual bank finance | 2047.20 | 1679.60 | 1550.38 | 2805.01 | 2805.01 |
| Difference | (+)700.00 | (+)52.75 | (–)891.23 | (–)445.65 | (–)226.68 |

### Working Capital Variance

The process of budgeting in ECIL has undergone substantial changes particularly after this decentralization of the organization into autonomous groups. Each group prepares its own sales estimate 9 to 10 months before the beginning of the next financial year and further revise the same at the end of the second quarter of the financial year. The group managers meet several times which are further translated into production requirements and costs by each group. After finalisation of the budget at group level it is presented to the head office for incorporation in the Master Budget.

The working capital budget gives the projected investment in the working capital components by calling data from each group reflecting their individual requirements. As per RBIs directions a detailed assessment is also made in the prescribed forms for quarterly submission to the Bank. Since this requirement leads to a constant review of working capital by banks, the budget receives greater attention by the company. As regards the method used for preparing the budget, it was revealed that ECIL used the technique of 'percentage increase/decrease in items over the previous year based on discussion and intuition.

No trend studies or advanced projection techniques were used for preparing the budget.

A comparison of the budgeted and actual working capital figures for 1985-86 led to a few interesting observations (Table. 11.9). It was found that there were no large variations in the working capital components. The percentage of variation is limited to 10 to 11. The higher variation in case of work in process was attributed to a change in the quantum of orders, specification of the product and delay in commissioning. The negative variation, though small, in the raw materials, reflected efforts by the company to reduce its investment in the component. By and large, the working capital position was close to the budgeted figures.

**Table. 11.9 Working capital variance in ECIL for 1985-86**

**(Rs.in lakhs)**

| Particulars | Budget for 1986 | Actual for 1986 | Variance | Percentage of variance over actual |
|---|---|---|---|---|
| Current assets including loans and advances | | | | |
| (a) Inventories | | | | |
| Raw materials | 36.96 | 36.85 | – 0.11 | – 0.30 |
| Work in progress | 15.61 | 30.45 | + 4.84 | + 23.67 |
| Finished stock | 6.23 | 7.02 | + 0.79 | + 11.25 |
| (b) Debtors | 26.47 | 28.69 | + 2.22 | + 7.74 |
| (c) Loans and advances and cash balance | 20.19 | 22,37 | + 2.18 | + 9.74 |
| TOTAL | 105.46 | 115.36 | + 9.92 | + 8.60 |
| Current liabilities | 58.22 | 62.12 | + 3.90 | + 6.28 |
| Working capital | 47.24 | 53.26 | + 6.02 | +11.30 |

### The operating cycle

The operating cycle of a firm begins with acquisition of raw materials and ends with the collection of receivables. It is divided into four stages i.e. raw materials, work in process, finished stock and debtors collection stage. The duration of the operating cycle is equal to the sums of the durations of each of these stages less the credit period allowed by the suppliers of firms. Expressed in terms of symbols, it is :

$$0 = r + w + f + d + c$$

where; 0 = duration of operating cycle

r = raw materials and stores storage period

w = work in process period

f = finished goods storage period

d = debtors, collection period

c = creditors payment period

The information pertaining to each distinct stage of the operating cycle, stated in days of relevant activity, has considerable significance. It can be used with some modifications, in arriving at the investment required in each of these stages for anticipated level of activity. The total of these investment would represent the estimated working capital requirements.

The figures for the last three years evidently point out significant improvement in the investment in over the periods (Table. 11.10). There has been constant reduction in the period of hold up in raw material and WIP inventory, debtors stage. The finished goods storage period is almost constant. In case of creditor's collection period, ECIL should plan to increase the duration so that its own investment could be reduced.

**Table. 11.10 Operating cycle of ECIL from 1983-84 through 1985-86**

**(No.of days)**

| | R | W | F | D | C | O |
|---|---|---|---|---|---|---|
| 1983-84 | 243 | 160 | 20 | 167 | 138 | 452 |
| 1984-85 | 227 | 142 | 21 | 155 | 155 | 390 |
| 1985-86 | 158 | 106 | 19 | 97 | 80 | 300 |

**Source: Compiled form the Annual Reports of ECIL from 1983-84 to 1985-86**

## Concluding Observations

ECIL has made significant improvements in its profitability and financial position during the last three years. In the area of working capital, it has adopted scientific methods for controlling inventories and debtors. The installation of Data Base Management System for providing on the spot information on critical working capital variables has helped in reducing investment in all types of inventories. However, the Corporation's policy on the working capital structure needs to be carefully examined. Indeed, the budget figures for 1986-87 indicate unfavourable trends in all the working capital variables as compared to its previous years. Moreover, the problem of adequacy of the present financing pattern for working capital has also come to the fore. On the whole, the study unfolds the following interesting features:

1. The four product groups out of seven, namely consumer electronics, control systems, computers and communication systems occupy significant position with regard to income, value of production and contribution to general administrative expenses. The savings in the working capital investment in these groups would be relatively more effective in adding to the profitability of the organisation. The control system should also be more stringent for these groups.

2. The investment of about 80% in the current assets speaks of a shortsighted policy in the financial structure of the organization. This has been one of the reasons of the low return in past years. Since the company has turned the corner only recently, it should concentrate in building up fixed capital base. There should be efforts to reduce the current ratio to 1.5 or less.

3. Raw materials constitute about 65 to 70% of the total inventory. A concerted effort is needed is controlling this kind of inventory through effective requisition based on accurate bill of materials, reduction in lead time for both imported and other items, effective utilization and quick disposal of slow moving and obsolete stocks. The cash in process and finished goods inventory seem to be within reasonable limit considering the manufacturing cycle and sales procedures respectively.

4. Government departments and undertakings are the major customers of ECIL. The credit terms for these customers require an outright payment of 90 to 95% and the balance to be paid within a period of one month. The outstanding dues of ECIL represent mostly the unpaid balance which stretches over a period of two years or more. Thus such portions of the outstanding amount should be carefully examined as to its early recovery. If there is a chance for further delay, they should better be written off. Present collection efforts should be further stepped up.

5. The corporation is using costly sources of internally generated funds in financing major portion of working capital gap. In times of rising profitability, this seems

to be an unfavourable practice. Rather, the company should carefully examine the possibility of recourse to sources like public deposit for working capital. Since it does not affect the permissible bank borrowing position as per Tandon Norms, the company can substitute this source for internal funds. The latter can be better utilized for building up capital formation which is very low at present.

6. There is a very narrow difference between the budgeted and actual working capital items for 1985-86. This implies that the actual working capital practice closely confirms with the budget and the budget is very effective. However, the element of pessimism in the preparation of the budget cannot be ruled out. This is evident in the 1986-87 budget figures, which reflect a higher investment in almost all working capital variables as compared to 1985-86. The budget share be optimistic and reflects bold efforts on the part of the organization to reduce investment in current assets without comparing its profitability.

7. It seems that ECIL does not plan its working capital requirements based on the operating cycle concept. Though the total operating cycle period has improved in the periods upto 1986, there are indications that it may go up in the future. This would be mostly due to a higher totaling period in the raw materials and work in process stage. It would be more effective if each product group compute the operating cycle and prepare its future working capital plan on the basis of the operating cycle period.

# 13

# Working Capital Efficiency under Inflation

## Theoretical Framework

The amount of sales revenue and working capital in any given period may be considered to consist of three components -

(a) The level obtained in the preceding period,

(b) Inflationary increase in it, and

(c) 'growth' achieved during the current period.

Of these components, inflationary increase is caused by price factors, which ruin exogenous to the company, and are not amenable to control. Separation of inflation - induced contents in sales revenue and working capital is necessary for effective control as it can only be so exercised on factors that are 'controllable'. Further, inter period efficiency in working capital management can be more meaningfully portrayed if the measure of efficiency is defined in a way that excludes inflationary increase.

We shall now try to isolate the inflationary increase in sales revenue by employing the Linked Chain Index (LCI) approach. Under the LCI approach price indices are formed with a changing base period, that is, immediately preceding period becoming the base for the period under consideration. Similarly the sales revenue is also related to the preceding period's level.

Let $P_t$ and $V_t$ represent the unit price of a finished product and volume of the product sold during period 't'. Sales revenue during period 't' is $S_t$. then,

$$S_1 = S_0 + S_0 \frac{(P_1 - 100)}{100} + g_1$$

$$S_2 = S_1 + S_1 \frac{(P_2 - 100)}{100} + g_2$$

$$S_t = S_{t-1} + S_{t-1} \frac{(P_t - 100)}{100} + g_t$$

'g' refers to the growth. This idea behind the decomposition of sales revenue into three components is to isolate the 'growth' in its distinguished form inflationary increase. Growth is period 't' can be obtained as

$$g_t = S_t - S_{t-1} - S_{t-1} \frac{(P_t - 100)}{100}$$

If we have access to price and volume data can readily obtain the growth value in period 't' as $(V_t - V_{t-1}) \times P_t$. This analysis is equally applicable to working capital also. The same price indices are assumed to be relevant for working capital also.

Then, $S_t = S_{t-1} + I_t^S + g_t^S$ for sales, and

$W_t = W_{t-1} + I_t^W + g_t^W$ for working capital, where :

$I_t^S = S_{t-1} \frac{(P_t - 100)}{100}$, the inflationary increase in sales and

$I_t^W = W_{t-1} \frac{(P_t - 100)}{100}$, the inflationary increase in

**Working Capital**

One way of viewing the issue of efficiency in working capital management is to compare the actual level of working capital for a period with the predetermined standard for the level of operations achieved. This may perhaps be viewed as absolute efficiency. It is generally considered that working capital turnover (defined as the ratio of sales revenue to working capital) or its reciprocal (i.e., working capital to sales ratio) adequately reflects the efficiency in working capital management. Other factors being the same, the higher the turnover, the greater would be the ROI, and the higher the degree of efficiency in working capital management. Alternatively, the lower the working capital management. In this analysis we take the working capital to sales ratio as an indicator of efficiency.

Working capital to sales ratio may be considered in four different ways. These can be grouped as absolute ratios and marginal ratios. Both absolute and marginal ratios can be either inflation adjusted of inflation unadjusted. These are as follows :

1. Working capital/sales revenue;

$$W_t / S_t$$

2. Incremental working capital/incremental sales revenue ;

$$(W_t - W_{t-1}) / (S_t - S_{t-1})$$

3. Working capital-inflationary content in working capital/Sales Revenue-Inflationary content in sales revenue;

$$(W_t - I^W_t) / (S_t - I^S_t)$$

4. 'growth' in working capital/growth in sales revenue;

$$(I^W_t / I^S_t)$$

The first ratio is the conventional working capital to sales ratio. From the point of view of control it is at a comparative disadvantage as it fails to netout inflationary increases from both working capital and sales revenue. Formulation (3) is superior to (1) as inflationary increases are netted out.

Marginal ratios, given by formulations (2) and (4) provide an idea of working capital to sales ratio at the margin. Since the marginal or incremental levels are much smaller than the total levels considered underformulations (1) and (3), one can reasonably expect wider fluctuations in the marginal ratios. Further these ratios can be negative also. Marginal ratios have to be interpreted taking into consideration not only the magnitude of the ratio but also the direction of change in both the working capital and sales revenue.

## Empirical Analysis

An attempt has been made here to apply the principles given in the earlier section to real life cases. Data on working capital and sales revenue are obtained from the published financial statements of some companies operating successfully in the Indian Corporate Sector. Since considerable amount of complicated calculations are involved, a computer utility called electronic spreadsheet is used. A five year period is chosen for the study from 1980 to 1984. Sales revenue figures are taken gross of excise duty. Working capital is defined in the conventional manner is the excess of current assets over current liabilities.

Relevant price indices are obtained from RBI Bulletins which have 1961-62 as the base year. No when a company's accounting year does not correspond with the financial year used for the price indices.

The price indices obtained are converted into Linked Chain Indices. For this purpose, each year's index is expressed as a percentage of the preceding year's index. The spreadsheet equations, final results are tabulated in Table 13.1.

**Table 13.1**

**Monitoring Working Capital Efficiency Under Inflation**

**Method Used : Linked Chain Indicates Approach**

**Name of the Company : BHEL**

| Year | Price Index (RBI Bulletin) | Sales Revenue | Price Index (LCI) | Increases in Sales (IS) | Inflationary Component | Growth Component | Working Capital (WC) | Increase in WC (IWC) | Inflationary Component | Growth Component | Working WC/ Sales | Capital IWS/ IS | Sales Inflation Adjusted WC/ Sales | Ratios Growth in WC/ Growth in Sales |
|---|---|---|---|---|---|---|---|---|---|---|---|---|---|---|
| 1999 | 205.00 | 79016.00 | 0.00 | 0.00 | 0.00 | 0.00 | 39031.00 | 0.00 | 0.00 | 0.00 | 0.00 | 0.00 | 0.00 | 0.00 |
| 2000 | 219.70 | 94639.00 | 107.17 | 15623.00 | 5666.03 | 9956.97 | 46368.00 | 7337.00 | 2798.81 | 4538.19 | 0.49 | 0.47 | 0.49 | 0.45 |
| 2001 | 226.70 | 117916.00 | 103.19 | 23277.00 | 3015.35 | 20261.65 | 52271.00 | 5903.00 | 1477.36 | 4425.61 | 0.49 | 0.25 | 0.44 | 0.22 |
| 2002 | 240.80 | 132472.00 | 106.22 | 14556.00 | 7333.99 | 7222.01 | 45536.00 | –6734.99 | 3251.09 | –9986.08 | 0.44 | –0.45 | 0.34 | –1.37 |
| 2003 | 256.40 | | 106.48 | | 8582.07 | | | | 2950.01 | | | | | |

## Working Data

| Name of the Industry | Type | Year | Price Index | Sales. Rs. Amt (in lakhs) | Working Capital (in lakhs) |
|---|---|---|---|---|---|
| 1 | 2 | 3 | 4 | 5 | 6 |
| 1. National Textile Corporation, (Andhra Pradesh, Karnataka Kerala and Maharashtra | Cotton Textile | 1995 | 191.2 | 5527 | 2217 |
| | | 1996 | 209.66 | 456 | 2390 |
| | | 1997 | 226.5 | 6562 | 2518 |
| | | 1998 | 231.7 | 7096 | 1265 |
| | | 1999 | 244.2 | 8199 | 2407 |
| | | 2000 | 252.3 | 8044 | 2115 |
| 2. The Fertilizers Corporation of India Limited | Fertilizers | 1997 | 260.6 | 8337 | 2649 |
| | | 1998 | 278.8 | 17680 | 352 |
| | | 1999 | 277.7 | 24970 | 10700 |
| | | 2000 | 262.5 | 32515 | 6481 |
| 3. Steel Authority of India | Iron-steels & Ferro-Alloys | 1995 | 256.2 | 153353 | 48776 |
| | | 1996 | 265.3 | 199598 | 62221 |
| | | 1997 | 315.3 | 218798 | 72852 |
| | | 1998 | 378.8 | 264859 | 104988 |
| | | 1999 | 409.8 | 305389 | 115141 |
| | | 2000 | 467.2 | 314771 | 81653 |
| 4. Bharat Earth Movers Limited | Transport Equipment | 1995 | 218.8 | 9856 | 5184 |
| | | 1996 | 253.8 | 12007 | 7375 |
| | | 1997 | 289.9 | 8791 | 8278 |
| | | 1998 | 307.9 | 22193 | 10223 |
| | | 1999 | 312.3 | 33510 | 16987 |
| | | 2000 | 320.0 | 38263 | 24423 |

### Working Data

| Name of the Industry | Type | Year | Price Index | Sales. Rs. Amt (in lakhs) | Working Capital (in lakhs) |
|---|---|---|---|---|---|
| 1 | 2 | 3 | 4 | 5 | 6 |
| 5. Hindustan Machine Tools Limited | Non-electrial Mechinary | 1995 | 211.6 | 16845 | 6391 |
| | | 1996 | 238.9 | 18275 | 8147 |
| | | 1997 | 271.2 | 18834 | 9822 |
| | | 1998 | 288.9 | 26046 | 12812 |
| | | 1999 | 310.0 | 26856 | 14201 |
| | | 2000 | 315.9 | 32941 | 16859 |
| 6. Bharat-Electronics Limited | Electrical Machinery | 1995 | 196.7 | 7638 | 3641 |
| | | 1996 | 287.4 | 8295 | 4806 |
| | | 1997 | 212.5 | 6891 | 5392 |
| | | 1998 | 226.3 | 12844 | 6420 |
| | | 1999 | 239.6 | 14228 | 8256 |
| | | 2000 | 249.4 | 15493 | 9918 |
| 7. Electronic Corporation of India Limited | Electrical Machinery | 1995 | 196.7 | 3406 | 1854 |
| | | 1996 | 287.4 | 3899 | 2272 |
| | | 1997 | 212.5 | 3484 | 1795 |
| | | 1998 | 226.3 | 5806 | 2511 |
| | | 1999 | 239.6 | 6675 | 3460 |
| | | 2000 | 249.4 | 7235 | 3572 |
| 8. Bharat Heavy Electricals Limited | Electrical Machinery | 1995 | 196.7 | 66154 | 25350 |
| | | 1996 | 287.4 | 74048 | 34822 |
| | | 1997 | 212.5 | 81227 | 39031 |
| | | 1998 | 226.3 | 94639 | 46368 |
| | | 1999 | 239.6 | 117916 | 52271 |
| | | 2000 | 249.4 | 132472 | 45536 |

## Working Data

| Name of the Industry | Type | Year | Price Index | Sales. Rs. Amt (in lakhs) | Working Capital (in lakhs) |
|---|---|---|---|---|---|
| 1 | 2 | 3 | 4 | 5 | 6 |
| 9. Hindustan Cables Limited | Electrical Machinery | 1995 | 196.7 | 4983 | 299 |
| | | 1996 | 287.4 | 5638 | 3791 |
| | | 1997 | 212.5 | 6885 | 3782 |
| | | 1998 | 226.3 | 8616 | 4140 |
| | | 1999 | 239.6 | 10327 | 5866 |
| | | 2000 | 249.4 | 12499 | 6456 |
| 10. Mazagon Dock Limited | Transport Equipment | 1995 | 218.8 | 2272 | 3256 |
| | | 1996 | 253.8 | 5358 | 2966 |
| | | 1997 | 289.9 | 8605 | 2576 |
| | | 1998 | 307.9 | 10367 | 6646 |
| | | 1999 | 312.3 | 9610 | 6830 |
| | | 2000 | 320.0 | 20780 | 8050 |
| 11. Hindustan Antibiotics Limited | Fertilizer | 1995 | 165.0 | 1643 | 889 |
| | | 1996 | 268.7 | 1739 | 1345 |
| | | 1997 | 260.6 | 2152 | 1665 |
| | | 1998 | 278.8 | 2788 | 1366 |
| | | 1999 | 277.7 | 3681 | 2676 |
| | | 2000 | 262.5 | 3190 | 2886 |
| 12. Indian Telephone Industries | Electrical Machinery | 1995 | 196.7 | 9293 | 6807 |
| | | 1996 | 287.4 | 10937 | 8037 |
| | | 1997 | 212.5 | 8631 | 9640 |
| | | 1998 | 226.3 | 15726 | 11602 |
| | | 1999 | 239.6 | 18205 | 15843 |
| | | 2000 | 249.4 | 21211 | 19597 |

From the four columns under the head 'working capital' to sales ratio we can draw some broad conclusions as to the relative efficiency of working capital management.

### Information Sheet for Working Capital Efficiency under Inflation

1. ***Technique Employed :*** Linked Chain Indices approach
2. ***Inputs :*** (a) Year
   (b) Price Index (RBI Bulletin)
   (c) Sales Revenue
   (d) Working Capital
3. ***Computer utility used :*** Electronic Spread Sheet
4. ***How to run the utility :***

**Step 1** : Load Floppy disc and input

**Step 2** : Press RETURN key twice.

**Step 3** : Load file
*Command :* /L
*Input :* File name as 'WORK'
And press RETURN twice.

**Step 4** : Read the files in column B

**Step 5** : If you want to input your own data, input in relevant fields (A12 : A18, B12 : B18, C12 : C18, of the faculty.

**Step 6** : Otherwise to calculate the various columns give command by pressing SHIFT & !

**Step 7** : To obtain printed results given the following command C
Command 1 : /0
Command 2 : p
Command 3 : B
Command 4 : A1 : K20 & L1 : O20

### Date Sheet for Working Capital Efficiency under Inflation

| Item | Description | Cell No | Value |
|---|---|---|---|
| 1. | Name of the company | C3 | |
| 2. | Year | A12 to A18 | |
| 3. | Price Index (RBI Bulletin) | B12 to B18 | |
| 4. | Sales Revenue | C12 to C18 | |
| 5. | Working Capital | H12 to H18 | |

# 14

# Case on Cash Management in Okey Engineering Company Limited

## Introduction

The Okey Engineering Co. Ltd., a state level public enterprise, is a nationally well known company manufacturing consumer durables and light engineering goods such as bus bodies, cooking ranges, gas cylinders, fans, voltage stabilizers and household steel furniture. It also fabricates steel structural and supplies mainly to public sector undertakings and the defence department.

The Okey was established in the early forties as a partnership company which was subsequently converted as a public limited company. It was managed in early years by managing agents. The state government took over the company ultimately about two decades ago.

The company is a leading engineering unit in the state with labour force in the neighbourhood of 4,000. It had grown from the very beginning around the concept of multi-product.

Over the year the financial position of Okey has deteriorated steadily and the company has been going through substantial stress and strain. On March 31, 2003, as against the paid-up capital of Rs. 203 lakhs, the accumulated loss of the company amounted to Rs. 69 lakhs. However, the turnover of the company has been improving slowly but steadily over the years.

## Growth Pattern

The turnover of the company increased from Rs. 277 lakhs in 1981-82 to Rs. 1623 lakhs in 2002-2003, an increase of nearly 500 per cent. The company has been able to achieve the growth by sustained efforts as increasing the share of the market by offering wide variety in products as well as in their range. The growth was also made possible by diversification pressures aimed at and achieved. The gross block of the company increased from Rs. 118 lakhs to Rs. 32 lakhs while the net block increased from Rs. 66 lakhs to Rs. 103 lakhs during the period under reference as can be seen from Table 14.1.

**Table 14.1 Growth Pattern**

**(Rs. in Lakhs)**

| | Gross Block | Net Block | Gross Turnover | Capital Turnover (Gross) |
|---|---|---|---|---|
| 2000-2001 | 118.00 | 66.00 | 277.00 | 2.00 |
| 2002-2003 | 312.00 | 103.00 | 1623.00 | 5.00 |
| Increase in Percentage | 164 | 56 | 488 | 150 |

## Operating Performance

(i) A detailed analysis of the operation performance of the company for the last four years is given in Appendix - I. The conciliated balance sheets of the company as at the end of the past four years are given in Appendix-II.

(ii) Capacity utilization in the company has been unfortunately low due to variety of reasons. Therefore the company has been able to increase its sales performance only marginally during the last few years and suffered a setback in 2001-02. Relaxation in the standards with regard to quality had also contributed to underutilization of its capacity. As on 2002-03, the capacity utilisation in the company's main unit was as shown in Table 14.2.

**Table 14.2 Capacity Utilisation**

| | Installed Capacity | Production | Utilisation |
|---|---|---|---|
| Consumer Durables | 60,000 Nos. | 30,000 Nos. | 50% |
| Steel Fabrication | 10,000 Nos. | 6,000 Nos. | 60% |

The underutilization of the company has had telling affect on the profitability of the company. The operation performance given in Appendix - I, indicates the impact of the pattern of capacity utilization over the years. While the manufacturing overheads accounted for only 6.9 per cent of the sales revenue, direct labour costs account for 11.9 per cent administrative overheads (including indirect labour) account for 14.2% and selling and distribution overheads accounted for 11.3% during the year 2002-2003. Due to high incidence of fixed costs (direct labour, administrative overheads and art of selling overheads aggregating 53%), the profit before interest and taxes has been reduced to a meager 1.6% of sales revenue of 2002-2003.

**Table 14.3 Sales Vs Cost of Production**

**(Rs. in Lakhs)**

| Net Sales | | | | Cost of Production | |
|---|---|---|---|---|---|
| For the Year | | Increase over the Previous Year | % Increase or % Decrease | For the Year | As % of Sales |
| 1999-2000 | 1072 | – | – | 720 | 67.2 |
| 2000-2001 | 1331 | 258.93 | 24 | 919 | 69.0 |
| 2001-2002 | 1063 | (–) 267.15 | (–) 20 | 868 | 81.7 |
| 2002-2003 | 1380 | 317.45 | 30 | 959 | 69.5 |

It may be noted that the principal reasons for the increase in the cost of production has been the steady increase in labour cost. In some years the spurt in sales was more than offset by higher percentage of increase in cost of production mainly due to wage rise.

(iii) The State Bank of Hyderabad (SBH) is the banker to the Okey Engineering, whose margin requirements are given in the next page. The SBH is not happy with the company for various resons one of which is its failure to adhere to repayment schedule in respect of clean cash credit. Therefore, the ban has been charging a penal rate of 17% on the entire clean cash credit of Rs. 45 lakhs. The rate of interest charged on other advances is 15.5%. Further the SBH has been charging a high rate of 16.5% on amounts exceeding the norms suggested by Tandon Committee. The company's existing credit limits and borrowings are as follows :

**( Rs. in lakhs )**

| | Credit limits | Extent to which limits were utilised as on 31.7.2003 |
|---|---|---|
| Cash credit | 450 | 445 |
| Bills Discount | 90 | 15 |
| Cash Credit Clean | 45 | 50 |
| | 585 | 510 |

The margin required by SBH as well as the estimation of working capital for **1986-87** in respect of various items is as follows :

| | Margin required | Total Amount | Bank Finance | Margin |
|---|---|---|---|---|
| Receivables | only up to 15 Lakhs are financed by SBH | 296 | 15 | 281 |
| Finished Goods | 30% | 198 | 139 | 59 |
| Work-in-progress | 35% | 99 | 64 | 35 |
| Raw Materials | 30% | 216 | 151 | 65 |
| Stores and Spares | 35% | 25 | 16 | 9 |
| Salaries and Wages | 100% | 30 | - | 30 |
| Other Expenses | 10% | 19 | - | 19 |
| Excise Duty on Showroom Stock | 30% | 30 | 21 | 9 |
| Advance Against Order | 30% | 40 | 28 | 12 |
| Sub-Total | 300% | 953 | 434 | 519 |
| Less: Trade Creditors | | 80 | - | 80 |
| Total | | 873 | 434 | 439 |

The company's working capital requirements are influenced by the seasonal demand for refrigerators. It has to build up stocks between August and January to meet the increased demand between February and July.

Considerable amount of receivable are overdue from some of the public sector enterprises due to disputes arising out of deviations and delayed deliveries of structural A sum of Rs. 119 lakhs has been outstanding for a period of more than one year.

The industry average of interest on net sales as per the study by the Reserve Bank of India of large size companies for 1986-87 ranged from 2.5 to 3.4 per cent, of net sales. The Company's record has been adverse when compared to these norms. The debts equity position of the company is as given below:

| 1999-2000 | 2000-2001 | 2001-2002 | 2002-2003 |
|---|---|---|---|
| 6.3 : 1 | 3.9 : 1 | 6.4 : 1 | 5.9 : 1 |

The Okey Engineering has been finding the going with the banker pretty tough and feels frustrated in managing its day-to-day operations. The banker on the other hand insists that he has stretched his neck far beyond the acceptable norms and the company must restore the imbalance in its debt-equity position to a reasonable and acceptable position. The banker is likely to be pacified if debt-equity position is brought to 2.5:1.

## Required

1. Calculate the different cash transmutation ratios for 2002-2003 as indicated in Appendix-6.
2. What steps would you suggest to improve the short and long-term effectiveness of cash management?
3. Can the stand of banker for a change in the capital structure be justified ?

## APPENDIX - I

### Okey Engineering Company Limited
### Operating Performance From 1999-00 to 2001-02

(Rs. in Lakhs)

| Particulars | 1999-00 | | 2000-01 | | 2001-02 | | 2002-03 | |
|---|---|---|---|---|---|---|---|---|
| | Amount | % to Sales | Amount | % to Sales | Amount | % to Sales | Amount | % to Sales |
| 1. Nett Sales | 1072 | 100 | 1331 | 100 | 1063 | 100 | 1380 | 100 |
| 2. Cost of Production/Sales | | | | | | | | |
| (a) Raw material consumed | 576 | 53.7 | 701 | 52.7 | 640 | 60.1 | 747 | 54.1 |
| (b) Stores & Spares | 20 | 1.9 | 26 | 1.9 | 22 | 2.1 | 26 | 1.9 |
| (c) Power & Fuel | 20 | 1.9 | 25 | 1.9 | 32 | 3.0 | 31 | 2.2 |
| (d) Direct Labour | 106 | 9.9 | 140 | 10.5 | 150 | 14.6 | 164 | 11.9 |
| (e) Other Manufacturing expenses | 14 | 1.3 | 15 | 1.1 | 24 | 2.0 | 13 | 1.0 |
| (f) Depreciation | 15 | 1.4 | 12 | 0.9 | 12 | 1.0 | 12 | 0.9 |
| Sub-total | 751 | 70.1 | 919 | 69.0 | 880 | 82.8 | 993 | 72.0 |
| Add opening : | | | | | | | | |
| Work-in-process (WIP) | 41 | 3.8 | 72 | 5.4 | 72 | 6.8 | 84 | 6.1 |
| Loss closing WIP | 72 | - 6.7 | - 72 | - 5.4 | - 84 | 7.9 | - 118 | 8.6 |
| Cost of Production | 720 | 67.2 | 919 | 69.0 | 868 | 81.7 | 959 | 6.5 |
| Add opening F.G. | 138 | 12.9 | 161 | 12.1 | 232 | 21.8 | 308 | 22.3 |
| Less closing F.G. | - 161 | - 15.1 | - 232 | - 17.4 | - 308 | - 29.0 | - 217 | - 15.7 |
| Cost of Sales | 697 | 65.0 | 848 | 63.7 | 792 | 74.5 | 1050 | 76.1 |
| Cross Profit | 375 | 35.0 | 483 | 36.3 | 271 | 25.5 | 330 | 23.9 |
| 3. Administrative and General Expenses | | | | | | | | |
| (a) Salaries, wages etc. | 155 | 14.5 | 207 | 15.6 | 202 | 19.0 | 196 | 14.2 |
| (b) Selling and Distr. Exp. | 15 | 1.3 | 13 | 1.0 | 6 | 0.6 | 7 | 0.5 |
| (c) Commission, Rebates etc. | 78 | 7.2 | 111 | 8.3 | 81 | 7.6 | 109 | 7.9 |
| (d) Advertisement | 13 | 1.3 | 15 | 1.1 | 13 | 1.2 | 14 | 1.0 |
| (e) Others | 18 | 1.7 | 19 | 1.4 | 13 | 1.2 | 26 | 1.9 |
| Sub-total (3) | 279 | 26.0 | 365 | 27.4 | 315 | 29.6 | 352 | 25.5 |
| Cross Profit before Interest | 96 | 9.0 | 118 | 8.9 | - 44 | - 4.1 | - 22 | - 1.6 |
| Interest | 60 | 5.6 | 104 | 7.8 | 106 | 10.0 | 102 | 7.4 |
| Profit before tax | 36 | 3.4 | 14 | 1.1 | - 150 | - 14.1 | - 124 | - 9.0 |
| Other Income | 23 | 2.1 | 20 | 1.5 | 64 | 6.0 | 112 | 8.1 |
| Net Profit | 59 | 5.5 | 34 | 2.6 | - 86 | - 8.1 | - 12 | - 0.9 |
| Prior period adjustments | | | (–) 2 | | (↓) 6 | | (+) 2 | |

## APPENDIX - II

### Okey Engineering Company Limited
### Balance Sheet

(Rs. in Lakhs)

| Particulars | 1999-00 | 2000-01 | 2001-02 | 2002 |
|---|---|---|---|---|
| **Assets** | | | | |
| Fixed Assets: Gross Block | 290 | 294 | 303 | 312 |
| Less depreciation to date | 173 | 185 | 197 | 209 |
| Net Block | 117 | 109 | 206 | 103 |
| Investments | ----- | 15 | 32 | 32 |
| Current Assets, Loans & Advances | | | | |
| Cash & Bank balance | 38 | 15 | 13 | 22 |
| Inventory: Finished Goods | 161 | 232 | 308 | 217 |
| Work-in-Progress | 72 | 72 | 84 | 118 |
| Raw material | 257 | 381 | 12 | 198 |
| Stores and spares | 18 | 12 | 18 | 36 |
| Sub-Total | 546 | 712 | 635 | 591 |
| Receivables | 154 | 216 | 247 | 262 |
| Loans & Advances | 88 | 100 | 85 | 116 |
| Total Current Assets | 783 | 1028 | 967 | 969 |
| Development Expenses | ----- | ----- | ----- | 3 |
| Total Assets | 905 | 1152 | 1105 | 1107 |
| **LIABILITIES** | | | | |
| Share Capital | 124 | 184 | 184 | 203 |
| Capital Reserve General | 11 | 11 | 5 | 5 |
| Reserve & P&L A/c. | (–) 11 | (+) 21 | (–) 59 | (–) 69 |
| Net work | 124 | 216 | 130 | 139 |
| **LOANS** | | | | |
| Bank Borrowing-Cash and Credit | 506 | 579 | 552 | 510 |
| Fixed Deposits | ----- | 10 | 43 | 32 |
| Short-term Loans as Advance | 10 | 49 | 24 | 20 |
| Total Loans | 516 | 638 | 619 | 562 |
| **CURRENT LIABILITIES & PROVS** | | | | |
| Sundry Creditors | 56 | 65 | 50 | 95 |
| Deposits from Dealers | 10 | 12 | 15 | 14 |
| Others | 199 | 123 | 149 | 146 |
| Total Current Liabilities | 265 | 200 | 214 | 255 |
| 4-year Current Warranty Receipts | ----- | 98 | 142 | 151 |
| Total Liabilities | 905 | 1152 | 1105 | 1107 |

## APPENDIX - III

### Ratios for Evalution of Cash Management

| Ratio | | Formula for Computation |
|---|---|---|
| **I. Liquidity Ratios** | | |
| (a) Current Ratio | : | $\frac{\text{Current Assets}}{\text{Current Liabilities}}$ |
| (b) Quick Ratio (Acid-test Ratio) | : | $\frac{\text{Current Assets - Inventory}}{\text{Current Liabilities}}$ |
| (c) Working Capital to | : | $\frac{\text{Working capital}}{\text{Capital employed}}$ |
| **II. Turnover Ratios** | | |
| (d) Cash Turnover | : | $\frac{\text{Sales}}{\text{Cash}}$ |
| (e) Raw Material Turnover | : | $\frac{\text{Cost of Materials Consumed}}{\text{Average Raw - material inventory}}$ |
| (f) Work-in-Progress Turnover | : | $\frac{\text{Cost of goods manufactured}}{\text{Average work - in - Process}}$ |
| (g) Finished Goods Turnover | : | $\frac{\text{Cost of Goods sold}}{\text{Average work - in - Process}}$ |
| (h) Debtors Turnover | : | $\frac{\text{Sales}}{\text{Average Sundry Debtors}}$ |
| (i) Loans and Advances | : | $\frac{\text{Sales}}{\text{Loans and Advances}}$ |
| **III. Structural Ratios** | | |
| (j) Cast | : | $\frac{\text{Cash}}{\text{Current Assets}}$ |
| (k) Inventories | : | $\frac{\text{Inventories}}{\text{Current Assets}}$ |
| (l) Sundry Debtors | : | $\frac{\text{Debtors}}{\text{Current Assets}}$ |
| (m) Loans and Advances | : | $\frac{\text{Loans and Advances}}{\text{Current Assets}}$ |

# APPENDIX - IV

## Operating Cycle

### Method of Computation

1. **Raw Material and Stores and Shares** : $\dfrac{\text{Average inventory of raw materials and stores}}{\text{Average materials and stores consumption per}}$

2. **Sundry Creditors** : $\dfrac{\text{Average trade creditors}}{\text{Average purchase per day}}$

3. **Work-In Process** : $\dfrac{\text{Average work - in - progress}}{\text{Average cost of production per day}}$

4. **Finished Goods** : $\dfrac{\text{Average inventory of finished goods}}{\text{Average cost of sales per day}}$

5. **Sundry Debtors** : $\dfrac{\text{Average book debts}}{\text{Average sales per day}}$

The average inventory on book debts can be arrived at by finding the mean between the relevant opening and closing balances for the year. The average dividing the respective annual figures by 365.

### Operating Cycle for Selected Companies in Engineering Industry Based on Published Accounts for 2003 - 04

| Period of Operating Cycle | Ashok Leyland Ltd. DAYS | Tho Indian Tube Co. Ltd. DAYS | Kirlo-skar Pneuna-tic Co. Ltd. DAYS | Kanani Engine-ering Cor. Ltd. DAYS | Preci-sion Bear-ings India DAYS | Metal Box Compny of India Ltd. DAYS | Pro-mier Auto-mobiles Ltd. Ltd. DAYS | Bajaj Auto Ltd. DAYS |
|---|---|---|---|---|---|---|---|---|
| Raw materials | | | | | | | | |
| Stores inventory | 28 | 101 | 185 | 241 | 436 | 134 | 74 | 150 |
| Less : Trade credit | 63 | 35 | 105 | 284 | 127 | 72 | 92 | 62 |
| | (35) | 66 | 80 | (143) | 309 | 62 | (18) | 88 |
| Work-in-Progress | 7 | 25 | 24 | 19 | 75 | 17 | 16 | 15 |
| Finished Goods Inventory | 66 | 22 | 9 | 56 | 22 | 18 | 31 | 2 |
| Sundry Debtors | 23 | 27 | 105 | 157 | 163 | 43 | 21 | 11 |
| Total Objective Cycle | 61 | 140 | 218 | 89 | 569 | 140 | 50 | 116 |

## APPENDIX - V

### Permissible Bank Finance
### Tandon Comittee Methods

(Rs. in Lakhs)

| Description | 1999-00 | 2000-01 | 2001-02 | 2002-03 |
|---|---|---|---|---|
| **Current Assets :** | | | | |
| Raw-material, stores & spares | 275 | 393 | 230 | 234 |
| Work-in-Process | 72 | 72 | 84 | 118 |
| Finishred Goods | 161 | 232 | 308 | 217 |
| Total Inventory | 508 | 697 | 622 | 569 |
| Receivables | 154 | 216 | 247 | 262 |
| Loans and Advances | 88 | 100 | 85 | 116 |
| Cash and bank balance | 38 | 15 | 13 | 22 |
| Total Current Assets | 788 | 1028 | 967 | 969 |
| **Current Liabilities :** | | | | |
| Bank borrowings - cash credit | 506 | 579 | 552 | 510 |
| Fixed deposits | ---- | 10 | 43 | 32 |
| Short-term loans and advances | 10 | 49 | 24 | 20 |
| Sundry Creditors | 56 | 65 | 50 | 95 |
| Deposits from dealers | 10 | 12 | 15 | 14 |
| Others | 199 | 123 | 149 | 146 |
| Total Current Liabilities | 781 | 838 | 833 | 817 |

## APPENDIX - VI

### The State of Art of Cash Management at Okey Engineering Company Limited

### A Trend Analysis from 1990-00 to 2002-03

| | | 1999-00 | 2000-01 | 2001-02 | 2002-03 |
|---|---|---|---|---|---|
| **I. Liquidity Ratios :** | | | | | |
| A. Current ratio | | 1.01 : 1 | 1.23 : 1 | 1.16 : 1 | |
| B. Quick ratio | | 0.36 : 1 | 0.39 : 1 | 0.41 : 1 | |
| C. Working capital to capital employed | Percentage | 5.6 % | 63.5 % | 55.8 % | |
| **II. Turnover Ratios :** | | | | | |
| D. Raw material turnover | No.of times | | 2.18 | 2.13 | |
| E. Work-in progress turnover | " | | 12.76 | 11.13 | |
| F. Finished goods turnover | " | | 4.32 | 2.93 | |
| G. Sundry debtors turnover | " | | 7.19 | 4.59 | |
| H. Loans and advances turnover | " | | 13.31 | 12.50 | |
| I. Cash turnover | " | | 88.73 | 81.76 | |
| **III. Structural Ratios :** | Percentages | | | | |
| Cash | | 4.8 | 1.5 | 1.3 | |
| Inventories | | 64.5 | 67.8 | 64.3 | |
| Receivables | | 19.5 | 21.0 | 25.6 | |
| Loans and advances | | 11.2 | 9.7 | 8.8 | |

### Operating Cycle Trend of Eng. Co From 2000-01 to 2002-03

| | Days | Days | Days |
|---|---|---|---|
| Raw material, stores and spares | 168 | 172 | |
| Less sundry creditors | (–) 26 | (–) 41 | |
| | 142 | 131 | |
| Work-in-progress | 29 | 33 | |
| Finished goods inventory | 85 | 124 | |
| Sundry debtors | 51 | 80 | |
| | 307 | 368 | |
| Number of cycles | 1.19 | 0.99 | |

## APPENDIX - VII

### Okey Engineering Company Limited Funds Flow Trends 1999-00 to 2002-03

| | 1999-00 | | 2000-01 | | 2002-03 | |
|---|---|---|---|---|---|---|
| | Sources | Uses | Sources | Uses | Sources | Uses |
| **A. Internal Generation** | | | | | | |
| Additions to reserves and surplus | 32 | --- | --- | 80 | | |
| Depreciation | 12 | --- | 12 | --- | | |
| | 44 | --- | 12 | 80 | | |
| **B. Longeterm Sources and Uses** | | | | | | |
| Additions to share capital | *60 | --- | --- | --- | | |
| Additions to fized assets | --- | 4 | --- | 9 | | |
| Capital reserve | --- | --- | --- | 6 | | |
| Investments | --- | 15 | --- | 17 | | |
| | 60 | 19 | --- | 32 | | |
| **C. Shortterm Sources and Uses** | | | | | | |
| Cash | 23 | 41 | 2 | --- | | |
| Finished goods | --- | 71 | --- | 76 | | |
| Work-in-process | --- | --- | --- | 12 | | |
| Raw material and stores and spares | --- | 118 | 163 | --- | | |
| Receivables/Sundry debtors | --- | 62 | --- | 31 | | |
| Loans and advances | --- | 12 | 15 | --- | | |
| Bank borrowings (cash credit) | 73 | --- | --- | 27 | | |
| Fixed deposits | 10 | --- | 33 | --- | | |
| Shortterm loans and advances | 39 | --- | --- | 25 | | |
| Sundry creditors | 9 | --- | --- | 15 | | |
| Deposits from dealers | 2 | --- | 3 | --- | | |
| Others | | 76 | 26 | --- | | |
| 4 year warranty receipts | 98 | --- | 44 | --- | | |
| | 242 | 327 | 286 | 186 | | |
| Total | 358 | 358 | 298 | 298 | | |

*Sales tax arrears to State Government converted into equity.

## APPENDIX - VIII

## An Extract from the Report of the Study Group to Frame Guidelines for followup of Bank Credit

### Working Capital Gap and Bank Finance

A banker's main role as a lender will be to supplement the borrower's resource in carrying a reasonable level of current assets in relation to his production requirements.

Stated differently, we would expect the borrower to hold only a reasonable level of inventory and receivables, according to the norms. The total current assets will be carried partly by a certain level of credit for purchases and other current liabilities, funds required to carry the remaining current assets may be called the working capital gap which can be bridged partly from the borrower's owned funds and long-term borrowings and partly by bank borrowings.

In the context of the above approach gap, i.e., total current assets less current liabilities other than bank borrowings and finance a maximum of 75 per cent of the gap; the balance to come out of long-term funds, i.e., owned funds and term borrowings.

(i) Bank can work out the working capital gap, i.e., total current assets less current liabilities other than bank borrowings and finance a maximum of 75 per cent of the gap ; the balance to come out of long-term funds, i.e., owned funds and term borrowings.

(ii) Borrower to provide for a minimum of 25 per cent of total current assets out of long-term, i.e., owned funds plus term borrowings. A certain level of credit for purchases and other current liabilities will be available and the bank will provide the balance. Total current liabilities inclusive of bank borrowings will not exceed 75 per cent of current assets.

(iii) Same as (ii) above, but excluding core current assets from total current assets on the theory that core current assets should be financed out of long-term funds, i.e., owned funds plus borrowing.

The three alternatives may be illustrated taking the following examples of a borrower's financial position projected at the end of the next year.

The last method would mean the banker financing unto a maximum of 75 per cent of the working capital gap of 220, i.e., 165 and the borrower providing at least 55 out of his long-term funds, i.e., owned funds plus long-term borrowings. This method gives a uniform current ratio of 1:1.

The second method would mean the borrower financing a minimum of 25 per cent of total current assets (92) through long-term funds and the gap, i.e., maximum of 128 (273 – 150), will be provided by the bank. This will give a current ratio of at least 1.3:1.

The third method would mean a further reduction in bank borrowing and strengthening of the current ratio.

### Suggested Norms for Inventory and Receivables

| Industry | Raw materials (including stores and other items used in the process of manufacture) | Stocks - in process | Finished goods | Receivables and bills purchased and discounted |
|---|---|---|---|---|
| (1) | (2) | (3) | (4) | (5) |
| (i) Cotton and Synthetic Textiles | 2 Cotton (Bombay and Ahmedabad areas)<br>3 (Eastern areas Bihar, Orissa, West Bengal and Assam)<br>2½ (Other than the above areas)<br>2 Other raw materials | ¾ (Composite site textile mills)<br>½ (other mills) | 2 ½ (combined) | 2 ½ (combined) |
| (ii) Man-made Fibre | 1½ | ½ | 1 ¾ (combined) | 1 ¾ (combined) |
| (iii) Jute textiles | 2½ | ¼ | 1 (For domestic sales)<br>1½ (For (exports) | 1½ |
| (iv) Rubber Products | 2 | ¼ | 1 ¾ (combined) | 1 ¾ (combined) |
| (v) Fertilisers | | | | |
| (a) For nitrogenous plants | ¾ (Units near near rofinery)<br>1½ (Units away from refinery) | Negligible | 1 (Where stocks are in plant site)<br>1½ (Where stocks are also in uncountry centres) | 1¼ |

| (1) | (2) | (3) | (4) | (5) |
|---|---|---|---|---|
| (b) For phosphotic plants | 2 (Units in port port areas) | Negligible | 1 (Where stocks are in plant site) | 1¼ |
| | 3 (Units away from port areas) | | 1½ (Where stocks are also in up-country centres) | |
| (vi) Pharma-ceuticals | 2¾ | ½ | 2 | 1¼ |
| (vii) Dyes in Dyestufis | 2¼ | | ¾ | 2¼ |
| (viii) Basic Industrial Chemicals | 2¾ | ¼ | 1 | 1¾ |
| (ix) Vegetable and Hydro-gonatod oils | 1 | Negligible | ——— ¾ ——— | |
| (x) Paper | 2-6 Bamboo and Wood (To be built up in stages from November to May and there after to be brought down) | | 1 (For con-trolled sales and<br>¼ (For free sales) | ¾ |
| | 2¼ Chemicals | | | |
| (xi) Cement | 2¼ Cypsum | ½ | ——— 1 ——— | |
| | 1¼ Limostone | | | |
| | ¾ Coal | | | |
| | 1½ Packing materials | | | |
| (xii) Engineering Automobiles and Ancillaries | 2¼ | ¾ | ——— 2 ½ ——— | |
| (xiii) Engineering consumer durables | 2 | ¾ | ——— 2 ½ ——— | |

| | | | | | |
|---|---|---|---|---|---|
| (xiv) | Engineering Ancillaries (other than Automobile Ancillaries) and component suppliers | 2 | ¾ —————— | 2 ½ —————— | |
| (xv) | Engineering Machinery Manufacturers and other Capital Equipment suppliers (other than Heavy Engineering)** | 2¾ | 1¼ —————— | 3 ½ —————— | |

**Notes :**

(i) Raw mateirals are expressed as so many months consumption. They include stores and other items used in the process of manufacture.

(ii) (a) Stocks-in-process are expressed as so many months cost of production.

(b) In individual cases, the bank may deviate from the norm for stocks-in-process if it is satisfied that the actual process time involved in any particular an uit, say, in view of the nature of production, past experience and technology employed, is more than the norm suggested.

(iii) (a) Finished goods and receivables are expressed as so many months cost of sales and sales respectively. These figures represent only the average levels. Individual items of finished goods and receivables could be for different periods which could exceed the indicated norms so long as the overall average level of finished goods and receivables does not exceed the amounts as determined in terms of norm.

# 15

# Project Appraisal and Finance

## PRELIMINARIES

1. A project has, by its very nature, to be time bound exercise and any delay in its implementation is bound to disturb the profitability projections and make its success difficult of achievement. Bearing this in mind, the Development Financial Instructions (DFIs) start the appraisal of the project as soon as the application is received with a view to complete the exercise of appraisal and section within 2 to 3 months.
2. After the initial decision to support a particular proposal is taken (this could be an internal exercise in the case of state level DFIs while at the all-India level, a senior executives meeting of all the institutions takes the decision.) A preliminary scrutiny of the application is done and details of additional information required are listed and called for. A site visit is planned; this is utilized to have an on-the-spot study of the location, the utilities and to have discussion with the promoters on various aspects that were known from the study.
3. After the site visit, the detailed appraisal is taken up. While the promoter, in his applications, professes that the unit would yield the products and the surplus on the basis of certain assumptions, the DFI gives the projects a second and independent look. The purpose of such a look is to spot the

weak areas and strengthen them so as to ensure success of the venture. Appraisal provides the basis on which the DFI takes an investment decision and while various well-defined techniques are applied during appraisal, the entire exercise is flexible, as weightages have to be given to different factors in each case. Primarily the appraising team of officers have to rely on their own knowledge and experience and, where necessary, draw upon information available from reputed source.

4. Any project which seeks institutional support has to pass the following five tests :
   (a) Managerial competence;
   (b) Technical feasibility;
   (c) Commercial viability;
   (d) Economic justification; and
   (e) Financial soundness

In analyzing these, the team should not be deterred by weak areas and to devise ways and means to rectify the same and render the project fit for support by the DFI.

## DETAILED APPRAISAL

1. *Management*

   The most input for the success of a business enterprise is the management and it is also the most difficult to evaluate. There are varieties of tools which can be applied to appraise the other four tests mentioned in the previous para but to assess management, there are no mathematical formulae or doctrinal approaches. This is particularly true of a new unit where the qualities of management will be tested after the unit goes into production. The entrepreneur who has conceived the project is basically an enterprise builder whereas the quality expected of a manager is the ability to develop an organization. Evaluation of management would call for assessment of

   (i) The Entrepreneurs;
   (ii) The Board of Directors;
   (iii) The Committee of Management;
   (iv) The Chief Executive and
   (v) The Departmental Heads

A study of the entrepreneur's background and discussions with him during appraisal would reveal whether he has, in abundance, the major traits commonly associated with builders of enterprises. (An entrepreneur can be defined as a person who has ingenuity, a good intellect, a healthy sense of self, an inner drive and a clear-cut purpose. He has more belief in hardwork than luck. He has effervescent optimism. He is a positive thinking achiever interested in opportunities. He has a vision.)

2. The Board of Directors should ideally be a well-knit multi-disciplinary team of peers acting as a well-motivated consultative group and offering guidance (which will be readily sought if they are effective) on how to improve the overall performance of a unit. The composition of the Board is arrived at, after considering the requirements of the proposed unit; where two or more technocrats join to promote a project. DFIs insist on appointment of an independent Chairman or Chief Executive in order to avoid any possible (and likely) difference of opinion among the promoter group and where the unit is in the joint sector or co-operative sector. DFIs insist on a pre-disbursement condition of broad-basing the Board by induction-independent professionals.
3. The committee of management which consists of a majority of independent directors and DGI nominees invests decision-making with collective thinking and imports the advantage of participative management. This is particularly useful in cases where the Chief Executive is not found to be up to the mark or the Board of Directors is tilted in favour of the promoters.
4. The Chief Executive, by virtue of his position, is the key person in ensuring the success of the venture. Even weak or inert Board will be activated by him by bringing vital issues before it for discussion; at the other end, a Chief Executive below par may not implement the decisions of the Board. The important qualities of a Chief Executive are dynamism, leadership, result-orientedness and the ability to deliver the goods and to absorb constructive criticism even from juniors. He should be a member of the Board of Directors or attend the Board meetings invariably as permanent Special Invitee; he should not be changed without prior consultation with the Board/DGI (This condition is warranted, for instance, in public sector units where the Chief Executive could be a government servant subject to frequent transfer).
5. The Chief Executive is assisted by departmental heads that should constitute a team of requisite expertise, adequate delegated authority and awareness about accountability. In suitable cases, it is desirable that some of the departmental heads are trained in the Collaborator's plant.

### Technical Feasibility

1. Technical appraisal involves a scrutiny of the manufacturing process, size of the plant, location, layout, and selection and procurement of plant and machinery, availability of inputs and schedule of implementation.
2. Where alternate process are available to manufacture the particular product, the process proposed by the entrepreneurs should be justified; if a new process is preferred to a conventional one, its workability at least on pilot scale should be established and the process-suppliers may be pursued to participate in the equity of the unit. In the case of collaborations, the track-record of the collaborator should be ascertained. The collaboration agreement

should cover all aspects, the more important of which are the nature of support in planning and designing, selection and procurement of equipment, installation operation, training, export, royalty and guarantees covering production performance.

3. The economic size of the unit would be related to the process, raw material availability, the capital investment and the market potential. The economic size of a plant will change with changes in technology, market etc. To cite an example, a spinning mill should have at least 25,000 spindles to be viable now, as against an economic size of 12,000 spindles a decade ago.
4. The location of the project is to be justified from the availability of a majority of the important factors such as land, raw materials, utilities, effluent disposal, transport, labour, social infrastructure etc. The requirement of land depends on the plant layout and buildings to be constructed with some provision for future expansion. The load-bearing capacity of land should be ascertained. The location should be near the raw material source if it is bulky or perishable. Prospects of regular supply of raw material should be examined and this would need examination of government policy in the case of import of raw materials as well as prospects of manufacturing the same locally; development of ancillaries should also be planned in suitable cases. Utilities like power are very important in the case of power-intensive, (mini-steel aluminium) and continuous process industries (glass, cold storage). While availability of water assumes importance for manufacture of paper, effluent disposal has to be examined very carefully and the agency putting up the system and the equipment to be used, call for detailed scrutiny. Transport facilities have an important bearing on the location (eg : near railway station with a siding if needed in the case of heavy raw materials/finished goods and near harbor for export-oriented units) while labour, though available in plenty, if not of adequate quality and abroad.
5. The selection of plant and machinery would be related to the manufacturing process and size of the unit, balancing of the different stages of production and the need to cover, if possible, the scope of changing the product-mix to suit the market. Equipment for utilities should necessarily match the needs of the main plant and machinery. The layout should take into consideration the process flow, flow of materials, storage needed for raw materials, consumable and finished goods, inter-linkging storage areas and material-handling facilities and aspect relating to environment and effluents.
6. Procurement of plant and machinery could be a turnkey basis or by placing orders on different suppliers. The lowest lender is so much a guiding factor as the quality of the machinery and level of technology, the track record of the supplies, delivery/payment terms and performance guarantee which consists of mechanical guarantees are, however, no substitute for the exercise involving proper selection of the quality of the machinery and assessment of the reputation of the supplier.

In case promoter proposes to fabricate any part of machinery, the expertise available with them and the cost as compared to new machinery should be discouraged unless justified by long delivery period of new machinery and certified, by a competent Indian authority about a reasonable long economic life of 10 to 15 years.

6. The schedule of implementation involves listing of all the possible activities from project identification to commercial production and projecting the time to be taken for each activity on a bar-chart. These would help indicate periods when more than one activity will be in progress and would also help improper planning and gearing up the material and human resources to attend to those activities. All activities should invariably be included and the time to be taken should be reasonable for completion of each activity.

8. In concluding that a project is technically feasible, some important questions should be satisfied; these are

   (i) The right process for the cost and the market.
   (ii) Plant and machinery suited for the process and the quality and quantity of finished goods.
   (iii) Technology and side effects like harmful effluents and environment pollution.
   (iv) Layout to ensure smooth flow and safety and
   (v) The whole concept designed for optimum utilization of land, labour and equipment

## Commercial viability

1. Market is one aspect which is not properly covered by most of the entrepreneurs except in a value manner and hence its appraisal calls for great care. Some of the tools of appraisal are :

   (i) Import substitution method
   (ii) Past trend method
   (iii) End-use method
   (iv) Correlation and regression and
   (v) Export.

   The source of information on market consist of the primary sources of information on market consist of the primary sources (the consumers, trade competitors, government sources, research/financial institutions, consultants etc.) and secondary source (published material relation to the product and the market, published by institutions, newspapers, journals and annual reports of companies). The information furnished by the entrepreneurs can be compared with the information available from the above sources.

2. While examining the market, the prevailing conditions like proces situation, controls, if any, by government and capacity utilization of competitors should be examined. Low capacity utilization could be caused by raw material scarcity or other bottlenecks or due to obsolete equipment or could even be deliberate. The whole exercise of appraisal should aim at getting a clear picture of demand and supply.
3. After studying the prevalent conditions the future prospects with reference to demand and supply (which would increases if other units are in various stages of production and would enter the market) have to be examined. Any gap between demand and supply need not necessarily establish the market for the product as other aspects like pricing, advertising and selling polices play important roles. Industrial goods call for proper distribution system and advertising. Selling arrangements through established agencies are advantageous but if the promoters are interested in such agencies, such arrangements are not normally allowed except for short periods in special circumstances.

## Economic Justification

1. The object of this exercise is to ascertain whether the project in question is the best for investment of the economic resources for optimum use from the national angel. The techniques used are
   (i) Economic Rate of Return (ERR)
   (ii) Effective Rate of Production (ERP)
   (iii) Exchange Ratio or Domestic Resources Cost (DRC)
2. ERR is used to determine the real cost of a project without taxes, subsidies etc. as they represent only transfer payments within the economy and hence tend to distort the value. The capital cost, the working capital and operation components are revalued using international prices, conversion factors and shadow wage rates respectively. ERR is the rate of discount which equates the economic costs of a project and is considered good.
3. ERP measures the net protecting available to a particular stage of manufacturing and its need arises from the fact that tariffs, import control and subsidies, used to encourage domestic industries might have already afforded protecting some of the inputs of the project in question.

   The formula used for ERP is $\frac{\text{DVA} - \text{WVA}}{\text{WVA}} \times 100.$

   Indicating the excess of the value added at domestic prices (DVA) over the value added at world price (WVA) as a percentage of WVA.
4. DRC indicates the amount of investment, in rupees, in a project to earn or save and indicates the long-term comparative advantage enjoyed by a country in the production of a particular product. In computing DRC, sales realization

is taken at border prices (c.i.f. for import substitute product and f.o.b for an exportable product). By deducting foreign exchange costs (c.i.f. costs of imposed inputs and charges of foreign capital employed) net savings or earnings from project capital are obtained. The cost in terms of domestic resources (rupee cost net of taxes) divided by net foreign exchange savings or earnings (in terms of dollars and expressed in terms of rupee per dollar) gives DRC.

5. DRC should be compared with the shadow for exchange rate or acceptable cut-off foreign exchange rate (15%); if it is less, the project will be worthwhile but if more it indicates that domestic resource cost is high and it may not be economically justifiable to spend scarce domestic resource to earn foreign exchange at any cost . However reliable up to 30% higher than the prevailing exchange rates may be assumed to give allowance for the inability of the new unit to earn foreign exchange at or below the official rate.

**Financial Soundness:**

1. Financial forecasting is to be done by the promoters to assess the profitability to decide on how to finance, to use as a controlling device and finally to gain the confidence of DFIs and the investing public.
2. Financial appraisal would start with checking the cost of the project and ensuring that all items are included and the cost is reasonable. The various items are
    (i) Land and land developments;
    (ii) Factory and non-factory buildings, other civil works and all attendant expenses like architect's fees;
    (iii) Plant and machinery, imported and indigenous inclusive of all charges (important duty, sales tax, freight, insurance, etc., and essential spares);
    (iv) Technical know-how and engineering fees including expenses of foreign technicians and training of Indian technicians abroad;
    (v) Miscellaneous fixed assets such as furniture, fixture, vehicles and other equipment (eg. fire fighting, effluent disposal);
    (vi) Preoperative expenses including interest and other expenses incurred during construction period;
    (vii) Preliminary, capital issue and mortgage expenses (stamp duty, registration and legal expenses);
    (viii) Initial working capital (margin money) and provision for cash losses in early years of operation;
    (ix) Start-up expenses necessary for starting the operations of the plant; and
    (x) Contingency provision of 10% on non-firm items of buildings and plant and machinery.

3. Appraisal of the above items is done with reference to various documentary evidence provided by the entrepreneurs and by inter-firm comparison; large variations have to be suitably explained. While verifying the cost of imported machinery, information may be obtained from foreign machinery journals or from our embassies. Preliminary and pre-operative expenses have to be checked with reference to the implementation schedule, the reasonableness of which should be first assessed. Margin money for working capital should include provision for holding large stocks of imported raw materials depending on their availability, country of origin, etc.

## Means of Finance (MOF)

1. The usual source of finance for a project can be broadly divided into equity and debt and equity can be further subdivided into promoter's contribution and other items of equity.
2. Promoters contribution would consist of the money brought in by the promoters by way of share capital and can also include the following;
   (i) Unsecured loans from promoters subordinated to the term loans with regard to rate of interest and repayment;
   (ii) Equity participation by collaborators;
   (iii) Equity from World Bank in high cost projects;
   (iv) Equity by state level DFIs in the case of joint sector projects and other projects where the DFIs give non-disposal and overrun undertakings;
   (v) Internal cash accruals of existing units; and
   (vi) Contribution to rights issue by existing shareholders including DFIs in the case of existing units.
3. The other items of equity are Ordinary Share Capital (other than what is brought in by the promoters). Preference Share Capital due for redemption after 3 years, premium on issue of shares, free reserves and surplus (less accumulated losses, arrears of depreciation, goodwill and miscellaneous expenses) Central/State subsidy and non-refundable deposits in the case of Co-operatives.
4. Debt would consist of long-term loans (in rupees and foreign currencies) and deposits including unsecured loans not subordinated to term loans, debentures (except that part which is compulsorily convertible to equity), deferred payments and preference shares redeemable within 3 years.
5. The proportion of debt and equity in the MOF of a project has to be acceptable as borrowed capital and own capital have to be serviced differently. The former is repayable as per a schedule while the latter is not ordinarily repayable; borrowed capital carries interest which is a pretax charge while

own capital has to be paid dividend from profits after tax. A proper mix of debt and equity would enable the unit to service both. The debt and equity ratio (DER) fixed from all projects is 2:1 (except for small scale industries for which it is 3:1) and it can be relaxed for high cost projects in the priority sector.

6. Certain norms are also prescribed for the promoter's contribution; it should at least be 22.5% of the project cost except in the following:
   (i) In the case of projects coming up in specified backward areas, it should be at least 20% of the project cost;
   (ii) In the case of projects prompted by technician entrepreneurs, it should be at least 17.5% of the project cost; and
   (iii) In the case of units coming up in non-industry districts, it should be at least 12.5% of the project cost

   It should be noted that the above levels represent the minimum amount of promoter's contribution and in case the promoters are able to bring in more funds, they should do so.

7. MOF does not merely mean typing up of the various sources of funds to finance the project. It should also be ensured that the funds would be no bottlenecks. Thus, the amount of subsidy should be advanced by the DFI (as this should be adjusted against the disbursement of subsidy). If a company were promoting a new project, it would be examined whether that company has invested (and locked up) its funds in any of its subsidiaries; it would not be advisable to assist such companies.

## Financial Projections

The financial projections, consisting of profitability estimates; cash flow estimates and projected balance sheets call for a careful examination and the assumption on the basis of which the projections have been made have to be verified (eg. assumption of a high-capacity utilization without a gradual build-up is justified in a new unit). Cost of production should include storage of scarce raw materials for a longer period than normal. The quantum of raw materials and utilities required for the production of the finished product of the estimated quantity and quality should be assessed carefully, as there is the crux of the whole exercise. Wages and salaries should be assuemd to increase by 5 annually. Insurance should cover against flood and earthquake. Repairs and maintenace should be commensurate with the type of industry; for example, it should be substantial for corrosive industries. Selling expenses would depend on the extent of market build-up needed. Administrative expenses should be kept down to avoid over-ostentation in the formative years but suitable administrative set-up including appropriate managerial support for the new entrepreneurs should be provided for sale price should be related to prices of alternate products and the international price. The implementation schedule should be carefully studied as the cost of the project would depend on timely implementation.

The cash flow statement aims at matching the inflow of funds with the out go and helps in fixing a reasonable repayment schedule for the loan. The debt servicing capacity of the unit should be measured; a DSCR (debt service coverage ratio) of 1.5:1 is acceptable to the DFIs.

The projected balance sheets tend to depict the status of the project at different future dates and are helpful in taking investment decisions.

A number of performance indicators are worked out to assess the intrinsic methods of the unit. Some of the important ones are briefly given below :

| | Indicator | Remarks |
|---|---|---|
| (a) | $\frac{\text{Capital employed}}{\text{Value of output}}$ | This ratio is useful for inter company comparision to appreciate economic significance of the project. |
| (b) | $\frac{\text{Capital employed}}{\text{net value added}}$ | Net value being net increase to national income, this ratio indicates the efficiency of the investment in increasing national income. |
| (c) | Percentage of (a) raw materials (b) salaries (c) interest to value of output | These indicate the comparative importance of the various items in the value of output. |
| (d) | $\frac{\text{Operating profit}}{\text{Sales}}$ | Measures profitability of sales. |
| (e) | $\frac{\text{Profit after tax}}{\text{Equity}}$ | Indicates the earnings on equity dividend should be lower than this so that reserves can grow. |
| (f) | Investment per worker and productivity per worker | These indicate cost of creating one job and the output therefrom |
| (g) | Break even point | This indicates the level of production where the sales cover the cost of production. |
| (h) | Unit cost of production | This is useful for inter-protect comparison |

| | | |
|---|---|---|
| (i) | Internal rate of return (IRR) | This is the rate of discount at which the present value of the net cash flow would be equal to the present value of capital expenditure. The IRR acceptable to DFIs is 15. In cases where IRR which is generally computed after tax, is below 15, IRR before tax called market rate of return (MRR) is worked out. If MRR is above 15, the project could be supported. |
| (j) | Sensitivity Analysis | This is used to determine the viability of the project in relation to slight changes in the assumptions of (i) critical inputs and (ii) inputs the cost of which cannot be correctly measured. If the analysis reveals raw material cost or selling price as critical factors, the unit should be strengthened by long term agreements regarding supply of raw material or sale of the products. |

***Conclusion :***

The purpose of appraising a project and fixing the MOF is to asses the viability of the project by means of the various tools and methods discussed above and to determine a resource-mix designed to help in implementing the project. The final decision on investment is based on the assessment and acceptability of the various risks in the project.

# GUIDELINES FOR CALCULATION OF RATIOS

## Part A

### Cannotations of terms used

**1. Debt (Term Liabilities)**

(a) Long-term loans/deposits (repayable after 12 months) including interest bearing unsecured loans from Government/Government agencies, promoters etc.

(b) Debentures (Convertible debentures to be treated as debt (except that part of debentures which are compulsorily convertible into equity) until they are converted, irrespective of the period of maturity.

(c) Deferred payment

(d) Preference shares due for redemption between 1 and 3 years.

**2. Equity (owned funds)**

(a) Ordinary share capital

(b) Preference share capital due for redemption after 3 years.

(c) Premium on issue of shares.

(d) Free reserves and surplus less accumulated losses, arrears of depreciation, goodwill and miscellaneous expenses (i.e. preliminary expenses etc.) Development rebate/investment allowance reserve, debenture redemption reserve, dividend equaliation reserve etc. Should also be treated as free reserves. Reserves created out of revaluation of assets should not be taken as free reserves.

(e) Amount of Central/State subsidy.

(f) Long-term interest-free unsecured loans from State Government or Government agencies (such as sales tax loans etc.) and promoters, usually subordinated to institutional loans (if not subordinated, such loans may be created as debt).

(g) Non refundable deposits in the case of co-operatives.

**3. Current Assets**

(a) Stocks of raw materials

(b) Stores

(c) Work-in-progress

(d) Finished goods

(e) Bad debts including debts on account of bills discounted

(f) Bill and other receivables

(g) Loans and advances

(h) Pre-paid expenses (such as advance payment of tax)

(i) Cash and deposit with banks

*Note :* Investments are not to be included in current assets.

**4. Current Liabilities**

(a) Sundry creditors

(b) Unpaid dividends, provision for taxation

(c) Provision for taxation

(d) Bank borrowings for working capital including bills discounted.

(e) Unsecured loans/deposits to the extent not treated as debt or equity.

(f) Preference shares redeemable within one year.

(g) Other current liabilities and provisions.

**5. Stocks of Finished Goods**

Closing stocks of finished goods.

**6. Annual sales (net sales)**

Income from sale of finished goods, net of excise duty, *less* discounts and returns. Non-operating income need not be included in net sales; however, such income should be shown separately to form part of turnover.

**7. Receivables**

The amounts of receivables and/or sundry debtors as given in the Balance Sheet, including bills discount sheet, including bills discounted.

**8. Stocks of raw materials**

Closing stocks of raw materials, chemical and bought-out components.

**9. Consumption of raw materials :**

Opening stock *plus* purchases made during the year *minus* closing stock of raw materials, chemicals and bought-out component.

**10. Net Block**

Net fixed assets (gross fixed assets *minus* depreciation) *plus* capital work-in-progress. Arrears of depreciation, if any to be accounted for in full while preparing the analysis of Balance Sheets and Profit and Loss accounts, even if not provided for in the accounts and shown as arrears (if necessary, give a suitable footnote).

**11. Net Worth**

(a) Equity share capital (paid-up value)

(b) Preference share capital (paid-up-value)

(c) Free reserves (i.e. reserves created out of revenue profits and not set aside specifically to meet depreciation, taxation or any other known liability, contingency or commitment): development rebate/ invest allowance reserve, debenture equalization reserve etc and Central/ State subsidy should be treated as free reserves. Reserves created by revaluating of assets should not be taken as free reserves.

(d) Surplus (if any in profit and loss account)

(e) Deduct from sum-total of (a to d) intangible assets, goodwill etc. and deficit (if any) in Profit and Loss account.

**12. Gross Profit**

Profit *before* interest, depreciation and tax.

**13. Operating Profit**

Profit *after* interest, and depreciation but *before* tax.

**14. Net Profit**

Profit after interest, depreciation and tax but *including* other income.

**15. Capital Employed (to be computed at the beginning of the year)**

(a) Net worth (as given at 11 above)

(b) Debentures

(c) Long-term loans including interest-free unsecured loans form State Government, government agencies etc.

(d) Deferred credits

(e) Short-term loans such as bank borrowings etc.

(f) Unsecured loans and deposits.

**16. Cost of Production**

(a) Cost of raw materials, chemicals, component and stores

(b) Utilities

(c) Labour and plant overheads

(d) Other factory overheads
(e) Administrative expenses
(f) Sales expenses
(g) Royalty and know-how payable.

**17. Value of output**

Net sales realization (net of excise duty and returns) *plus* value of closing stock. So finished goods and work-in-process *minus* value of opening stock of finished goods and work-in-process.

**18. Gross value added**

Value of output *minus* cost of raw materials, fuel, power, water and other direct material input like consumables, stores and spares etc. (Net value add equals gross value add *minus* depreciation).

**19. Variable Cost (for calculating break-evenpoint)**

(a) Raw materials
(b) Bought-out component, chemical etc.
(c) Stores and spares
(d) Utilities (power, water, fuel etc.)
(e) Packing materials
(f) Interest on working capital borrowings
(g) Direct selling expenses
(h) Royalty (variable)
(i) Other expenses varying proportionately with output
(j) Contingencies relating to the above items.

**20. Fixed and Semi-Variable Cost (for calculating break-even point)**

(a) Wages and salaries
(b) Factory and plant overheads
(c) Repairs and maintenance
(d) Administrative expenses
(e) Interest on term liabilities
(f) Selling expenses (other than variable items)
(g) Fixed know-how fees/royalty payments
(h) Depreciation
(i) Contingency relating to the above items.

## Part - B

## Interpretation of Ratios

***Balance Sheet Ratios***

(i) Debt-equity ratio $= \dfrac{\text{Term liabilities}}{\text{Owned funds}}$

This ratio denotes the relationship between long-term debts and owned of a company and helps in assessing the capital gearing.

*The following points may be noted while working out debt-equity ratio:*

(a) In the case of existing companies having investements in other companies the extent to which such investements are considered to be non-realizable, may be deducted from the amount of equity. Whether an investement is non-realizable or not should be decided taking into account various relevant factors.

(b) Free reserves would mean reserves created out of revenue profits and not those set aside specifically to meet depreciation, taxation or any known liability, contingency or commitment. Reserves created by revaluation of assets should not be treated as free reserves.

(c) Debt-equity ratio should not be expressed in terms of percentage but as a ratio showing equity as 1 and calculating debt up to one decimal point. Also expression of the ratio in the reverse order may be avoided.

(d) Debt-equity ratio may be worked out as on the date of completion of a project both for new as well as expansion cases.

(ii) Current ratio $= \dfrac{\text{Current assets}}{\text{Current liabilities}}$

This ratio is an indicator of a company's liquidity position and ability to meet the current obligations.

*Note :* Current ratio should not be expressed in terms of percentage but as a ratio showing current liabilities as i and calculating current assets up to one decimal point.

(iii) Percentage of stocks of finished goods

$$= \frac{\text{Closing stockfinished goods}}{\text{Net sales}} \times 100$$

This ratio reflects the funds blocked in finished goods in relation to sales. Quick turnover of stocks (or as low ratio of finished goods to sales) is an indicator of good management of production, sales and stock of finished goods.

(iv) Percentage of receivables to annual sales

$$= \frac{\text{Receivables and / or sundry debtors including bills rediscounted}}{\text{Net sales}} \times 100$$

The ratio points to the average period of conversion of sundry debtors to cash i.e. the number of days' credit enjoyed by sundry debtors or the credit period allowed and thus the money with sundry debtors.

*Note :* Since receivables would normally include excise duty element, the ratio may be calculated on the basis of turnover including excise duty and where the elements of excise duty is significant, a specific mention may be made.

(v) Percentage of stocks of raw materials to annual consumption

$$= \frac{\text{Closing stock of raw material, chemicals and components}}{\text{Consumption of raw materials, chemicals and components}} \times 100$$

The ratio revealing the cost structure is an indicator of stocks of raw material to annual consumption and indicates the efficiency in inventory management.

(vi) Ratio of new block to equity $= \dfrac{\text{Net fixed assets}}{\text{Net worth}}$

This ratio indicates the extent to which the cost of fixed assets is met out of owned funds.

*Note :* As indicated earlier full depreciation should be accounted for, even if not provided in the accounts and shown as arrears.

(vii) Ratio of net block of debt $= \dfrac{\text{Net fixed assets}}{\text{Term liabilities}}$

This ratio indicated the extent to which cost of fixed assets is met out of borrowed long-terms funds.

(viii) Ratio of net block of long-term resources

$$= \frac{\text{Net fixed assets + long-term investements in subsidiaries etc.}}{\text{Net worth and term liabilities.}}$$

This ratio indicates the extent to which fixed assets and long-term investements in subsidiary companies are financed out of long-term resources, indicating the margin available for working capital.

## Profit and Loss Account Ratios

(i) Percentage of gross profit to sales = $\frac{\text{Gross profit}}{\text{Net sales}} \times 100$

The percentage of gross profit to sales indicates whether the average mark up on goods sold is sufficient normally to cover all expenses and to show a profit.

(ii) Percentage of operating profit to sales = $\frac{\text{Operating profit}}{\text{Net sales}} \times 100$

This ratio denotes the margin of profit on sales revealing the operational efficiency of the unit.

(iii) Percentage of profit (before tax and interest) to capital employed

$$= \frac{\text{Gross profit}}{\text{Capital}} \times 100$$

As an indicator of return on investment, this ratio helps in assessing the merit of the project.

(iv) Percentage of profit after tax (net profit) to equity capital

$$= \frac{\text{Profit after tax minus preference dividend for the year}}{\text{Equity share capital (paid up value)}} \times 100$$

As this ratio is intended to the return on equity share capital, dividend payable (for the year) on preference capital is deducted from profit after tax.

(v) Percentage of raw materials to cost of production

$$= \frac{\text{Cost of raw material components and consumable stores}}{\text{Cost of production}} \times 100.$$

(vi) Percentage of salaries and wages to cost of production

$$= \frac{\text{Salaries and wages}}{\text{Cost of production}} \times 100$$

(vii) Percentage of interest to value of output = $\frac{\text{Total interest}}{\text{Value of output}} \times 100$

Ratios at (v) and (vi) above indicate the cost components of raw materials and salaries and wages in the cost of production and the ratio (vii) indicates the share of interest payment to the value of output.

**Important performance Indicators**

(i) Gross value added to capital = $\frac{\text{Gross value added}}{\text{Capital employed}}$

(ii) Gross value added per worker

$$= \frac{\text{Gross value added}}{\text{Number of workers and salaried employees}}$$

(Productivity per worker)

(iii) Investment per worker = $\frac{\text{Capital employed}}{\text{Number of workers and salaried employes}}$

These ratios reflect the capital intensity and labour productivity of the project.

**Other Important Indicators**

(i) Debt Service Coverage Ratio : (DSCR)

$$= \frac{\text{Profit after tax + depreciation + interest on term borrowings and deferred credits}}{\text{Repayment (installments of on term borrowing and deferred credits + interest on term borrowings and deferred credits}}$$

This ratio indicates the ability of the unit to meet its liabilities by way of payment of installments of term loans and interest thereon from out-of-cash accruals and forms the basis for the fixation of the repayment schedule in respect of the term loans raised for the project. DSCR may be calculated as an average for the total loan amount covering the whole repayment period after commencement of production. Hence, the values in the denominator and the numerator of the ratio may be taken as the sum total to the values for the entire period of the proposed term loans commencing from the year in which commercial production starts. (DSCR may also be worked out as an average of the annual ratios).

(ii) Unit cost of production

The unit cost of production may be worked out in the enclosed proforma as shown in the cost sheet appearing in Chapter 17 on page 290 which are self-explanatory.

(iii) Break-even point (at installed capacity)

$$= \frac{\text{Fixed and semivariable cost capacity utilizatian}}{\text{Contribution (i.e. sales minus variable cost)}}$$

Break-even point is the point at which the cost of production equals sales realization. Normally , in the break-even analysis, costs are segregated into fixed, semi-variable and variable components. It is assumed that in the short run, the fixed and semi-variable costs would not materially vary with the level of output and that the variable costs vary directly with the level of output. In the case of highly capital-intensive projects like fertilizers, automobile tyres, paper, cement, petrochemicals etc., and break-even point may also be calculated on a can basis (i.e.) excluding depreciation as a cost factor.

An illustrative example for working out the break-even point is given in Chapter 17 on page 285.

(iv) Internal rate of return (IRR) (Financial)

Cash receipts are to be taken (after tax) for the life of the project (say 15 years) and the net cash flow be discounted. The gross cash receipts for the 15$^{th}$ year should also be taken into account the salvage value.

## ECONOMIC APPRASIAL

### A. Economic Rate of Return

The method to be adopted for calculation of economic rate of return can be best described as 'Partial Little-Mirrless'. This is because while international prices are used for valuation of tradable inputs and outputs, an attempt is to be made to independently estimate the true value of non-tradable, according to the procedure outlined by Little-Merrlees.

International prices are considered as the relevant economic prices and accordingly it is necessary to substitute market prices with international prices for all non-labour inputs or outputs. In the case of tradable inputs where international prices or social cost data are not directly available , a standard conversion factor of 1.5 is to be used. However, there are some items like electricity, transport etc. (non-tradable), for which it is not possible to obtain international prices. In these cases, the procedure is to break up the physical components of marginal inputs used in production of the goods (or supply of a service) into labour, tradable goods and residuals. The tradable components are revalued at international prices, and labour at its shadow-wage rate, to obtain marginal social cost of non-tradable.

In practice, the non-tradables are divided into several broad categories such as electricity, transport, buildings and construction, and conversion factors are used to value them a their social costs. These conversion factors break up non-tradable into their tradable and labour components as well as revalue the tradable components.

For calculating the Shadow Wage Rate, the following formula is to be adopted:

$$SWR = \frac{c-m-a}{1.5}$$

Where, 'c' is the industrial wage rate, 'm' is the marginal product of an average worker in rural areas (which is assumed to be equal to the median value of per capita consumption in rural area), and 'a' is the average savings rate out of wages (which is assumed to be equal to the provident fund contribution, Employees' State Insurance contributions and income-tax deducted at source, if any). In this formula, 1.4 is the conversion factor for deriving the social (or tradable) cost of the incremental consumption of labour due to industrial employment. On this basis, a SWR of 0.5 may be used.

To summarize, the capital cost of the project, the working capital requirements and the operating costs are disaggregated into tradable, non-tradable and labour components, which are revalued using international prices, conversion factors and shadow wage rate, respectively. The project benefits are also revalued at the international process. Finally the revalued components are segregated and the new flow is discounted to obtain the economic rate of return.

## B. Effective Rate of Protection

Effective Rate of Protection (ERP) expressed as a percentage is calculated by using the following formula:

$$\frac{\text{Value at domestic prices minus value at world prices}}{\text{Valued added at world prices}} \times 100$$

Data required for calculating ERP may be obtained in the form indicate below:

(Rs. per tonne/kg/unit)

| | At domestic prices | At world prices (c.i.f/f.o.b) |
|---|---|---|
| (a) Selling price (ex-factory) | | |
| (c) Input cost: | | |
| Traded | | |
| Non-traded | | |
| (d) Value added | | |

Calculations are made on the both Balassa (which keeps non-traded inputs as part of the total input cost) ad corden which included non-traded inputs in the value added methods.

All the necessary data for ERP calculations need to be obtained from applicant companies along with the information on other aspects of the proposal. Domestic selling price poses no problem (since selling price is always taken net of taxes and excise duties). The selling price is inclusive of a reasonable "world" or "international" price is the c.i.f. price of imports or f.o.b. price of exports. However, when information is not available from applicant companies, statistics on foreign trade or the relevant industry association may be consulted.

In calculating input costs, the following items of cost are to be treated inputs:

(a) Raw materials and stores

(b) Power, fuel and water

(c) Repairs and maintenance

(d) Selling expenses

(e) Part of administrative overheads.

The division between traded (for which domestic price and world price are calculated) and non-traded (for which only domestic price is calculated) items is to be made according to the following rules:

(a) *Raw materials and stores :* In general, these are taken as "traded" goods and their value at both domestic and world prices should be estimated. Occasionally, it may be difficult to obtain c.i.f. equivalent for raw materials procured indigenously. These should then be estimated according to import prices or ruling prices in important foreign markets.

Raw materials that, which are of low-value and high bulk also involve disproportionately high transport costs (e.g. silica, wood for pulp etc.) which are not actually imported are to be treated as non-traded ones.

(b) *Power, fuel and water :* These are usually "non-traded". However, in cases where fuel is in the form of oil and/or coal, and where fuel costs are a high proportion of the total cost (as in the steel and cement industries), an attempt should be made to value it at international prices also.

(c) *Repairs and maintenance :* This is again "non-traded". However, in rare cases, when it consists of substantial and recurring consumption of spares and chemicals (not included in raw materials) this is treated as "traded" and appropriate international prices should be obtained.

(d) *Selling expenses* : This is also "non-traded".

(f) *Factory supervision and factory overheads :* This usually include some labour costs and office expenses, such as rent, insurance, audit fees etc. All labour components in this cost item is excluded from computation of input cost (this goes into value added). Rent, insurance, and fees are considered non-traded.

## Calculation of Value-Added

This is the "residual". Value-added is simply selling price minus all input costs and consists of payments to capital and labour and depreciation.

## C. Domestic Resources Cost (DRC)

The domestic resource cost (per US dollar saved or earned) measures the international competitiveness of the product manufactured.

**Calculation of DRC**

DRC is calculated by using the following formula

$$\frac{\text{Domestic cost}}{\text{c.i.f. (or f.o.b.) price of output (minus) foreign exchange cost}} = \text{Exchange rate}$$

For calculating DRC, data may be arranged in the form indicated below:

(Rs. per unit)

| | Indigenous/domestic | Imported |
|---|---|---|
| **Operating Costs** | | |
| Raw materials | | |
| Power, fuel and water | | |
| Repair and maintenance | | |
| Consumable stores | | |
| Labour | | |
| Administrative overheads and expenses | | |
| Selling expenses | | |
| *Capital Costs* | | |
| Capital employed (at the charge of 10%) | | |
| Depreciation (at the rate of 6%) | | |

**Capital Employed**

Capital employed comprises total capital cost of project (fixed plus working capital). This is split into indigenous component and imported component. After deducting the element of taxes and duties (which are transfers) from the indigenous component (e.g, excise duties, sales tax) and imports components (e.g. customs duties), charge on capital employed is input at 10 percent.

**Depreciation**

Depreciation on capital is taken on the basis of 6 per cent and split into indigenous and imported parts depending upon the split up of capital in these segments. Calculating depreciation, all duties, land (ground and site development) costs, and 50% of preliminary pre-operative expenses are to be ignored.

**Operating costs**

Raw material cost is taken net of excise/custom/duty/other taxes. Also, wherever possible, discriminatory taxes on utilities and labour, such as power costs, income tax etc. are to be removed.

## I. Standard conversion factors for economic appraisal

*Note :* "TC" refers to the "tradable component of non-tradable item; "WC" to the labour or "wage component " and "RC" to the "residual component".

Similarly, "MP" is the market price – understood to include the price actually received for the product as well as the per unit cost of an item bought. "WP" is the "World Price" of a good taken to be either the c.i.f. or f.o.b. price of the item or the price of a non-tradable item obtained by revaluating its component parts at world shadow prices.

The Shadow Wage Rate (SWR) used is 0.50. This factor is applied to unskilled and semi-skilled labour only. Management wages are revalued at 0.80 skilled labour taken on par.

### 1. Capital Cost of Project

(a) Land — WP = MP / 1.5

(b) Buildings and construction — WP = TC + (WC × SWR)

(c) Transport — WP = TC + (WC × SWR)
= 0.65 MP + 0.245 MP × SWR

(d) Indigenous plant and machinery — WP = 0.70 MP

(e) Foundation and refection expenses — WP = TC + (WC × SWT)
= 0.50 MP × 0.70 + 0.50 MP × SWR

(f) Miscellaneous fixed assets — WP = 0.70 MP

(g) Technical know-how fees etc.:

(i) Overseas fees — WP = Actual foreign exchange cost + (Rupee cost/1.5)

(ii) Indigenous fees — WP = 1.5 MP

(h) Capital issue expenses and preliminary and pre-operative expenses:

(i) Capital issue and capitalized interest charges, mortgage fees and insurance (included under preliminary and preoperative expenses)

(ii) *Other preoperative expenses :* WP = 0.02 × Mp
WP = MP

**2. Working Capital**

(a) *Finished goods, work-in-progress, receivables :* $WP = \frac{\text{WP of output}}{\text{MP of output}}$

(b) *Raw materials and stores :* $\frac{WP = \text{WP of raw materials of stores}}{\text{MP of raw materials \& stores}}$

(c) *Working expenses :* $WP = TC + (WC \times SWR)$
$= 0.50\ MP + (0.50\ MP \times SWR)$

**3. Operating expenses**

(a) *Electricity, water, fuel and steam :* $WP = TC + (WC \times SWR)$
$= 0.50\ MP + (0.17\ MP \times SWR)$

(b) *Transport :* As above under capital cost of project

(c) *Administrative salaries :* WP = 0.80 MP

(d) *Repairs and maintenance :* WP = TC (wage component included under labour) = MP/1.5

(e) *Administrative and other overheads :* WP = MP/1.5

(f) *Selling expenses :* $WP = Tc + (WC \times SWR)$
$= MP^* / 1.5 \times 0.22 + (MP^* / 1.5 \times 0.49 \times SWR)$

* MP or 3% of sales expenses, whichever is less.

(g) *Royalty :*

(i) *Foreign :* At foreign exchange cost

(ii) *Indigenous :* WP = 1.5 MP

**II. Conversion factors for revaluating non-tradable**

Indigenous Equipment –Tradable value is 70% of actual price other equipment – Estimated on the basis imported (c.i.f) cost of similar assets.

Transport – 65 % is tradable and 25% is labour.
Land – Tradable value is actual price/1.4
Buildings & Construction – 50% is tradable and 25% is labor
Local Engineering and Other Fees – Tradable value is actual price × 1.5

*Banking Charges :* Tradable value is 2 per cent of actual interest paid
Pre-operative Expenses – Tradable value is 100 pe rcent of actual
Stock of finished Goods, Work-in-process, Receivables – Tradable value is:

$$\text{Actual} / \frac{\text{Domestic Price of Final Products}}{\text{World Price of Final Product}}$$

*Raw Materials & Stores :* Tradable value is actual amount divided by the weighted average difference between the c.i.f. price of raw materials and actual prices paid by project.

*Working Expenses :* 50% is tradable and 50% is labour

Electrical = Divide 'actual' by 1.4; tradable is 71 [percent of this labor is 13 per cent]

| | | |
|---|---|---|
| Administrative Salaries | – | Tradable value is 'actual' minus 20% |
| Repairs and Maintenance | – | Tradable value is actual/1.5 |
| Other overheads | – | Tradable value is actual/1.5 |
| Selling expenses | – | Divide 'actual (up to a maximum of 3% of sales) by 1.5. Tradable value is 22 per cent of this and labour is 49 per cent |

**III Rules for calculation of non-tradable**

(i) *Land :* The social value of land is the capitalized value of its marginal product at international prices. In principle, this should require an estimation of the marginal product of land in its alternative use for the life of the project. Instead of attempting this rather difficult and uncertain exercise, the actual market price of land representing the capitalized value of its marginal product at domestic prices may be assumed. The tradable value may be derived by applying the SCF of 1.5.

(ii) *Transport costs :* These are to be broken into tradable (T), labor (L) and residual (R) in proportion of 65 per cent, 25 per cent and 10 per cent.

(iii) *Buildings and constructions :* This may be broken down into T, L and R in proportion of 50 per cent, 25 per cent and 25 per cent.

(iv) *Engineering Fees :* Tradable values of fees paid to local engineering services may be obtained by multiplying the actual value of SCF of 1.5, This reveals that engineering fees in India are lower than abroad, and its tradable value is, therefore, higher than the actual market cost. Engineering and other fees paid to foreigners are valued at their actual foreign exchange cost.

(v) *Banking charges :* Banking costs, included in the project cost, normally consist of interest payments and insurance charges to the banks during construction period. Interest payments, of course have to be ignored for the purpose of rates of return calculation; however, it may be taken at 2 per cent of the actual interest as representing the cost of the services provided by the banking sector. This entire amount has been taken as representing social cost.

(vi) *Pre-operative expenses :* These consist of travel expenses and salaries of administrative personnel involved in promoting and setting up the entire amount under this head is to be assumed as a social cost.

(vii) *Administrative salaries :* The social cost of administrative salaries is assumed to be equal to total salaries minus taxes and provident fund contributions. It is to be assumed that here is no social benefit attached to the consumption of the administrative staff, and that their entire consumption is, therefore, social cost. Consumption may be taken at 80 per cent of salaries and the tradable value of their consumption can be assumed to be same as its domestic value.

(viii) *Repairs and maintenance and "other overheads" :* Tradable value has been derived by applying the SCF of 1.5.

(ix) *Selling expenses :* The marginal social cost providing this service has been obtained by applying the SCF of 1.5 to actual value (upto 3 percent of sales). The cost is to be broken down into T, L and R in proportion of 22:49:29 respectively.

(x) *Electricity :* The social marginal cost of supplying electricity to projects is to be estimated by dividing the actual values by a factor of 1.5. This cost is broken down into T, L and R in the proportion of 17:13:16.

# 16

# Capital Budgeting

## Non-Discounting Criteria

*Urgency :* Based on Judgement
Subjective Decision

*Payback period :* Where 'Product Obsolescence' and 'Technology Obsoloscence' are Fast this criteria will be useful.

## Accounting Rate of Return (ARI)

*ARI :* Average Profit after taxes over the life of the project

Average book investment during the life of the project after depreciation.

## Discounting Criteria

*Net Present Value (NPV)*

$$NPV = \sum_{t=1}^{n} \frac{At}{(1+k)^t} - I$$

or

$$NPV\ 2 = \sum_{t=0}^{n} \frac{At}{(1+k)^t}$$

Initial outlay indicated with - sign.

At = Net Cash Flow for the year 't'

k = Discounting factor (to take care of inflation and opportunity cost)

n = Life of the project

I = Initial investment

### Internal Rate of Return (IRR)

The value of 'k' when

$$I = \frac{At}{(1+k)^t}$$

### Interpretation of IRR

1. IRR represents rate of return on uncovered balance.
2. IRR represents the compound rate of return earned on initial investment for the life of the project. This implies that the firm reinvests intermediate funds at IRR.

Since the reinvestment of the intermediate funds at IRR may or may not be possible the first interpretation is more realistic.

### Profitability Index (PI)

$$PI = \frac{\frac{At}{(1+k)^t}}{I}$$

$$PI = 1$$

### Comparison Among Discounting Criteria

Normally NPV, IRR, and PI give similar ranking for projects.

The Ranking Tend to be different when

1. The shape of cash flows differ
2. The projects have substantially different costs
3. The projects have substantially different lives.

### Project Life Cycle Comparison

Physical life

Economic life

Common horizon approach

Optimisation Techniques can be used in Selecting Projects

## Project Risk and Uncertainty

*Risk* - Associated with losses uncertainity-Neutral.

*Project risk* - Situation where the likelihood of a particular consequence could be quantified.

*Project uncertainty* - Situation where the likelihood of a particular consequence cannot be quantified.

The distinction between risk and uncertainty is not very rigid.

## Assessment of Uncertainity

*Steps involved*

1. *Definition :* Through a sensitivity analysis, the key components are first identified. Uncertainties which could affect the values of these components are then listed. These uncertainties will have to be defined in terms of quantifiable measures.
2. *Structuring :* Two types.
   (a) Decomposition of the uncertain variables into smaller, simpler component which are easier to assess directly rather than complex ones.
   (b) Structuring for attaining technical advantage in assessment.
3. *Preliminary Assessment :* Assessing an uncertain variable consists of listing the possible values the variable can take and the associated chances. Mathematical models can be used for this purpose.
4. *Consistency Checks :* After preliminary quantification is done checking for consistency is essential.
5. *Revision, Modification and Refinement :* Basing on additional information obtained-revision, modification and refinement may be necessitated.

## Project Uncertainty and Risk Analysis

1. *Sensitivity Analysis*

Examining the magnitude of change in the NPV or the rate of return from the project for a small change in individual components.

*Limitations :*

(a) In larger or complex projects measuring the sensitivity of the NPV or rate of return to the changes in individual components is at best. A fragmentary approach which gives a partial view.

(b) The values of the variables are generally changed in an *ad hoc* manner. Systematic analysis is not followed.

2. *Decision Theory*

Offers a basis for analysing the risks, involves in investment decisions and helps the investor arrive at a decision under conditions of uncertainty.

3. *Simulation Analysis*

Sensitivity analysis indicates the sensitivity of the criterion of merit (NPV/IRR) to variations in basic factors. The decision maker would also like to know the likelihood of such occurrence. This information can be generated by simulation analysis.

*Steps Involved :*

(a) Identify the factors which have a bearing on NPV, IRR etc.
(b) Obtain the probability distribution of these factors.
(c) Select at random a value for each of these factors.
(d) Determine the NPV for the set of values obtained in step (c).
(e) Repeat steps (c) & (d) a very large number of times to get a very large number of values of NPV.
(f) Plot the frequency distribution of the NPV values obtained.
(g) Calculate the mean and standard deviation and other parameters of interest for this frequency distribution.

From the above the probability of NPV being some value can be calculated.

**Project Risk Profile**

| Market Volume | NPV (Rs. lakhs) | Probability | Remarks |
|---|---|---|---|
| 1000 | −0.41 | 0.10 | If fashions favour |
| 1200 | −0.25 | 0.25 | pastel shades |
| 1600 | 0.08 | 0.45 | |
| 2000 | 0.40 | 0.15 | Mixed trend |
| 2400 | 0.72 | 0.05 | If teenage market picks up |
| Weighted average | 0.0285 | | |

**Approaches for Incorporating Risk in Investment Decisions**

1. Risk adjusted discounting rate method

$$\text{NPV} = \frac{\text{At}}{t = 1(1 + k + d\,i)^t} - I$$

Where di = Adjustment factor for risk. If project under consideration to more risky than ongoing activities di = 0. If project under consideration less risky di = 0. If project as much risky as ongoing activities di = 0

2. Firm risk equivalence method. Here risk is supposed to change with time discount rate is adjusted for risk differential.

$$NPV = \frac{di + At}{t = 1(i + k)^{t}} - I$$

Lt = Firm risk equivalence coefficient for year t.

## Project Risk

*Practical Approaches*

1. Conservative estimate of revenues
2. Safety margin in cost figures
3. Flexible investment yardsticks
4. Acceptable over-all certainty index

| Factor | Certainty Index |
|---|---|
| Raw material availability | 70% |
| Power availability | 60% |
| Freedom from competetion | 80% |
| Overall certainity index | $= \frac{70 + 60 + 80}{3}$ <br> = 70% |

***Issues and Problems in Capital Budgeting***

1. Realistic Assessment (estimation) of project costs inclusion of all relavent costs including cost of infrastructure, provision of contigency, provision for cost escalation (inflation)
2. Realistic estimation of revenue basing on ___________
   Capacity Utilisation
   Market conditions
   Price
   Govt. policies
3. Discounting factor
   How realistic we are in considering the discounting factor
4. Sensitivity Analysis
   Are we systematic ?
5. Project Risk
   Are we identifying the risk factors ?
   Are we quantifying the risk ?
   Are we presenting the projects profiles with the associated risks ?

6. Management tools and techniques

   Are we taking advantage of the management tools like OR, computers to ensure that our investment decisions are correct ?

7. Database & Documentation

   Are we making any efforts at the micro or macro levels to document the data and information to provide us the data base for taking advantage of management tools & techniques ?

8. Sharing information & experiences, are we moving in the right direction ?

9. Are we using managment tools and techniques as aids for decision making

   OR

   Are we using management tools and techniques to rationalise our decisions ?

# 17

# Cost Concepts and Break Even Analysis

The term *cost* consists of essentially three ingredients in respect of particular product viz., materials, labour and overheads. The term also is equally useful not only for particular product but also services and operations. The utility of cost identification in respect of, particularly, in the matters of price fixation, profit planning, cost reduction, cost control, productivity etc.

The term cost in divided into the following components.

(i) Director material

(ii) Direct labour

(iii) Direct overheads

(iv) Prime cost : ____________

[(i) + (ii) + (iii)] ____________

(v) Indirect material

(vi) Indirect labour

(vii) Indirect overheads

(viii) Factory cost ____________

[(iv) + (v) + (vi) + (vii)] ____________

(ix) Selling and distribution costs

(x) Cost sales ________________

[(viii) + (ix)] ________________

(xi) Add profit ________________

Selling : rice : ________________

In order to have better control over controllable and uncontrollable costs are again divided into three types viz., fixed costs, and variable costs which are discussed below :

**Diagrammatic Representation of Total Cost**

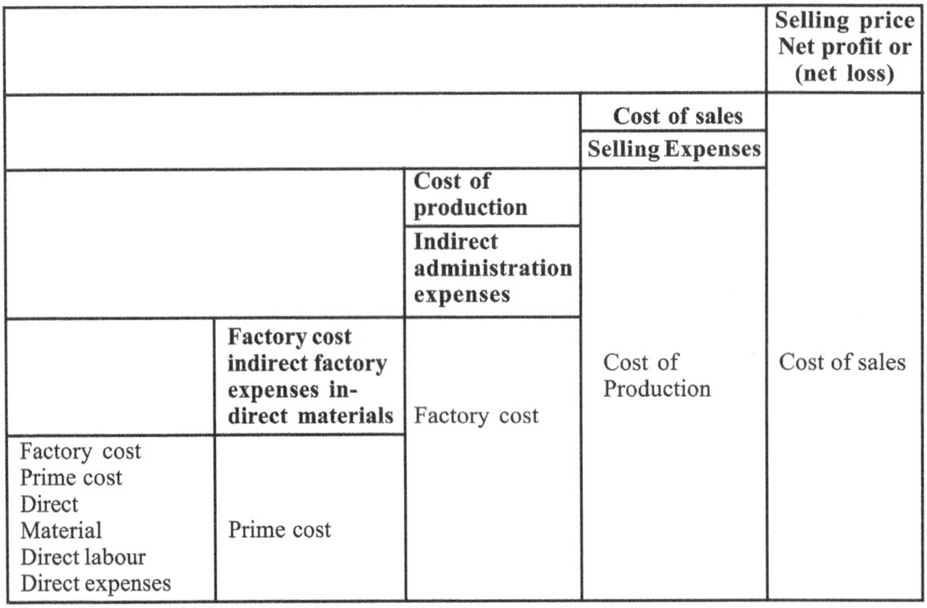


**Interchangeable Words**

| General Terms | | Interchangeable with |
|---|---|---|
| Prime cost | - | Flat cost; first cost; direct cost |
| Factory cost | - | Works cost; production cost; manufacturing cost. |
| Cost of production | - | Office cost; gross cost |
| Cost of sales | - | Selling cost; total cost; distribution cost |
| Factory cost | - | A charge to be made against each job to cover miscellaneous expenses, e.g., cleaning; experiments. |
| Office cost | - | Administration expenses such as rent, salaries; management cost. |
| Overhead charges | - | A term applied to any item comprising on cost. |

## Fixed Costs

These costs are incurred in order to build up production capacity. A business unit purchases land, building and machinery. If these assets are acquired through borrowings the interest is payable on the loan. Further depreciation is to be provided on building and machinery. Taxes are also to be paid on property. Thus, interest, depreciation, and taxes are costs which are incurred for owning fixed assets. All these costs are to be incurred periodically even when the production is completely suspended and the plant shut down. These are period costs. All period costs are fixed costs.

The business also requires trained personnel. Retention of at least a minimum number of employees involves certain fixed costs. However, such cost usually are fixed within a specified volume of production. Certain other costs are incurred for long range planning, product development, research, training etc. These costs also do not change with the volume of production upto a certain level and hence these are fixed costs.

The fixed costs change over a period of time by managerial decisions on additions to fixed assets, recrement of trained personnel etc. In a sense every fixed costs is variable at sometime. The fixed costs are incurred on the basis of anticipation of business and therefore it is called capacity cost. From the bracer point of view there are no costs which do not change at sometimes or other with the changes in the volume of production.

## Semi Fixed Costs

These are fixed costs upto a certain level, where upon they behave like variable costs.

## Variable Costs

In addition to the costs associated with building up productive capacity mentioned above, there are certain other kinds of cost which vary directly in production to the volume of production. The latter costs relate to materials, certain kinds of labour, supplies and services. These costs tend to increase or decrease proportionately with the volume and are called variable costs of marginal costs. All prime costs and variable overheads are marginal costs.

## Analysis of Cost

It would be seen from the cost analysis table that total cost is generally taken as the sum of material cost, wages and other expenses. However, the cost accountant tries to analyse the total cost in greater detail and in various ways to suit his purpose. Total expenditure may be analysed thus in the following Table 17.1.

**Table 17.1 Analysis of cost**

| | | | | |
|---|---|---|---|---|
| Material cost | = | Direct material cost | + | Indirect material cost |
| + | | + | + | + |
| Wages | = | Direct wages | + | Indirect wages |
| + | | + | | + |
| Expenses | = | Direct expenses | + | Indirect expenses |
| **Total cost** | = | **Prime cost** | + | **Overheads** |

It is clear from the above table that prime cost is the aggregate of all direct costs and overhead is the aggregate of all indirect costs. So total cost is the sum of prime cost and overhead.

The ICMA terminology has given the following pictorial representation of the elements of cost related to typical manufacturing organization.

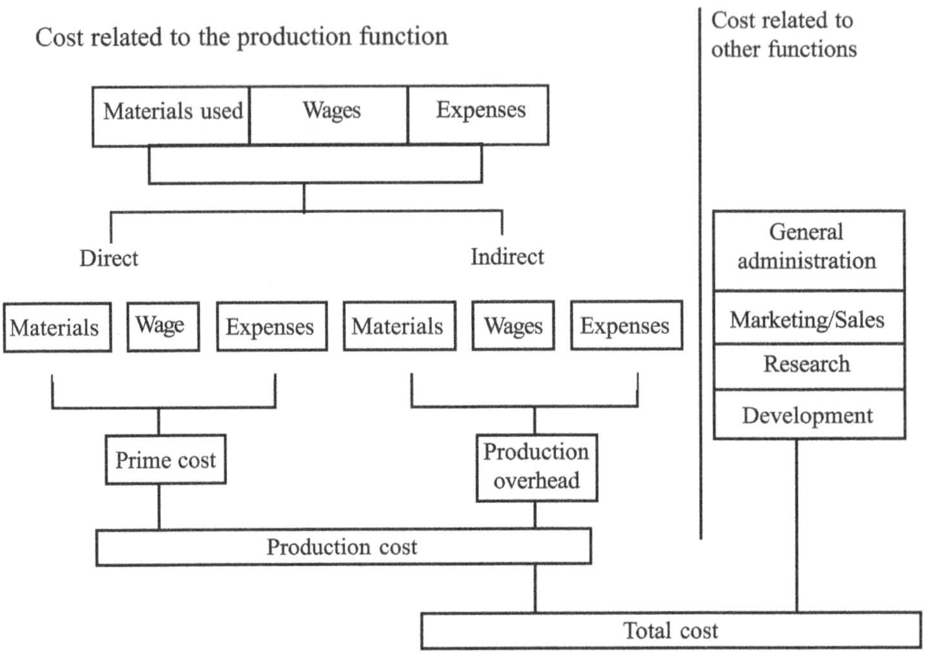


These elements of cost are explained with the help of a cost sheet.

## Cost Sheet

The analysis for different elements of cost of the product is shown in the form of a statement called "Cost Sheet". Cost Sheet is a schedule or document which presents the estimated detailed cost with respect to a cost center or a cost unit. It is only a memorandum statement and is not a part of the double entry cost accounts. The statements summarize the cost of manufacturing a particular list of products and discloses:

(i) The prime cost (ii) The works cost

(iii) The cost of production, and (iv) The total cost

When the department cost is divided by the number of units produced, the quotient is the average cost per unit of the work performed. Separate columns could be provided for the total and the unit cost of each element of cost. Column could also be drawn for the current and the past periods. Cost Sheet is prepared at weekly, monthly, or other interval. A specimen is given below.

## A Case on Cost Estimation Concerning SIRBM Co. Limited

In May 1971, Mr. Adi, the Managing Director of SIRBM CO. LIMITED, decided to undertake a study of cost estimating his company's products. This was the first time in the history of the company that such a study was being attempted. The problem arose because the company's research division had developed a new product.

The company was started 22 years ago with small capital and was the first to make razor blades in country. Slowly with better equipments and with the help of foreign technicians the product improvement was achieved in 10 years.

For another ten years the company struggled hard to maintain its leadership among the middle and lower classes and face the competition in the market where foreign blades were available and many Indian-made as well. Most of the home competitors had better and more modern equipment. The equipments in the company were old and there was a complete breakdown in 1964-65. Major repairs and overhands were undertaken. By 1967 most of the competitors had overtaken this company in terms of not only sales but also in terms of leadership in introduction of stainless steel blades.

Mr. Adi had the responsibility of taking up the challenge to regain the company's position. With the U.S. collaboration, he went ahead to put up a brand new plant. By 1969, new stainless steel blades with 'SIRBMCOL' as brand name; were introduced. The response was good and sales started picking up.

Meanwhile research division was working on improving the shaving edge and struck the depositing platinum on the edge. Immediately preparations were made for manufacturing these on a large scale. In the other parts of the world also these blades had just come up, so SIRBMCOL was one among the world, competitors and wanted to capture its due share in the market. Of course whatever could be made in India could all be sold within the country itself. But at the same time Mr. Adi was very keen in foreign exchange. He was not very sure what price he should fix for his product in the world market. If he underquotes he would unnecessarily lose a chunk of profits coming in the form of foreign exchange. If he overquotes he might run the risk of losing orders.

He therefore called a meeting of his officers M/s Arumgam-Commercial; Ananth-Technical; Barathan-Financial; and Chandran-Research and introduced the problem.

Sri Arumgam analysed the situation as follows. The world-reputed brands were selling at about Rs. 72/- per 100 blades. They gave about 20 shaves each, against 10 shaves of the company's brand. So it could be valued at Rs 36 per 100 blades. In addition because if the blade has no name in the market it could not be priced above 400 per cent of the price of foreign-reputed brands i.e., about Rs. 29/- per 100. This was the maximum price to be quoted.

Mr. Chandran felt that if Indian blade is a platinum blade like the others there would have been difficulty in selling it at even Rs. 72 per 100. According to him the ideal price would be a little below Rs. 60/- per 100.

Mr. Ananth felt that exports were not for making money but for earning a name for the company and foreign exchange to import stainless steel strips required for making blades.

Mr. Barathan made a quick calculation as follows :

| | |
|---|---|
| Direct material | 6 |
| Direct labour | 4 |
| Packing | 2 |
| Overheads : Factory 3 | |
| H. O. 3 | 6 |
| **Total** | **18** |
| Selling expenses | 12 |
| Exercise duty | 3 |
| Advertising | 12 |
| **Total** | **27** |
| Total cost of sales | 45 per 100 blades |
| Cost of Research (if absorbed in one year) | 20 per 100 blades |
| Cost of Research (if absorbed in five years) | 5 per 100 blades |

He also gave the following facts :

- Import license worth 50% FoB value of exports will be granted.
- Cash discount of 10 percent is also admissible on exports
- 25 percent draw back is permitted.

He also prescribed 15 per cent as the profit margin to be added to the estimated cost for quoting.

Mr. Adi summed up saying that none was able to give a foolproof way of cost estimation for an optimal price. Ceiling price was brought out but no floor price was conceived by anybody. He now wants to determine the floor price for exports based on the principle that the company should benefit equally from internal sales and export sales.

## Techniques for the analysis of cost-volume-profit relationships

The profit and loss statement merely tells what profit has been earned on a specific volume of business done during a particular period. In order, however, to have proper planning and control of operations, volume of business must be treated as a variable factor. Under such conditions, costs and income are also variables which depend to a great extent upon the volume of the business proposed to be done by analysing the relationships among the variable such as costs, volume and profit. Volume affects profit in two ways. It affect the revenue goes down and unit cost goes up. It is possible to plan for a certain level of production and to examine its effect on profits. The results of such analysis are usually presented in the form of break-even charts. An understanding of the relationships among the items like costs, volume ancprofits together with the information relating to the effects that changes in volume will have on the business is helpful to the management for proper appreciation of problems relating to planning and control. In order, however to appreciate the effect of changes in volume of sales on the profit of the company, it is essential that all the costs are properly analysed and segregated between fixed costs and variable-costs. If however, any planning for the future operations of the company is made on the basis of the figures in the income statements as published, it may not be possible to reach the correct estimate. Thus to a management the income statement as published periodically for the information of shareholders, creditors and others is not very useful. The information in these statements have to be divided into the fixed and variable elements and these information may enable the management to make a more realistic assessment of its earnings from the future operations.

**Example**

| Conventional profit and loss account | | Break-even profit and loss account | |
|---|---|---|---|
| Sales | Rs. 600 | Sales | Rs. 600 |
| Total costs (100 units @ Rs. 4 per unit plus fixed expenses of Rs. 150 | 550 | Variable costs (66 2/3 of sales) | Rs. 400 |
| | | Contribution | Rs. 200 |
| | | P/V ratio | 3343% |
| | | Fixed expenses | 150 |
| Net profit | Rs. 50 | | 50 |

## Break-even point

The break-even point indicates the volume of sales which the company must achieve in order to cover its total costs. At this stage the company merely recovers the total costs. It is possible to recover the fixed costs when the sales proceeds of the company are in excess of marginal or variable costs. The difference is called contribution. If the company can sell more than the break-even volume, it earns profit provided the sales proceeds of additional units are more than the variable costs thereof. The higher the volume of sales the larger is the amount of profit as every contribution after the break-even level of sales adds to the total revenue of the company. In the case of a company producing more than one product the profits depend upon a proper balance of selling price, produce mix, volume and costs.

| | | |
|---|---|---|
| Marginal cost | = | Prime costs + Variable overheads |
| Contribution | = | Sales – Marginal costs |
| Profit | = | Contribution – Fixed costs |
| Profit + Fixed costs | = | Sales – Marginal costs or P + F = S – M |

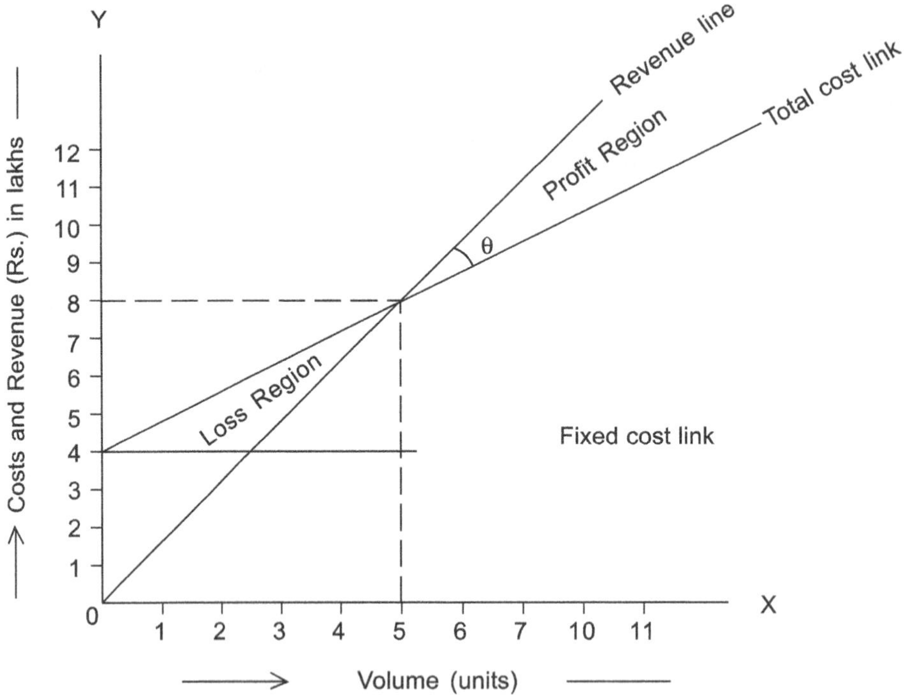


Break-even point is that point where the fixed costs are recovered through contribution.

$$BEP = \frac{\text{Total Fixed Costs}}{\text{Contribution per unit}} \text{ or}$$

$$\text{BE volume} = \frac{\text{Total Fixed Costs}}{\text{Per Unit Ratio}}$$

**Example**

| | | |
|---|---|---|
| Sales | | 100 units |
| Selling price per unit | Rs. 6 | |
| Variable cost per unit | Rs. 4 | |
| Fixed costs | Rs. 150 | |

Find out the break-even point of sales

**Solution**

| | |
|---|---|
| Selling price per unit | Rs. 6 |
| Variable cost per unit | Rs. 4 |
| Contribution or Marginal income | Rs. 2 |

Contribution of Rs. 2 is derived from 1 unit

Contribution of Rs. 1 is derived from 1/2 unit

Contribution of Rs. 150 is derived from 1/2 × 150 units or 75 units

Break-even volume of sales 75

Break-even amount of sales 75 × Rs. 6 = Rs. 450

**Formula**

Sales at break-even point

$$(\text{Bal}) = \frac{\text{Fixed costs} \times \text{sales}}{\text{Sales} - \text{Marginal costs}}$$

$$\text{BEP} = \frac{F \times S}{S - M}$$

$$\text{HEP (in terms of volume)} = \frac{F}{S - M}$$

The fixed costs are recovered from contribution of each unit. If the company sells 50 units only it recovers Rs. 100 towards fixed costs and thereby incurs a net loss of Rs. 50. It is only when it sell 75 units, it recovers the entire cost and the net working result at this stage is neither profit nor loss. It earns profit only by selling additional units over the 75 units. Other things remaining the same, the profit directly varies with volume of sales.

There are a few basic assumption underlying the break-even concept :

(a) Cost should be divisible into fixed and variable categories

(b) There is no change in investment of fixed assets

(c) Variable cost remains constant per unit

(d) Selling price does not change during the period

(e) If there is more than one product the sales mix remains constant through the period under consideration.

(f) Productivity remains constant

### Break-Even Chart

It is a visual device which helps the management of company to appraise its performance on the basis of its present and the estimated profit. There are two lines on the break-even chart, one is the sales line and the other is the cost line. The point of intersection of the two lines is called the break-even point. In order to draw the revenue and cost lines it is necessary to have scale of quantities in order to give value of these lines. Profit and loss can be measured on the chart for any volume of sales. Changes in fixed costs change the break-even point while in changes in variable costs change break-even point and profit volume ratio.

### Margin of Safety

Margin of safety is the percentage of excesses sales over those at the break-even point, to the actual sales. It indicates as to what extent the sales may decline before the company starts incurring losses. In the break-even chart, the distance between break-even point and the point of actual sales indicates the margin of safety. Using the figures in the foregoing example we may work out the ratio as follows :

| | | |
|---|---|---|
| Actual sales | Rs. | 600 |
| Sales at break-even point | | 450 |
| Excess sales | Rs. | 150 |

Margin of safety $\dfrac{150 \times 100}{600}$

$= 25\%$

In other words the company will incur losses if the sales decline by more than 25%.

### Break-Even Analysis - Some Basic Examples

A pen manufacturer sells his pen at an average price of Rs. 5 variable costs incurred in manufacture are Rs. 5 variable costs incurred in manufacture are Rs. 3 and fixed expenses Rs. 25,000 per year.

Contribution $= 1 - \dfrac{3}{5} = \dfrac{2}{5} = 40\ \%$

$$\text{Sales at break-even point} = \frac{\text{Rs. } 25{,}000}{0.40}$$

Break-even sales volume = Rs. 12,500 pens per year

Thus, the unit should aim to sell at least 11,500 pens per year, to break-even.

In practice, it may not be possible to estimate the fixed and variable costs exactly. However, by treating all *expenses other* than raw materials costs as fixed costs, the approximate break-even point can be calculated.

A product X sells for Rs. 25 per piece. Materials costs (consisting of raw materials and packing) are Rs. 15 per piece and fixed expenses amount for Rs. 1 lakh per year.

$$\text{Break-even sales} = \text{Rs. } \frac{(100{,}000)}{\left(1 - \frac{15}{25}\right)}$$

$$= \text{Rs. } 2{,}50{,}000/\text{-}$$

and Break-even sales volume = 10,000 pieces per year

The break-even point is therefore reached when 10,000 pieces are sold per year.

Calculating the break-even point is a slightly more complicated exercise, when a unit manufacturers a number of products with varying contribution margins. In such cases, the weighted average of the contribution margin has to be calculated, to find the break-even point.

A unit manufactures four products, A, B, C and D. Contribution margins are 40%, 30%, 35% and 50% (defined help as sales revenue less material cost) respectively. The unit expects to realise 50%, 35% 15% and 10% of its sales revenue from A, B, C and D respectively. Fixed expenses are Rs. 10 lakhs per year.

$$\begin{aligned}\text{Weighted average of contribution margin} &= (0.40 \times 0.50) + \\ &= (0.30 \times 0.25) + \\ &= (0.35 \times 0.15) + \\ &= (0.50 \times 0.10) \\ &= 0.3775 \text{ or } 37.75\%\end{aligned}$$

$$\text{Break even sales} = \frac{(\text{Rs.}10 \text{ lacs})}{(0.3775)} \text{ per year}$$

or Rs. 26.49 lacs per year

## Exercises

**1. The following details relate to IPE Ltd. Prepare a Cost Sheet showing different components of Cost for 2003.**

| | | | in Rs. |
|---|---|---|---|
| Raw Materials consumed | | – | 8,00,000 |
| Wages paid to labourers | | – | 2,00,000 |
| Directly chargeable expenses | | – | 40,000 |
| Oil and Waste | | – | 4,000 |
| Wages of Foreman | | – | 20,000 |
| Storekeeper's wages | | – | 10,000 |
| Elcctric powcr | | – | 10,000 |
| Lightining : | Factory | 10,000 | |
| | Office | 4,000 | 14,000 |
| Rent : | Factory | 40,000 | |
| | Office | 20,000 | 60,000 |
| Repairs & Renewals : | | | |
| | Factory Plant | 10,000 | |
| | Machinery | 20,000 | |
| | Office Premises | 4,000 | 34,000 |
| Depreciation: | | | |
| | Office Premises | 10,000 | |
| | Plant & Machinery | 4,000 | 14,000 |
| Consumables stores | | | 20,000 |
| Manager's salary | | | 40,000 |
| Director's fees | | | 10,000 |
| Office printing & stationery | | | 4,000 |
| Telephone charges | | | 1,000 |
| Postage & Telegrams | | | 2,000 |
| Salesmen's Commission & salary | | | 10,000 |
| Travelling expenses | | | 4,000 |
| Advertising | | | 10,000 |
| Warehouse charges | | | 4,000 |
| Carriage Outwards | | | 3,000 |

**Hint :**

**Prime Cost:** It consists of costs of direct material, direct labour, and direct expenses. It is also known as basic, first or flat cost.

**Factory Cost:** It comprises prime cost and, in addition, works or factory overheads which include costs of indirect material, indirect labour and indirect factory expenses. This cost is also known as works cost, production or manufacturing cost.

**Office cost:** It comprises of factory cost and office and administration overheads. This is also termed as total cost of production.

**Total cost:** It comprises of cost of production and selling and distribution overheads. It is also termed as Cost of Sales.

**Components of Total Cost**

| | |
|---|---|
| Direct material<br>Direct labour<br>Direct expenses | Prime Cost or Direct Cost or First Cost |
| Prime Cost Plus<br>Works overheads | Works or Factory cost or Production Cost or Manufacturing cost |
| Works cost plus office &<br>Administration overheads | Office cost or Total cost of production |
| Office cost plus Selling &<br>Distribution overheads | Cost of Sales or Total Sales |

**Answer - 1.**

**Cost Sheet for IPE Ltd for 2003**

| | Rs. | Rs. | Rs. |
|---|---|---|---|
| Direct Material: Raw materials consumed | - | - | 8,00,000 |
| Direct Labour: Wages paid to labourers | - | - | 2,00,000 |
| Direct Expenses: Directly chargeable expenses | - | - | 40,000 |
| PRIME COST | | | |
| Add: Factory Overheads: | | | |
| Indirect Material : | | | |
| Consumable Stores | 20,000 | | |
| Oil & Waste | 2,000 | 22,000 | |
| Indirect expenses : | | | |
| Electric power | 4,000 | | |
| Factory lighting | 10,000 | | |
| Factory rent | 40,000 | | |
| Repairs & Renewals : | | | |
| Plant 10,000 | | | |
| Machinery 20,000 | 30,000 | | |
| Depreciation: | | | |
| Plant and Machinery | 4,000 | 88,800 | 1,40,000 |
| | | | 11,18,000 |
| FACTORY OR WORKS COST | | | |
| Add: Office or Administrative Overheads: | | | |
| Indirect material: | | | |
| Office Printing & Stationery | | 4,000 | |
| Indirect labour: | | | |
| Manager's salary | 40,000 | | |
| Director's fees | 10,000 | 50,000 | |

*Contd. Cost Sheet for IPE Ltd. for 2003*

| | Rs. | Rs. | Rs. |
|---|---|---|---|
| Indirect Expenses: | | | |
| Office lighting | 4,000 | | |
| Office Rent | 20,000 | | |
| Repairs &Renewals premises | 4,000 | | |
| Depreciation on premises | 10,000 | | |
| Telephone charges | 1,000 | | |
| Postage & Telegrams | 2,000 | 41,000 | 95,000 |
| TOTAL COST OF PRODUCTION | | | |
| Add: Selling & Distribution overheads: | | | |
| Indirect labour: | | | |
| Salesmen's Commission & Salary | | 10,000 | |
| Indirect expenses: | | | |
| Traveling expenses | 4,000 | | |
| Advertising | 10,000 | | |
| Warehouse charges | 4,000 | | |
| Carriage outward | 3,000 | 21,000 | 31,000 |
| COST OF SALES | | | 13,06,000 |

——□——

**2. Complete the following Cost Sheet:**

**Cost Sheet for June, 2001**

| | | |
|---|---|---|
| Opening Stock of raw materials | 1,00,000 | |
| Add: Purchases | | ........... |
| | 5,00,000 | |
| Less: Closing stock of raw materials | 1,20,000 | |
| Raw materials consumed | ........... | |
| Direct wages | | 3,00,000 |
| Other direct expenses | | 20,000 |
| | | ........... |
| **a) Prime Cost** | | |
| Add: Factory overheads : | | |
| Indirect material | 60,000 | |
| Indirect labour | .......... | |
| Indirect expenses | 10,000 | 90,000 |
| **b) Factory or Works Cost** | | - |
| Add: Office or Administration overheads | | 1,70,000 |
| **c) Cost of production** | | - |
| Add: Opening stock of finished goods | | 1,40,000 |
| Less: Closing stock of finished goods | | 1,50,000 |
| Selling and Distribution overheads | | 80,000 |
| **d) Cost of goods sold** | | 10,30,000 |
| Sale of finished goods | | 13,30,000 |
| **e) Profit for the month** | | - |

**3. Prepare a Cost Sheet with the help of the following details :**

| | |
|---|---|
| Raw Materials: | |
| Opening stock | 20,000 |
| Purchases | 1,00,000 |
| Closing stock | 40,000 |
| Direct wages | 40,000 |
| Chargeable Expenses | 8,000 |
| Machine hours worked | 16,000 |
| Machine hour rate | Rs. 2 |
| Office overhead | 10% of works cost |
| Selling overhead | Rs. 1.50 per unit |
| Cash discount allowed | 1,000 |
| Interest on Capital | 2,000 |
| Units produced | 4,000 |
| Units sold | 3,600 @ Rs. 50 each |

(**Hint:** Cash discount and interest on capital are to be excluded from costs).

**Answers - 3.**

Prime Cost Rs. 1,28,000; Works Cost Rs. 1,60,000; Cost of Production Rs. 1,76,000; Cost of Sales Rs. 1,63,800; Profit Rs. 16,200

**4. Calculate (a) Value of raw materials consumed; (b) Total Cost of Production; (c) Cost of Production of goods sold; and (d) The amount of profit from the following particulars:**

| | |
|---|---|
| Opening stock: | |
| Raw materials | 50,000 |
| Finished goods | 40,000 |
| Closing stock: | |
| Raw materials | 40,000 |
| Finished goods | 50,000 |
| Raw materials purchased | 4,00,000 |
| Octroi paid on raw materials | 40,000 |
| Carriage inwards | 60,000 |
| Direct wages paid | 2,00,000 |
| Direct expenses | 20,000 |
| Rent, rates and taxes | 50,000 |
| Power | 20,000 |
| Factory heating and lighting | 20,000 |
| Factory insurance | 10,000 |
| Experimental expenses | 5,000 |
| Office management salaries | 40,000 |
| Office printing and stationery | 20,000 |
| Salary of a salesman | 6,000 |
| Advertising | 3,000 |
| Carriage outwards | 1,000 |
| Sales | 10,00,000 |

(**Hint:** (a) Rs. 5,10,000; (b) 8,77,000; (c) Rs. 8,67,000; (d) Rs. 1,03,000)

# 18

# A Case Study on 'Financial Decision-Making Process'

## The Well-fit Enterprises Limited

The Well-Fit Enterprises Ltd., a company specializing in the production of high quality boots and shoes and other footwear for men and women, has been operating for a number of years. The annual profit and loss accounts are in use as well as in some form, not so adequate for controlling the issue of materials.

The competition in the industry has become intense and the directors are concerned with the reduced profit margin and are afraid of the enterprise entering into red, for the reason that some of the cost centers are incurring losses. They feel that the accounting and other office staff could provide much more information to aid the management for enhancing the profitability of the enterprise.

At present, an unqualified accountant, who rose from the rank and file and does not believe in professionalisation, heads the Finance and Accounts department. The only qualified accountant in the whole of the undertaking who used to supply some data to the Managing Director on costs and inefficiencies was side-tracked from the mainstream and was vindictively posted in an unconnected line with the designation as '*Officer on Special Duty*' by the chief of Finance and Accounts. None is interested to make good of his professional expertise, lest, the ignorance of the senior officers in the FPA department should be exposed out. There is also a rumour that a qualified accountant may also leave the enterprise shortly.

*The production Division is divided into following departments:*

1. Skin Room and Store.
2. *Clicking Room :* This department is concerned with the cutting of the uppers from the skins. Certain other operations are also carried out in this department.
3. *Machine Room :* All the various parts of the uppers are machined together.
4. *Lasting Room :* In this department the skins are jointed together by sewing or riveting.
5. *Finishing Room :* The sole and heel of each shoe is ground down to give a smooth finish, they are also coloured, dried and polished.
6. *Press Room :* This department is concerned with cutting up the sole leather and bottoms. Once the operations are carried out the appropriate numbers of each size are transferred to the lasting room.

There is no planning and coordination at present in the enterprise. Quite often the M.D. comes to know the inter-departmental quarrels or trivial issues leading to production losses.

One of the main difficulties being encountered by the company is that the sales fluctuate considerable between winter and summer. The spring and summer represent 80% of normal capacity, but the winter sales are only around 50 of the capacity, mainly in respect of the 'cost centers' indicated in the undermentioned paragraph.

**Cost Data**

**Production at 50% of Production Unit Price (10 lakh pieces)**

| | | | |
|---|---|---|---|
| (a) | Variable costs | | |
| | Skins | 25 | |
| | Chemicals, Colour, etc. | 10 | |
| | Other overheads | 5 | 40 |
| (b) | Fixed cost | | 25 |
| | Total cost | | 65 |
| (c) | Selling price | | 60 |
| (d) | Loss per unit | | 05 |

There are no immediate plans for any large expansion, but the Directors would like to eliminate idles capacity. Due to changes in the fashion and keeping of stocks of finished goods is impracticable. The enterprise's last year turnover is of the order of Rs. 45 crores, making a loss of Rs. 1.5 crores approximately and this is expected to continue to be the same for current year. Suddenly, the enterprise received and exports order from Zambia to supply 10 lakh pieces of shoes at the rate of Rs. 58 on an average, while the actual cost of production tends to be @ Rs. 65/-. With the assistance of an outside Cost Consultant the management could obtain the cost data as above, in respect of the above 'Cost Center'. The 'Cost Center' has an idle capacity of 50% of production.

## Required

1. Suggest ways of overcoming the problem of idle capacity
2. Whether to accept the above export offer or not and the justification for the same.
3. An explanation of budgetary control system, which could be suitable for the Well-Fit Enterprises Ltd., and modus operandi of the system.
4. The benefits the Directors can hope to achieve from the installation of the system.

******

(You may please make any assumptions which you may deem it fit)

# 19

# Standard Costing for Management Control

## Standard Costing for Management Control

Standard costs are pre-determined measures of what costs should be under specified conditions. Fixing standard costs and analysing the variances of actual costs from standard costs helps management control and in judging and improving the performance.

## Budgets and Standards

In many organisations budgeting system means static budgets master budget is prepared and evaluation is not beyond simply comparing the actuals with the master budget. This is basically what is obtaining in the Government also.

For better control and rational approach, a flexible budgeting system has to be evolved which requires developing standards for major costs. Standard costs are carefully pre-d determined costs. They can also be called target costs or costs that should be attained. Such standardisation helps to build up budgets, gauge performance, obtain standard costs, give estimates and even save book-keeping costs. Standardisation of cost is a pre-requisite for flexible budgeting and feed-back system.

Standardisation specified how a task should be accomplished and how much it should cost. Once the task has been accomplished, the actual cost incurred is compared with the standard cost to reveal variances. From this feed-back, better ways of achieving the targets could be evolved. If need be even the standards could be altered. Standard cost is a unit concept and based on the number of units proposed to be achieved, from this the budgeted cost is developed as a total concept.

## Levels of Standard Cost

Perfection, Ideal, maximum efficiency or theoretical standard costs reflect a dreams approach. These are absolute minimum costs that are possible under the best conceivable operating conditions, using given specifications and equipments. They are more for psychological satisfaction than for practical application.

Attainable standard costs mean the costs that should be incurred under very efficient operating conditions. They are difficult and challenging, but at the same time possible of achievement. Obviously, they are more generous than ideal standards, because of provisions for normal spoilage, ordinary break-down, lost time etc., built into it. At the same time attainable standards should be set tight enough, so that the operating people will consider achieving the same a satisfying accomplishment. In fact variances are more likely to be slightly unfavourable than favourable, though favourable variance are not ruled out. Attainable standards are the practical and most widely used ones, because the resulting standard costs serve many purposes simultaneously and have the most enthusing and motivating impact on the employees. Currently attainable standards can be used for master budget, motivation, incentives and for product costing. They are also very useful for the preparation of cash flow predictions.

## Developing the Standards

The standards setting and budget preparation process in an organisation is primarily the responsibility of the line personnel, directly involved. The relative tightness or otherwise of the budget is the result of shop floor discussions and bargaining between the manager and his superior. The Accountant, the Industrial Engineer and marketing managers extend necessary technical assistance and advice, but the final decision is that of the line manager. He is the one who should accept the challenge and achieve the targets.

Thc Accounting Department helps in pricing the physical standards and reporting actual performance from time to time, in comparison with the standards.

It shall not be thought that standard costs are always based on technical engineering studies and rigorous specifications. Although a rigorous approach is desirable, a practical approach has to be finally chosen. Accurate measurements have to be modified to suite practical conditions and to motivate the staff in a responsible way.

## Variances

Though standard costs could be fixed with all the care and consideration, the actuals will vary from the standards. This is because of the difference in day-to-day working conditions, quality of raw-materials, prices paid for the raw-materials, labour efficiency differing from individual to individual etc. The variation of the actual cost from the standard cost is called a variance. In management control performance such deviations from the standard are analysed under cost of materials, cost of labour, flexible overheads and fixed overheads. Further, sub-division under each is also possible and desirable.

From the revenue point of view sales and receipts are analysed under sales variance.

## Sales Variance

Sales variance indicates the difference in receipts from sales between budgeted figures and the actuals. This may be due to a deviation in the anticipated volume of sales of anticipated sales price. The variance due to volume called sales volume variance and is given by the following formula :

Sales volume variance = (Budgeted units – Actual units) × Budgeted price.

The variance in revenue due to difference in prices only, is given by the following formula :

Price variance = (Actual price – Budgeted price) × Actual quantity or units sold

## Direct Material Cost

The variance in the cost of direct material consumed for the number of units produced is called material cost variance. This is further sub-divided and analysed under price variance and efficiency variance.

Price variance is the difference between actual unit price and budgeted unit price multiplied by the actual quantity of raw material consumed.

Efficiency variance is given by the difference between the actual quantities or units of raw-material consumed and the standard quantity or units of raw-material multiplied by the budgeted price.

The purpose of this approach is to separate defects of price fluctuations and efficiency fluctuations. The production personnel are not normally responsible for the price fluctuations, whereas they are answerable for efficiency fluctuations. Similarly the purchasing personnel are responsible for price variance and not for efficiency variances. The management can have both the variances for taking necessary follow up action.

## Labour Cost Variance

In many organization, because of the wage agreements etc., labour cost could be foreseen with some accuracy. However, labour efficiency involves supervision, motivation and control. As such labour cost variance is analyzed under labour rates variance and labour efficiency variance, in a manner similar to material cost variance.

Labour price variance can be traced to subsequent escalation in the labour rates.

Labour efficiency variance is a much more complicated affair. Time standards are usually set for various operations. A master operation list is prepared for each activity and from time standards, the standard units of time for the activity is fixed. However, the practical achievement will vary from this. Absentism can dramatically affect the efficiency. So a time frame will be set up to prepare the tools and make them ready before starting the manufacturing activity. It is common for batch production and depending on the size of the batch, its impact on the number of labour hours per unit produced will vary. Morals of the labour, go slow tactic, efficiency of machines, where machine work is involved etc., all contribute to labour efficiency variance.

## Cost Benefits Approach to Variances

A highly refined method for monitoring each cost and its variance could be developed. But the need for the same and the benefits accruing to the organization from it should be carefully looked into. Under certain circumstances standard costs system and variance analysis could itself be more costly than the normal system. But if standard costs system is run without parallel actual cost system, then the cost could be considerably reduced. In fact, in many organizations standard cost system has been adopted with a view to saving record keeping costs.

The variance shall not be looked at individually. Many times, managers trade off among the variances. When he has got an opportunity to take advantage of bargain purchases, the quality of raw material may contribute to adverse materials efficiency variance. If the sum total of the two is favorable to the company, then the trade off has to be arranged. As such the approach shall not be that of a straight jacket but a comprehensive one. There are too many interdependencies among the activities. The sum total shall always be looked at.

## Responsibility of Variances and Corrective Steps

Price variances are the responsibility of purchase department. They are often regarded as a measure of forecasting policy rather than the failure to put at specified prices. Some control over the price variances is obtainable by getting many quotations, by buying in lots, taking advantage of cash discounts and selecting the most economical means of delivery. It can also be achieved by perfecting the method of forecasting prices.

However, failure to meet the prices standard may also result from sudden rush of sales orders or changes in production schedules which will necessitate hurried purchases at uneconomical prices or will require more costly delivery. In such cases, the responsibility rests with the production manager or sales manager and not the purchase manger. Similarly, labour efficiency variances value be traced to shape floor management or maintenance department or to the labour welfare department.

Material efficiency variance depends on the accuracy of detailed engineering production schedule and also on the quality of the materials supplied. Through a periodic summary of excess material requisitions the total material efficiency variance is arrived.

When and how far the variances should be investigated depends on management's judgment. This again depends on whether the variances are significant enough to warrant management's attention. For variance analysis and follow up also involves costs. Normally variances, above certain amount are investigated in detail. Here also cost benefit test has to be applied.

Along with standardization of costs, limited range of variation from that has also got to be accepted.

### Overheads Variance

The variable factory overheads consist of many items including power, repairs, indirect labour, idle time etc. The best way to analyze when the actual performance done not agree with the standards is to be investigated all possible causes one by one.

Variable overheads by their very definition are proportionate to the actual production and as such the variable overheads variance is given by multiplying the difference between actual units produced and standard units assumed by standard overhead per unit.

Fixed factory overheads consist of all such overhead expenses like rent, taxes, insurance, etc. including varies with the level of production or activity, within limits. The total fixed cost for budgetary control is unaffected by the specific projected volume of production sales or any other activity.

For practical purposes, in order to charge fixed overhead, per unit rate is arrived at by dividing the budgeted total fixed factory overheads by the budgeted volume of production or activity. From this assumption or standard fixation, the variances are calculated.

The most perplexing and complex of all variances is that of fixed overheads. The budgeted figures will never agree with the actual charged or recouped. This is due to variation in the volume of production, efficiency, calendar periods etc. The total fixed overheads variance could be analysed under single head, two heads and three heads. Under single head it is the difference between the budgeted and the actual amounts. While analyzing under two heads it is split into volume variance, efficiency variance and calendar variance. Value variance can be further split into calendar variance, idle capacity variance, activity variance etc.

It shall be noted that the accruals will bray for the budgeted and the budgeted will vary from the applied overhead costs. All the differences are ultimately set off against the profits arrived at by applying standard cost.

In conclusion, it can be said that standard costs help in arriving at rebel estimates for given quotations and for management control over the expenditure periodically. But the success of the system depends upon the accuracy with which the standards are set. Further, the variances will have to be regularly analyzed and appreciated for applying correctives.

# 20

# A Case on Cost Control and Cost Reduction for Executives of State Level Public Enterprises

## Introduction

This case exercise is designed and developed for training the executives of Business Enterprises the reader may assume himself/herself as an executive and, thereby, do the role play. This case exercise would help participants to gain an understanding of finance function of their organisation. The exercise aims :

1. to make participant understand the basic concepts in Financial Management.
2. to relate the concepts to their work experiences.
3. to identify and discuss the elements of financial management within ones job responsibility which needs improvement.
4. to analyze and formulate financial efficiency strategies.
5. to develop an action plan for such improvements and examine their implications in the overall organisation context.

## Methodology

This exercise is a self learning exercise. The exercise enables participants to relate various concepts in financial management to real life experiences of Executives. It is done at individual level, then through group discussions and conference.

### *Stages of the exercise*

1. Brief introduction by the faculty.
2. Individual exercise (Exercise I).
3. Classroom discussion.
4. Individual exercise (Exercises II and III)
5. Group discussion (Exercises IV and V)
6. Classroom discussion.
7. Group discussion (Exercise VI)
8. Classroom discussion and summing up.

## EXERCISE I

## (INDIVIDUAL EXERCISE - SELF ASSESSMENT)

1. **Name of the participant :** ______________________________

2. **Designation :** ______________________________

3. **Work place :** ______________________________

4. **What are the financial objectives of executives in your organisation? Briefly specify.**

   ______________________________

   ______________________________

   ______________________________

   ______________________________

   ______________________________

5. **Briefly state the financial objectives of executives at your level of the organisation.**

   1. ______________________________

      ______________________________

   2. ______________________________

      ______________________________

   3. ______________________________

      ______________________________

   4. ______________________________

      ______________________________

6. **Redefine the financial objectives of your organisation.**

   1. ______________________________

   2. ______________________________

   3. ______________________________

   4. ______________________________

   5. ______________________________

**7. Redefine the financial objectives at your level of operation.**

1. ____________________________________________

2. ____________________________________________

3. ____________________________________________

4. ____________________________________________

5. ____________________________________________

**8. Specify your financial authority.**

(a) ____________________________________________

(b) ____________________________________________

(c) ____________________________________________

(d) ____________________________________________

**9. Do you think you have sufficient budget powers to complete your task in time?**

______ Yes ______ No In no explain the reasons.

**10. Who sets your financial target ? Suppose if you are a Senior Executive who sets your budget/standard for the expenses at drill site assuming that you are associated with an oil exploration organisation.**

## EXERCISE II
## (INDIVIDUAL EXERCISE)

**Each participant is requested to list out the different items of expenses, they are incurring at different levels of operations. Suppose if the participant is working at field level i.e. drill site he/she is requested to list the expenses at field level.**

| Name of the expense | Type of Expense | Variable/ Fixed | Controllable/ Non-controllable |
|---|---|---|---|
| 1. Cashing Pipe | ________ | ________ | ________ |
| 2. Tubing | ________ | ________ | ________ |
| 3. Drill Pipe | ________ | ________ | ________ |
| 4. Other pipe and pipe fittings | ________ | ________ | ________ |
| 5. Well heads | ________ | ________ | ________ |
| 6. Repair charges of video | ________ | ________ | ________ |
| 7. Maintenance charges | ________ | ________ | ________ |
| 8. Travel expenses | ________ | ________ | ________ |
| 9. Diesel expenses | ________ | ________ | ________ |
| 10. Over time expenses | ________ | ________ | ________ |
| 11. ____________ | ________ | ________ | ________ |
| 12. ____________ | ________ | ________ | ________ |
| 13. ____________ | ________ | ________ | ________ |
| 14. ____________ | ________ | ________ | ________ |
| 15. ____________ | ________ | ________ | ________ |
| 16. ____________ | ________ | ________ | ________ |
| 17. ____________ | ________ | ________ | ________ |
| 18. ____________ | ________ | ________ | ________ |
| 19. ____________ | ________ | ________ | ________ |
| 20. ____________ | ________ | ________ | ________ |

## EXERCISE III

## (INDIVIDUAL EXERCISE)

**From the above exercises you have to identify and list out 10 areas where cost reduction is possible in descending order of importance.**

**The area for cost reduction**

1. ______________________________

______________________________

2. ______________________________

______________________________

3. ______________________________

______________________________

4. ______________________________

______________________________

5. ______________________________

______________________________

6. ______________________________

______________________________

7. ______________________________

______________________________

8. ______________________________

______________________________

9. ______________________________

______________________________

10. ______________________________

______________________________

## EXERCISE IV
## (GROUP EXERCISE)

**Discuss your list (Exercise IV) in a group of 3-4 participants and prepare a common/agreed list of 10 areas where cost reduction/financial improvement is possible.**

1. ______________________________

   ______________________________

2. ______________________________

   ______________________________

3. ______________________________

   ______________________________

4. ______________________________

   ______________________________

5. ______________________________

   ______________________________

6. ______________________________

   ______________________________

7. ______________________________

   ______________________________

8. ______________________________

   ______________________________

9. ______________________________

   ______________________________

10. ______________________________

    ______________________________

## EXERCISE V

## (GROUP EXERCISES)

### Long Term Plan

| | Areas of cost reduction | Action plan | Possible savings |
|---|---|---|---|
| 1. | ______ | ______ | ______ |
| | ______ | ______ | ______ |
| 2. | ______ | ______ | ______ |
| | ______ | ______ | ______ |
| 3. | ______ | ______ | ______ |
| | ______ | ______ | ______ |
| 4. | ______ | ______ | ______ |
| | ______ | ______ | ______ |
| 5. | ______ | ______ | ______ |
| | ______ | ______ | ______ |
| 6. | ______ | ______ | ______ |
| | ______ | ______ | ______ |
| 7. | ______ | ______ | ______ |
| | ______ | ______ | ______ |
| 8. | ______ | ______ | ______ |
| | ______ | ______ | ______ |
| 9. | ______ | ______ | ______ |
| | ______ | ______ | ______ |
| 10. | ______ | ______ | ______ |
| | ______ | ______ | ______ |

# 21

# Cost Reduction

The objective of any industrial organization is to make profit. No business can continue to operate unless a profit is made. All activities within a company should be so organised and co-ordinated that their overall effect and ultimate aim is to increase the profitability of the business. The introduction of any new activity or the modification of existing one should be critically examined to ensure that it assists the company to achieve this objective. This in effect depends upon the effective utilization of the resource deployed in the business or the productivity of the organization.

Figure 21.1 The productivity of certain set of resources (input) and the amount of goods or services in terms of increase in industrial efficiency or productivity must ultimately be reflected in reducing costs. The effects of which can be so far-reaching as to warrant the active interest of the entire industrial community. But notwithstanding the apparent awareness of the need for increased productivity there is as yet little evidence to indicate that organised efforts in the field of cost reduction are being made. The two problems are closely related. This can be seen from the following statement of the two-fold aspect of cost reduction.

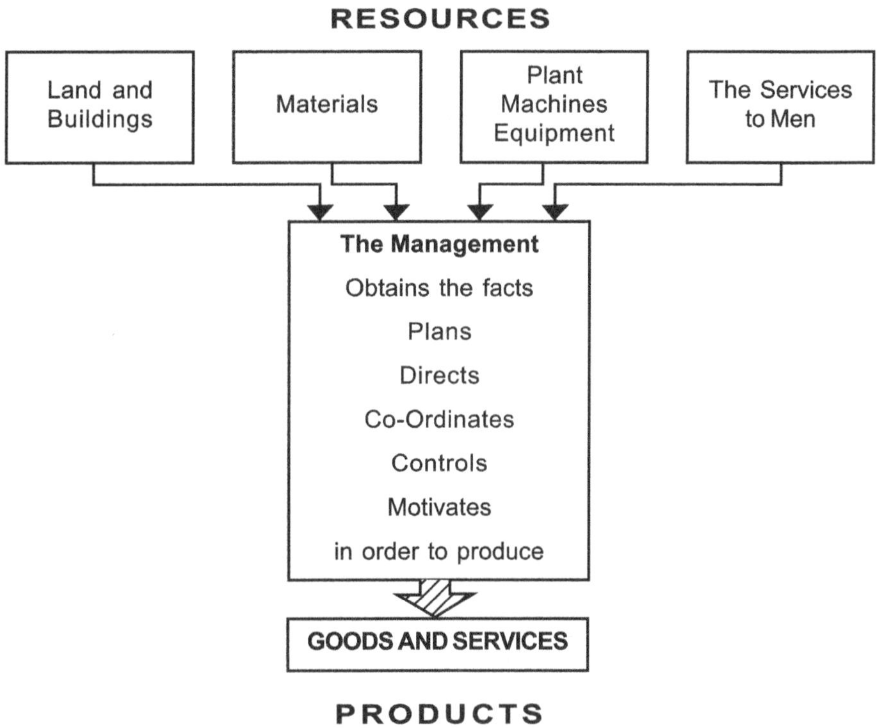


**Fig. 21.1** The role of the management in co-ordinating the resources of an enterprise.

*Cost Reduction Embraces*

(i) Unit-Cost reduction by expenditures reduction in respect of a given volume of output; and/or

(ii) Unit-Cost reduction by an increase in productivity (i.e., an increase in output, yield or rate of output for a given expenditure)

In practice, cost reduction will ultimately be achieved by the combination of these influences and it will probably be impossible to assess the contribution which each has made to the overall savings.

## Definition

1. Cost reduction is to be understood as the achievement of real and permanent reductions in the unit cost of goods manufactured or services rendered without impairing third suitability for the use intended.
2. From this definition it will be seen that the retention of the essential characteristics and quality of the product is assumed, and the term cost reduction must be confined to genuine savings in the costs of manufacture,

administration, distributing and selling, brought about by the elimination of wasteful and in essential elements from the design of the product and from the techniques and practices carried out in connection therewith.

3. Reductions in cost to consumer as a result of reductions in taxation or similar government action or the effect of price agreements are not to be regarded as cost reduction.

### Cost Control and Cost Reduction

1. Methods of scientific management are already in use in many businesses as a result of an increasing recognition of the advantages, which this approach to the control of business operations has to offer.
2. Amongst the techniques which have become popular in the management feels are budgetary control and standard costing, which often lead to improved efficiency, revealing as they do divergences from predetermined plan and thus furnishing a useful tool for cost control. Cost control, however, as generally practiced, lacks the dynamic approach to many of the factors affecting cost, which planned cost reduction demands. The tenancy is to accept standards once they have been fixed and to leave them unchallenged over a period, although the variance from standards receive close attention, often resulting in some contribution improving operating efficiency.
3. In cost reduction, on the other hand, standards must be constantly challenged for improvement. There is no phase of the business which is exempt from cost reduction. Products, processes, procedures and personnel are subject to continuous scrutiny to see where and how they can be reduced in cost. Under cost control methods variances show the effectiveness of control almost daily. In cost reduction the potential savings are buried in the standards and can only be dug out by continuous and planned research. A programme of cost reduction never stars of its own volition; it must be planned and followed up.

### Areas of Cost Reduction

A thorough analysis of the components of manufacturing time depicted in Fig. 21.2 would help to envisage cost reduction under three major areas viz.

1. Material cost reduction.
2. Labour cost reduction.
3. Overheads cost reduction.

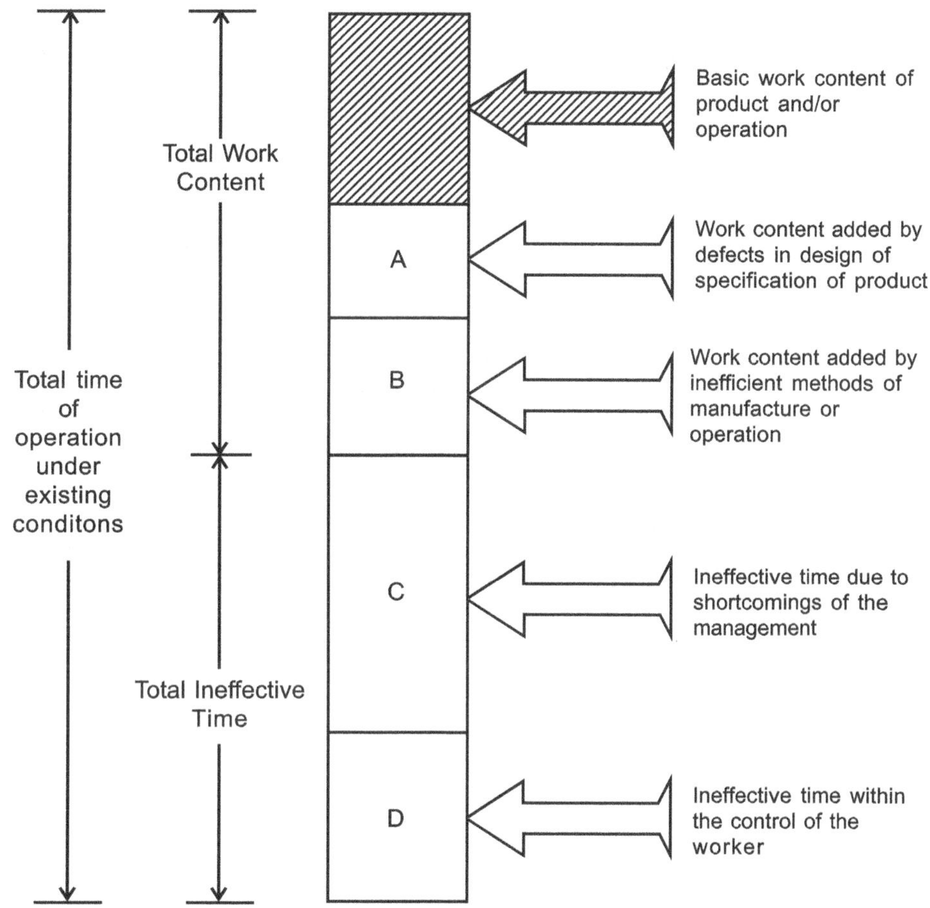


**Fig. 21.2** How manufacturing time is made up.

### 1. Material Cost Reduction

In manufacturing industry material takes a major share (50% to 70%) of the cost. Hence there is a scope for maximum cost reduction in this area. The material cost is to a great extent enhanced by

(i) Defective design of the product and its components.

(ii) Wrong selection of raw material in terms of type or of quality, and

(iii) Poor manufacturing methods leading to excessive scrap and rejection.

It is apparent Fig. 21.3 that to the true basic cost of material, costs are added due to various factors, which could be controlled by the proper use of techniques available to the management.

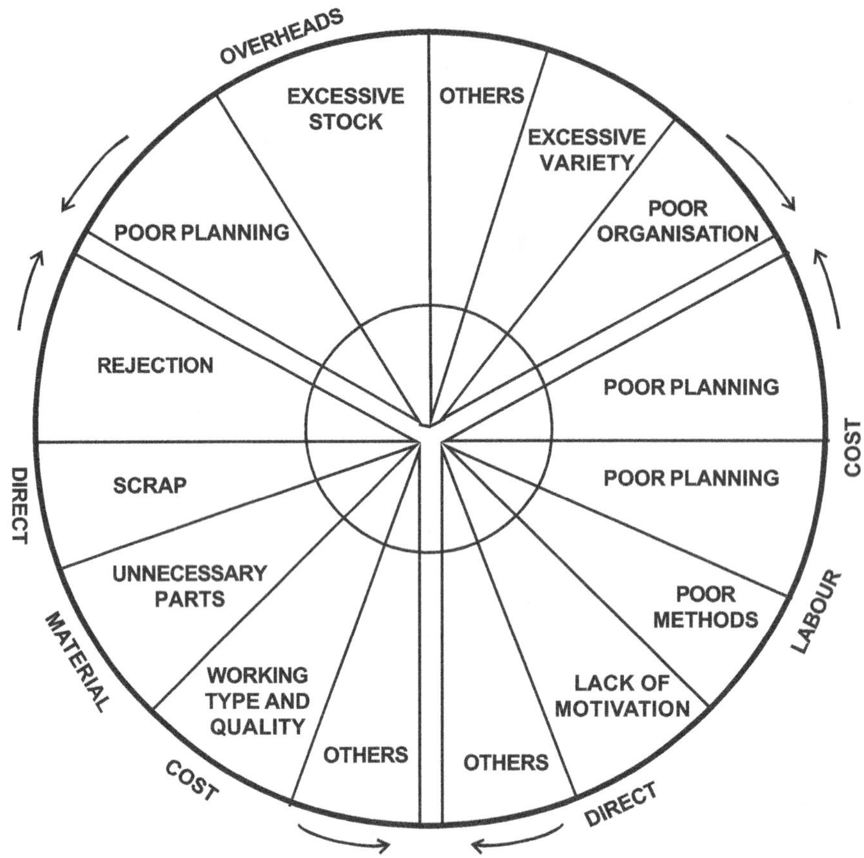


**Fig. 21.3** Constituents of total cost with probable reasons for exective cost.

*The following are a few illustrations :*

(i) In a rubber works, manufacturing caps for penicillin vials, the rejection for various reasons was found to be as much as 38%. Hence the direct material cost of the product for this factory is 60% higher that what it ought to be.

(ii) A maker of wiring clips was using a 1.5/8 strip for punching out 1.1/2 clips and the utilization of material was only 40%. By using a wider step and punching out two clips in the opposite direction this company was able to increase the utilization of material to 81%

(iii) At the Pontao Division of General Motor, the original design for the manufacture of recoil spring casing for an automatic aircraft cannon required a 6 lb. Casting to be machined from a 56 lb. Forging 50 lb of steel clips going to scrap. The new design was to weld a steel tube to 14 lb. Cylindrical forging from which only 8 lb of metal has to be removed, i.e., a 75% reduction in the cost of direct material.

(iv) A manufacturer of electronic equipment in Mumbai found by investigation as he could obtain 18.8% saving in the component cost of unitized Gamma Ray Spectrometer by eliminating a few of the components and substituting cheaper ones of the others without affecting the quality of the instrument.

The above examples will show that the direct material cost is to a great extent enhanced by:

(i) Defective design of the product and the component
(ii) Wrong selection of raw material in terms of type quality.
(iii) Poor manufacturing methods leading to excessive scrap and rejection.

We must understand, therefore, that eventhough higher vast through direct material is attributed to the shop supervision; the foreman has limited chances of controlling material costs. All he can do is the prevention of scrap and waste. It is the responsibility of the designer or the engineer to specify the type of materials and tools to be used which will lead to a lower basic cost of material. Also it is the Purchasing Department or the buying section, which can control the prices paid for them and secure maximum value for the money paid. The responsibility for controlling material can be divided amongst:

(i) The designer - for reducing the basic costs
(ii) The purchasing officer - for reducing the price paid.
(iii) The foreman - for reducing scrap, rejection, and wastage in use.

Probably the greatest scope for cost reduction throughout industry lies at the stage of product design. The cost of manufacturing, warehousing, and distributing will depend greatly on the decisions taken at this stage. The far-reaching effect of design upon product cost makes it imperative that a systematic consideration be given at this stage to all aspects contributing to its cost. Some of the factors are:

(i) Standardization and variety reduction;
(ii) Compactness of the finished product leading to economy of packing and transportation;
(iii) Use of materials considering their cost, machining and handling property, yield factor, and storage requirements; and
(iv) Influence of design upon manufacturing cost in terms of tolerances, tools, jigs and fixture, and processing time.

Once the designer has decided on the parts and components of the product and the materials to be used based on the above considerations, and the relative economy, it is left to the purchase section to buy it from the most competitive supplier.

Value analysis is concerned with a detailed discussion of the price of every component of the finished product purchased or manufactured to find out whether the best value for the money spent on it is obtained. Application of Value Analysis for purchasing has reduced the prices of items in many instances by 70% to 90%, 40% being quite common.

Typical industrial instance show poor utilization of material due to excessive scrap and rejection. Hence the control and reduction of usage of material in industry merits a very thorough in inquiry by the cost reduction team. To start with, a study of the yield, i.e., the relationship between the gross weight of materials purchased and the net weight of the finished product may point the way for further investigation into process inefficiencies. This may lead to the recognition of wastage of material at various stages and their elimination by using:

(i) Material of proper size and type.

(ii) Adequate but not excessive manufacturing tolerance.

(iii) Better equipment.

(iv) Better training of workers.

(v) Better operating methods.

(vi) Adequate supervision.

(vii) Adequate stage inspection.

**2. Labour Cost Reduction**

Eventhough material cost reduction was presented by the most potential area for cost reduction due to being a major part of the cost in manufacturing % labour turning industries, labour cost control has received more attention due to its easiness to handle. Another reason for its receiving favourable consideration from management and consultants is the extent to which reduction is possible. While material cost could be reduced from 60% to 50% or even 40% labour cost with mechanization can be almost brought down from 5% to 10%.

The direct labour cost normally, Fig. 21.3 shown on the cost sheet includes true labour cost (payment for the time booked) which cannot be reduced and a major portion of costs added due to various factors, such as poor manning, poor planning, poor working methods, and lack or motivation.

***Poor Manning :*** In many industries work study and labour control techniques have received favorable attention, because the management is aware that they are burdened with more men as a result of poor manning policy also lead to lower wages since a company's total wage bill is limited by its ability to pay. Poor manning does not just mean excessive men, since there are cases where inadequacy of men of required skill has led to a lower productivity and a higher cost.

***Poor Planning :*** No proof is required to show that bad planning of work orders adds to idle time of men and machines. Lack of raw materials of the required quality, at the right time, and at the right place, also due to defective planning adds to labour cost by increasing the ineffective time of meant. The influence of poor planning on labour cost can be summarized thus:

(i) Non-availability of men of the required skill.
(ii) Non-availability or inadequate supply of material.
(iii) Non-availability or inadequate supply of material.
(iv) Non-availability of work when all other facilities are available

***Poor Methods :*** Work content and hence labour cost of almost every job in the industry is enhanced by inefficient method of manufacture or operation. The following, among many other factors, lead to excessive amount of man-hours wasted or ineffectively utilized:

(i) Defective design demanding removal of excessive material;
(ii) Wrong machine and tools used leading to a lower output;
(iii) Process not operating properly, i.e., equipment run at sub-standard feeds and speeds;
(iv) Bad layout factory, shop, or workplace leading to excessive movement of men;
(v) Too tight tolerance and quality standards demanding great care on the part of the operatives and leading to more rejection and reprocessing; and
(vi) Bad working methods of the operatives causing waster motion and efforts.

***Lack of Motivation :*** Another factor, which adds up labour cost, is the attitude of the worker himself due to lack of proper motivation. Management by proper planning can provide work, material, and equipment, but if the man is not willing to return, on the labour investment will be much below standard.

The solution to a reduction of labour cost lies in the elimination of the factors enumerated before as leading to poor utilization of manpower. To summarize, labour productivity can be enhanced, and labour cost consequently reduced by:

(i) Reducing the work content of jobs: this can be achieved by –
    (a) Modifying the product design;
    (b) Providing adequate tolerances;
    (c) Eliminating unnecessary activities;
    (d) Rearranging and combining necessary activities; and
    (e) Improving the materials and equipment used.
(ii) *Providing adequate work :* Proper sales forecasting and planning of production can even ups and downs in production demand, and provide a steady work for the men employed. Also of great importance is the provision of only the required number of men for the work.
(iii) *Recognizing extra effort :* Recognition plans like merit-rating, for the purposes of giving merit increment and promotions, incentive schemes for paying a man according to his contribution of work, and suggestion

system to share the gains of experience and participation can provide the required pep for men to work and meet the standard of the level of performance established by management techniques like Work Study.

(iv) *Worker Working :* The most important of all is the willingness of the worker to work productively for a greater proportion of time and an understanding that the industry is dependent on his work and not his presence.

### 3. Overheads

Overhead cost in almost every industry is excessive. This may be attributed to factors like poor planning, poor inventory policy leading to excessive stocks of raw material finished goods, tools and spare parts, lack of standardization, and poor organization

***Poor Planning :*** Poor planning adds up unnecessary overhead expenses also in addition to direct material and labour expenses, also in addition to direct material and labour costs. It is regrettably true that the management's concern for efficiency in manufacture often appears to be continued to the more obvious factors like production methods, factory layout, and operator efficiency, while other potential sources of considerable savings go untapped. A few of this source are:

(i) The supply and utilization of power, fuel and water.
(ii) Maintenance.
(iii) Inspection.
(iv) Clerical services.
(v) Personal services.

Only when these services are recognized as important areas of expenditure and potential sources of cost reduction, and accorded the same enthusiastic interest as other branches of industry, can the objectives of a cost reduction program be fully achieved.

***Inventory Control :*** The importance of stock control arises from the demand which investment in stocks places upon the available liquid capital. It is of far greater significance from the point of view of cost reduction by virtue of the fact that stocks can give rise to the following sources of cost:

(i) Storage cost.
(ii) Handling cost.
(iii) Stock-taking and other clerical expenses.
(iv) Deterioration and its prevention.
(v) Pilferage.
(vi) Insurance and stock room security.
(vii) Obsolescence.

***Standardization :*** The effects upon costs and the general manufacturing efficiency of a wide diversity of products, components, equipments and methods are sufficiently important to warrant special consideration of this factor.

A reduction in variety means longer rush with fewer changes on the production line, more mechanization, higher production and lower unit cost.

The wheels of industry turn to the orders of many persons having various degrees of authority, and the contribution that a properly defined chain of responsibility and channels of communication can make towards a deduction of costs is difficult to measure.

Finally, cost reduction and control is continuous process and a program once commenced should be coordinated and controlled, atleast the benefits achieved by improved performance may easily be dissipated.

*Techniques that are commonly adopted to affect cost reduction are :*

1. Work Study.
2. PERT/CPM.
3. Value Analysis.

# 22

# Budgeting Scope and Behavioural Process

## Introduction

Budgeting is an important management accounting technique which can benefit all forms of business enterprise if fully understood and properly operated.

## Definitions

### *Budget*

"A quantitative analysis prior to a defined period of time, of a policy to be attained in a given objective."

### *Budgetary Control*

"The establishment of departmental budgets relating to the responsibilities of executives to the policy, and the actual with budgeted results, either to secure by individual action, the objective of that policy or to provide a basis for its revision."

The first excludes qualitative factors, which in themselves may be vital to the successful achievement of the given objective. However, a significant amount of descriptive information is likely to accompany the budget document.

The budget therefore initially serves as a guide to management in the implementation of the selected strategy, but during the actual budget period it will serve as a management control device.

## Reasons For Budgeting

1. *Periodic Planning :* Budgeting aims to ensure the effective and efficient use of scarce resources by determining the best way to achieve the objectives of the organisation.

   Unfortunately, not everyone is a compulsive planner but budgeting creates a formal planning framework that forces managers to take account of likely future activities. It also provides specific and uniform periodic deadlines for each phase of the planning process.

   It must be emphasised that budgeting by itself does not guarantee successful attainment of budgets requires acceptance and execution of these plans by human beings.

2. *Co-ordination, Co-operation and Communication :*
   (a) Budgeting provides an opportunity for the exchange of ideas and aspirations between managers from the various organisational segments.
   (b) Top management are provided with a vehicle to communicate their expectations to lower-level managers.
   (c) Budgets serve as a communicator during the budget period, as reference to the budget reminds everyone of the agreed targets and the progress to date.
   (d) Managers of interdependent segments need to co-operate and to co-ordinate their activities in order to maximise the utilisation of available resources.
   (e) As the size of the organisation increases, interrelationships/ interdependency grows more complicated. Co-ordination then becomes essential in order to avoid sub-optimisation and the budget serves as the linkage that holds the various departments together, and ensures that actions being taken are towards the attainment of objectives.

3. *Quantification and Cost Awareness*

   Due to the limited supply of resources, organisations must compare costs and benefits of each potential activity and select those that are considered to result in the most optimal resource allocation.

   In most circumstances, costs usually present to problems but problems may arise as to the quantification of benefits to be derived, particularly in respect of non-profit organisations.

   Accountants by nature are concerned with the cost implication of proposed activities, and budgeting forces all managers to think in terms of costs and benefits.

4. *Performance Evaluation and Control*

   What is success ? Can we be regarded as being successful simply by doing better than last year ? comparison of present performance with past performance may be inadequate, particularly if activities are not compatible.

   Budgeted performance reflects estimates of future events, and what is considered acceptable performance. Comparing actual results for the total organisation with budgeted results (measured on the same volume basis) provides meaningful information and indicates the need to analyse and investigate the variances.

   The action taken on the variances is possibly the most important aspect of the control system. Corrective action should be taken quickly at the right time and in the right place. It must also be stressed that only intended future activities will be affected or influenced by such decisions, which will be aimed at minimising and controlling future costs.

   This reporting system does not simply lend itself to reporting overall results of an organisation, in fact from a control view-point this would be unsatisfactory. Therefore, reporting on performance within areas of responsibility automatically provides a basis for managerial/employee performance evaluation and can act as a motivator, provided that the correct circumstances prevail.

5. *Goal orientation*

   Ideally the budget process is a means of implementing major policy decisions. If a long-range plan exists, this will govern the preparation of short-term budgets. The long-range plan shows the estimated revenues and expenses, over each of the next few years that are implied in policy decisions which have already been taken. Such plans indicate management's impression as to the future survival and growth of the organisation in terms of markets, products, production processes, distribution channels and financing.

   The long-range plan is likely to be reviewed on an annual basis and if changes are required these will then be reflected within the short-term budgets.

   Budgets should therefore reflect plans that are considered likely to achieve organisational goals and objectives.

   Top managements must formalise the organisational goals so that operational goals can be developed throughout the organisation. This should result in a more effective budgeting process.

   Successful budgeting is not an automatic outcome but the budgeting process is more likely to succeed when the following conditions are prevalent :

1. top management involvement and support;
2. a clear definition of long-term objectives within which budgeting operates;
3. an organisational structure which has clearly defined responsibilities and authority;
4. full acceptance and involvement of line managers;
5. an effective accounting information system that is supportive and not threatening;
   (a) expenditure/performance reports relating to responsibility;
   (b) timely and accurate reporting system; and
   (c) ability to provide additional information upon request;
6. regular revision of budgets and targets in the light of new circumstances.

## Limitations of Budgetary Control

A budget is merely a document and as such it does not possess the capacity for doing anything. It is no more than the representation of future operations and expectations.

During the budget period, management should be reminded of the following limitations of budgetary control :

1. Budgets are formulated using estimates and therefore deviations are not unexpected.
2. Rigid adherence to the budget is not as important as the managers ability to adapt to new conditions.
3. Budgets should not be used or perceived by managers as simply a reward/punishment device.
4. The execution of a budget is not automatic. Managers must be educated and informed as to benefits of budgets before they can become effective tools of management. Many of the problems that originate are due to lack of understanding of both the techniques and the behavioural conditions involved.

## Approaches to Budget Preparation

There are three types of approaches that can be adopted to derive the estimates that are to appear in the final budget-imposed, participative and negotiated.

1. *Imposed budgets* : Referred to as a "top-to-bottom" budget; top management decides upon the budget quantities, which are in turn communicated downward to lower-level managers. Lower-level managers are responsible for the execution of the budgets but have virtually no say about what is expected of them.

*Advantages*

(a) Planning decisions are made by managers who have a wider perspective of the organisation's operations and the interactions of the different sub-activities.

(b) Top management are fully aware of the resources available for the coming year and allocate them in an unbiased manner.

(c) Budget preparation is cheap, relative to the small number of people involved.

*Disadvantages*

(a) Top management may not be fully aware of specific information relating to production/marketing processes or how the available resources should be allocated in the light of this information so as to attain organisational goals.

(b) Imposed budgets may reduce the commitment of lower-level managers to their responsibilities and duties.

2. *Participative Budgets :* Information is sought from lower-level managers and their estimates are then co-ordinated and communicated upwards : referred to as a "bottom-to-top" budget.

*Advantages*

(a) Attainment of goals is logically more likely as a direct result of lower-level managers having an active role in establishing budgets.

(b) Due to daily involvement in departmental activities, lower-level managers intimately know best the abilities of their department and the necessary resource requirements.

*Disadvantages*

(a) Lower-level managers may inflate the importance of their own department, and may not be aware that inter-dependencies exist.

(b) Unrealistic estimates may be made; requesting more resources than are needed, or setting output goals at easily achievement levels.

(c) Participative budgets are more costly to supervise and to co-ordinate than imposed budgets.

3. *Ncootiated budgets :* This approach is more realistic, whereby there is a certain degree of information being exchanged between top and lower-level managers. It aims to take advantage of the favourable features of the first two approaches, i.e., it combines the broad perspective of top managers with the precise knowledge of lower-level managers and it achieves the personal commitment of the lower-level managers.

*Steps involved in this bargaining process :*

(a) Preliminary goals are communicated downwards and the available resources are delineated within an overall perspective.

(b) If these are unaccepted by lower-level managers, they are encouraged to suggest alternatives either in terms of resources of expectations.

(c) Top management will either secure additional resources or amend their expectations.

Managerial approaches to budgeting reflect the fact that it is only a part of a complex and highly political process by which organisational resources are allocated to undertain courses of action.

## Technical Aspects of Budgeting

### *Budget preparation*

The length of time needed to prepare the budget varies according to the size of the organisation and the approach adopted. Nevertheless, it is often left until as late as possible in order to reduce uncertainties, concerning predictive sales volume and selling prices, production levels and related production costs and other functional expenses.

### *Budget period*

The time period to which the plan of action relates : the specified time period is usually one year but it may be for a shorter or longer period, depending on the needs of the organisation.

### *Control period*

For control purposes the budget period is divided into shorter periods, known as control periods. The frequency with which comparisons of results are made and the appropriate reporting is carried out is dictated by the control periods.

### *Budget centre*

Efficient control requires that due recognition must be given to the fact that costs are best controlled at the point at which they are incurred. Suitable areas of control have to be selected. The areas selected should comply with the natural responsibilities of supervisors and executives. Such areas are known as budget centres.

### *Controllable and Uncontrollable Costs*

Clearly distinguishing between controllable and uncontrollable costs aids the tracing of responsibilities. Controllable costs are normally influenced by internal factors, uncontrollable costs by external factors. Fixed overhead costs are incurred as part of policy, managers who can change policy can thus control these costs. The variable overhead costs are generally controllable by employees below the ranks of policy-making management.

**Illustrated Budget preparation**

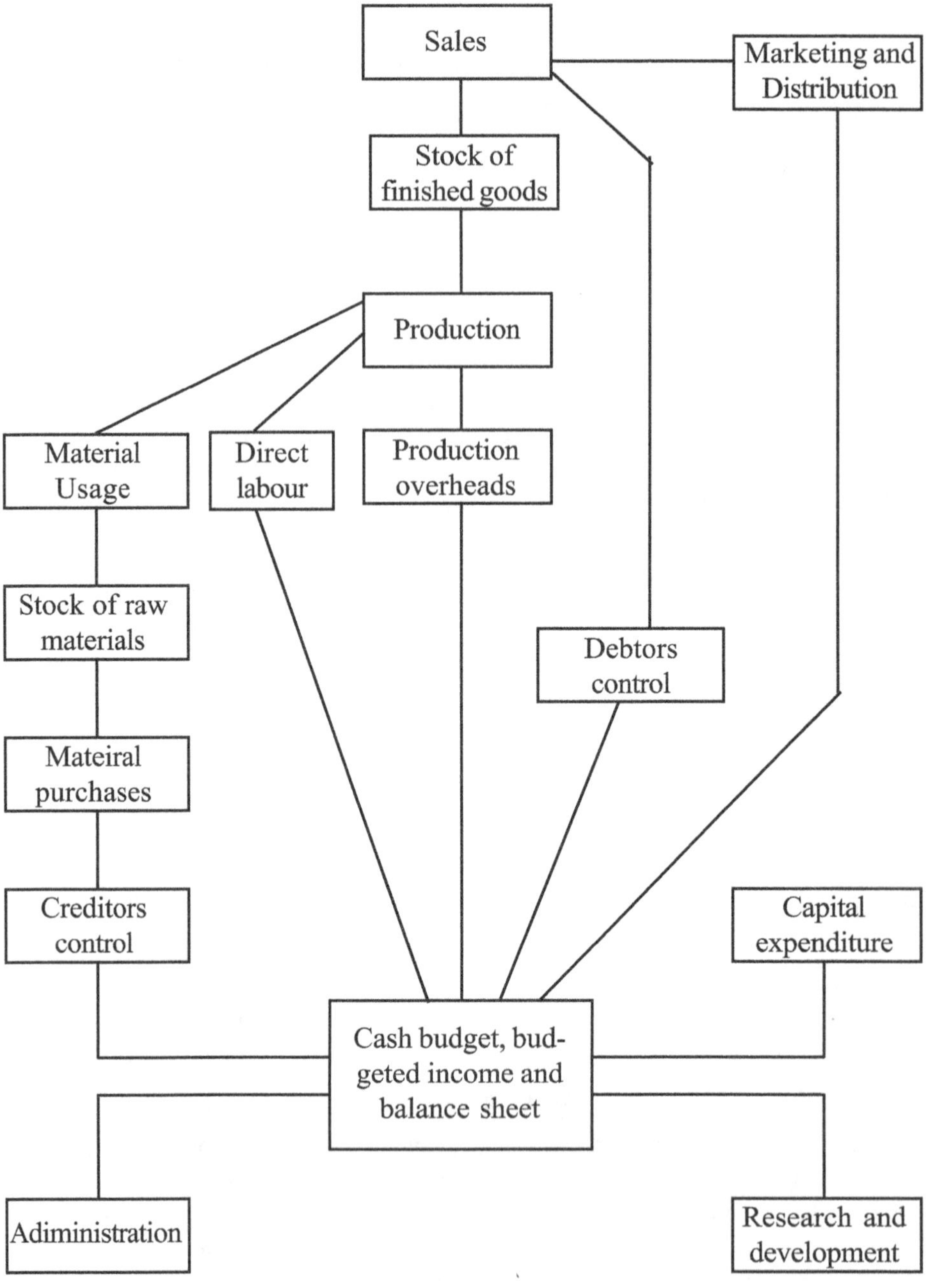

### *Fixed budget*

This employs a fixed budget level of activity and thus considers all costs and revenues pertinent to this level of activity.

### *Flexible budget*

From the point of view of managerial control, i.e., to aid in cost control, it is useful to indicate to management what costs they should incur at varying levels of activity. The essence of a flexible budget is the presentation of estimated cost data at various levels of volume and this requirement makes a knowledge of cost behaviour even more essential. It is a budget which is designed to change in accordance with the level of activity actually attained. Preparing a flexible budget in effect is simply a matter of analysing the overhead into fixed and variable and determining the extent to which they will vary within the normal range of activity.

### *The operating budget*

*This is usually in two parts :*

(a) a programme budget and

(b) a responsibility budget

This represents two different ways of depicting the overall plan of operations for the business.

The programme budget describes the major programmes the company plants to undertake. It may be arranged, for example, by product line and show the associated revenues and costs associated with each product.

The responsibility budget sets out plants in terms of the persons responsible for carrying them out. It is therefore primarily a control device, since it sets a standard against which actual performance can later be compared. So in a factory, for example, there may be a responsibility budget showing the costs which are controllable by the foreman of each department. If the costs in a responsibility centre are expected to vary with volume, the responsibility budget should be prepared in the form of a variable or flexible budget. This shows the expected behaviour of costs at various volume levels.

### *Master budget*

The budgeted profit and loss account and balance sheet will indicate the enterprise results to be expected by the end of the period. If the results are judged to be unsatisfactory the functions are re-budgeted. This process continues until an overall satisfactory budget is drafted. The budget is then accepted by top management and upon acceptance the budget is termed the master budget. From that moment on it ceases to be rely a plan, it also becomes an executive order.

### *Budget manual*

A document which sets out standing instructions governing the responsibilities of individual managers, and the procedure, forms and records relating to the preparation and use of the budget.

***Budget committee***

This committee is responsible for the overall budget preparation and administration. Those actually involved will depend on the management structure and policy but the committee normally includes a representative from each of the functional areas.

**Principle budget factor**

The identification of the factor which imposes a limitation on the level of activity; it is usually sales demand but there may be a limitation as regards a factor of production (raw materials, skilled labour or machine time). This must be determined and its value assessed before any other functions can be budgeted.

## Functional Budgets and the Master Budget

Budgets are prepared in draft form and then amended in the light of new developments or discussions between departmental managers or between managers subordinates and superiors. If sales demand is the factor, restricting budgeted activity, however, the sequence of budget preparation will be as follows :

1. The sales budget is prepared first. This will incorporate decisions about selling prices and expected sales volume for each item of product (or service) and also the changes in the level of debtors.
2. The departmental budgets for marketing, sales and distribution would also be made at an early stage, because estimates of spending on sales promotion, advertising and salesmen will be necessary to gauge the expected volume of sales.
3. Having prepared a sales budget, it should be possible to estimate production requirements however, a decision must first be taken about stocks of finished goods. A decision to increase stocks would mean that production for the period must exceed sales volume; on the other hand, a decision to reduce stock levels (so as to improve the organisation's cash position) would mean that production volume would be less than sales volume by the amount of the run-down in stocks.
4. The production budget is then prepared, specifying the expected quantities of each product to be made, in each factory or manufacturing department, followed by the budgets of resources for production, i.e.,
   (a) materials usage budget;
   (b) labour budget;
   (c) production overhead budget (indirect material, indirect labour, machine utilisation and other related costs).
5. A material-purchasing budget is also required, specifying the expected quantities and price of each stores item for raw materials, bought-out components, and stationery. In order to prepare purchase budget, a decision must first be taken about stock levels. Purchase requirements

(in quantity) are the usage requirements, plus any increase in raw material stock or less any decrease in stocks. Also consideration would be given as to change in creditors.

6. A capital expenditure budget, specifying the need to replace or acquire additional fixed assets.
7. The cash budget cannot be prepared until the functional budgets in items 1 to 6 have been decided. The importance of this budget cannot be overstressed, if adequate control is to be exercised over the flow of cash and if the continual solvency of the business is to be assured. It will reflect the expected cash inflows, each month for the budget period. Shorter control periods may be necessary but will be dictated by the needs of the business.
8. These budgets will then be amalgamated to prepare the budgeted profit and loss account and year-end balance sheet.
9. Once approved by top management (perhaps by authorisation of the budget committee) these budgets become the master budget for the coming year.

## Behaviour Aspects of Budgeting

*Budgets aim to serve a variety of purposes :*

- planning of essential economic resources;
- co-ordination of interrelated activities;
- delegation of managerial authority;
- motivation of managers and employees.

There is a tendency for organisations to expect results simply by understanding and concentrating on the technical procedures of budgeting, failing to recognise that effective use and application of budgeting depends on the actions of the responsible individuals.

Budgetary systems can and do influence behaviour and action but unfortunately not always in the anticipated or desired direction. Nevertheless, despite these behavioural problems being recognised, and considerable research having been carriedout, it is still difficult to form broad generalisations as the findings are complex and often contradictory.

However, there is general agreement that budgeting is not a neutral, objectives and purely technical process, and it is necessary to appreciate the importance of sound inter-personal relations and to obtain the co-operation of participants.

T. Lucey suggests that an idea budgeting system is one which :

(a) encourages goal congruence;
(b) develops motivation and
(c) avoids dysfunctional effects.

## Goal Congruence

"The need to create situations in which each individual, in attempting to satisfy his own needs, will be making the greatest possible contribution to the accomplishment of the goals of the organisation". (R. N. Anthony).

Goal congruent is achieved when the personal goals of individuals coincide with the goals of the organisation. Research demonstrates that to achieve goal congruence, requires consideration of a broad range of human needs in addition to those that can be satisfied by economic rewards. Although money is an excellent motivator for satisfying lower-level needs, concentration on organisational policies relative to job enrichment, management by self-control and participative leadership may provide better motivation for achievement of higher level needs.

It would be unrealistic to assume that this ideal is attainable in its entirety but at the same time it would be unwise to select and implement organisational goals without consideration of personal goals.

McGregor's Theory X and Theory Y characterise the two extremes of management styles and attitudes which are reflected in the way the budgeting system may be operated.

***Theory X***

Supportive of an authoritarian management style, which views people as :

(a) inherently lazy;
(b) requiring coercion and control;
(c) avoiding responsibility and
(d) only seeking security,

This is the theory of scientific management, with its emphasis on control and extrinsic rewards.

***Theory Y***

Supportive of a more democratic and participative management style and views people as :

(a) liking work, which is as natural as rest or play;
(b) now having to be controlled and coerced if they are committed to the organisation's objectives and
(c) under proper conditions not only accepting but also seeking responsibility.

Theory X is based on the assumptions derived from scientific management developed by Taylor and Gilbreth which is clearly operational but can create frustration and prevents personal development. The trend in behavioural research suggests that benefits may be derived from implementing a leadership style as suggested by Theory Y, through participation.

## Motivation

Defined by T. Lucey as : "The need to achieve a selected objective and the resulting drive that influence action towards the selected objective".

Budgets are used to motivate members of the organisation by serving as targets and mechanisms for gaining involvement and commitment. Budget reports are not solely used to measure the performance of the organisational segments as economic entities but also the performance of the individual responsible for their administration.

Some empirical evidence indicates that clearly defined objectives, and the active participation by managers in the planning process, can induce motivation in a positive manner. Likewise the control process is aided by active participation in the investigation of variances, and in the evaluation and selection of appropriate solutions. Motivation is improved, therefore, by appropriate emphasis on positive achievements rather than simply concentrating on the adverse variances.

The budget becomes a target intended to induce an active and possibly pressured organisational atmosphere, which it is believed will result in higher levels of performance within the organisation. (Stedry)

Research by Argyris suggests that budgets are considered by managers/employees as pressure devices and that undue pressure was the core of the budgeting problem. The budgets were regarded as part of a policing system, which tends to result in negative motivation. Therefore, to foster motivation requires the full involvement and continuous participation by all levels of managers in the planning and control processes, their acceptance of the budgets and attainable levels of performance being set.

### *Dysfunctional behaviour*

Caplan suggests that there is simple evidence to support the premise that behaviourally naive management accounting techniques, such as budgeting, can serve as a deterrent to goal congruence and under certain circumstances, can be a source of such undesirable behaviour responses as frustration, conflict and rigidity.

This results in dysfunctional behaviour which has the effect of reducing the overall effectiveness and efficiency of the organisation, and can be evidenced by the following responses :

1. *Reaction to pressure :* Budgets are definite in nature. There is little room for manipulation or escape if results are not going to turn out as expected. Constant pressure leads to a gradual erosion of rationality which is replaced by mistrust, hostility and lower performance levels. Discosts, a clear definition of responsibilities and establishing appropriate standards of performance will help to relieve such pressure.
2. *Over-emphasis on the short run :* Too much emphasis is given to activities relating to short-term profitability which may be detrimental to the long-term prospects for the organisation. For example, a manager may fail to

take advantage of a special purchasing offer as this would result in spending above the budgeted amount. Opportunities should be made available to the managers to explain their actions, which may not be clear within the context of budget reports.

3. *Poor communication :* Where a Theory X style of management is employed there is the risk of managers manipulating results, so that top management receive the performance summary that they expect or an unwillingness to transmit information. These tactics are used by managers who feel that their survival justifies the use of such tactics. The reluctance to communicate information will seriously impede the efficiency of the planning and control processes.

   There is also the potential conflict between the line managers and the accounting department. This is particularly possible where the accounting department reports directly to a higher level of management, as opposed to those directly responsible for the activities being reported. Line managers are likely to become suspicious and react against the budgeting system.

   This can be avoided by altering the reporting system to ensure that line managers receive performance reports, either prior to or simultaneously with the high-level managers, together with an opportunity to comment on the results.

4. *Sub-optimisation :* Budgeting pressure can lead to sub-optimisation which is where individual or departmental goals are pursued to the detriment of the organisational goals. For example, one department may take actions which are beneficial to that department without regard of the unfavourable effects on other departments, resulting in a net loss to the organisation.

   Such action may be due to the measures of performance being used for individual departments which does not highlight the degree of inter-dependency between departments. Alternatively, it may be due to the apparent rigidity of budgets, whereby managers feel compelled to spend the amount of money allocated in their budget, so as to avoid a possible reduction in subsequent budget periods, whereas the unnecessary amount spent could have been diverted to another department which may have improved the total performance of the organisation.

   Basically the avoidance of dysfunctional behaviour is not easy but organisations must ensure that genuine participation is present, because Agyris observed that some firms professing to use participative budgeting were not really using it at all. He suggested that it would probably be much wiser for such firms to follow authoritarian budget practices and honestly admit it than to engage in the pretence of pseudo-participation.

   In order to achieve the motivational advantages of true participation necessitates top management accepting a certain degree of budgetary slack.

## Budgetary Slack

According to Schiff and Lewis, managers create slack in budgets by under-estimating revenues and overestimating costs. They are motivated to do this because it introduces a degree of flexibility into the budgets, so as to guard against the possible failure to attain the budgets.

It is regarded as necessary, since failing to attain budget levels is perceived as a social stigma and can cause a reduction in aspiration levels, goals and performance. Some slack may be desirable to allow the achievement of personal goals while at the same time meeting the organisation's goals. However, excessive slack is clearly detrimental to the best interests of an organisation.

Therefore budgetary slack exists to provide individuals with room to manoeuvre within a budgetary constraint.

Tightness of budgets and performance levels

*Research on aspiration levels provides the following conclusions :*

1. the constant achievement of too easily attained goals may adversely affect motivation and performance;
2. the constant failure to achieve goals which have been set too high can also have a negative influence on motivation and performance and
3. individuals tend to set higher expectations and work harder to achieve those expectations when they have been directly involved in the goal-setting process and have developed a personal commitment to their achievement. (Caplan)

This indicates a relationship between targets and performance but how does this come about ? Mcclelland's theory on achievement motivation suggests that individuals possess a desire to be challenged and to be innovative.

Hofstede found that up to a certain degree of tightness, budgets became stronger motivators as they became tighter, although thereafter motivation declined.

Therefore budget levels that are set too high can cause individuals to become discouraged and ignore these targets. Alternatively, budget levels that are set too low may cause individuals to become self-satisfied and inefficient and perform below their real potential.

## Ideal Budgets

These are budgets which assume that the organisation can operate at maximum capacity with maximum efficiency at all times.

Highly unlikely to be achieved and viewed as unreasonable. Research supports this view and concludes that ideal budgets are not the best approach to achieve motivation.

### Currently Attainable Budgets

These should be achieved under normal working conditions, i.e., tight enough to prevent inefficiency and at the same time generate personal satisfaction on achievement. A difficult feat to accomplish since management need a thorough knowledge of their workforce's ability, previous experience of the methods of work and a degree of commonsense, aside from the technical problems of obtaining accurate and relevant estimates for inclusion in the budge.

## Summary

Recognition of both technical and behavioural aspects of budgeting are essential if organisational goals are to be achieved. To date the required knowledge to design and operate an ideal budgeting system has not been provided. Budgeting is not simply a purely technical process, it includes nemerous behavioural problems which can be particularly disruptive if managers do not participate in the setting of budgets or if budget levels are perceived as unattainable. Every budgeting system must be tailor-made and its success should be measured by the extent to which it provides the necessary motivation for individuals to make their maximum contribution to the achievement of organisational goals.

# 23

# Budgeting and Budgetary Control

We are all familiar with the term "budget" and at some stage or other we have all used budgets in our personal affairs. There is the holiday budget and the one for the purchase of furnishings, or a new house.

Budgeting, therefore, simply means fabrication a plan for the future. In the case of a business, with which we are here concerned, it is a plan for the future operation of business; the requirements of capital before it can become established, and subsequently, the planning for and control of revenue and expenditure, and the general operation of the business.

The modern business enterprise is a highly complicated organisation, frequently with a considerable investment in land and buildings, machinery, raw materials, etc., all managed by people for the purpose of satisfying a consumer demand for goods and services. All these varied activities are inter dependent, and unless the whole structure is knitted together to work as a team in order to achieve the common goal, there will be no real measure success.

Accordingly, while we may have volume of sales built on a sound marketing policy, these goods must be delivered at the right place on time. This inturn involve sound production planning, which needs the right equipment and personnel to operate it. Production needs all the necessary materials with planned availability, and all this adds up to a planning forward for the financial arrangements to allow it to be carried out.

Budgets, while looking forward and laying plans for future operations, cannot entirely ignore the past. Past records will be examined, related to market conditions and current price levels, and possible trends in the future. We can express this another way by saying that a budget is based on past events but considered in the light of future probabilities, be capable of attainment, and should present a positive objective for a volume of sales sufficient to produce a satisfactory profit. It will be seen as these lectures on budgets and budgetary control proceed, that the sales budget is the all-important one. We all know that there can be no profit without sales and consequently there is no profit on goods however efficiently they may be produced, if they continue to lie in the warehouse.

It is a common business practice to budget carefully for a new enterprise. No businessman would embark on a new venture without considering the following factors :

1. What are the *risks* involved ?
2. Will the *profit* provide an adequate return on the capital invested ?
3. What *time* will be required for normal development ?
4. What is the *effort* required ?

These are first principal questions and particular ventures may pose additional problems such as location and climate. Basically, however, a thought analysis of the above will uncover the required information.

One of the first considerations in the budget program is that in item (2), which will involve the task of estimating the total income and expenditure for the venue, any excess of the income over the expenditure will, broadly speak, be the net profit which can be expected.

These estimates of income and expenditure, or the budget itself, will subsequently be used to make comparisons with actual results, and the degree to which the analysis of the estimates is made will determine the intensity of the comparisons and their effective use for purpose of control.

If a business is to operate successfully, it must continually plan its activities in advance. The budget thus prepared becomes the standard for the business, which are closely related, but we must always keep in mind that there is a distinction between the two. A business may have a budget and exercise budgetary control without utilizing a standard costing. Similarly, it may be said that standard costing does not itself create a budget, although it would normally presuppose its existence.

We have been considering some of the principles of budgeting and why we should have budgets. The basic considerations formulated previously can be expanded into the following objectives:

1. To present the future operations of the enterprise as concisely as possible;
2. To co-ordinate the efforts of all those concerned by formulating a unified plan;
3. To provide a constant remainder of the ultimate element on all business transactions – finance;
4. To reduce costly instituting automatic control and consequently, by the elimination of weaknesses, to increase profits;
5. To provide a centralized executive control over the internal operations of the business without decreasing the responsibility of employees;
6. To control the investment in stocks and stores within reasonable maximum and minimum levels;
7. To co-ordinate production activities with sales demands at seasonal and peak levels;
8. To control all revenue expenditures in a logical manner by bringing items of expense under regular review;
9. To regulate capital expenditure and prevent any undue expansion of fixed assets.

Let us again summarize these purposes and advantages of budgeting and budgetary control in the following terms :

(a) *Establishment of objective* for the whole undertaking.
(b) *Executive policy* for future operations.
(c) *Authority* for expenditure.
(d) *Finance :* Co-ordinate statement of funds to be received and expended.
(e) *Progress :* Comparison of results of operations achieved.
(f) *Training* of personnel in forecasting, planning and organization.

There should always be an appreciation of the limitations of budget and it must be remembered that budgeting is an aid to management, not an end in itself. Budgets, being based on estimates will not execute themselves and accordingly must always be backed up with competent amazement if they are to become realities and the budgeted profit realized.

It is possible to have a budget without budgetary control, which is little better actually than having no budget at all. But obviously we cannot have control without a budget.

The following are essentials before any budget plan can be completely followed out :

1. A complete system of general accounting to provide basic information
2. A system of cost accounting integrated or co-ordinated with the financial encodes and from which information on production volume and cost can be determined;
3. Adequate records of stock and stores to provide information on usage;
4. Monthly profit and loss statements for the whole undertaking;
5. A defined chart of accounts to allow correct comparison to be made between budget and actual figures.

This brings us to the rather obvious principle in all matters in connection with the budget. This may be especially appointed. Whatever may be the appointment, the official in the position of budget officer has a number of clearly defined duties.

1. To receive from heads of departments, periodic estimates and to approve the form in which these are made ;
2. To verify that all activities are co-ordinated and to place these estimates before the budget committee formed to finalise the budget.
3. To attend all meetings convened to deal with the preparation of the budget and to supply supplementary information.
4. To convey the decisions of the budget committee to the heads of departments in the appropriate form.
5. To follow the working of the budget plan and to receive reports on operations;
6. To inform heads of departments of any changes in original estimates;
7. To maintain close liaison with all departments in order to ensure correct co-ordination;
8. To take out periodic comparisons between budget and actual results and to ensure that these are correctly tabulated and reported to management.

One of the first steps in preparing a budget is to settle on the period. While this is usually one year, it may not necessarily be so. It is further necessary that all departmental estimates must cover the same period so that eventually they can be co-ordinated.

There is no fixed method of determining the period of the budget but the following are considerations :

1. Length of accounting period;
2. Length of stock turnover period;
3. Market conditions;
4. Adequacy of past period;
5. Length of production period;
6. Financial considerations.

### Accounting Period

The whole purpose of a budgetary system will be defeated if the planning is not checked against actual results. In order to effect comparisons therefore it should be seen that the beginning and end of the budget period coincide with the stage of the financial period.

### Stock Turnover Period

Sales are frequently effected by seasonal demands and accordingly the greater portion of the year's sales can occur at a particular peak period. Production however must be carried on for a period before hand in preparation for the peak period so that the budget must cover the whole of the turnover period, that is, from when production commences to the time when sales occur.

### Market Conditions

Variations and instability in market conditions tend to make budgeting more difficult and could also mean more frequent revisions in the budget figures. Where such conditions exist the budget period must be as short as possible. On the other hand, where conditions are stable and prices more or less constant, long range planning can be made with more confidence.

### Adequacy of Past Records

Future planning is frequently based on past records in the light of future probabilities. Hence, records of past operations and trends are important in giving an indication of what can happen in the future. Should the business be a new one there will be little or no antecedent information and the budget should be as short as possible, to be extended as further information becomes available.

## Financial Considerations

A sound financial policy dictates that the budget must cover a period for which adequate financial arrangements to cover operations can be made well in advance.

Most business experience peak demands for financial requirements, and all planning must be sufficiently long to carry the business over these periods.

## Budget Preparation and Presentation

Figure 23.1 depicts the budget process.

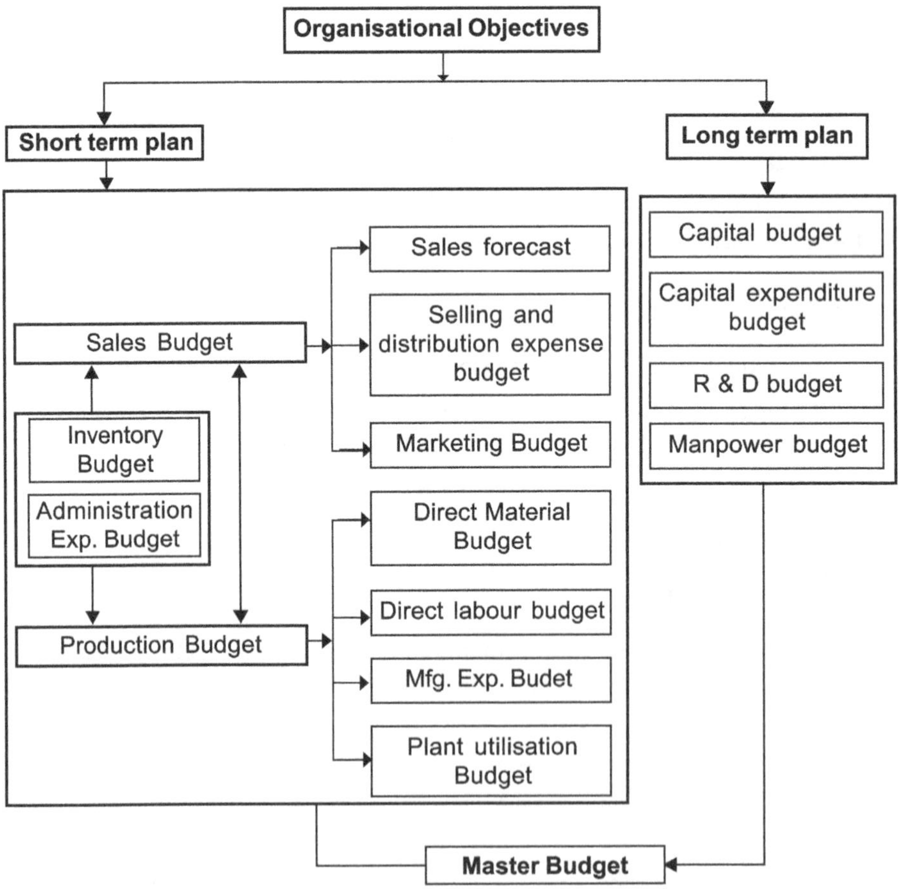


**Fig. 23.1** Budget Process.

Budgets fall into two main classes :

1. Financial budgets
2. Operational budgets

The main operating budget or, as it is commonly called, the master budget, is in effect a projection of the profit and loss statement and it combines the following :

(a) Sales
(b) Production
(c) Administration expenses

The production budget can again be sub-divided into :

(a) Sales
(b) Selling and distribution
(c) Sales administration

The financial budgets can normally be sub-divided into :

(a) Cash receipts and expenditure
(b) Capital expenditure.

It must be kept in mind that the subdivision of budget can go on almost interminably. For instance, the materials budget can be divided into raw materials and maintenance stores, and further again into foreign and local purchases. Sales advertisements which may form a very considerable part of selling expenses and be subject to a special individual vote from the board, may warrant a budget of its own within the framework of selling expenses. And so we can go on.

Let us go back for a moment of the same chapter on budgeting wherein we considered first considerations :

1. Risk
2. Profit
3. Time
4. Effort.

On these considerations, the most important is that of profit. To achieve the required profit, selling policies and production planning may have to be reconsidered and expenses reviewed. The amount of profit required will determine whether the sales expected are adequate and the expenses low enough. Profit is the ultimate figure towards which the budget plan must steer.

### Profit

The amount of profit required will be based on the total capital invested in the business and the risks involved. The rates of interest on first-class securities, interest on long-term loans, dividents to shareholders and provisions for future expansion, will all have to be considered. The calculation could follow somewhat the following lines.

**Table 23.1**

| Items for consideration | Last year Rs. × 1000 | This year Rs. × 100 |
|---|---|---|
| Dividents to shareholders | 7,500 | 9,000 |
| Provision for Taxation | 1,500 | 1,800 |
| Reserves | 1,000 | 1,200 |
| Total profit required | 10,000 | 12,000 |

This Table 23.1 is shown in condensed form and the figures are quite imaginary, but it does shown the method used in determining the starting point of all budgeting namely, the total profit required by the organisation for the coming year which as the Table 23.1 shows is Rs. 12,000,000.

## Budget Committee

The actual work of carrying out the preparation of the budget as explained in the previous chapters now become the responsibility of the budget committee which, for example, could consist of :

1. Top management
2. Departmental managers : Sales, Production, Personnel, Finance and Planning.
3. Chief Engineer
4. Any other major departmental heads
5. Budget officer.

The budget committee should be sufficiently compact to allow for quick reference and decisions but also sufficiently representative to allow for through consideration of all the problems connected with operations. Accordingly, while the Budget Officer is finally responsible for the presentation of a completely co-ordinated budget, it cannot and should not be regarded as entirely his work, a good budget is the result of the combined skill of the executives responsible for their own particular phase of the activities of the organisation.

## Sales Budget

The next stage in the preparation of the budget is the estimating of sales. This is an extremely wide phase of budgeting, and methods will vary widely with different types of business. The detailed methods used in determining a realistic volume of sales for the year do not lie within the scope of this book. The task is the responsibility of sales personnel and ultimately of the Sales Manager or Marketing Manager/ Director.

In a business of any magnitude the forecasting and planning of sales volume is the all important part of the budget plan. As there can be no profit without sales, this aspect cannot be too strongly emphasised. In the task of compiling the sales budget, the Sales Manager becomes a co-ordinator within the sales department. While it could of course be the case in many retail establishments, it is seldom that a product finds its sales in one compact area in the case of a manufacturing industry. Accordingly the sales budget is divided into its smallest element, which may be a town area. These estimates are then assembled into territories and hence into regions or states, with a final total assembly for the whole enterprise.

The form of sales budgets used will naturally be many and varied, and accordingly, those shown in Fig. 23.2 and 23.3 are for illustration purposes only.

### Budget for Selling Expenses

Selling expenses can be broadly divided into two main classes :

1. Those which can be linked directly with a product, i.e., direct selling expenses;
2. Those of a general nature, i.e., indirect selling expenses.

The selling expenses budget will be considered in relation to the volume of sales, as many items such as commission, delivery charges, etc. will vary directly with sales. The form of budget will commonly take the form sales. The form of budget will commonly take the form outlined in Fig. 23.4, condensed for the sake of convenience.

### Administrative Expenses Budget

This budget will normally follow a simple pattern. Some items are capable of reasonably close estimation while others will be subject to external factors beyond the control of the enterprise. Estimation is further facilitated by working through the year month by month. A common form is shown in Fig. 23.5 suitably condensed.

### The Production Budget

This budget while ultimately preserved in a summarised form showing the co-ordinated result of estimates of operations, actually falls into three main sections :

1. The materials (or purchases) budget ;
2. The labour budget ;
3. The factory expense budget.

and accordingly will be dealt with separately.

**Figure 23. 2 Sales Budget - Territory No. 1**

**For Year Ending ______**

| Products | Area A | | | | Area B | | | | Total for Territory | | | |
|---|---|---|---|---|---|---|---|---|---|---|---|---|
| | Last Year | | This Year | | Last Year | | This Year | | Last Year | | This Year | |
| | Quantity | Value | Quantity | Value | Quantity | Value | Quantity | Value | Quantity | Value | Quantity | Value |
| | | | | | | | | | | | | |
| Total | | | | | | | | | | | | |

**Figure 23. 3 Sales Budget - Region / Zone**

**For Year Ending ______________**

| Products | Territory 1 | | | | Territory 2 | | | | Territory 3 | | | |
|---|---|---|---|---|---|---|---|---|---|---|---|---|
| | Last Year | | This Year | | Last Year | | This Year | | Last Year | | This Year | |
| | Quantity | Value | Quantity | Value | Quantity | Value | Quantity | Value | Quantity | Value | Quantity | Value |
| | | | | | | | | | | | | |
| Total Sales Cost of Goods Sold | | | | | | | | | | | | |
| Gross Profit | | | | | | | | | | | | |

**Figure 23. 4 Budget of Selling Expenses for Year Ending**

| | Territories | | | | | | |
|---|---|---|---|---|---|---|---|
| **Sales (as per budget)** | **A** | **B** | **C** | **D** | **E** | **F** | **Total** |
| | | | | | | | |
| **Department Selling Expenses** | | | | | | | |
| Sales salaries | | | | | | | |
| Advertising | | | | | | | |
| Commission | | | | | | | |
| Salesmen's Expenses, etc. | | | | | | | |
| Sub-Total | | | | | | | |
| **Other Selling Expenses** | | | | | | | |
| Administration, etc. | | | | | | | |
| Sub-Total | | | | | | | |
| **Total Selling Expenses** | | | | | | | |

**Figure 23. 5 Budget of Administration Expenses**

**For Year Ending ____________________**

**(Monthwise) - for 12 months**

| | January | | February | | November | | December | | Total | |
|---|---|---|---|---|---|---|---|---|---|---|
| | Last year | This year | Last year | This year | Last year | This year | Last year | This year | Last year | This year |
| | | | | | | | | | | |
| Total | | | | | | | | | | |

The materials budget involves factors which have not so far effected those considered previously. Sufficient detail must be prepared to show not only the quantities of materials required to take care of budgeted production, but in addition :

1. The quantities of materials which must be in stock during each budget period :
2. The dates by which materials must be available;
3. Budgeted cost of the materials.

In other words, the purpose of the materials budgets is to ensure that adequate quantities of the materials used are available when required, and also to enable the purchasing officers to organise their activities to the best advantages. This involves estimates of the volume of production, which in turn will depend on the volume of sales. To secure a balanced production programme therefore it would seem that the sales budget and the production budget should be compiled almost simultaneously and, indeed, co-ordination between the two at all times is a necessity.

The situation in practice - will in most cases resolve itself into the question of supply and demand. Where the supply exceeds the demand, the significant determination is what can be sold, so that the volume disclosed by the sales budget will very largely determine the volume of production. On the contrary, should demand exceed supply, it will obviously be the best policy to sell all that can be made, in which case production will determine sales. Limiting factors to any determination on the above basis could be the availability of finance and manufacturing capacity. A sample of a form normally used in shown in Fig. 23.6.

The information compiled in the previous budget, as shown in Fig. 23.6, is again summarised in the form shown in Fig. 23.7 to give the total quantity and value of purchases for the budget period.

## Labour Budget

The labour budget sets up an estimate of the labour cost and the personnel requirements over the budget period.

The actual form of budget will vary according to the type of industry and the diversity of the labour employed but generally it will follow the form shown in Fig. 23.8.

### *Manufacturing Expenses Budget*

Budgeting for expenses serve three purposes :

1. Financial planning ;
2. Calculation of recovery rates ;
3. Control of expenditure on operations.

Expense budgeting has special problems because of the different nature of the items involved. These can be classified into :

1. **Fixed expenses** (invariable) which remain unchanged under varying conditions of operations (e.g., rent, taxes, insurance etc.);
2. **Semi-fixed expenses** (semi - variable) which tend to vary with changes in volume of activity, but not necessarily in fixed ratio; repairs, power and light
3. **Variable expenses** which not only vary with a change in the volume of activity but also maintain a direct ratio to that volume - such as consumable stores, services etc.

In preparing the budget, past records must be taken into account and future probabilities considered in regard to operations.

Fixed expenses should not present any major problems, as they can be estimated substantially from past records, and are not effected by any changes in output.

Variable and semi-variable expenses will however present some problems. Supplies and directly variable expenses can be calculated from the units of production expected, and then multiplied by the budgeted volume to give the total expense. In every case a check must be made on past performance and care taken to ensure that inconsistencies have been examined. It may be found that indirect or non-productive wages may conform to a fairly regular percentage of productive wages and this can be re-checked against foreman's estimates.

A suggested form of budget for manufacturing expense is shown in Fig. 23.9.

## The Cash Budget

The cash budget is of great importance in any budget programme. All business activity ultimately resolves itself into terms of finance and financial management. Planning for operations should not be put into effect without a full examination of the capacity of the business to provide the necessary finance. A knowledge is therefore, required of cash receipts and expenditure so that the availability of funds is in balance throughout the budget period.

The cash, or financial budget, in addition to presenting a plan for the management for the finances of the business is also a means whereby expenditure can be authorised, and this aspect will be discussed at a subsequent chapter.

The cash budget is more conveniently prepared in two stages and these are illustrated in Fig. 23.10 and Fig. 23.11.

Budgeting for capital expenditure will be the subject of a separate section, but for obvious reasons it appears as an item in the financial budget presented.

A final submission will logically be the master operating budget shown in Fig. 23.12 which summarises the presented individual budgets.

**Figure 23. 6 Material Budget (Purchase)**

**For Month Ending ________________**

**(For each Production Department)**

| Item | Code No. | Unit | Quantities Required | | Quantity on hand at beginning of period (c) | Purchase (a) + (b) – (c) | Rate | Amount |
|---|---|---|---|---|---|---|---|---|
| | | | For Production (a) | For end of period (b) | | | | |
| | | | | | | | | |

**Figure 23. 7 Material Purchase Budget**

**For Year Ending ____________________**

**(Monthwise for 12 Months for all Departments)**

| Item | Code No. | Unit | January | | December | | Total | |
|---|---|---|---|---|---|---|---|---|
| | | | Quantity | Value | Quantity | Value | Quantity | Value |
| | | | | | | | | |

Figure 23. 8 Labour Budget

For Year Ending ________ (Monthwise for 12 months)

| Department | Classification | Rate of Wage | January | | February | | November | | December | | Total Cost |
|---|---|---|---|---|---|---|---|---|---|---|---|
| | | | No. | Amount | No. | Amount | No. | Amount | No. | Amount | |
| | | | | | | | | | | | |
| | | Total | | | | | | | | | |

**Figure 23. 9 Manufacturing Expenses Budget (Factory)**

**For Year Ending ____________**

| STATISTICS | Total | Service Departments | | | Production Departments | | |
|---|---|---|---|---|---|---|---|
| (Basic for Appointment) | | 1 | 2 | 3 | A | B | C |
| 1. Floor Space | | | | | | | |
| 2. Direct Labour Hours | | | | | | | |
| 3. Plant Horse Power | | | | | | | |
| 4. Capital value, plant and machinery | | | | | | | |
| 5. Capital value, land and building etc. | | | | | | | |
| **FIXED EXPENSES** | | | | | | | |
| 1. Municipal Taxes | | | | | | | |
| 2. Fire Insurance | | | | | | | |
| 3. Rent | | | | | | | |
| 4. Depreciation | | | | | | | |
| 5. Management, etc. | | | | | | | |
| Total Fixed Expenses | | | | | | | |
| **VARIABLE EXPENSES** | | | | | | | |
| 1. Indirect labour | | | | | | | |
| 2. Consumable stores | | | | | | | |
| 3. Light and power | | | | | | | |
| 4. Repairs | | | | | | | |
| 5. Service Dept., Distribution, etc. | | | | | | | |
| Total Expenses | | | | | | | |

**Figure 23. 10 Cash Budget**

**For Year Ending __________**

| Item | January | February | March | October | November | December |
|---|---|---|---|---|---|---|
| **RECEIPTS** | | | | | | |
| 1. Sales - cash | | | | | | |
| 2. Sales - credit | | | | | | |
| 3. Other income | | | | | | |
| 4. Total Receipts | | | | | | |
| **DISBURSEMENT** | | | | | | |
| 5. Capital items | | | | | | |
| 6. Purchases | | | | | | |
| 7. Wages | | | | | | |
| 8. Administration Expenses | | | | | | |
| 9. Selling Expenses | | | | | | |
| 10. Manufacturing Expenses | | | | | | |
| 11. Other Expenses | | | | | | |
| 12. Total Disbursements | | | | | | |
| 13. Opening cash balance | | | | | | |
| 14. Balance for month (4 - 12) | | | | | | |
| 15. Closing Cash Balance (13 + 14) | | | | | | |

**Figure 23. 12 Cash Budget Summary**

**For Year Ending __________**

| Month | Dr. or Cr. | Opening Balance | Estimated Receipts | | Total Available | Estimating Expenditure | | Dr. or Cr. | Closing Balance |
|---|---|---|---|---|---|---|---|---|---|
| | | | Capital | Revenue | | Capital | Revenue | | |
| January | | | | | | | | | |
| February | | | | | | | | | |
| March | | | | | | | | | |
| April | | | | | | | | | |
| May | | | | | | | | | |
| June | | | | | | | | | |
| July | | | | | | | | | |
| August | | | | | | | | | |
| September | | | | | | | | | |
| October | | | | | | | | | |
| November | | | | | | | | | |
| December | | | | | | | | | |

**Figure 23. 13 Sales Budget Report**

**For Month of ________________**

**(Department____________________)**

| This month | | | | | Year-to-Date | | |
|---|---|---|---|---|---|---|---|
| No. | Budget | Actual | Over or Under Budget (%) | | Budget | Actual | Over or Under Budget (%) |
| | | | | | | | |

# 24

# Budgetary Control : Reporting

## Introduction

We have seen in previous chapters in this book the purpose of budgeting and the methods used in the preparation and presentation of the budget.

To summarize at this stage, with all budget preparation complete, we could find that we have the following:

(a) ***The long-term budget*** to provide for items of capital expenditure requiring advance preparation.

(b) ***The main budget*** or the plan for the normal period of operations. This is usually one year to recompile with a normal accounting period. This, together with a normal breakdown of the budgeting into shorter periods, say, of one month provides the fixed budgeting for the whole period.

(c) ***Flexible budgeting*** by means of which the appropriate budgeted expense is computed for the output actually achieved so that adverse tendencies may be examined and corrective action applied.

This now brings us to the implementation of the budget programme by means of budget reports and this, to be effective, must be on a short-term basis. These reports must be made available to responsible personnel as soon as possible after performance.

First-line supervisors or minor executives will receive reports within the scope of their individual responsibilities and these will incorporate all the relevant details necessary to enable appropriate action to be taken at their particular level. Reports for senior management will cover a wider field and even possibly longer periods.

*Reports, basically, should contain the following information :*

(a) Budgeted performance and the budgeted costs of that performance;

(b) The budgeted cost of actual performance;

(c) The actual performance at actual cost;

(d) The differences or variances between budget and actual;

(e) The value of all reports made for purposes of budgetary control is increased when the information is furnished cumulatively. In other words, the results for the current period and also those for the budgeted period of date.

It must be emphasized again that budget reports are most essential part of the budgetary control system. A budget without budgetary control is no better than budget at all. The reporting must be planned on a routine basis and timely action taken to institute any necessary corrective measures.

One of the budget means of deciding what action should be taken on budget reports, is the establishment of a budget committee, which holds regular meetings to consider reports and take decisions. Follow-up procedures then instituted at various levels of supervision and management to implement the decisions made at these committee meetings.

We should now examine some of the more important aspect of reporting for budgetary control.

There is a principle common to all budgetary control, which is that control will be exercised through the use of variances, i.e. the deviation of actual results from the budget. This provides for examination by the principle of exception on only those items, which call for action, revive the attention of the personnel concerned.

***Variances from budget are of three main kinds :***

1. ***The Realization of Income*** **:** The main purpose for any enterprise being in business is the sale of its goods and services. Accordingly, it may be claimed that the comparison of actual and budgeted sales becomes the first and most important in the control process. Variations must be followed up promptly for the reason, as we have already seen, that all subsequent considerations stream from the principal activity of the business-its sales volume.

2. ***Production :*** Here, we will find the accent placed very largely on quantitative control; the flow of materials and the utilization of equipment and labour. In this area we must have an appreciation of budget variances disclosing over-production and under-production should serve a valuable purpose.

3. ***Analysis of Variances :*** There is always the possibility that the examination of budget variances may disclose inaccuracies or invalidity in the budget itself. These may be caused by unforeseen changes in trading contains, i.e., for reasons beyond the control of the budget is preferable if budgetary control is to be the most effective.

A further consideration will naturally be the form of the actual reports to be used. Individual enterprises will naturally be required to develop a form of reporting suited to their own particular requirements so that any presentations in a book of this nature can only follow basic lines for special adaptation as required.

Before we consider the actual form of the report the following observations are important:

1. The prime purpose of budget reports must not be over-looked: they must déclassé the extent to which actual results are meeting budget targets.
2. Reports must be as concise as possible without sacrificing useful information. The concise report is more likely to receive the attention required from management than the voluminous on provident basically the same information.
3. Use can be made of graphs and charts whenever practicable.
4. The actual form of the report required is frequently determined by the level of management for which it is required. As we have seen already, top executives require, primarily, the over-all picture. Lower levels require more detail in their own spheres of responsibility.

## Reports

1. A form of ***sales budget report*** is illustrated in Fig. 24.1. As mentioned above, this form is basic only and further analysis will be determined from the requirements of the particular business concerned. A detailed examination of budget variances may be necessary for sales personnel to take any required action, while top management will be interested in the broader picture, and only in the details if considered necessary.
2. ***The production budget report*** shown in Fig. 24.2. The comparison of actual quantities of production with those budgeted for is a valuable guide in disclosing the extent to which there has been effective co-ordination between the production and sales.

   Production at less than the planned levels may result from a number of causes and these must be examined and the necessary action taken. Conversely, over production will result in an excess inventory, which if not corrected may result in losses due to obsolescence or deterioration for the stocks.

3. ***The purchases budget report*** illustrated in Fig. 24.3 is complimentary to the production report shown in Fig. 24.2 in that it disclose the variation of the actual cost of purchases from that initially planned and could provide some of the explanation required when analyzing the results of production. The form can also be expanded, if necessary, to show the variance between the initial planning presented in the fixed budget, with the revision computed from the flexible budget.

***Labour Budget Report***

This report provides for an analysis of the variance between the volume and rates of pay planned for the labour force and the actual results of that planning. Once again it could be complementary to the quantitative production budget. An illustration of the report form is shown in Fig. 24.4.

***Expenses Budget Reports***

These reports will all follow a similar pattern and, in particular, in regard to flexibility without which there can be no true measure of control. The form is illustrated in Fig. 24.5.

***Finance Budget Report***

These reports will usually follow a conventional pattern, and an illustration is given in Fig. 24.6. The last column on the form " Estimated for next month" may be expanded to cover a longer period, by the insertion of additional columns as required. Cash budgeting in summary form is presented in Fig. 24.7. Actual results are entered at the top of the form as the year proceeds and any revisions necessary incorporated for the balance of the period.

***Non-Operating Income and Expense***

This form is illustrated in Fig. 24.8 and is self explanatory.

***Master Operation Budget***

Finally, there is the report on the total operations of the business for the period under review. This is and it will present in total the information given in the reports illustrated above. The form can be adapted to present the cumulative results for the year to date and this is conveniently effected by transferring the "item" column to the center of the form and presenting the current months figures on the left side of the form and those for the year to date on the right side. The form is illustrated in Fig. 24.9.

**Figure 24.1 Sales Budget Report**

**For mont of**

**(Department)**

| This month | | | | | Year-to-Date | | |
|---|---|---|---|---|---|---|---|
| No. | Budget | Actual | Over or Under Budget (%) | | Budget | Actual | Over or Under Budget (%) |
| | | | | | | | |

**Figure 24.2 Production Budget Report**

**For Ended 200_**

| Item | Unit | Budget | Actual | Over Budget | % | Under Budget | % |
|---|---|---|---|---|---|---|---|
| | | | | | | | |

**Figure 24.3 Material (Purchase) Budget Report**

**For Ended 200_**

| Classification | Fixed Budget | Flexible Budget | Actual | Over Budget | % | Under Budget | % |
|---|---|---|---|---|---|---|---|
| | | | | | | | |

**Figure 24.4 Labour Budget Report**

**For the month of**

| Department or Cost Centre | Classification | Fixed Budget | | Flexible Budget | | Actual | | Over Flexible Budget | | | Under Flexible Budget | | |
|---|---|---|---|---|---|---|---|---|---|---|---|---|---|
| | | Hrs. | Amt. | Hrs. | Amt. | Hrs. | Amt. | Hrs. | Amt. | % | Hrs. | Amount | % |
| | | | | | | | | | | | | | |

**Figure 24.5 Factory Expenses Report**

**For month of**

| Items of Expenses | Fixed Budget | Flexible Budget | Actual | Over Flexible Budget | | Under Flexible Budget | |
|---|---|---|---|---|---|---|---|
| | | | | Amount | % | Amount | % |
| | | | | | | | |

(The same form can be used for Selling and Distribution Expenses and Administration Expenses)

**Figure 24.6 Finance Budget Report**

**For month of 200_**

| Item | Budget | | Actual | Variations | | Estimated for next month |
|---|---|---|---|---|---|---|
| | Original | Revised | | Original | Revised | |
| **RECEIPTS** | | | | | | |
| **Sales** | | | | | | |
| 1. Cash | | | | | | |
| 2. Accounts receivable | | | | | | |
| 3. Other income | | | | | | |
| 4. Total Receipts | | | | | | |
| **DISBURSEMENT** | | | | | | |
| 5. Capital expenditure | | | | | | |
| 6. Purchases | | | | | | |
| 7. Labour | | | | | | |
| 8. Selling and Distribution | | | | | | |
| 9. Administration expenses | | | | | | |
| 10. Factory expenses | | | | | | |
| 11. Other expenses | | | | | | |
| 12. Total Disbursement | | | | | | |
| **SUMMARY** | | | | | | |
| 13. Opening Balance (Cash) | | | | | | |
| 14. Balance for month (14 - 12) | | | | | | |
| 15. Closing Cash Balance | | | | | | |

**Figure 24.7 Cash Budget Summary Report**

**For year ending 200_ Presented for month of**

| Month | Dr. or Cr. | Opening Balance | Receipts | | Total Available | Disbursements | | Dr. or Cr. | Closing Balance |
|---|---|---|---|---|---|---|---|---|---|
| | | | Capital | Revenue | | Capital | Operations | | |
| **ACTUAL** | | | | | | | | | |
| January | | | | | | | | | |
| February | | | | | | | | | |
| March | | | | | | | | | |
| April | | | | | | | | | |
| May | | | | | | | | | |
| **ESTIMATED** | | | | | | | | | |
| June | | | | | | | | | |
| July | | | | | | | | | |
| August | | | | | | | | | |
| September | | | | | | | | | |
| October | | | | | | | | | |
| November | | | | | | | | | |
| December | | | | | | | | | |

**Figure 24.8 Report on Budget of Non-Operating Income and Expenses**

**For month of 200_**

| Items | | Budget | Actual | Over Budget | | Under Budget | | Remarks |
|---|---|---|---|---|---|---|---|---|
| | | | | Amount | % | Amount | % | |
| INCOME | | | | | | | | |
| | TOTAL | | | | | | | |
| EXPENSES | | | | | | | | |
| | TOTAL | | | | | | | |

Figure 24.9 Master Operating Budget

Report for Month Ended 200_

| Items | Fixed Budget | Flexible Budget | Actual | Variations from Flexible Budget | | | |
|---|---|---|---|---|---|---|---|
| | | | | Over | % | Under | % |
| Sales | | | | | | | |
| Cost of Good Sold | | | | | | | |
| Selling Expenses | | | | | | | |
| Administrative Expenses | | | | | | | |
| Total Costs and Expenses | | | | | | | |
| Net Operating Profit | | | | | | | |
| Non-Operating Income | | | | | | | |
| Total Profit | | | | | | | |
| Non-Operating Expenses | | | | | | | |
| Net Profit | | | | | | | |

The value of presenting cumulative results in all reporting should not be overlooked where it serves a useful purpose. The form illustrated in this text has been shown concisely for the sake of convenience.

**Budgetary Control : Flexible Budgeting**

Essential and basically, budgetary control is that form of control which is exercised through the regular comparison of actual results with those shown in the budget. If the work entailed in drawing up the budget has been done conscientiously and the presentation can be approached with confidence, then any differences arising between the budget and actual results must be examined promptly by management to see what can be done to rectify the position.

It is equally basic that control through budgeting must also have as its counterpart system of accounting, which can produce actual results promptly. It is also necessary that the accounting figures used for comparative purposes should be on the same basis as the budget. As an example, to know that sales have fallen by Rs. 5,00,000 short of the budget is only relatively significant. It becomes most pertinent when a comparison of details discloses that there has been a decline of Rs. 6,00,000 worth of goods in department A and a further decline of Rs. 4,00,000 in department B offset by and increase in department C of Rs. 5,00,000.

Budgetary control makes the task of management easier by concentrating attention on these phases of business activity which have been below budget figures. Or in other words, the budget provides the facilities for a quick comparison to indicate which departments need attention and those which do not need any special treatment at the moment.

It is necessary at this stage to introduce into our study on budgetary control, an explanation of the distribution between those budgets of a fixed nature such as we have been discussing and those which have regard for flexibility.

Budgets which give the greatest control are those which are flexible. A budget which has no flexibility will serve as and absolute measure, but if it is to stand throughout the total operation period, it will only serve a real purpose if there is no change in the volume of operations.

*Let us explain this in another way :*

Should the sales volume indicate a significant surplus of deficiency, as the case may be, over budget, there is no means of ascertaining from a fixed budget whether the optimum profits have been earned. The budget as it stand will provide satisfactory measures of comparison in regard to actual sales, as this is the starting point, but should this volume be much larger or smaller over the budget period are reasonable.

For example, sales may be budgeted at Rs. 10,00,000 and expenses estimated on this basis. If, to exaggerate the illustration, sales reach only Rs. 7,00,000, it is obvious that expenses should be well below the budget to a lower sales volume and not in any way due to any action on the part of the executives controlling costs could be excessive and that such excesses would not be disclosed. If on the other hand, sales increased to Rs. 5,05,00,000 it would be unjust to expect costs to remain at the same level fixed for a sales volume of Rs. 10,00,000.

To overcome the problem of satisfactory comparisons occasioned by sales fluctuating from budget, it is necessary to prepare a budget in table form setting out the expenses applicable at the various levels of sales. This table then becomes in effect a multiple budget from which the expenses at the required level can be taken off and compared with the actual. By this means, true budget variances will be disclosed. It has been condensed for convenience and can be expanded to deal with a wider range of results as required. All figures would normally be calculated on a monthly basis.

To complete this multiple budget, it will be necessary to have estimates of what the various expenses will amount to at the various sales levels (or activity levels) which may be encountered. With the fixed or original budget, there is definite goal to which the enterprises are striving and by comparing budget sales and profit with the actual sales and the budget of expense, and be seen how the selling efforts of the sales departments have contributed to the final results of operations.

The profit shown in the flexible budget itself varies from the fixed budget because of volume changes and not through inefficiencies in the usage, for example, of material, labour or indirect expenses. Consequently comparison of flexible budget with the actual results provides for the determination of responsibility for any other alteration to the profit. For instance, any variations between the budgeted material and labour costs of actual sales, and the actual cost itself will be disclosed.

Let us now consider the illustration of a flexible presentation of a master buget as shown in Fig. 24.10.From this example, it will be seen that the fixed budget has forecast a sales volume of Rs. 20,000 which has been estimated to produce a profit of Rs.1,825. The actual sales for the period however have exceeded the budget by Rs. 4,000 of and the profit be Rs. 275 more than budget.

The question, therefore, is whether the extra profit of Rs. 275 is adequate for the extra Rs. 4,000 in sales; or putting the question another way, are any of the

**Figure 24.10 Master Budget for (month) (year)**

| Details (all figures × 1000) | Fixed Budget | Flexible Budget | Actual | Variation from Flexible Budget |
|---|---|---|---|---|
| **SALES** | Rs.20,000 | Rs. 24,000 | Rs.24,000 | |
| **Cost of Manufacture** | | | | |
| Materials | 8,000 | 9,800 | 9,900 | +100 |
| Labour | 4,500 | 5,400 | 5,600 | +200 |
| **Fixed Expenses** | | | | |
| Rent and Taxes | 800 | 800 | 800 | |
| Insurance | 50 | 50 | 50 | |
| Depreciation | 300 | 300 | 300 | |
| Repairs and Renewals | 200 | 200 | 200 | |
| Factory Manager's Salary | 100 | 100 | 100 | |
| Sub Total | 1,450 | 1,450 | 1,450 | |
| **Semi-Variable** | | | | |
| Indirect Wages | 570 | 630 | 700 | |
| Non-Productive Wages | 245 | 290 | 280 | +70 |
| Compensation Insurance | 110 | 140 | 140 | −10 |
| Fuel and Power | 500 | 590 | 630 | + 40 |
| Supplies | 100 | 120 | 100 | −20 |
| Sub Total | 1,525 | 1,770 | 1,850 | |
| **Total Cost** | 15,475 | 18,420 | 18,800 | +380 |
| | 4,525 | 5,580 | 5,200 | |
| Selling Expenses | 1,800 | 2,000 | 2,100 | +100 |
| Administrative Expenses | 900 | 1,000 | 1,000 | |
| | 2,700 | 3,000 | 3,100 | |
| Net Profit | 1,825 | 2,580 | 2,100 | −480 |

actual expenses higher than they should be. The answer to this is given in the flexible budget, and the figures can be reconciled as follows :

| **Increase in Profit as per Budgets** | | |
|---|---|---|
| Flexible | 2,580 | |
| Fixed | 1,825 | 755 |
| **Less Variations** | | |
| Materials | 100 | |
| Labour | 200 | |
| Indirect wages | 70 | |
| Non-productive wages | –10 | |
| Fuel and power | –40 | |
| Supplies | –20 | |
| Selling expenses | 100 | 480 |
| **Equals** | | |
| Actual profit | 2,100 | |
| Less fixed budget | 1,825 | 275 |

By preparing statements of this kind we can eliminate the effect of changes in volume of sales and present the items showing excess expenditure for further examination.

We should give some further consideration to the methods used in compiling the expenses for purposes of budgetary control through the medium of the standing date which would be entered in the table as illustrated in the Fig. 24.11.

### Variable Expenses or Costs

In most enterprises, direct labour and materials will be classed as variable. These items are traceable and chargeable directly to each job, product, or process. The cost of labour and material is a very definite and as certainable part of the cost of the product, and in a factory where there is efficiency in production planning and control, the same product should always retire basically the same amount of labour and materials for its manufacture. The total cost of labour and material for any period, therefore, would be determined by the kind and quantity of the product manufactured.

The most accurate and reliable method of budgeting the labour and material cost is by the use of standard in a standard costing system. Where standards are not in existences, however, estimates will have to be made and those in turn expressed as percentages of sales. By either method, determination of the cost of labour and materials should not present any great difficulty.

**Figure 24.11 Flexible Budget for (month) (year)**

| Pencentage of Capacity | 65 | | 70 | | 75 | | 80 | | 85 | | 90 | | 95 | | 100 | |
|---|---|---|---|---|---|---|---|---|---|---|---|---|---|---|---|---|
| Class of Expenses | Fixed | Var. | Fixed | Var. | Fixed | Var. | Fixed | Var. | Fixed | Var. | Fixed | Var. | Fixed | Var. | Fixed | Var. |
| | | | | | | | | | | | | | | | | |
| Sub Total | | | | | | | | | | | | | | | | |
| TOTAL | | | | | | | | | | | | | | | | |

### Fixed or Non-variable Costs

These expenses cover items which recur regularly during the year or which are incurred or paid annually, such as the cost of occupancy, municipal taxes, insurance and depreciation, etc.

There are generally no problems in budgeting first such items either for the fixed or flexible budget as they basically remain the same irrespective of the volume of operations. As exception to this rule could be items such as additional rent for temporary storage to cope with and exceptional volume they must be treated as excess costs.

### Semi-Variable Costs

These expenses or costs present the difficulty in forecasting. They increase in sales and decrease when sales volume falls, owing to their semi-variable nature however, there is no fixed relationship to operations as the case of truly variable costs such as direct labour and materials. As the costs are fixed and some that are variable, and it is necessary therefore to find out what these elements are.

Having found the fixed element and separated it, it is possible that the remaining part may be found to vary indirectly with the volume of operation, or approximately so.

As a simple illustration of method, it is proposed to submit a flexible expense budget from the following date :

| | | |
|---|---|---|
| 1. | Office salaries | Rs. 2,000 |
| 2. | Fixed expenses - office | Rs. 1,500 |
| 3. | Advertising | Rs. 2,000 |
| 4. | (a) Salesman - allowances and salaries<br>(b) Commission is paid at 1% on actual sales effected | Rs. 6,000 |

5. Transport and delivery as estimated at 5% on total sales
6. Agency commission is 7½% on sales effected
7. A total expense budget is required for the following sales:

| | Salesmen | Agency | Total |
|---|---|---|---|
| A. | 1,25,000 | 15,000 | 1,40,000 |
| B. | 1,42,500 | 17,500 | 1,60,000 |
| C. | 1,62,500 | 17,500 | 1,80,000 |

**Flexible Expenses Budget**

For ................ended .....................20

| | A | B | C |
|---|---|---|---|
| **Estimated Sales** | **140,000** | **160,000** | **180,000** |
| ***Fixed Expenses :*** | | | |
| Office Salaries | 2,000 | 2,000 | 2,000 |
| Office Expenses | 1,500 | 1,500 | 1,500 |
| Advertising | 2,000 | 2,000 | 2,000 |
| Salesmen | 6,000 | 6,000 | 6,000 |
| | 11,500 | 11,500 | 11,500 |
| ***Variable Expenses :*** | | | |
| Commission-salesmen | 1,250 | 1,425 | 1,625 |
| Transport and Delivery | 7,000 | 8,000 | 9,000 |
| Commission - agency | 1,215 | 1,312 | 1,312 |
| Total | 20,875 | 22,237 | 23,437 |

There is an assumption in this example that fixed costs over the range of sales volume will not change. In practice, this will have to be tested by actual experience.

## Capital Budgeting

Capital budgeting has acquired great significance in the recent past for the following three major reasons:

1. *Differences in capital projects :* Not two capital projects are alike. They differ in many respects such as the period, cash outlay, profits, which can translate all these differing variables into some common denominator, so that meaningful comparisons can be made.
2. *Need for rationing the capital resources :*There would have been no need for a comparative study of capital projects had there been abundant resources available with every company for capital investments, given a chance, every manager is capable of submitting a proposal for huge capital investment which, according to him, is absolutely essential. However, the finances available to a company are very limited and it will not be possible for any company, however capital investments, put forward by its managers. The available capital has to be rationed among the applicants. The need for rationing the limited capital among several projects forms the basis for developing certain tools and techniques of evaluating and ranking various capital projects.

3. *Different from revenue budgeting :* Unlike the decisions related to a revenue budget, the capital budgeting decisions are more complex because of four basic reasons:
   (a) The cash outlay involved is comparatively heavier, many times running to, perhaps, several crores of rupees. (The burden of cash outlay is of course relative to the size of a company).
   (b) The impact of a capital expenditure decision will be felt over a longer period of time. If a machine is purchased, there are many long-term implications in the form of annual depreciation charges, repairs, maintenance expenses, etc.
   (c) A revenue budget has a time horizon of just a year and so many things can be reasonably forecast and estimated. But it is very difficult to make such a forecast in the long-run because of many uncertainties such as technological changes, potential competition, future of national economy, etc.

In the chapter, we shall examine the various issues related to capital budgeting decisions, in depth. It is essential to remember that certain mathematical knowledge becomes essential to understand the tools and techniques of capital budgeting.

**Reasons for Capital Investments**

(a) Projects, which are meant to maintain or improve profitability :

1. Certain projects may result in cost reduction, e.g., replacement of manual operations by labour saving devices.
2. Certain projects may lead to increased output and therefore increased earnings.
3. It may become necessary to invest in certain projects in order to protect the company's earning potential, in view of growing competition. It may be either a protective investment or even an investment, meant to ward off competition.
4. Many capital investments become necessary because of technological changes and innovations. If a machine with a better design comes into the market, the existing machines (in the same line) become obsolete. If a new manufacturing process is developed (which results in greater economy and / or more output), the existing process has to be discarded.
5. Certain investments may be mad because of strategic reasons. If a company wants to acquire or maintain leadership in the industry, it spends vast sums of money on research and development which may in some cases appear to be out of proportion to its existing level of activities.

The primary motive in making the above types of investment is profitability in contrast to the five types of investments classified under (b) below. What we are going to discuss in this chapter is relevant to the investments which are made for reasons of profit.

(b) Projects for which profitability is not the criterion: here are certain projects, in which every company has to invest funds, through such projects do not have any direct impact on increased profitability either in the short-run or in the long-run.

*Examples*

1. Projects, which are statutorily required e.g., effluent clearing plant in a fertilizer factory, dust collector in cement factory, special equipment to treat noxious gases released by a chemical factory.
2. Service department projects e.g., Buildings and furniture for administrative, finance, legal departments, etc.
3. Welfare projects such as Health Clinic, Recreation Club for employees.
4. Educational projects such as schools for employees children.
5. Safety projects e.g., fencing equipments, special protective cages, etc.

However, it does not mean that some of these projects do not result in increased productivity and profitability in long-run. They may. But what is necessary to remember is that in making these investments. Profitability is not the chief criterion.

***Factors to be considered in Capital Budgeting***

Before we discuss the standard techniques which are used to evaluate capital expenditure, it is important to keep in mind the following important factors, which have a direct bearing on any capital expenditure decision. The dependability of the techniques of capital budgeting is directly related to the assumptions, which go into them.

1. *Cash Flow :* In capital expenditure analysis we should not deal with the accounting profits which may be influenced by several factors such as accruals, provisions for certain anticipated expenses, and also many notional charges. We consider here only the cash outflows and cash inflows because a capital expenditure decision has to be made considering its impact on net increase in future operation cash flows. Accounting profit (or losse) is not relevant here.

   ***Example***

   In January 1977 a company purchased a machine costing Rs. 2 lakhs. It can manufacture 1,000 units per month each of which can be sold at Rs. 5. The cost of producing and selling transpose them (without including depreciation charges) is Rs. 3 per unit. The machine is estimated to have a life of 10 years, with no scrap value at the end. This company follows the written down value method of depreciation at 20% p.a.

| | |
|---|---|
| A. Cash inflows - sales 1000 units × 12 months × Rs. 5 | Rs. 60,000 |
| Cash outflows expenses 1000 units × 12 months × Rs. 3 | Rs. 36,000 |
| Net cash flow | Rs. 24,000 |

B. Reported Accounting Profit - First year

| | | |
|---|---|---|
| Sales | | Rs. 60,000 |
| Less : Expenses | Rs. 36,000 | |
| Depreciation | Rs. 40,000 | Rs. 76,000 |
| Loss | | Rs. 16,000 |

In this fashion, the accounting profits (or losses) may vary from year to year. What is given above is a very simple example. The results may be totally different if different policies are adopted for inventory valuation or for depreciation. Hence, for capital budgeting we consider only the actual cash outflows and inflows but not the accounting profits (or losses).

2. *Cash outlay for the project :* A careful estimates has to be prepared for the cash outlay required for the project. Understandably heavy outlay is needed in the first or second year. Subsequently also it may become necessary to pump in fresh money for overhaul and periodical replacements. These should also be estimated and included in the project outlay. It should not be forgotten that every new project requires certain additional working capital which has to be also financed from one source or the other. Many times experiences suggests that working capital estimates for new projects tend to be rather on the lower side, because of either ignorance or errors in judgement on the part of the promoters. But in a large number of cases, this underestimation of working capital requirements is due to a deliberate practice intended to bring down the total project costs, so that the financial institutions may be happy with the higher returns projected on this lower investment base. Apart from deliberate practice, it has to be agreed that making a correct estimation of working capital needs for new projects is rather really more difficult than is the case for existing projects or activities. Therefore, the management has to be extremely careful in this aspect to ensure that the total project cost is inclusive of the capital cost of assets and also the additional working capital requirements.

3. *Scrap value :* It is necessary to estimate the scrap value, which will be realized at the end of the effective life of the asset. It is difficult to make a 100% accurate estimate in this respect, because it is not possible today to forecast what type of technological changes may take place by the time the economic life of the asset ends. For all that one may know, the asset may just become useless and there may not be any scrap value at all. On the other hand, in certain cases, such as real estate located in an important urban area the realizable value at the end of a specified period may go up many times.

4. *Estimates of time :* Where are two important estimates relating to time. Which have to be made :

   (a) The time at which cash flows are expected to take place. This relates to the forecast of the time when the initial capital expenditure takes place and also the time when the cash inflows begin to take place, for certain projects the entire expenditure may have to be incurred in the very first year and in some other cases it can be spread over two or more years. Similarly, cash inflow may start, in certain cases, in the very first year; but in a large number of cases, after three or five years. This estimation of time pattern is of importance in any exercise in capital budgeting.

   (b) Expected production life of investment. This is the crux of the matter. Profitability or otherwise of a project is greatly influenced by the span of its productive life. A project with relatively small annual profits may be extremely viable if only its productive life is much longer than another project with relatively higher annual profits and lower productive life. It is not a simple estimate, which can be made by either an engineer or by a finance manager. What we are asset, which, in this context, means economically productive life, which can be seriously affected by technological changes resulting in newer and cost-saving assets. The innovatios can suddenly shorten the productive life of an existing asset. Keeping these complexities in mind, a realistic estimate of productive life has to be made.

5. *Tax implications :* There are many tax implications to be carefully studied in connectior with capital expenditure decision, because every rupee of tax saved results in greater net cash flows. The important tax implications are given below in a nutshell. (The sections referred to here are from the Income Tax Act. 1961).

   (a) *Investment allowance :* Under section 32A, a sum equal equal to 25% of the actual cost of machinery or plant is allowable as investment allowance if installed after 31-3-2000 for the purpose of production of items specified in the ninth schedule to the Income Tax Act. This allowance is given in respect of the previous year in which the machinery is insalled in the immediately succeeding previous year in which it is irst out to use.

   (b) *Scientific research allowance :* Under section 35, where any expenditure is laid out on scientific research related to the business carried on by the assesses including any expenditure of a capital nature, the whole of such expenditure including capital expenditure incurred in any previous year can be deducted in that previous year.

   (c) *Tax benefits in backward areas :* Under section 80 HH, the Income Tax Act allows with effect from 1-4-1998 a deduction equal to 20% of the profits and gains from the income of those industrial undertakings or business of an hetel which have begun or begin to manufacture articles after 31-12-1994 in any backward area as specified in the eighth schedule to the Act. This deduction will be allowed in computing the total income in respect of the ten assessment years beginning with the assessment year relevant to the previous year, in which the industrial undertaking begins to manufacture articles or the business of hotel starts functioning.

(d) *Tax holiday benefits :* Under Section 80J, newly established industrial undertakings or ships or hotels will be allowed in computing the total income, a deduction from such profits of so much of the amount thereof as does not exceed the amount calculated at the rate of 7.5% per annum of the capital employed. This benefit is available for five assessment years since the commencement of commercial production.

It has to be understood that these tax implications are discussed above only in a brief and simplified manner ; for greater details, you may refer to any standard book on Income Tax.

6. *Acceptable rate of return :* This is the most controversial question to be tackled in capital budgeting. If we ask "what is the acceptible rate of return in your company?" the likely reply may be some 10% or 12%, etc. But if we ask the managers to explain why 10% or 12% and why not 8% or 15%, it may not be possible to get a satisfactory answer. This acceptable to the Managing Director or the Board of Directors or any other person. (If so, there will be a great deal of inexplicable arbitrariness). It refers to the rate which is acceptable to the company in relation to the cost of the capital funds employed by it. It is worth remembering that I have mentioned in chapter 4 that the concept of cost of capital can be useful in capital budgeting decision. Cost of capital operates the minimum acceptable rate of return (called "cut-off rate" or "hurdle rate") for any of capital projects. If a particular project does not yield at least a rate of return, cost of capital, then it is not worth being pursued.

However, it is necessary to remember that in certain practical situations, it may become difficult to identify projects in the same lines of business if cost of capital is applied as the acceptible rate of return. This happens when a particular firm's cost of capital is rather high due to greater dependence on equity and the conditions in that particular line of business are rather dull. In such cases, the cut-off rate is not the cost of capital (which is influenced by the shareholders opportunity cost) but the opportunity cost of the company itself. Otherwise, it may not be possible to salvage a company (which is currently in difficulties) by allowing it to expand or diversity.

### Capital Budgeting Techniques

Having understood the preliminary aspects relating to capital budgeting we shall now examine some of the important techniques of capital budgeting. There are three such techniques, which are most commonly used. We shall see below their relative merits and demerits.

**A. Report on investment**

This is a age-old technique used for evaluating capital projects. It has been defined in many ways, which Jad Peter Drucker to say that ROI is "a rubber or infinite elasticity". However, the most widely used formula for ascertaining ROI is given below :

$$\text{ROI} = \frac{\text{Average additional profit p.s.}}{\text{Average amount invested}} \times 100$$

The following points have to be considered while using the Return on Investment technique :

1. Capital employed includes
   (a) Fixed assets at net value or replacement cost less depreciation.
   (b) Net current assets (i.e., Current Assets minus Current Liabilities) but excludes investments made outside the business and also all intangible and fictious assets such as goodwill, deferred revenue expenditure, etc.
2. The profit figure, as reported in a traditional Profit and Loss Account, should be adjusted for :
   (a) Any abnormal or non-recurring losses or gains such as losses due to fire or gains on account of exchange devaluation, etc.
   (b) Depreciation based on replacement cost, rather than the hostorical cost; and
   (c) Non-operating income, such as dividends received from external investment.
3. Depreciation, for this purpose should be usually calculated on replacement cost basis. In a project meant for plant replacement, depreciation should represent the money, which is forfeited by not disposing of the old machine.
4. *Residual value :* Whatever residual value is received on sale of old machine should be deducted from the price paid for the new machine.
5. *Average Investments :* If a machine, with 5 years life, is purchased for Rs. 20,000, and its value at the end is, say, Rs. 2,000, the average investment

$$\frac{\text{Initial outlay} + \text{Residual value}}{2}$$

$$\frac{\text{Rs. } 20{,}000 + \text{Rs. } 2{,}000}{2}$$

$$= \text{Rs. } 11{,}000$$

*Example*

| | Project A | Project B |
|---|---|---|
| Average Investment | Rs. 50,000 | Rs. 1,50,000 |
| Net profit during the life of project (adjusted as above) | Rs. 30,000 | Rs. 75,000 |
| Project life | 10 years | 5 years |
| Annual return | Rs. 3,000 | Rs. 15,000 |
| Return on investment | 6% | 10% |

Therefore, Project B is preferable.

*Merits*

1. It is a very simple and easy method which can be understood by all managers. It is, in fact, this simplicity of the method which accounts for its wide popularity.
2. Each project is considered in its totality; the entire life of the project is taken into account (unlike the payback period method, to be discussed).

*Drawbacks*

1. There are many debatable issues about each factor which has to be considered for calculation of return on investment:
   - Why should depreciation be taken on replacement cost basis?
   - Why not on historical cost?
   - Is it practicable to calculate depreciation on replacement cost basis?
   - Why should average investment, not the original one, be considered?
2. It is based on reported profits; but not cash flows. As already explained in the previous section, reported profits do not represent as correct a situation as cash flows in the context of capital budgeting. As cash flows are not considered, it is not possible to consider the time pattern of cash flows.

Because of these two major limitations, the ROI technique is not useful to make sophisticated analysis for capital budgeting decisions.

**B. Pay-back Period**

As capital projects have a long gestation period, during which time many uncertainties may creep in, the degree of risk assumed by a company when planning capital expenditure is directly related to the length of time required to recover the investment from the cash flows generated by the project. The pay-back period takes care of this important aspect of risk in investment decisions.

The Pay-back period is the time required for the net cash flows to equal the amount invested. It stress of time that is necessary for a company to recoup its investment from the net cash flows.

If there are two or more competing projects priorities among them set on the basis of pay-back period are selected, because the risk elements is the least in such a project.

*Example*

| | **Project A** | **Project B** |
|---|---|---|
| Investment (Rs.) | 10,000 | 20,000 |
| **Net cash inflows :** | | |
| I year | 3,000 | 5,000 |
| II year | 3,000 | 5,000 |
| III year | 4,000 | 5,000 |
| IV year | 3,000 | 5,000 |
| V year | 3,000 | 5,000 |
| Pay-back period | 3,000 | 4,000 |

Therefore, Project A will be preferred to Project B.

*Merits*

1. It is easy to calculate. It can be understood by non-financial executives also easily.
2. When year money conditions are prevailing in the country, the pay-back method is very suitable, because the emphasis in this technique is on the quick recovery of the investment through cash flows.
3. The risk element, involved in capital budgeting will be taken care of by the pay-back method, as it prefers a project, which recoups the investment in the shortest possible period.
4. The guess work and uncertainties are quite limited in calculations, because it is not necessary to forecast cash flows throughout the life of the project.

*Drawbacks*

In spite of the above advantages, the pay-back method is not an unmaxed blessing. Its use has been rather restricted due to the following limitations:

1. The cash flows generated throughout the life of the project are not considered. It ignores the cash flows which arise after the pay-back period. What is important is the life after pay-back:

*Consider the following example :*

| | Project P | Project Q |
|---|---|---|
| Investment | Rs. 60,000 | Rs. 1,20,000 |
| Life of the Project | 10 years | 15 years |
| Annual cash flows | Rs. 15,000 | Rs. 24,000 |
| Pay-back period | 4 years | 5 years |
| Life after pay-back | 6 years | 10 years |
| Cash flows during life after pay-back | Rs. 90,000 | Rs. 2,40,000 |
| Post-pay-back cash flows as a percentage of investment | 150% | 200% |

In the above example, the pay-back method suggests that Project P should be preferred to Project Q. However, when we consider the total life of each project, Project Q emerges more profitable than Project P.

2. Another serious drawback is that the pattern of cash flows over a period of time are considered to be uniform. Time value of money is ignored. It is necessary that the cash flows received in earlier periods should be given more value than the cash flows received in the later periods, A rupee received today is more valuable than a rupee to be received one year later because this one rupee of today can in the meantime earn some interest. Pay-back method does not take into account this important aspect.

   After studying the two methods-the ROI and the pay-back which do not consider time value of money-we now examine two more methods, which make time adjusted calculations.

**C. Time-adjusted methods**

Money has a time-value. Cash flows received in different years should not be treated to have uniform value. Today's rupee is more valuable than a rupee to be received a year later. At this stage, it is suggested that the readers should go through Appendix-I to this chapter regarding the essential mathematics, which explains the background logic relevant to time adjusted cash flows.

*There are two time-adjusted methods, used in capital budgeting :*

(a) Trial and Error Method or Internal Rate of Return

(b) Net Present Value Method

Both these methods use the Present value tables given in Table A appended to this chapter. But there is one major difference between these two methods. Under the first method, no discount rate is assumed; it is found out by trial and error. But in the second method, the calculations are made with the help of a given rate of discount.

(a) *Trial and Error Method or Internal Rate of Return :* When there are two streams of cash-flows - an outflow and an inflow it is possible to equate both of them, when they are discounted at a particular rate, in terms of present values. The trial and error method seeks to find out that particular rate of discount, which equates the cash flows – both inflows and outflows – in terms of their present values. A number of trail calculations are made to establish the exact rate of discount.

***Example***

Suppose there are 2 machines A and B. A requires a cash outlay of Rs. 50,000 whereas B needs 60,000. The net cash flows (i.e., inflows minus outflows) of these machines are as under:

| Year | A<br>Rs. | B<br>Rs. |
|---|---|---|
| 1. | 20,000 | 5,000 |
| 2. | 15,000 | 10,000 |
| 3. | 10,000 | 15,000 |
| 4. | 10,000 | 25,000 |
| 5. | 5,000 | 15,000 |
| 6. | 5,000 | 10,000 |
| | 65,000 | 80,000 |

We are going to make two trial calculations to find out the exact rate of discount:

**Cash Flow –Machine A**

| Year | Cash Inflow(Rs.) | Trial No. 1 Discount 11% p.a. | | Trial No. 2 Discount 10% p.a. | |
|---|---|---|---|---|---|
| | | PV of re.1 | Net PV Rs. | PV of re.1 | Net PV Rs. |
| 1. | 20,000 | .901 | 18,020 | 0.909 | 18,180 |
| 2. | 15,000 | .922 | 12,180 | 0.826 | 12,390 |
| 3. | 10,000 | .731 | 7,310 | 0.751 | 7,510 |
| 4. | 10,000 | .659 | 6,590 | 0.683 | 6,830 |
| 5. | 5,000 | .594 | 2,970 | 0.621 | 3,105 |
| 6. | 5,000 | .537 | 2,685 | 0.565 | 2,825 |
| | 65,000 | | 49,755 | | 50,940 |
| *Less* : Investment | | | 50,000 | | 50,000 |
| Net Present Value | | | (-)245 | | (+)840 |

Thus from the above table it appears that the actual rate lies somewhere between 10% and 11% which can be found out by using the following formula:

$$\text{Actual rate of discount} = \text{Discount rate of the low trial} + \frac{\text{Excess PV of low Trial}}{\text{Excess PV of low trial over deficit PV of high trial}} \times \text{Difference between high and low discount rates}$$

$$= 10\% + \frac{840}{840-(-245)} \times 1\ \%$$

$$= 10\% + \frac{840}{1085} \times 1\ \%$$

$$= 10\% + 0.77\%$$

$$= 10.77\%$$

It means that the discount rate of 10.77% equals the cash outflows and cash inflows of machine A . In other words, it is the Internal Rate of Return of machine A. Now we have to similarly ascertain the discount rate which equates the cash flows of machine B.

**Cash Flow - Machine B**

| Year | Cash Inflow(Rs.) | Trail No. 1 Discount 11% p.a. | | Trail No. 2 Discount 10% p.a. | |
|---|---|---|---|---|---|
| | | PV of re.1 | Net PV Rs. | PV of re.1 | Net PV Rs. |
| 1. | 5,000 | .901 | 4,545 | 0.926 | 4,630 |
| 2. | 10,000 | .826 | 8,260 | 0.857 | 8,570 |
| 3. | 15,000 | .751 | 11,265 | 0.793 | 11,895 |
| 4. | 25,000 | .683 | 17,075 | 0.735 | 19,375 |
| 5. | 15,000 | .621 | 9,315 | 0.681 | 10,215 |
| 6. | 10,000 | .564 | 5,640 | 0.630 | 6,300 |
| | 80,000 | | 56,640 | | 60,985 |
| *Less* : investment | | | 60,000 | | 60,000 |
| Net Present Value | | | (-)3,900 | | (+)985 |

$$\text{Actual rate of discount} = 8\% + \frac{985}{985-(-3900)} \times 2\% = 8.4\ \%$$

It implies that the internal rate of return machine B is 8.4 % p.a. Based on the above data, we can conclude that machine A is preferable to machine B, as the internal rate of return of machine A is higher than that of machine B.

It is significant to note at this stage that there is an underlying assumption when we use the internal rate of return of machine A in the above example is 10.77% p.a. We are assuming that the net cash flows garter by the machine can be invested every year so that they can yield a compound interest of 10.77% p.a. (Because discounting and compounding are two sides of same coin, as explained in the appendix). But supposing that the company can earn today only 85 p.a. on its funds, where is the possibility that it can employ the net cash flows of machine A to yield a compound interest of 10.77% p.a. Under such circumstances when the investment opportunities open to company are limited in their yields, the internal rate of return, which is higher than the available or the possible yield, is not practically relevant for capital budgeting decisions.

Reverting to our example, discussed just now, where the company can earn today only 8% p.a. It is apparent that for that, company any project which has an internal rate of return higher than 8% stands on the same footing. Hence, it cannot make a choice between A and B. Perhaps, both of them can be accepted, if there are adequate financial and other resource.

That is why the second technique namely the Net Present Value method, came into vogue. It assumes a particular rate of discount, which operates as the cut-off rate.

(b) *Net Present Value method/DCF* : Under this method the discount rate is assumed. Usually this assumed discount rate should be equal to the company's weighted average cost of capital. Unless capital project is expected to yield at least as much as the cost of capital, the project should not be accepted. Otherwise, by getting into such uneconomical projects, the company runs the risk of lowering its profits and the earnings per share in the long-run.

***Example***

The average cost of capital of M/s Ramson Limited is 16%. Examine the feasibility of the following two projects :

| Year | Project A<br>Investment Rs. 40,000<br>Cash Flow Rs. | Project B<br>Investment Rs. 40,000<br>Cash Flow Rs. |
|---|---|---|
| 1. | 10,000 | 7,000 |
| 2. | 12,000 | 10,000 |
| 3. | 15,000 | 12,000 |
| 4. | 12,000 | 12,000 |
| 5. | 10,000 | 15,000 |
| 6. | 5,000 | 10,000 |
| | 64,000 | 66,000 |

**Discount Cash Flow**

| Year | Discount Factor @ 16% | Project A(Rs.) | Project B(Rs.) |
|---|---|---|---|
| 1. | .862 | 8,620 | 6,034 |
| 2. | .743 | 8,916 | 7,430 |
| 3. | .641 | 9,615 | 7,692 |
| 4. | .552 | 6,624 | 7,124 |
| 5. | .476 | 4,760 | 7,140 |
| 6. | .410 | 2,050 | 4,100 |
| | | 40,585 | 39,620 |
| Less Investment | | 40,000 | 40,000 |
| Net Present Value | | (+) 585 | (–) 480 |

Based on the above data, we can say that if decisions are made based only on the volume of Net Present Value, it is quite likely that the decisions may not always be correct as shown in the following example:

| | Project X (Rs.) | Project Y(Rs.) |
|---|---|---|
| Investment | 1,00,000 | 2,00,000 |
| Net present value (at a discount rate of 12%) | 13,550 | 18,880 |

In a case as the above, Project Y seems to be preferable to Project X because the net present value of the former is greater than that of the latter. But a minute's reflection will suggest that the quantum of net present value is a function of the quantum of investment. A project with higher investment is likely to generate a higher net present value than the other project with a lower investment. We are not, to be sure interested in the absolute quantum of net present value, unless it is related to the quantum of investment itself. If net present value is expressed as a percentage of the investment, the position of the two projects will be as under:

| | Project X | Project Y |
|---|---|---|
| $\frac{\text{Net present value}}{\text{Investment}} \times 100$ | 13.55% | 9.44% |

It is now clear that Project X is preferable to Project Y because its percentage of net present value to investment is higher than that of project Y. You might have noticed by now that this additional calculation of percentage is not necessary when a comparison is made between two or more projects, which require the same amount of investment (as was the case in the example on the previous page).

In this chapter we have seen a few examples of various capital budgeting techniques to ascertain the rate of return. The risk element, as such, can also be quantified with the help of sophisticated statistical techniques, which are beyond the scope of this book. I suggest that you may attempt to solve the exercises provided at the end of this chapter, so that you can consolidate the knowledge you have gained in this chapter.

# 25

# Zero - Base Budgeting*

> *When budgeting for next year, most companies use the current budget as starting point, but one company prefers to start from scratch*

In 1960s Arthur F. Burns, then Counsellor to the President, addressed the Annual Dinner Meeting of the Tax Foundation on "The Control of Government Expenditures". In this speech burns identified the basic need for what we at Texas Instruments have come to call *zero-base budgeting*. He stated that :

"Customarily, the officials in charge of an established program have to justify only the increase which they seek above last year's appropriation. In other words, what they are already spending is usually accepted as necessary, without examination. Substantial savings could undoubtedly be realized if it were required that every agency make a case for its entire appropriation request each year, just as if its program or Programs were entirely new. Such budgeting produce may be difficult to achieve, partly because it will add heavily to the burdens of budget-making, and partly also because it will be resisted by those who fear that their pet programs would be jeopardized by a system that subjects every activity to annual scrutiny of its costs and results.

---

* Base on Peter A. Pyhrr's Monumental Contribution on Zero Base Budgeting.

Burns was advocating that government agencies start from ground zero, as it were, with each year's budget and present their requests for appropriations in such a fashion that all funds can be allocated on the basis of cost/benefit or some similar kind of evaluative analysis. TI is using this approach to budgeting in its business operations, building on cost benefit techniques, and has had a considerable measure of success with it.

The need for effective zero-base budgeting of this kind is increasingly apparent in both industry and government today, since all institutions must adapt to an environment in which the allocation of limited resources presents a constantly depending challenge. However, as our experience at TI demonstrates, this kind of budgeting need not "add heavily to the burdens of budget-making." In fact, efficiently planned and properly managed, it can actually reduce them.

As developed at TI, this kind of budgeting separates out the basic and necessary operations from those of a more optional or discretionary character so that management can focus special attention on this second, softer group. The basic steps to effective zero-base budgeting are :

- Describe each discrete company activity in a "decision" package.
- Evaluate and rank all these packages by cost/benefit analysis.
- Allocate resources accordingly.

Naturally these steps cannot be applied quite so easily as they can be stated.

I hope the following description of Ti's practices and results will help the executive who is interested in pursuing this approach to budgeting think through the problems of applying it in his own company.

### *Where to use it ...*

The first thing to understand about zero-base budgeting is that it is best applied to service and support areas of company activity, rather than to manufacturing operations proper.

A corporation's level of manufacturing activity is determined how much the company shall spend on labour, materials, and overhead. A decision to increase company expenditures for these items does not necessarily bring increasing benefits in the form of increased sales, although it does tend to boost production volume. Hence there is not the same simple relation between costs and benefits here as there is in the service and support areas, where the manager can trade off a level of expenditure on a project against the direct returns his investment in the project will bring him.

Thus, cost benefit analysis, which is crucial to zero-base budgeting, cannot be straightforwardly applied to decisions to increase or decrease expenditures in the manufacturing area.

In industry, then, zero-base budgeting finds its main use in areas where expenditures are not determined directly by manufacturing operations themselves in areas, that is, where the manager has discretion to choose between different activities (and between different levels of activity) having different direct costs and benefits. These ordinarily include marketing, finance, quality control, maintenance, production planning, engineering, research and development, personnel, data processing, and so on.

In passing I might note that although areas such as quality control and maintenance may be heavily influenced by the manufacturing level or by changes in this level, the zero-base budgeting process can still be used in these areas because the manager's decision to fund quality control or maintenance activities depends on the relative benefits he thinks these activities will ultimately provide to the central manufacturing operations.

## How to begin

When a company applies zero-base budgeting in its service and support areas, it must explain the *decision package concept* to all levels of management and then present guidelines for the individual manager to use in breaking his area's activities into workable packages of this kind. Next, it must set in motion a ranking on consolidation process whereby the package sift upward toward the top in such a fashion that the decision packages of less importance are winnowed for top management's study and judgement. Let me now explain these two procedures in more detail.

## The decision package concept

The decision package is a document that identifies and describes a specific activity in such a manner that management can (a) evaluate it and rank it against other activities competing for the same or similar limited resources and (b) decide whether to approve it or disapprove it. Management may use quantitative or subjective evaluation techniques in ranking each package (I shall discuss evaluation techniques and ranking procedures later), giving a higher priority or rank to packages that satisfy minimum operating and legal requirements and a lower rank to the more discretionary packages.

The specifications in each package must provide management with the information it needs to evaluate the activity. These may include a statement of the goals of the activity, the program by which the goals are to be achieved, the benefits expected from the program, the alternatives to the program, the consequences of not approving the package, and the expenditures of funds and personnel the activity requires.

There are two basic types of decision packages :

1. Mutually exclusive packages identify alternative means for performing the same function. The best alternative is chosen, and the other packages are discarded.
2. Incremental packages reflect different levels of effort that may be expended on a specific function. One package, the "bare package", may establish a minimum level of activity and others identify higher activity or cost levels.

The following example begins with a set of three mutually exclusive decision packages formulated by a production planning manager for handling the production planning of product X. Of the three, the recommends the first, which represents the current level of activity in the area, and states the other two as alternatives to be discarded. The three mutually exclusive packages are as follows :

***Recommended package A :*** Retain five production planners at a cost of Rs. 60,000. This level of effort would maintain production and shipping schedules and inventory reporting at the level the manufacturing superintendent desires.

***Alternative package B :*** Estimate the production planners and let line foremen do their own planning. This strategy will result in zero incremental costs for foremen, but will also result in excessive inventories, inefficient production runs, and delayed shipments.

***Alternative package C :*** Combine production planning for products X, Y and Z. This procedure eliminates two supervisors at a total cash saving of Rs. 30,000. However, this alternative entails a number of consequences. The foremen on each product line will fear lack of specialized service, peak workloads on all product lines will coincide, creating excessive burden on the foreman supervisor to manage operations effectively and although it is desirable to locate the planning function close to the production lines the production facilities for X, Y and Z are so widely separated that this desirable proximity would have to be scarified.

Once he has defined the basic alternatives and selected the one he considers best, the manager should complete his analysis by describing the incremental variations (if any) of this chosen alternative. And, specifically, for his recommended alternative A, he should describe packages that call for more or less than five production planers for product X. In this particular case, the manager believed that he could eliminate one planner from the group and still satisfy the minimum requirements for planning. Hence, he identified these base and incremental packages for his recommended alternative. A, as follows :

***Base package (satisfies requirements for minimum operating level) :*** Retain only for planners to support coordination between marketing and manufacturing and to establish production schedules and reports. Consequently, long-range planning, inventory control, and marketing support for special product modification will be reduced. The required allocation for this is Rs. 45,000.

***Incremental package 1 :*** Add back one planner to the basic package. This will increase forward planning of production and shipping schedules from a two-week horizon to a four-week horizon, allow in process inventory control reports to be updated daily rather than every other day, and help marketing management accommodate customers who require special product modification. The allocation increment required is Rs. 15,000. (This incremental package represents the status quo.)

***Incremental package 2 :*** Add one OR analyst to evaluate optimal production lots versus optimal inventory levels by color and size. The allocation increment required is Rs. 15,000. (Note that savings of 1% in production cost or 5% in inventory would offset this price tag.)

This example, summarized in *Exhibit I*, roughly illustrates the format used to display decision packages at TI in its 1971 budgeting, although it omits a good deal of detail. Note that it shows both the total cost of the level of activity that the manager considers minimal (Rs. 45,000), and that it also identifies the two discarded alternatives and another possible increment for the basic package. This kind of format encourages the manager to scrutinize each operation for all possible cost reduction and operating improvements for base and incremental packages, as well as all discretionary packages.

The Appendix to this article suggests some guidelines for identifying various categories of packages and offers a number of additional, rough examples of particular packages.

## Formulating packages company wide

Decision packages are usually formulated at the "ground level". This promotes detailed identification of activities and alternatives and generates interest and participation by the managers who will be operationally responsible for the approved budget. *Exhibit II* shows the basic formulation process.

A logical starting point for determining next year's needs is the current year's operations. Each manager takes his area's forecasted expense level for the current year, identifies the activities creating this expense, and calculates the cost for each activity. At this stage, he should simply identify each activity at its current level and method of operation and not try to identify alternatives or increments.

After he has broken his current operations into preliminary decision packages, the manager looks at his requirements for the upcoming year. To aid him in specifying these requirements, upper management should issue a formalized set of assumptions primarily because it provides him and his peers with uniform bench marks for estimating their funding requirements for next year's budget. However, it fills several other important functions as well :

## Exhibit I. Decision Package Format

Department : Product X planning Package No. 500
Package name : Base package for product X planning Manager: John Harrison

**Goals :**

1. Provide minimum level of planning activities for 199,000 units of product X.
2. Maintain in-process and finished goods at current inventory level.
3. Provide minimum marketing co-organization with manufacturing foremen.

**Statement of program :**

1. Maintain updated production and shipping schedules for two weeks in advance (currently maintaining schedules four weeks in advance)
2. Provide finished goods inventory reports daily and in-process inventory reports every other day (currently being done daily).
3. Maintain perpetual inventory system on raw material to maintain a two-weeks supply on hand and a two-weeks supply on order.

**Benefits :**

1. This is the minimal level of planning required to deliver product X on schedules.
   Personnel : 4
   Cost : Rs. 45,000

**Consequent of non-approval :**

Elimination of planners would force li ne foremen to do their own planning with zero incremental cost; but excessive inventories, inefficient production runs, and delayed shipments would result in an expensive, constant sales loss.

**Incremental packages :**

1. Add back long-range planner at Rs. 15,000 (Recommended package)
2. Add operations research analyst at Rs. 15,000

**Alternative package :**

Combine production planning for departments X, Y and Z. A poor logistic setup would result.

**Resources required :**

| | | | |
|---|---|---|---|
| 1969 | Rs. 60.000 | (Personnel : | 5) |
| 1970 | Rs. 45.000 | (Personnel : | 4) |
| Change | – Rs. 15.000 | | – 1 |

- It brings inaccurate assumptions or misunderstandings to light. As a consequence, it is often easier for the manager to analyze any unusual cost variances that might have occurred during the current budget year.
- It provides a focal point for reviewing and revising assumptions and indirectly helps keep the number of such revisions under control.
- It helps everyone keep track of revisions in the list of assumptions and of the changes in activity levels and costs that these revisions entail.

**Exhibit II. Formulation of Decision Packages at the Lowest Operational Level or Cost Center**

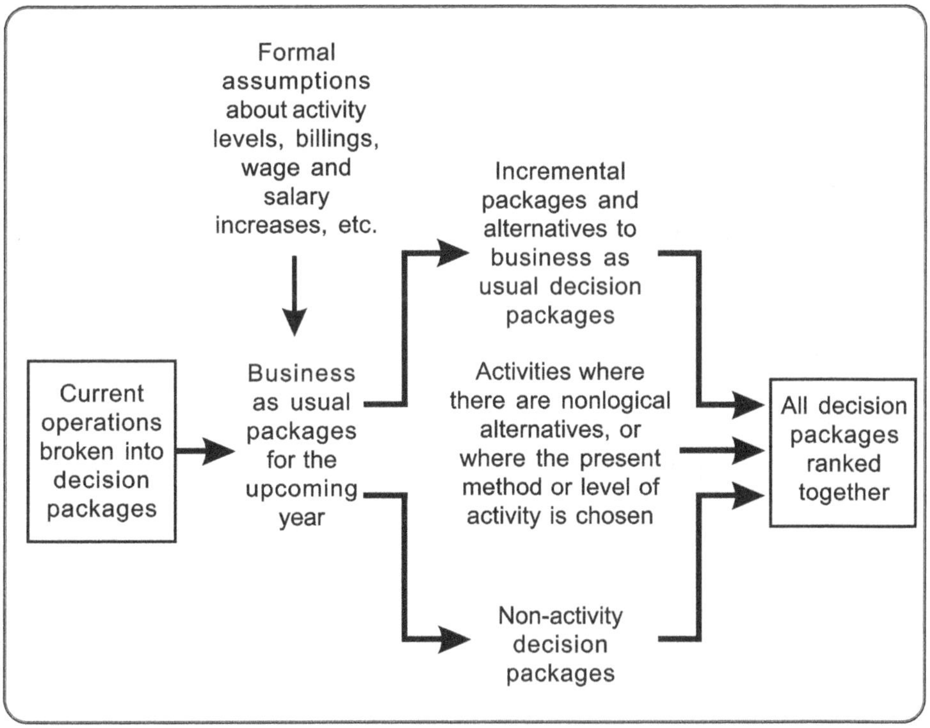


Once the manager has formulated his preliminary list of decision packages and has received the formalized set of assumptions about the next year's operations, he translates the packages in his list into "business as usual" packages for the upcoming year. These packages merely cast this year's operations in terms of next year's costs.

To determine next year's costs, each manager simply adjusts costs for changes in activity level, for salary and wage increases, and (on an annualized basis) for personnel and operations expenditures not incurred during the present budget year or which will not be incurred during the upcoming budget year.

Next comes the real starting point in determining next year's budget. The manager now develops his final set of decision packages from his business as usual packages by segmenting each of them into mutually exclusive and incremental packages wherever possible and noting the discarded alternatives as the final items on the decision package document. If he should happen to decide that one of these alternatives is a more reasonable or realistic base package for a particular activity than the one he has listed for this activity in his business as usual group, he just swaps the two and develops a set of incremental packages around the new base package.

Finally, at the same time the manager is looking into his current and ongoing activities, he should identify all new activities in his area for the upcoming year, develop decision packages that handle them, and attach them to his final set.

At the conclusion of the formulation stage, then the manager will have identified all his proposed activities for the upcoming year as follows :

1. Business as usual packages in which no variations are possible or impossible, so for as he can see. Here the manager merely exhibit the present level and method of activity in decision package format.
2. Decision package each consisting of a base package and incremental packages (with alternatives noted at the end for all other ongoing activities.
3. Decision packages for new activities.

The manager is now ready to rank his packages.

## The Ranking Process

The ranking process provides management with a technique to allocate its limited resources by making management concentrate on these questions. "How much should we spend" and "Where should we spend it ?".

Management constructs its answer to these questions by listing all the packages identified *in order of decreasing benefit to the company*. It then identifies the benefits to be gained at each level of expenditure and studies the consequences of not approving additional decision packages ranked below that expenditure level.

Theoretically, one ranking of decision packages can be obtained for an entire company and judged by its top management. But while this one, single ranking would identify the best allocation of resources, ranking and judging the high volume of packages created by describing all the discrete activities of a large company would impose a ponderous, if not impossible, task on top management. At the other extreme, ranking only at the cost-center level is obviously unsatisfactory, since it does not offer upper management any opportunity to trade off expenditures among cost centres or other, larger divisions of the company.

One can begin to resolve this dilemma by grouping cost centers together naturally, according to types of activity, and producing consolidated rankings for each grouping. The organizational width and depth of such groupings are determined by three factors.

1. The number of packages involved, and the time and effort required to review and rank them.
2. Local management's ability and willingness to rank untamiltar activities.
3. The need for extensive review across organizational boundaries to determine trade-oils in expense levels. (This factor is particularly important when deep cuts in expense levels are required to combat poor profits).

The initial tanking should of course occur at the cost-center level, where the packages are developed, so that each manager can evaluate the relative importance of his own activities and tank his packages accordingly.

Then the manager at the next level up the ladder reviews these rankings with the cost center managers themselves, and uses their rankings as guides to produce a single, consolidated ranking for all the packages presented to him from below. At lower levels of an organization, an individual can sometimes do the ranking without any consultation if he has detailed knowledge of the areas involved. In general, however, and particularly at higher levels of the organization, we have found that the expertise necessary to rank packages is best obtained by the use of a committee. At each ranking level the committee membership should consist of all the managers whose packages are being marked and a manager from the next higher organizational level to serve as chairman.

As *Exhibit III* indicates, the consolidated ranking for cost centers, $D_1$, $D_2$ and $D_3$ would be worked out by a committee chaired by the manager of $C_2$ with the managers of $D_1$, $D_2$, and $D_3$ as members. The manager of $C_2$, together with the managers of $C_1$ and $C_2$, would then serve as a member of a committee chaired by the manager of $B_2$. At these sessions all three managers from Level C would present the consolidated rankings from their areas for further consolidation. This process continues to the top. (This "consolidation" hierarchy usually corresponds to the ordinary hierarchical organization of the company, but logical groupings of similar functions may be useful even where these cut across normal organizational boundaries).

## Voting Mechanisms

At TI, each committee produces its consolidated ranking by voting on the decision packages presented by its members. As at the cost-center level, the most important or most beneficial packages are ranked highest and the least important or beneficial lowest. (I should note, incidentally, that the base package is always ranked higher than the incremental packages clustered around it, so that the base can easily be retained even it the increments are rejected.)

**Exhibit III. Consolidation levels in a four-level structure**

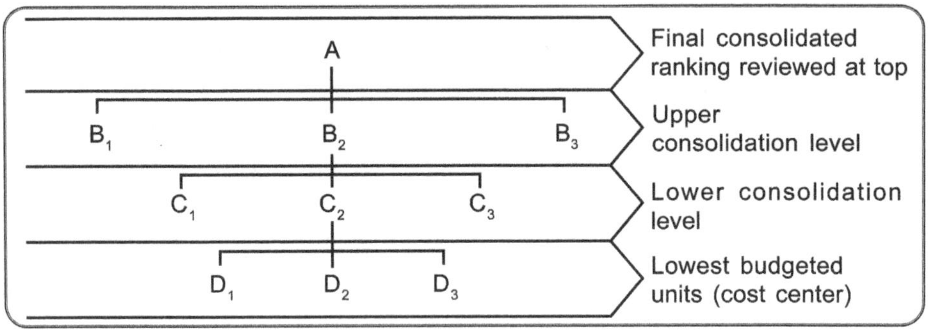


The voting mechanism can be simple or complex, depending on the number of criteria on which the package must be evaluated, the committee's ability to rank the packages against the criteria, the number of packages, and the time allotted for the process. Three basic voting schemes are in use :

1. Each member gets one vote on a fixed scale.
2. Each member votes on several different criteria, with even or weighted values.
3. A combination of the first two schemes is used, the first to establish a preliminary ranking and the second to established a detailed ranking around the cutoff level after one has been established.

*Exhibit IV* shows a voting scale. This scale was designed for overhead and support activities, but can easily be modified from qualitative to quantitative criteria if appropriate information on the packages being ranked is available.

**Exhibit IV. A Voting ballot**

| Rank | |
|---|---|
| 6 | Package ranked here should definitely be funded (a) to satisfy minimum operating or legal requirements or (b) because they have a high probability of significant impact. |
| 5 | |
| 4 | Package ranked here should definitely be funded (a) to satisfy minimum operating or legal requirements or (b) because they have a high probability of significant impact. |
| | ← *Decision point goal expenditure level* |
| 3 | Package ranked here some muscle and these would be the first packages to add if the goal expenditure level were increased. |
| 2 | |
| 1 | Package ranked here should not be seriously considered, given the current expenditure goals. |

We have found it helpful to have a review session after the detailed ranking, in which the votes of the members are displayed, misunderstandings of package content and differences of opinion are discussed, and a final ranking is established.

## Controlling the Volume

We encountered three problems with the ranking process :

First, although the consolidated rankings encompassed only two small divisions, staff and research, the number of decision packages generated overwhelmed top management's ability to evaluate them thoroughly and rank them in the allotted time. The two divisions comprised 100 cost centers, in each of which 3 to 10 packages were identified.

Second, managers had conceptual difficulty in ranking, packages they considered to be legally or operationally obligatory.

Third, they expressed concern about their own ability to judge the relative importance of dissimilar activities, especially in areas like staff, where almost all the packages required subjective evaluation and ranking.

The second and third problems caused little or no practical difficulty, for reasons that will shortly be evident. The first problem, however-that of volume was serious because in any application of this technique the total volume of packages was bound to increase greatly with each consolidation, at each successive level.

If the problem was serious, the solution was simple. To reduce the number of packages to be reviewed in detail by successively higher levels of management and to concentrate top management's attention to the lower ranked activities, a cutoff expense line was established at each organizational level. Management at that level then reviewed in detail and ranked only the decision packages involving expenditures below that cutoff line in any detail.

Packages above the cutoff line were, and indeed should be, briefly reviewed at each successive level to give management a feel for the entire operation and to allow top management to verify to its own satisfaction the relative importance of the packages above the cutoff line versus the ones below it that is, the ones being studied in detail and ranked.

Since the total number of packages to be reviewed does increase at each higher level, the cutoff line must be made more stringent at each higher level if the volume of packages to be reviewed at successive levels is to be kept under control.

## Setting the Cutoffs

In practice, it is best to establish the cutoff line at the highest consolidation level first, and then establish the cutoff lines for the lower levels. The most effective way to establish this first cutoff is for management at the highest consolidation level to estimate the expense that will be approved at the top level and then set the cutoff far enough below this expected expense figure to allow the desired trading-off between the divisions whose packages are being ranked. Lower consolidation levels then set less stringent cutoffs for their own use. It is important to note that these cutoffs must be set before consolidation at any level begins.

At the highest consolidation level, for example, management might set the cutoff at 80%. This means that at this level - call it Level B management would glance over the package rankings handed up to it from Level C, skim off the highest ranked ones until the expenditures represented by the skimmed packages added up to 80% of last year's budget for the areas in question, review these packages for reasonableness, and then seriously scrutinize and rank the remaining, low-ranked, and more discretionary packages into a consolidated series to be passed to the top.

At Level C, let us assume, a cutoff line of 50% had been set. When Level D had handed up its rankings, management at Level C would have glanced over all the packages, skimmed the top ones up to a total value of 50% of last years expenditures in the areas in question, checked these for reasonableness, and then evaluated and consolidated the rest in its own, new ranking to be handed up to Level B. (Naturally, cutoff lines can be expressed just as well in absolute dollars as in percentages).

Thus the conceptual difficulty and concern that management initially expressed over the ranking process proved to be unfounded. Managers did not concentrate their time on packages that were legally or operationally required, rather, they concentrated on discretionary activities. Note that the relative order of "required" packages is unimportant, even if these packages fall above the cutoff at the next consolidation level.

Furthermore, managers did not spend too much time worrying whether package 4 was more important than packages 5, but only assured themselves that packages 4 and 5 were more important than package is, and that package 15 was more important than package 25, and so forth.

The ability to achieve a list of ranked packages to any given organizational level allows management to evaluate the desirability of various expenditure levels throughout the budgeting expenses. Also, this ranked list provides management with a reference point to be used during the operating year to identify activities to be reduced or expand deal is allowable expenditure levels change or if the organization is over or under budget during the year.

### *Conclusion*

The decision package ranking process is general procedure for achieving zero-base budgeting. It provides management with an operating tool to evaluate and allocate its resources effectively and efficiently and provides the individual manager with a mechanism for identifying, evaluating, and communicating his activities and alternatives to higher levels of management.

As this process expanded from the staff and research divisions to the manufacturing divisions within 11, the general procedure and philosophies remained the same, although some mechanical details of implementation such as information package, decision criteria used to evaluate and the rank the packages, the level to which the packages are ranked, and so forth has been modified to fit the specific needs to each operation.

This process was also adopted during 1970 to identify and evaluate benefits and alternative expenditure levels and cash flows for major facility projects, with the subordinate ranking consolidated into one ranking for the entire corporation.

Zero-base budgeting is a flexible and powerful tools. It has greatly simplified the budgeting procedure at T1, and brought about better resource allocation to boot. We believe it is potentially useful to great many companies in a great many industries, and, if our success with it is any indicator, it will be applied widely in the future.

## APPENDIX

### Aids for Identifying Packages

To break down their department activities into packages, management should think in terms of three broad categories : service and support, capital expenditure, and labour, material, and overhead expenses directly associated with manufacturing.

**1. Service and Support Packages**

These packages focus on five kinds of subjects : people, projects or programs, services received, services provides, and cost reduction.

People provide the most common subject for decision packages because they both spend money and create expenses through their wages and salaries. The subject of a package is likely to be personnel in an area where (a) costs are predominantly people-related, (b) people perform several tasks or functions and a level of personnel effort can be identified, or (c) the function of specific individuals can be condensed or eliminated. The following base package suggests a personnel reduction.

*Decision package :* Combined Sales Manager for Region A and Region B.

*Cost :* $ 45,000

*Statement :* Combine sales regions A and B into one region, eliminating Sales Manager A.

*Benefits :* Combining regions saves expenses of Sales Manager A and secretary ($ 40,000).

*Consequences of nonapproval :* The manager for the combined region will have less time for market surveys and problem solving for smaller customers, but negative sales impact should be minimal due to sales levelling and expected economic slump for sales of the largest customers in Region A.

*Alternatives :*

* Maintain sales manager in Region A at an additional cost of Rs. 40,000. (This might been an incremental package).
* Combine sales regions A and C.

*Projects or Programs* are likely to be the package topic where costs are generated by personnel and services provided. The following package is an example.

*Decision package :* Automated Inventory System.

*Cost :* Rs. 60,000.

*Statement :* A ready-success, perpetual inventory system for in-process and finished goods. Two many years of programmer effort are required, with Rs. 10,000 expense for computer charges.

*Benefits :* This will reduce production and shipping delays due to stockouts, and reduce inventory levels by 25%. The costs will be repaid in one year.

*Alternatives :*

* Eliminate the system. However, this would eliminate the stated benefits and waste the Rs. 20,000 already spent on the development.
* Delay installation from September 2001 to April 2002, for a Rs. 10,000 savings in 2001.
* Eliminate the ready-access capability of the system (Rs. 5,000 reduction in package cost).
* Expand the system to include raw materials inventory (Rs. 15,000 additional cost).

*Services received* is an appropriate subject wherever costs for services are paid to sources external to the managers area of activity. The managers should identify separate decision packages or include these costs within other packages. For example, the following base package for a quality control activity represents a cutback to the minimal level in percent service costs paid out by the product X production department.

*Decision package* : Reduced Quality Control for product X.

*Cost :* Rs. 100,000

*Statement :* Inspect 35% of finished goods for product X within one hour of assembly completion.

*Benefits :* This sample will identify repetitive process errors and ensure 90% probability of consumer acceptance.

*Consequences of nonapproval :* Greatly increased customer ejection and probable sales losses, process errors will continue if the present level of testing is reduced.

*Alternatives :*

* Increase sample tested to 35%. This will increase the probability of customer acceptance to 95% (Rs. 30,000 additional cost).
* Reduce sample to 20%. This will reduce probability of consumer acceptance to 80% (Rs. 65,000 reduction in package cost).
* Retain present level of testing activity, but delay inspection to four hours after assembly completion to reduce peak-testing loads and overtime (Rs. 10,000 delayed into next budget year).

*Services provided* is a helpful category wherever charges can be specified or estimated. If services are directly charged to the customer the budget should be determined from a list of packages developed in conjuction with and approved by the customer. (In some cases, of course, customers are too numerous for individual packages to be developed for each one, or perhaps customers will not assume commitment for any planned service level because of uncertainty.) If the customer is not directly charged for services received, the service package, identified will follow the normal ranking and review procedures.

*Cost reduction* : Incidentally, is a kind of package, that is useful when a cost incurred for receiving or providing a service is not recovered during the same budget period. The net cost of the package should be shown as the total cost minus savings during the budget year. (If the cost is offset in the same period, the manager should incorporate the reduction in the appropriate decision package.)

### 2. Capital Expenditures Packages

This category is chiefly useful for breaking cost major expenditure not included in other packages. This frequently occurs when (a) capital projects have a long lend time, (b) benefit will not be realized during the budget year, (c) expenditure rates can vary, (d) projects are deferrable, or (e) cash flow problems require trade off between expense and capital dollars budgeted. Capital packages may also conveniently identify expenditure related to cost-reduction programs.

Capital packages frequently identify variable expenditure schedule for meeting normal operating needs. The following package is an example.

*Decision package :* Expenditure schedule for Expanding Dollars chemical facility.

*Cost :* Rs. 1 million in 2001 Rs. 1.5 million in 2002 Rs. 0.5 million in 2003.

*Benefits and consequences of nonapproval :* Marketing studies justify capacity at this rate.

*Alternatives :*

* Delay necessary plant expansion for six months by going to full-capacity operation at existing facilities on Saturdays and Sundays.
* Slip expenditure and completion schedules.
* Compress construction schedule and in 5% to 10% acceleration premium.
* Reduce capacity on the chemical storage tanks to minimum requirements (Rs. 2000,000 reduction in total project cost).

Once managers understand the formats they should use, they can begin formulating package for their areas of activity.

### 3. Labour, material, and overhead expenses directly associated with manufacturing

Although the zero-base concept will probably not apply here, the manufacturing area may use decision package to identify alternatives and discretionary activities, allowing management to rank these packages with packages identified for other areas.

# Answers to Review Questions

**Chapter 1**

| | | | | | |
|---|---|---|---|---|---|
| **1.1** (b) | **1.2** (b) | **1.3** (d) | **1.4** (b) | **1.5** (d) | **1.6** (c) |
| **1.7** (d) | **1.8** (b) | **1.9** (c) | **1.10** (c) | **1.11** (c) | **1.12** (b) |
| **1.13** (a) | **1.14** (b) | **1.15** (d) | **1.16** (a) | | |

**Chapter 3**

| | | | | | |
|---|---|---|---|---|---|
| **3.1** (c) | **3.2** (c) | **3.3** (b) | **3.4** (b) | **3.5** (a) | **3.6** (c) |
| **3.7** (c) | **3.8** (b) | **3.9** (c) | **3.10** (a) | | |

**Chapter 4**

| | | | | | |
|---|---|---|---|---|---|
| **4.1** (d) | **4.2** (b) | **4.3** (b) | **4.4** (d) | **4.5** (b) | **4.6** (d) |
| **4.7** (d) | **4.8** (a) | **4.9** (c) | **4.10** (b) | **4.11** (b) | |